PUGILATUS

TED SPOON

ILLUSTRATIONS & FRONT COVER

NICK DANGEROUS

Published 2014
by Berforts Group Ltd

ISBN 978-1-908616-62-3

Printed and bound in the United Kingdom

Typeset in Garamond & **KNOCKOUT NO.49**

Corbis & Gettys Images

"Of one thing I am certain, Boxing will never die...not while men are born with ambition, or with hands that can be curled into fists."

- T B. Shepard, The Noble Art

PREFACE

It's nonsensical to champion one sport over another. The different rule sets leave us with apples and oranges. If we were to rank them merely in terms of seizing attention, few, perhaps none stop you in your tracks quite like boxing.

With its one-on-one element tennis has a few similarities, but as Randall 'Tex' Cobb put it, "If you screw up in tennis, it's 15 love. If you screw up in boxing, it's your ass." Historian Pierce Egan referred to the process of punching as having "a kind of consanguinity to murder attached to the transaction." The idea is to hit and not get hit, but the goal is to incapacitate, and every blue moon somebody will pay the ultimate price. Critics look upon fighters as savages but the risk they take is what sets them apart from every other athlete. Mixed Martial Arts also shares this raw ingredient, however, though it may equal boxing in terms of grit it lacks finesse. In theory MMA offers the ultimate guise of combat. In practise contests often degrade into wrestling or shoot-outs. The liberal rule set leads to confused tactics and rapidly winded fighters. There isn't that sustained dynamism, and because many come from a handful of disciplines you don't get those vivid style clashes. Artistry is sacrificed for excess. Moreover it breaks the sacred rule of hitting a man while he's down. Boxing is still The Noble Art.

Contrary to its bloody foundations, boxing can be very tactical, so much so that violence becomes an afterthought. Solid punches will land, and the pace may be hectic, but so well-taught are some that the spectacle lies in the affinity they have for their craft. Anticipating and negating each other, fighters become linked in a kind of dance except, as Jack Handey quipped, "There's no music, no choreography and the dancers hit each other."

More so than a celebration the purpose of this book is to provide a coherent overview of the last 300 years, detailing each era to reveal their connection. It is a common decision to separate the London Prize Rules and Marquess of Queensberry Rules on the basis of their differences, ignoring their similarities. And this is important to keep in mind because, despite all the changes, the core principles which resuscitated boxing are still in effect. The real science behind drumming skulls did not upgrade in tandem with the quality of film. The old timers, the Jack Dempseys and the Benny Leonards are receiving more credit these days, but it is a kind of dutiful respect, one that lacks understanding. It was Egan, not A.J. Liebling, who first referred to pugilism as "the sweet science", a whole two centuries ago when Sugar Ray Robinson wasn't even a twinkle in his great grandmother's eye.

Just as it is essential to know how to hold your hands before throwing a punch, to understand boxing it is essential to connect the dots starting with James Figg, when fist-fighting started to make sense. This is not a catalogue. Many great fighters are missing and there is no record index. Particular themes have been chosen for each era, both to deliver more personal pen-pictures and to help give a sense of progression. In each of the seven Queensberry chapters it gives the page number for at least one of fifteen fight stories; a collection of some of boxing's most famous encounters. Popular myths behind each are addressed while contemporary opinion does its best to give you a ringside seat.

It's of no consequence whether or not you agree with my opening sentiments, but to fully appreciate this book it *is* important that you don't subscribe to the defective theory that boxing is like most sports and continually improves. Boxing changes, evolves, and not for the better but according to its surroundings. As methods undergo revision older ones are forgotten. Older never to be associated with inferior as Bernard Hopkins would suggest through studying the movements of Ezzard Charles, or of Henry Armstrong nailing spikes into a railroad because he heard Jack Dempsey did it. All information is relevant. Sure there are extremes; we shouldn't expect Tom Cribb to outbox Muhammad Ali in Madison Square Garden any more than we should expect Ali to outlast Cribb in the open country, but wed them in 1900 and their differences would discover a middle ground. Fighters are moulded by their eras, not chained to them.

As a final word the origins have been left untouched. Those Egyptian reliefs and Greek ornaments would lend nothing but gristle. Boxing, at least the boxing we know, officially began with Jack Broughton's 1743 set of rules. This book has lent the Latin term for boxing, Pugilatus. Information may dither the further you go back, but the sport is indebted to that warrior's spirit, something which continues to lure brave souls into the ring.

LIST OF CONTENTS

LPR = London Prize Rules

MQR = Marquees of Queensberry Rules

PUGILATUS

WHAT WAS A BARE-KNUCKLE FIGHT?

Before one begins to read into pugilism it would help first to address the nature of a bare-knuckle fight, for what can be understood (save for their protracted violence) is so vague that inquiries are prone to get lost in the bloodshed. In a sense that is not at all misleading.

The vast majority of bare-knuckle contests, up until the gloves ruled, were instances of human butchery, served up as raw as you like. The simple ruling that they were fights to the finish had a habit of degrading the most skilful beginnings into gory submissions. When a man was felled, either by a punch or throw, he had a whole thirty seconds to come back 'up to scratch' to start over, and before 1838 altered the policy a pugilists' seconds frequently carried their men back to continue; that when they were barely conscious. It may seem ridiculous but such measures actually helped fighters gain the day, as it was termed, therein capturing the spirit of:

> "*England, that never did nor never shall*
> *Lie at the proud foot of a conqueror.*" [1]

The taboo label never left pugilism, where bouts were held the law often tagged along, but with a microcosmic appeal in bravery and sportiness you could say it pulled the strings of England's heart, attracting men from all classes; even some dukes were known to dress down and take their place among the seedier supporters come nightfall. A prize-fight assembled all the different threads of society to create one big, unstable mass of jeering, pickpocketing and gambling. Although the term 'The Fancy' would come to help denote early day fans, the greater percentage would have simply been the curious who enjoyed a good dose of bear-baiting. There were no sanctioning bodies, no referees (not in the sense you're thinking) no security guards, and a fighter's seconds were not outside but *inside* the ring. Rules existed but stipulated more of a general aim in contrast to today's fussy supervising. It was all very impressionable. As a result many underhanded tactics were successfully implemented, both by the fighters and their seconds. Claiming fouls when things weren't going well, dropping illegally to earn a break, and general assistance like wiping the blood from a fighter's face during a round.

With that said, any half decent fighter was painfully aware that if you didn't have an inkling of the science, you didn't stand much of a chance. It is important to note that for all the sustained injury there was a preferred code of conduct which appreciated minimal wrestling, exhibiting your abilities, and all the while maintaining that basic honour; not hitting a man on the way down or falling on him with your knees. It was

---

[1] Shakespeare, William, 'King John', Act 5, Scene 7

desirable to strike with the first two knuckles because they did not dislocate as easily. Fighters did not turn their punches over but rather punched with the fist aligned vertically. Unconditionally a man had to think his blows through in a fight which was fair game to last over an hour. In turn, this fine punch placement meant the best fighters had to be good defensively. Tom Cribb was renowned for his durability because of his unique method of milling on the retreat whereby he caught punches while going backwards, sapping most of their power. Fighters needed not just to look out for body punches, but your eyes, ears, nose and throat were very susceptible. Without a pair of gloves to reduce the gaps there was less room for error.

Scrapping after a drink was commonplace, whether in anger or self-defence, but such tales have dirtied the fact these men were also disciplined. By the ninteenth century training had gone from a remote activity to an essential drill. There were some questionable detox measures like induced vomiting and dehydration; the idea seems to have been to purge and then rebuild. Writer William Hazlitt summed up the process of training as "exercise and abstinence". Sparring kept you sharp, dumb-bells and the broadsword strengthened your arms, running improved your stamina. Tom Cribb's famous 1811 camp in the Scottish Highlands may read like a wild goose chase but he ran set distances and varied his pace. Hills sprints were almost certainly part of the routine. Thirteen years later Ned Turner prepared in the Welsh mountains; apparently the benefits of high-altitude training were not unknown. Helping them through the physical toil was a high-protein diet. Raw eggs, mutton, fowl and beef were staple foods. Bread and potatoes helped sustain energy levels until the sun disappeared, at which point they weren't long for bed. A far cry from today's standards but (generally) pugilists came to the ring fit and with a game plan.

Nothing can be as informative as first-hand observation, but the efforts to decipher styles and draw comparison should help you appreciate not just what these men achieved in their time, but what they contributed towards the context of boxing. So we're going back to where things started to take form, eighteenth century London, 'The Big Smoke'; a desperate time with 1666's Great Fire having eliminated the vast majority of the city, leaving it to be hurriedly rebuilt to an appalling state. Unwholesome water drove most to gin, manual labour often led to an early grave, and wretched conditions spread disease. Most men lived recklessly outside of factory work and many women, if not able to steer clear of the streets through laundry or domestic services, were left to whore themselves out. Actually, so popular was prostitution that you could even purchase guides to help find a female to suit your preference. To at least give yourself a chance you needed a skill.

CHAPTER I

BECOMING

"To lay aside the destructive weapons of war invented by art, and make use of those which nature has provided." [2]

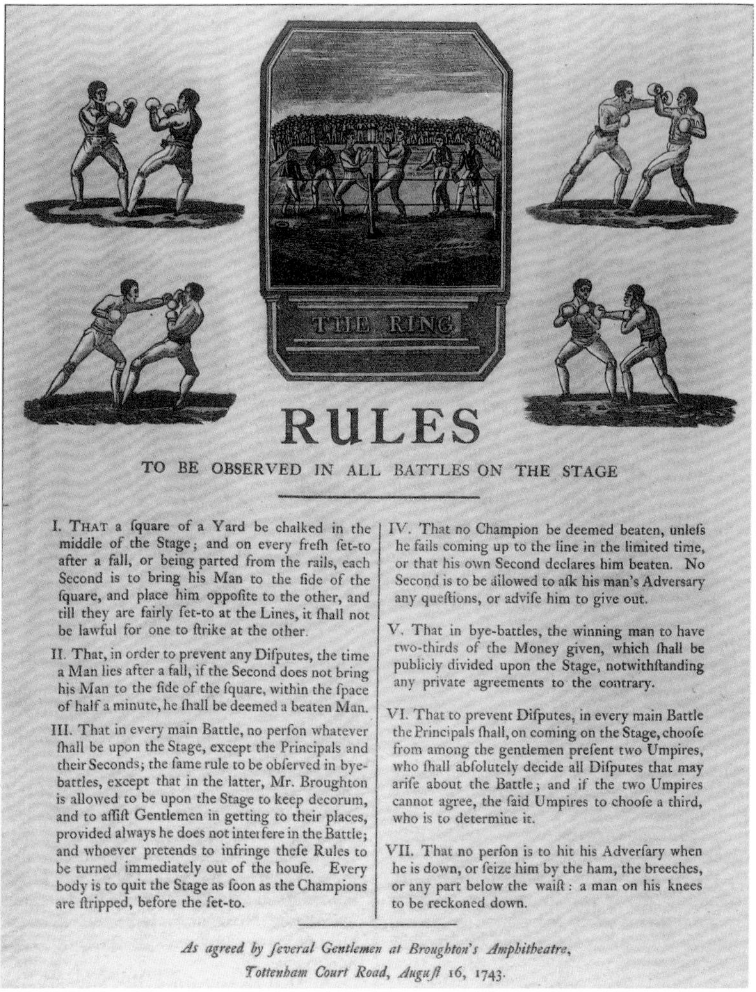

THE RING

RULES

TO BE OBSERVED IN ALL BATTLES ON THE STAGE

I. THAT a ſquare of a Yard be chalked in the middle of the Stage; and on every freſh ſet-to after a fall, or being parted from the rails, each Second is to bring his Man to the ſide of the ſquare, and place him oppoſite to the other, and till they are fairly ſet-to at the Lines, it ſhall not be lawful for one to ſtrike at the other.

II. That, in order to prevent any Diſputes, the time a Man lies after a fall, if the Second does not bring his Man to the ſide of the ſquare, within the ſpace of half a minute, he ſhall be deemed a beaten Man.

III. That in every main Battle, no perſon whatever ſhall be upon the Stage, except the Principals and their Seconds; the ſame rule to be obſerved in bye-battles, except that in the latter, Mr. Broughton is allowed to be upon the Stage to keep decorum, and to aſſiſt Gentlemen in getting to their places, provided always he does not interfere in the Battle; and whoever pretends to infringe theſe Rules to be turned immediately out of the houſe. Every body is to quit the Stage as ſoon as the Champions are ſtripped, before the ſet-to.

IV. That no Champion be deemed beaten, unleſs he fails coming up to the line in the limited time, or that his own Second declares him beaten. No Second is to be allowed to aſk his man's Adverſary any queſtions, or adviſe him to give out.

V. That in bye-battles, the winning man to have two-thirds of the Money given, which ſhall be publicly divided upon the Stage, notwithſtanding any private agreements to the contrary.

VI. That to prevent Diſputes, in every main Battle the Principals ſhall, on coming on the Stage, chooſe from among the gentlemen preſent two Umpires, who ſhall abſolutely decide all Diſputes that may ariſe about the Battle; and if the two Umpires cannot agree, the ſaid Umpires to chooſe a third, who is to determine it.

VII. That no perſon is to hit his Adverſary when he is down, or ſeize him by the ham, the breeches, or any part below the waiſt: a man on his knees to be reckoned down.

As agreed by ſeveral Gentlemen at Broughton's Amphitheatre, Tottenham Court Road, Auguſt 16, 1743.

Jack Broughton's 1743 ruleset

---

[2] Boxing Reviewed, or the science of manual defence, based on rational principles…, 1790, Thomas Fewtrell, p.38

James Figg dug up an old artefact in pugilism. In terms of aptitude he was better rehearsed in the practice of the small-sword, quarter staff and cudgel, but despite this, for its gritty novelty, fist-fighting intrigued. An illiterate, and to put it lightly, coarse member of society, Figg nonetheless charmed the Earl of Peterborough following an exhibition on the village green. As he built his reputation, which would eventually lead to being decorated as the first Champion of England in 1719, Figg lent his services to the public, teaching and training. One student in particular, Captain Godfrey would testify to the informative, if somewhat painful lessons in his 1747 publication *A Treatise On The Science Of Defence.*

With Figg's headquarters at the Adam and Eve pub (as it was then), the attraction towards pugilism began to root itself into the nation, being entertaining to watch and practical to study. This was the *Useful* science of self-defence; while undeniably brutal there was the opportunity to improve your health, decrease your susceptibility or go one further and attempt a career as a fighter.

At 6' and a well-proportioned 185lbs, Figg proved to have too much of everything for his time, retiring as champion in 1730. The impact he made was considerable (as King George I having a ring constructed in Hyde Park for public use demonstrates), but due to the lack of structure, and possibly because of Figg's multiple disciplines, pugilism remained in its infancy. His 1727 contest with pipe-maker Ned Sutton consisted of three challenges; one with the broadsword, one in a fist-fight and finally one with the cudgel. He won his contests with the broadsword and cudgel rather easily, but the fist-fight was, regardless of the skill shown, a product of when there were virtually no rules. While it was in the interest of a pugilist to appease the crowd with well-struck blows it did not omit the fact you could go as far as gouging one's eyes or 'purring' an opponent (raking them with spiked shoes whilst on the floor). Boxing was the model of fighting, but once you closed on your man you could strangle, scratch and just about do as you pleased; glorified street fighting is not far off the mark.

Just four years after retiring Figg passed away in his home at Oxford Road leaving a wife and several children. In the concluding years of his life a young apprentice by the name of Jack Broughton stood ready to fill the void left by the great man. Two men were considered champion in the six years which bridged the retirement of Figg and crowning of Broughton. First there was Tom Pipes who held it for four of them, and then George Taylor who held it for the other two. A basic silhouette of Pipes read that he was not a strong man but more than made up for this with his cunning and gameness, which was (it now seems rather obscurely) known as 'Bottom'. Taylor was a stockier, more imposing obstacle with learned abilities but is thought to have lacked courage. All three were notable talents under Figg's wing, but in 1736, having defeated Taylor, Broughton took the ball that his mentor had brought back into play and began to run with it.

To the liking of contemporary poet Paul Whitehead, his summary of Broughton was thus: "Were I to attempt a Description of your Qualifications, I might justly have Recource to the Majesty of Agamemnon, the Courage of Achilles, the Strength of Ajax, and the Wisdom of Ulysses..."[3] So rather good then.

Historian and lifelong fight fan, Pierce Egan's physical summary of him read: "Broughton was a remarkably well-made man, almost on purpose, it might be said, to form a complete pugilist. He was about 5' 11", and nearly 14 stone. He had a piercing eye, that seemed to penetrate the souls of his adversaries; his arms were rather long, but nevertheless they did not destroy the fine symmetry of his frame."[4] Aside from being a flawless specimen, much of Broughton's success came down to his quality of person; he was educated, eloquent and consequently a magnet for higher patronage, like the Duke of Cumberland who wagered on him many times. Figg had revived that appeal all fight fans share for the guts and glory of battle, but Broughton blew the audience barriers as far as all of England, attracting many who previously stood off, not wanting to be part of a questionable clique.

Decades later *The Times* newspaper would confess, "Boxing to the disgrace of the times, has been introduced to the public as a national art."[5] Indeed it was, "the brutal, though fashionable custom of boxing." The last remark had a kind of begrudged acceptance behind it. Although pugilism was not to be treated with first page exposure it was unavoidably a big part of English society. To strip at the waist, come up to scratch and set-to quickly became an iconic procedure. Broughton's moniker of 'The Father of Boxing' is almost an historical cheap shot to Figg, but the actions he took not only helped strengthen the bond between boxing and the public but gave the ring its honour.

The formation of the rules is thought to have been a result of the 1741 encounter between Broughton and the aspiring but ultimately overmatched, George Stevenson. After forty minutes of torrid fighting Broughton sunk in a blow under the heart which debilitated the younger man. Paul Whitehead's 1744 publication known as *The Gymnasiad* paid tribute; the following verse depicts Stevenson's sad destiny:

> "*Now droop'd the Youth, urging all his Might,*
> *With feeble Arm still vindicates the Fight.*
> *Till on the part where heav'd the panting breath,*
> *A fatal Blow impress'd the Seal of Death.*" [6]

Death itself did not come quickly; his failing body insisted on surviving for about a month after the contest, but throughout the weeks of a futile recovery Broughton sparked up a friendship with the stricken fighter. Away from the noise of an indecent crowd came quiet, solemn reflection, coming to its climax when Stevenson passed

[3] The Gymnasiad, Paul Whitehead, 1744, p.v

[4] Every Gentleman's Manual, 1845, Pierce Egan, p.53

[5] The Times, 1788, Jan 8th, p.2

[6] The Gymnasiad, Paul Whitehead, 1744, p.32

away in the champion's arms. It was time for a change, and so to lessen the risks seven revolutionary rules were put into action, giving pugilism its crucial framework. Fighting began to receive its praises on not just a manly basis, but a graceful one as well. The implications of these rules urged fighters to really *think* about their strategies. Elusive, defensive manoeuvres; initially thought to be cowardly were restyled as artful niceties.

With the growing number of people tracking down Broughton's amphitheatre, it soon became apparent how impractical it was to train with bare fists. Men and women weren't exactly sissies back in eighteenth century London, but it was preferable to learn minus the black eyes and broken noses. In February 1747 the *Daily Advertiser* had a segment which explained Broughton's willingness to teach people with the aid of "mufflers" (gloves). Promising to execute these lessons "with the utmost tenderness and regard to the delicacy of the frame and constitution of the pupil", those gentlemanly manners continued to smitten the curious, and while newcomers were shown the ropes, Jack remained the man to beat.

Come 1750, and with fourteen years of championship pedigree under his belt, Broughton fought a man named Jack Slack. The butcher who is now dramatically remembered as 'The Knight of the Cleaver' had fallen against men that Broughton had trounced. Although thirty-seven, an age in boxing which would signify disaster, Broughton's legend was such that his Royal compadre put £10,000 behind his fists. The huge investment, along with the intellectual differences between the two culminated in pugilism's first major drought. The battle wasn't fifteen minutes old when Broughton was rendered blind having suffered a cracking blow by the thought-to-be helpless butcher. It wasn't long then until the game champion is written to have uttered "By God I'm done!" cementing the most unpopular victory in all of boxing. Particularly sore over his loss, the Duke closed down Broughton's amphitheatre and took on an entirely negative view of the phenomenon (that was) boxing. Slack's legacy was sealed upon victory, but with the day won he led pugilism into a prolonged wilderness. The best part of half a century passed before boxing flourished again. A host of varied talents handed the championship down through years of much foul play, fixing, and generally decreased interest. Duggan Fearns vacated the championship of England in 1779 where it was to lay dormant for eight years.

JACK BROUGHTON

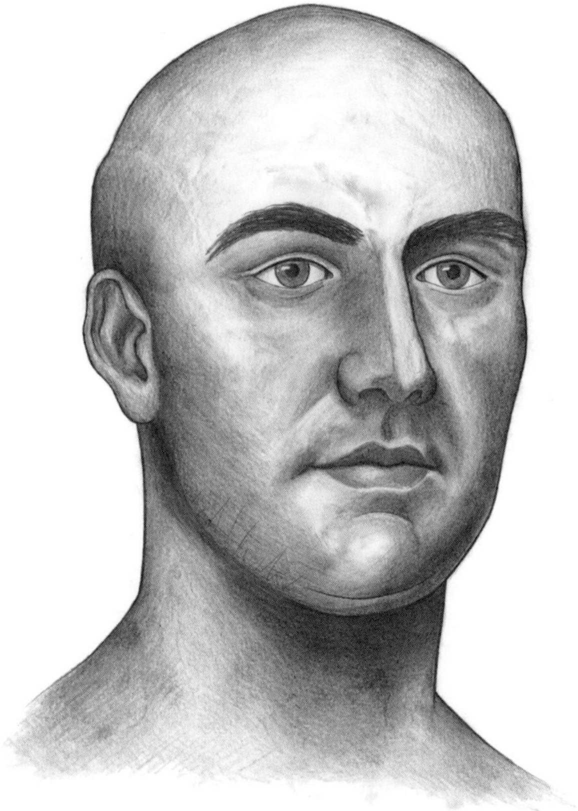

Height: 6'

Weight: 200lbs

Jack Broughton had size, but he also possessed imagination. The shaven-headed boxer had a genuine love for pugilism which separated him from his contemporaries. For at least fifty years he was the best thing boxing had ever produced.

Jack stressed straight punches; one of the first to recognize their superiority in speed and accuracy to round blows. He scouted habits before making his move and proved how deadly a clean punch to the body can be. When blows were directed at *his* body he beat them down with his forearms.

Broughton's square stance appears to be an impractical one, offering poor balance. Jack used this seemingly undecided footing to either advance or retreat with the left or right leg, striking diagonal postures with each step. This ambidextrous movement made him difficult to read.

Jack's hands were big and calloused enough to catch punches. When he anticipated correctly, Broughton would catch the opponent's blow with one hand and strike out with the other.

CHAPTER II

RENAISSANCE

"The beauty in boxing is in hitting clean, guarding, fending, and keeping off blows with judgement, all which depends on the eye, but hugging, more properly, belongs to wrestling." [7]

Tom Johnson vs. Isaac Perrins
Painting by Conrad Martin Metz

[7] Modern Manhood; or, the art and practise of English Boxing, Henry Lemoine, 1788, p.87

After all Broughton had done, pugilism came close to slipping into another deep sleep. The officiating degraded, and with it, so did the fighting. Styles had little method or grace which shaped many ugly encounters during a period that "must be considered very much inferior to what it was in Broughton's time."[8] The passion which had transmuted fist-fighting into a British treasure was absent for the best part of fifty years, but as the Industrial Revolution waved its wand over the country, a few men once again injected their money and enthusiasm into The Noble Art for its glorious rebirth. The public were still at the mercy of abundant disease like smallpox and consumption, but nearer the end of the eighteenth century many of those who were previously secluded to agriculture were presented with the means to venture downtown and join in the city madness. Horse racing and the atrocious instances of bear-baiting continued to appeal, but once again, the ring was to become the point of focus.

"Johnson is so much superior in every other requisite, that the science of pugilism, practised as it is by him, seems a new invention since the days of Broughton."[9] Thomas Jackling, better known as Tom Johnson, rekindled that empathy between fighter and spectator. So the story goes, before he made his name in the ring, Tom utilised his considerable strength to carry two sacks of corn to get both his, and a friend's wages, until the latter was healthy to return. These selfless efforts stopped his pal from losing the job. It is more likely the depiction of his character though than the legend of the great corn-carrier that endeared Johnson to the public. 1783 was the year he made his mark with a victory over Jack Jarvis, claiming the top spot, and not until 1791 did he budge.

A first-rate pugilist, calm and efficient, Johnson fought out of a comparatively awkward stance which required great strength in the loins (the lower abdominal region); legs very much bent with the torso thrust forward, hiding the body. Such a style did not look fit for mobility, but with speed and cunning he averted punches and ground his man down. Similar to Broughton, he is said to have devised pre-fight strategies. His finest hour arrived when all seventeen stones of Birmingham's Isaac Perrins threatened his title. Seventy-five minutes (sixty-two rounds) of tooth and nail clobbering ended with the giant Perrins stretched out. Shortly after his signature victory, Johnson briefly retired only to then make an unsuccessful bid to keep his title.

Benjamin 'Big Ben' Brain, a thirty-seven-year-old veteran but formidably powerful put an end to Johnson's tenure. It was to be a short lived stay as champion however for his damaged liver saw to it that a proposed February bout against Will Wood never was. Instead, Benjamin passed away a couple of months later in 1794. A second of Johnson's named Richard Humphries happened to be a fighter also, and a very good one at that. Throughout Tom's championship reign he had participated in three battles which did not just prove instant classics but marked a pivotal change in the evolution of prize-fighting. His opponent, Daniel Mendoza, fashioned from a curious blend of Spanish and Jewish heritage, went far beyond making his mark. His insatiable

[8] Boxing Reviewed, 1790, Thomas Fewtrell, p.45

[9] Boxing Reviewed, 1790, Thomas Fewtrell, p.87

appetite to teach had a ground-breaking effect on the boxing landscape. Mendoza's core objective was to convey the overlooked grace in pugilism. "(Boxing) though not perhaps the most elegant, is certainly the most useful species of defence…To render it not totally devoid of elegance has, however, been my present aim."[10] In fact, Mendoza wished to show how boxing was "equal to fencing, in point of neatness, activity, and grace."

5'7" and 160lbs, Mendoza was not physically capable of locking horns with the bulls out there, therein discovering the potential in playing matador. By today's standards a natural middleweight, Mendoza utilised original manoeuvres to conquer his larger rivals. The science of boxing, a subject of a fairly elusive nature, was to formally introduce itself. Going back, even Jack Slack was thought to have put in "some little dodges that Broughton was not up to, which bothered his old dove-tailed system of milling."[11] The lazy notion that Mendoza was the first man to not just stand and swap blows is not at all accurate. What Mendoza *did* do however was take the concept of the cerebral assassin and, just as Broughton had with boxing, supply its parameters.

One tale depicts the young Mendoza to have sporadically set-to as a last resort. Then, one day, from a sudden influx of paying fights, Mendoza went from skirting around a competition which had turned sour to not only climb its summit, but invest in its future. This passion reeled in figures of notoriety like the Prince of Wales and Duke of Hamilton. Feeling the buzz they made sure to frequent the ring's perimeter, once again giving it that national stamp of approval. The sheer breadth of talent about to flourish was like nothing before, but as the flagship pugilist Mendoza lacked familiarity.

Back when Figg ruled the roost, a Venetian fighter named Alberto Di Carni challenged one of his students, Bob Whitaker. Although Bob prevailed, during a moment of doubt, there was, as Captain Godfrey wrote, "a general foreign huzza on the side of the Venetian pronouncing our countryman's downfall." No doubt when Daniel leapt on to the apron; hair curled, radiating with strange mannerisms, the majority would have felt that basic reservation towards the unknown. And when he started to move around in that calculating, unfamiliar manner, it is most likely that dislike overcame the reservation. Though an educated fighter, Mendoza's plea for style unsettled the purists. By most accounts he was not a hard puncher, and although this was the result of the blatant weight disparity, it robbed Mendoza of that basic magic to smite his antagonist with one blast. Smite he did though. In a sizeable career, which Pierce Egan had at thirty-five bouts, Mendoza faltered only three times. During his first set-to with Humphries he received such an injury around his loins from falling that he was rendered physically unable to stand. Throughout a contest that he was thought to have had the better, Mendoza healed up and came back to settle their celebrated trilogy 2-1 in his favour.

---

[10] The Art of Boxing; with a statement of the transactions…, Daniel Mendoza, 1789, p.vi

[11] Every Gentleman's Manual, 1845, Pierce Egan, p.35

Mendoza the Jew, as he liked to be styled, held the championship from 1792-95. He released two publications; *The Art of Boxing* (1789) and *The Memoirs of the Life of Daniel Mendoza* (1816), later dubbing himself "The Father of Scientific Fighting" during his farewell gathering at Fives Court. Near the time of his separation from the championship there were plenty of capable fighters, but the one who would relieve Mendoza of his prolific status was cut from some especially rare cloth.

'Gentleman' John Jackson was a man of so many endearing qualities you could almost say a few of them were in danger of being gratuitous. For his sculpt-worthy frame and cultural knowledge he was loved by the higher ranks, and for his remarkable strength and hardiness he was respected by the masses. In reference to his hardiness, during a fight with George Ingleston where he suffered a broken leg, Jackson offered to continue if he could stipulate that both of them be strapped to chairs to swap punches from then on. Much to his dismay, this resourceful measure did not allow for the bouts continuation.

At 5'11" and close to 15 stone, Jackson was a large heavyweight. It was not size though but strength which baffled comprehension. His all-round athletic ability (if even close to being accurately recorded) was truly remarkable. In dead-lift fashion he is credited to have shifted over 'ten-hundred weight' (1000lbs); a striking feature which ran in tow with his reputation as a first-class sprinter and high-jumper. And then there was his boxing. It was a style similar to Johnson's with the waist pushed out, legs squat and arms very much in front. The paltry number of recorded fights for Jackson owes much to his high position in society where an initial interest in pugilism led for many years of amateur practice. When, at nineteen, he saw it fit to introduce that presence to the useful William Futrell or Fewtrell, he cleaned up impressively in sixty-seven minutes.

Jackson, as had Mendoza, made considerable efforts to connect the public to pugilism, but the difference was that Jackson was chums with a pliable aristocracy. Harvey Christian Coombe (Mayor of London) and George Gordon (Lord Byron) befriended him, not solely out of respect for pugilism's fame, but with a genuine interest to learn the profession. Now both are remembered to have been partial to boxing; an aspect which must be largely attributed to Jackson and his further efforts to cultivate. After Jackson left the ring injured, he retired for some time. The proverbial return in 1795 came with a championship showdown against Mendoza. In a greatly attended contest, aside from brief moments of resistance, Jackson dramatically overpowered Mendoza in ten minutes and thirty seconds. What will forever be remembered however is that fifth round when Jackson got hold of Mendoza's excess hair to pummel him silly with the spare hand. Cries of "Foul!" were of no consequence and the weary champion was left with little choice but to resign four rounds later. Although permanent retirement followed, leaving behind a grand total of only three fights, victory over the Jew cemented Jackson as one of the greats. He formed a pugilistic club in 1814 to try and regulate fighting. The closing of it in 1824 was an example of the crumbling state of pugilism, but before the dip comes the peak.

DANIEL MENDOZA

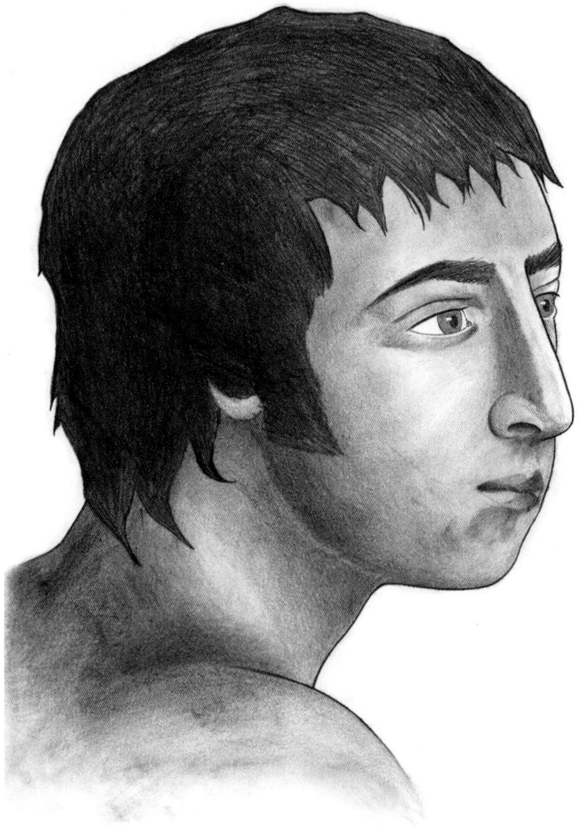

Height: 5'8"

Weight: 160lbs

The Mendoza model of fighting promised elegance along with manliness. Specifically, keeping 'the mark' guarded, pulling back after exchanges, and switching attitudes helped limit the chances of receiving a blow. Due to the lesser effects an 11 stone 8 lbs man has on men of 13 stone and upwards, it was of great importance to Mendoza about where he should strike; the throat, eyes and nose were prime targets.

Here Mendoza is in stance. The slight advancement of the left leg and arm was an alteration which has remained up till today.

The chopper blow was one for the big bullies. To defend against a round blow you could wrap your arm around the side of your head with the idea of greeting a fist with your elbow. Having defended, unravelling the arm to a quick snap, you could do awful things to noses with the back of your fist.

CHAPTER III

A GOLDEN ERA

"The kind and nature of popular sports and exhibitions of a people, whether just emerging from barbarism, or passing through the various stages of development, or arrived at the highest pitch of refinement, serve to measure, as a scale, the different degrees of their advancement in civilization." [12]

Painting by Henry Alken

[12] Pancratia, 1812, W. Oxberry, p.3

Nearing the dawn of the nineteenth century, off the back of its political influence and trading business, the British Empire watched its newly appointed capital develop into the largest city in the world. And pugilism, just like London, was scheduled to have its masterstroke. Within a little matter of ten years the ring would trickle out a series of unforgettable personalities and landmark battles, one after the other. Considering the evident wellbeing of boxing it's not surprising that there were plenty of good fighters, but even still, what emerged in such a short space of time (predominantly from Bristol) leaves one pointing to a tired axiom; that there really must have been something in the water.

A couple of decent pugilists gained ownership to the title while Jackson's presence continued to sizzle. Thomas Owen won the vacated title in an elimination contest against William Hooper. Sixty-four minutes of hard fighting ended with Owen standing and Hooper nursing a dislocated shoulder he gave himself from misguiding a punch. Not even twelve months were to pass as champion though for a seasoned bruiser called Jack Bartholomew relieved him of the championship in thirty minutes of well-contested fighting. Bartholomew was not at all a bad pugilist but these quick transactions were to be made to look trivial. An especially promising amateur called Jem Belcher made his grand appearance. He happened to be the grandson of the man who had defeated Broughton (Jack Slack) so fighting was part of his heritage. He was to live at an especially fast rate; the fact he didn't make it to thirty-one echoes this, but using that time to its fullest he set-to with an energy that destroyed opponent's and buzzed the audience.

Adopting the family tradition with real gusto, Belcher demonstrated ring smarts beyond his eighteen years when he clashed with Bartholomew. In what would have proven a painful lesson for any other fighter so young, Belcher secured a return bout with a draw after fifty-two rounds. The champion and his backers were confident of doing away with Belcher next time and thought it a dead-cert when the youngster was smashed to the ground; a black pigeon was released to signal his defeat. Unluckily for Bartholomew, Belcher got up and put him into the realms of insensibility with one, heavy cross-buttock. In round seventeen, after twenty minutes, he could do no more. Another of those popular tales works its way into the plot here when Belcher was said to have encountered a quartet of assailants in Chelsea of whom he managed to fend off four days prior to his fight with Andrew Gamble. And in due course, when the larger Gamble stripped and opposed Belcher he was hammered to defeat in nine minutes. Some reports have Belcher taking away £20,000 for his troubles.

Joe Berks or Bourke is well introduced as a man whose "ferocity was so out and out, upon all occasions, that he might be consistently styled the Emperor of Ruffians."[13] Not the happiest of chaps, but that ferocity at least gave something for Belcher to chew over. He first made it a point to challenge the champion while attending a prize-fight. In a manner most dear to him, Berks issued his challenge by trying on a punch. The blow was negated but it did not stop a spontaneous fight. Belcher walked away victorious inside twenty minutes but Joe earned himself an official rematch as he

[13] Every Gentleman's Manual, 1845, Pierce Egan, p.86

seemed to trouble Jem some, which, considering the champion's tyranny, was reason enough to warrant a title shot.

The stronger, hot-headed challenger was no slouch, giving it everything he had in the rematch. Some contemporary opinion surmised that not since Benjamin Brain dethroned Tom Johnson had such a fierce contest occurred. Berks had his moments, causing the usually sharpshooting champion to fight a little "round", but he could not survive Jem's blows and was mercifully pulled out by his seconds after twenty-five minutes. Their 1802 rubber match, save for one dramatic instance, ended in ten minutes. This instance involved Berks hoisting Belcher up by the legs in the fifth and dropping him on his head. That the champion may have suffered a broken neck was not out of the question, but to everyone's amazement, calmly he got up and knocked all the fight out of Berks. Still only twenty-one, there wasn't a Brit going who had not heard of Jem Belcher, the man with many more years of masterful demolitions sure to come. As it happened, just one more victory against Jack Firby materialised as the champ was involved in an accident playing rackets which maimed his left eye in 1803. Severely handicapped, regardless, Jem's exit was some time off.

And so the daunting task to fill Belcher's shoes presented itself to pugilism, but no better man could have rose to the occasion than fellow Bristolian, Henry Pearce. Hen (an abbreviation which led to his alias of the 'Game Chicken') was an apprentice of Jem's who got going with a twenty minute win over common opponent Jack Firby. Pearce was a stocky, muscular figure, barely 5'9" and around 13 stone. He wasn't a speedy assassin like Jem but sported a good defence along with an adamant constitution. As a fighter he was thought of as vigilant; cautiously dismantling his opponents with a combination of fine skill and strength. These qualities were too much for Berks, Elias Spray and Tom Carte, guiding Pearce towards his principal acid test. An equally precocious fighter by the name of John Gully had got himself into a spot of bother with debt, and wound up imprisoned. Apart from being a fellow Bristolian, Gully also happened to be a friend of Pearce's whom he is thought to have had a gloved exhibition with during a visit. When time came for Gully's release, Hen was ready for a formal challenge. There to seize this open window, Fletcher Reid, a man of sporting notoriety, convinced Gulley to try his hand at the champion. When all was said and done, Gully left the ring a beaten fighter, but not before seventy-seven minutes (sixty-four rounds) of some of the most desperate fighting had ever occurred. Pearce is written to have said to Gully after the curtain call, "You're a damned good fellow; I'm hard put to it to stand; you are the only man that ever stood up to me."[14]

Gully would go on to indemnify such praise with the championship stuck to his name, but in between the natural order of things, the sad, depleted and resentful figure of Jem Belcher returned to issue a challenge in 1805. The prospect of fighting with one eye could not stem the aspirations of a man (still just twenty-four) who had yet to be beaten, or relieved as Champion of England for that matter. With a weakened body and half his vision, Belcher managed splendidly in the early goings, but the insurmountable figure of Pearce took it all to exact his physical superiority. Thirty-five

[14] Every Gentleman's Manual, 1845, Pierce Egan, p.138

minutes expired, and along with it Jem's hopes for victory. In an act typical of the day to demonstrate one's remaining strength, Pearce exited and then re-entered the ring via somersault.

Beaten but broiling with heavy emotions, Belcher had yet to exercise his ring demons. And as for Pearce, heading down a path typical of the day, he drifted from the ring to encounter the dastardly pitfalls of Old England. Life was to be cruelly cut short, but not before a flash of heroics. Entering a blazing house in 1807 to rescue a trapped woman, Pearce demonstrated to the most avid boxing cynics that pugilists were capable of compassion. Consumption put its tight squeeze on the remainder of his life, and in 1809, at thirty-two years of age, Henry drew his last. The leave of Pearce effectively closed a chapter that was to resonate for a lifetime as Jem Belcher's miserable incarnation took a while longer to acknowledge that boxing embraced him no more. Tragic as life was, death did not linger.

In 1807 Gully returned to do away with Bob Gregson; a mauling 6'2" and 15 stone pugilist with a taste for poetry. Confirming common belief that he was the next best man, Gully won a thriller lasting one hour twenty minutes (thirty-six rounds) which again saw technique overcome strength. A rematch stretched to one hour fifteen minutes (twenty-four rounds) but Gregson received a more clinical beating. His last fight completed, Gully went on to make a fortune through horse racing. From booking to breeding he amassed considerable wealth. Ever ambitious he was elected as a Member of Parliament for Pontefract in 1832, serving two terms, and favourably left this world in his eightieth year. Gulley's retirement left the public again scanning for notable aspirants. Two men were identified; battle-worn Gregson, and the man whom Gully had decided against to fight, Tom Cribb.

With a body like gravel from relentless stints of coal-heaving, Cribb epitomised the idea of a bare-knuckle warrior. He was heavily built for the day, 5'10", 14 stone and, clearly not the fencing type, fought contests of pure attrition. His somewhat awkward style of 'milling on the retreat' was not to everyone's taste but, when it came to fighting to the bitter end, proved undeniably effective. His innovative style consisted of "drawing his opponents after him, and then punishing and irritating them in their pursuit, so as to have the effect of making their distances incorrect, (consequently, their blows were frequently thrown away, and generally too feeble to do any execution, from his ingenious mode of fighting)."[15]

Having served in the British Navy, Cribb entered the ring to fight an incredible five times in 1805 alone. What's more daunting is the total fight duration, which came to six and one half hours. All challengers were humbled, save for one. George Nichols dealt Cribb his sole defeat. In a ninety minute struggle, Cribb shockingly uttered "Enough!" It had been a tremendous showing by Nichols but it was an opinion that Cribb faulted "during his novitiate; at a time when he was considered little more than a bottom man." And in 1807 it was this tactical naivety that resurrected the bitter wrath of Jem Belcher.

---

[15] Boxiana or, Sketches of ancient and modern pugilism, Pierce Egan, 1830, p.198

The one-eyed pugilist must have appeared helpless next to the muscled mass of Cribb, but when the latter lay grovelling on the floor after the eighteenth it looked as if the former champion had done the extraordinary. Targeting the throat, Belcher brought Cribb down heavily, but what followed, thought to be a squabble about the odds, gifted Cribb with extra recovery time. Belcher continued with a wrist injury and diminished as the rounds went on until fifty-five minutes proved enough. Belcher would try one more time to get back what was once his, but first Cribb fixed the man who had defeated his brother, George Horton, and then defeated Gregson to solidify the championship in 1808. Cribb was completely exhausted upon concluding forty-five minutes having suffered multiple throws, but his shtick of countering on the retreat had done enough damage.

While Cribb's technical improvements merited attention the current powers of Belcher, "which were decreasing daily", laid the script for a rematch. The gameness of Jem could never be questioned, but panting through the claret, and with fists miserably sliced he waved the white flag. The fate of Belcher was to treat him no better than it had Pearce. The evil that was gin mugged his liver and a contracted virus encouraged pneumonia to put him at death's door in 1811. Only thirty, and caught in that familiar penniless rut, Belcher passed away.

Victorious against every man worthy of taking the opposing corner, Cribb had proven himself beyond dispute. Whatever moments of crises or doubt had marred past times, Britain could do little but praise the endless resolve of their new hero. "If Napoleon invades, we'll set Tom Cribb on him" was a familiar quip during the war, but what would come to immortalise the 'Black Diamond' was on the horizon. A dark brew of crudeness and terrible strength had broken from the shackles of Virginia to land in the British ring. Cribb's next contest garnered unforeseen international importance, one in which he would become well acquainted with a shadowy hulk. A man simply dubbed 'The Moor'.

JEM BELCHER

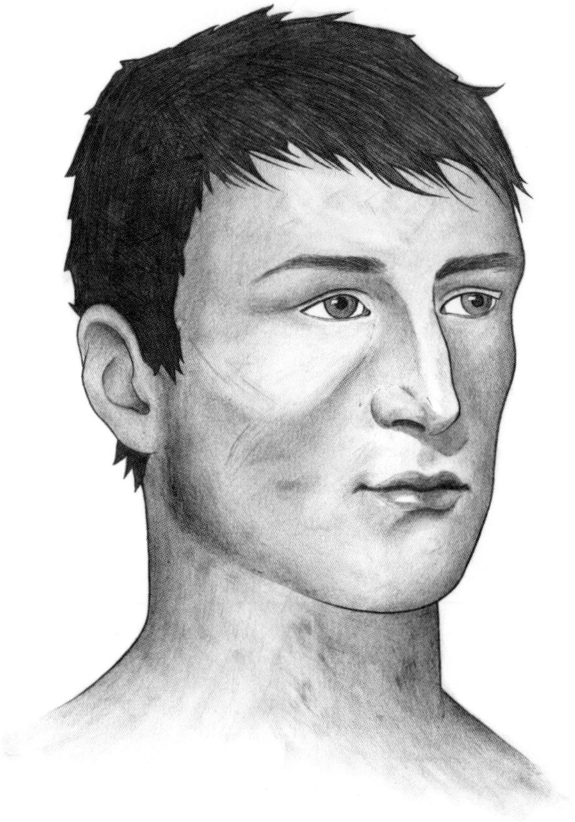

Height: 5'11"

Weight: 165lbs

Belcher was the perfect example of a natural fighter. His style was said to be "quite original", more "intuitive, than gained by practice". With tremendous speed and precision he got rid of his opponents in half the time it took most pugilists. The average prize-fight lasted around fifty minutes. The average length of a Jem Belcher fight is just half that at twenty-eight. However, if we remove the three futile comeback fights we get an average of twenty-four minutes, and further still, if we only consider his championship years we then get a fight average of just seventeen minutes. With straight punches and vicious throws, the slender figure of Belcher was able to overwhelm his adversaries in a manner that was particularly rare for the prize-ring.

Here Belcher can be seen jumping into a straight lead.

The Cross-Buttock was a heavy, Judo-esque throw, favoured by Broughton and a big weapon for Belcher. Placing your right leg behind your adversary's right, you took him by the shoulders and threw him over your hip. It was common to exacerbate injury by falling on the opponent in the same motion.

CHAPTER IV

INFAMOUS & UNSTABLE

"At the present moment, the English Nation stands on an eminence, if not decidedly superior, it must be admitted, to any other country in the world." [16]

Tom Cribb vs. Tom Molineaux
Copy of 1811 etching

[16] Boxiana, 1818, Pierce Egan, p.vi

Cherished as it was for the Englishman to prove his courage, only a matter of time stood before men from overseas threatened Britain's ownership to the ring; more specifically the ascribed 'men of colour'.

For the best part of 300 years the Atlantic Slave Trade had been transporting persons of African heritage to work free of charge, typically through agriculture or working as domestic servants. Nearing the nineteenth century the rise in the public conscience to abolish slavery offered the black man a chance to seize his freedom. Bill Richmond was the first African pugilist to make it in England. Working as a servant in Staten Island, Richmond observed all the mannerisms and nature of conversation of which he would later utilise as an English gentleman. More importantly he quickly learnt to humbly acknowledge his coloured disposition; white but not quite. Regardless of the racial jeers, with his speedy style and sharp eye the charismatic Richmond fought markedly well for a 150lbs man.

Many quality victories were achieved, but against a figure like Cribb there was little hope to overcome him in a fight to the finish. With Tom Molineaux there was plenty of hope. This Virginian slave possessed the type of body that Richmond needed; 14 stone condensed into a height that did not reach 5'9". There wasn't an ounce of spare flesh. Molineaux was given the means to elope from the U.S. having made his gambling owner wealthy with his fists. Upon landing on British soil in 1809 he adorned himself with an unofficial American championship; regardless, the sheer formation of him secured a reputation. With his boxing academy in London, Richmond found financial stability, but the phantom of Cribb remained. With Molineaux, Bill had found his exorcist.

An infant next to Richmond in terms of the science but physically a giant, Molineaux was taught the finer points and received constant earache on how to behave around whites. These cultural lessons would spectacularly fail, but Richmond fought his corner until the fight with Cribb became an internationally-gripping reality. What exactly transpired on December 18th, 1810, history hasn't specified, but through decades gone by the popular notion of foul play remains strong. Enveloped by a winter frost, Molineaux matched the champion blow for blow to come within a whisker of claiming his title. In one of the all-time classics Molineaux crumbled in the fifty-fifth minute. Electric as the battle was, the subsequent tale of a riot to protect Cribb's title went on to eclipse the fight. And when the rematch everyone had been waiting for drew near, Molineaux made sure he did not get a second chance; soaking up his national celebrity, indulging in every possible sin. Meanwhile, under the supervision of Captain Barclay, Cribb was subjected to a gutsy sixteen week training program, jaunting all over the Scottish Highlands, so thoroughly shedding any excess weight that "he would not reduce farther without weakening." When they set-to the year later Molineaux met defeat in less than twenty minutes. Wheezing out of a heavy chest, the usually resourceful Virginian suffered a broken jaw before his rival put him to the floor in dominant fashion. For Cribb, retirement made too much sense to pass up.

Richmond lost all faith in Molineaux and disowned him, leaving the big lug to carry on his mischievous path. Ireland was where his liver crashed in his thirty-fourth year. By contrast, drawing off those cultured roots which had served him so well Bill was honoured at the coronation of King George IV and lived on until he was sixty-six.

A great quiet commenced as Cribb, standing over his era like a colossus, kept the title. Champion of England; the one title pugilism offered to men of all weight made things rather unfair, but it would be an historical *faux pas* to link up the gold again without mention of two of the lighter masters. Appropriately installed as 'the phenomenon', Jewish Samual Elias was said to have fists like iron; a description not fantastically intended but a commonly held study. Popularly styled as 'Dutch' Sam, his 140lbs knew no bounds and, incredibly, is said to have been the other half of over 100 bouts. Tom Belcher, brother of brilliant Jem, lacked too much an element of the ruffian to thrive under the rule set, but made up for it with skill that astounded all who were witness. Out on the famed Fives Court, it was with the gloves that Belcher conveyed the nuances of boxing better than any prize-fighter.

The pair set-to thrice and each time the strength of Sam overcame Belcher's superior knowhow. Cameos of brilliance often left Sam swiping at the air; in fact, one opinion read "it is no exaggeration to say, he is by far a better boxer than Sam"[17], but with a style more designed to frustrate than pummel, Tom could not halt the ever advancing Jew.

Sam may have been the first pugilist to encourage one to consider a boxer's worth, pound-for-pound. As Pierce Egan thought, "take him for all in all" (all 9 stone 4 pounds of him) he had no equal."[18] His fearlessness also knew no bounds, once reported to have thrown down the gauntlet to then champion Henry Pearce in a fight he would have conceded the best part of 50lbs. His career reached its summit in 1804 during the highly anticipated clash against Westminster's supreme lightweight, Caleb Baldwin. At that time Caleb was said to have won forty-two contests consecutively without fault. Baldwin started as the favourite and looked to substantiate those odds when Sam fell under his accurate fist in quick time. Maintaining his early advantage, Caleb however bared the misfortune of catching one of Sam's terrible swings which got the blood flowing. Both men wore a red mask as the pace slowed and the odds evened, but it was the Jew's incredible reserve which got the better of Baldwin. The only contest that Sam is recorded to have lost was against a baker named Knowlesworthy. This set-to occurred ten years after the one with Baldwin and saw a forty-two-year-old, gin-guzzling (ten glasses per morning had become the norm) weakened version of the Jewish battler fail to last. Ending such an illustrious career on a low note, the want for conditioning quickly turned into a want for stable health. 1816 marked his death.

The best part of ten years passed when a protégé of Cribb's known as Thomas Winter began to seduce fist-fighting's hierarchy under Tom Spring. The artfully intended 'Light Tapper' represented a very different mould of fighting from Cribb's, but the courageous and learned manner in which he performed once again had people surrounding the ring by the thousand. Cribb agreed with the praise and handed over that championship. Spring made his claim against Ned Painter in 1818 but lost his

[17] The Times, 1807, Aug 21st, p.3

[18] Every Gentleman's Manual, 1845, Pierce Egan, p.101

only bout in the rematch when an early blow cursed him for the remainder. Bill Neat and Tom Oliver were two venerable forces. Spring scored victories over both.

The anticipated encounter with Neat is said to have lured no less than 30,000 of the nation to its scene, but the back-to-back marathons with Irish champion John Langan a year later brought an already outstanding career to its climax. The great length of each battle may be attributed to Spring's calculating ways, but Langan fought through every round with uncommon spirit, dragging Spring into states of dismal fatigue. The first bout ended after two and a half hours, and is thought to have claimed the life of one and injured many when part of the stage collapsed. The second bout adhered more to the rules but lost nothing in vigour. Both competitors required their seconds to help them come to scratch whilst waiting for their second, third, and fourth winds. The champion's swollen fists made it near unbearable to throw a punch, but for all of the Irishman's bravery, he could not seal the deal. With Spring's delicate weapons battered, and having proven his mastery, he left the prize-ring making him the fourth champion in a row to abandon the title. A national celebrity for the rest of his days, he later inherited the famed Castle Tavern from Tom Belcher and stayed put until his death in 1851, aged fifty-six. The next twenty years yielded a good crop but fatal encounters and foul play drove pugilism into another recession.

Tom Cannon, 'The Great Gun of Windsor', may be thought of as the man who led pugilism into its autumn. He had been competing alongside Spring and snuck his way into the history books with a twenty minute victory over Josh Hudson, a popular figure known as John 'The Bull'. He repeated this feat a few months later and then lost his claim to a fighter renowned for skulduggery. Jem Ward, another Black Diamond, tore the title away from Cannon in just ten minutes. Rumours of a fix were spread but Ward gained much respect on the scorching day when he blitzed the champion. Ward was previously beaten by Hudson but he pleased the audience with his fine technique. Victory over Cannon helped reinstall faith after Jem's shameful pantomime with Bill Abbott, but in 1827 Peter Crawley overpowered him in twenty-six minutes. Crawley encouraged Ward into a brawl, dispelling his advantageous boxing. He then retired to invest his fortune, leaving Jem to go on and become the first champion ever to regain the title. The roughhousing Jack Carter couldn't stop Ward and then Irish heavyweight Simon Bryne failed in seventy painful minutes. Not wanting to break the trend, Jem then decided to retire as champion, leaving Bryne and another large contender who he had refused to defend against called James Burke. It was at this point that the prize-ring was to endure one of its most threatening periods.

Bryne had previously experienced the darkest abyss when Scottish opponent Alexander McKay suffered a fatal beating by his hand. Frantic attempts were made to revive him but, "the poor creature was at length borne from the ground in a state of insensibility." Distraught but eager to continue, Bryne went on to join what must be one of the most miscellaneous of groups, becoming the victim, having been the survivor of a death-related bout. For the victor, affectionately labelled the 'Deaf un' for an obvious reason, it was a gloomy coronation. As had Simon he went to court for his actions but was acquitted of the charges. Regardless, as if pugilism had not already been sniffed at, Burke felt the aftershock for some time which urged him to continue his career over in America; the first British fighter to do so. Through touring and trying in vain to goad Ward out of retirement, Burke's next bout did not occur until four years later in 1937 against Samuel O' Rourke which was cake. Tom O' Connell was then handily defeated in New York before Burke returned to England. The absence had attracted a new customer, one who ended up pinching that title when Burke was penalised for hitting his downed man.

The loss of the championship often stigmatised yesterday's hero with hardships. Burke continued to fight for another four years but was dead within six. He fought a couple more times after departing from the title but soon contracted tuberculosis and died a very poor man in 1845. Now more than ever, pugilism was finding it hard to remain relevant. In response to Byrne's death a fresh set of rules entered in 1838, which most crucially barred seconds from helping their pugilist back to ring centre. With its comparative serenity, the turf did not suffer the vicissitudes of boxing. Horse racing offered social gambling grounds where one need not endanger their reputation. As for the ring, weary from legal whiplash, the spectacle called pugilism saw its Napoleonic heyday sail into the night. The days when the crowds roar could be heard for miles had slowly dithered. Old notions of barbarity regrouped.

As Egan saw it, "however the march of intellect may have done great things for the improvements of the arts and sciences, I must confess that improvements in pugilism have not kept pace with it, nay even on a jog trot."[19] Nevertheless, fists would defiantly remain for a further twenty years, lest the critics forget their own sentiment that "if the very devil wanted to fight, he would find an Englishman who would accommodate him."[20] Hard times spawned another batch of powerful, skilful and (as the pugilistic demography shifted) more westerly boxers.

---

[19] Every Gentleman's Manual, 1845, Pierce Egan, p.145

[20] The Times, 1825, Jul 20th, p.2

TOM BELCHER

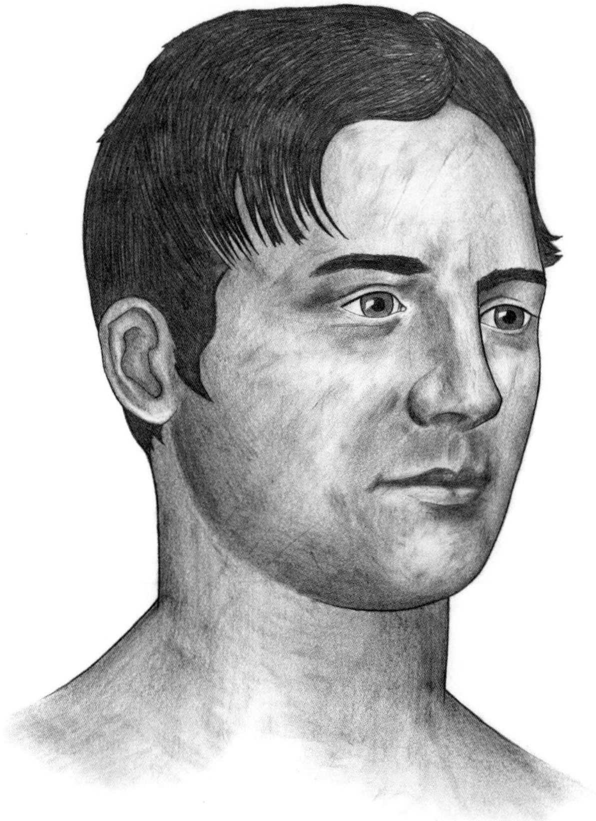

Height: 5'9"

Weight: 152lbs

Tom Belcher is an historical curiosity. He was both behind and ahead of his time; not tough enough to be the best prize-fighter but second to nobody when the gloves were on. It wouldn't be incorrect to say that gloved fighting unofficially existed alongside prize-fighting. At Fives Court sparring was a big attraction, and when the public came down to see Tom perform "those persons who were fond of the art of self-defence, experienced a treat."

(Overleaf) Here is Tom performing with the mitts at the Fives Court (the hotspot for boxing in between championship fights), demonstrating the strength behind science. With a bare-knuckle record of eight victories in thirteen bouts he was no pushover though when your brother is Jem Belcher it doesn't help. Inevitably there was a little imitating, firing his leads in that swift manner, but more impressive was his ability to take the play away. Tom would maintain space between himself and the opponent, stopping blows with a flexible guard. When it was time to fire back he did so with great accuracy and was known for his one-two; the rule-set didn't favour long combinations but punches *were* linked to capitalise. Reputedly, nobody got the better of Tom with the gloves, not when they kept to sparring. The long list of opponents included John Gulley, Tom Cribb, and Tom Molinueax.

CHAPTER V

THE NEW WORLD

"The ring is always constructed of a certain size for the express purpose of restraining the combatants within certain bounds, and within those bounds a man has a perfect right to retreat and jump about as long as he likes." [21]

Tom Sayers vs. John C. Heenan
Drawing by W.L. Walton

[21] Tom Sayers, Sometime Champion of England, 1866, S.O. Beeton, p.97

A year prior to the amended rules Queen Victoria began her sixty-three year reign over Great Britain; a period in which a previously non-existent middle class would reduce the gulf between poverty and riches. A huge number of people from east Europe poured into America, and with greater public involvement through new voting rights a closer knit society took its first steps into the new world. In fashion and architecture change was all around while train tracks were frenetically lay, offering a cheaper way to connect from town to town. Underneath the noise of steam trains and factories poverty had yet to loosen its deadly grip. The population boom reduced wages painfully so, leading to child labour, and the level of contamination terrorised all with disease; if you made it to thirty you may have been considered blessed.

One who became convinced on the last remark was the last of twenty-one children, part of a set of triplets, known to the pugilistic fraternity as 'Bendigo'. Born into a religious Nottingham home, William Thompson retired back into his pious roots, encircling a colourful life inside the ropes. As a young lad Bendigo excelled as an athlete; in stone-throwing, cricket and somersaulting to name a few, but his indulgence in the latter would cause for a three year absence. Thompson was the man who had relieved Burke of the title when the 'Deaf Un' got disqualified for head-butting. Bendigo had a knack for infuriating, laughing his way through tough times. To add to these confusing ways he fought out of a southpaw or left-handed stance, being credited as the first to do so.

His legacy, as is tradition, stemmed from a bloody saga with another boxer; in Bendigo's case the 6'2", 200lbs Ben Caunt. The imposing 'Torkard Giant' also hailed from Nottingham and went on to fight his hometown rival thrice. Each contest was drawn out and well fought but all terminated due to a foul; in two of them it was Caunt who suffered the penalty. The original occurred under Broughton's rule set; something that proved troublesome to the bigger man. Bendigo often dropped after getting through with a decent blow, a tactic all too common for the time. Caunt tried to contend with the better schooled boxer but largely fell victim to the round-ending trick, mentally as well as physically. Failed efforts were coroneted with laughter, eventually compelling Ben to walk up to his seated pest and thump him. The rematch, though not technically a championship bout, nonetheless attained championship significance. Bendigo's supporters, a nasty throng known as the 'Nottingham Lambs' made their noisy way to the scene. Though getting the better of things again, Bendigo was penalised for going down without receiving a blow. Bendigo's seconds claimed their man had slipped, owing to the fact he was not wearing the recently banned spiked shoes, but to no avail. When the decision was rendered, Caunt may have preferred a loss as Bendigo's lambs stormed after him. With fists, feet and clubbing weapons they tried to get at Caunt, but fortunately for him he managed to jump on a horse bareback and flee.

A month after defeating Burke the new champion incurred a knee injury while performing his favourite acrobatic stunt. This mishap forced Bendigo into temporary retirement, allowing Nick Ward (younger brother of Jem) to exact his weak grip on the title. Caunt was again disqualified for allegedly hitting Nick when down. The belt was swapped again in a rematch. It was during these trivial interactions that pugilism in the United States made its stand.

Before the 1840s contests occurred largely due to "personal grudge, or sprung from sudden and heedless chaffing."[22] James Ambrose or Sullivan, famous under 'Yankee Sullivan' helped to change all that. Though only a middleweight Sullivan used his wit to dumbfound the larger, unrefined sluggers. A twelve month stint in the U.S. convinced him to return but first he turned heads by defeating the highly touted John 'Hammer' Lane. John was unfortunate to have broken his forearm early on, but you've probably figured that sympathy was not one of the prize-ring's selling points; to Yankee's credit he is reported to have fought well before the incident, conducting himself in a manner "which proved that there was nothing of the novice in his pretensions."[23] When back in the States, Sullivan's Sawdust House bustled with customers. Over the next decade he would propel that fame to the tip of every American's tongue. Popular victories over Tom Secor, William Bell and Bob Caunt each claimed sizeable column space until it was time for America's first super-fight with New Yorker, Tom Hyer.

Hyer put himself in the picture by defeating George McChester in a two hour and fifty-five minute marathon back in 1841. He was better schooled than many of the native boxers and retained all the strength of his 6'2", 180lbs frame. An enjoyably complimentary pen picture of him read thus, "He is a tall, splendid looking fellow, of some six feet two inches in height, with regular and handsome features and a form that is a happy combination of Hercules and the Apollo Belvidere."[24] Sullivan trained rigorously for the $10,000 fight, which is thought to have sprouted from a pub brawl. He ran many miles and was said to have punched upwards during his dumbbell exercises to help prepare for the inevitable incline when delivering his blows. Unfortunately for him, when the time came for the anticipatory roars to quell, only seventeen minutes were needed to see Hyer emerge the victor. It's possible that Yankee's thirty-eight years played a part in this quick exit, but it's unlikely to have changed the result. Sullivan charged at Hyer unfazed, but the strength differential not only nullified his wrestling ability but ended up turning into a trap as he was repeatedly overpowered and twisted to the ground. Hyer made sure to fall on his chest in the same motion.

Sullivan had enchanted America, but Hyer capitalised to become their first champion. The loser briefly got his title back when Hyer decided to retire two years after their fight. Tom never fought again and died from cardiac dropsy aged forty-five. Sullivan lost the title to John Morrissey due to an officiating squabble (a fight he had won). He then retired and wound up dead in a jail cell; suicide or murder? Both the motives and circumstances of the incident are hazy.

Things were very slow during Morrissey's unremarkable reign which included four years without a defence. Over the Atlantic, Bendigo had been drawn from the alcoholic banter of his inn and back to the British ring. A further two hours and ten

[22] The American Fistiana, 1849, H. Johnson, p.1

[23] The Life and Battles of Yankee Sullivan, 1854, A. Winch, p.14

[24] The Life and Battles of Yankee Sullivan, 1854, A. Winch, p.38

minutes ended the trilogy with Caunt in the champion's favour and without a single cry of enough. The loser went on to take an interest in pigeon-racing; a hobby which lured him into the winter frost where he contracted a nasty cold. This eventually advanced into pneumonia and brought about his death aged forty-six. The champion took five years out, only to return and try his luck against future champion Tom Paddock. Although nearing forty, the vitality displayed by him delighted the crowd and he won on a foul.

Bendigo almost fell into the abyss of liquor when an evangelist preacher by the name of Richard Weaver encouraged him to improve his current form which had produced twenty-eight jail sentences. Retirement offered far too much spare time for a goalless drunkard. He dedicated the rest of his life to public speaking until his sixty-eighth year when a tumble down some stairs dealt him fatal internal injuries. A few months after the Paddock fight, a veteran named William Perry almost fought Bendigo. Many men had fallen before the 'Tipton Slasher' but it was victory over Tass Parker that put Perry neck-and-neck with Bendigo, essentially reprising the role of champion in between those long absences. Perry wasn't, as his nickname hinted, the artful type; he used his 6' frame and 13 stone to settle disputes in a more familiar, vicious manner. These clubbing methods failed to tame the giant American Charles Freeman in 1842; a man who is listed to have risen nearly 7' and weighed close to 300lbs. After getting the better of Parker, a unification of sorts came about when Paddock and Perry set-to in 1850. As had become customary, the title was claimed on a foul, and then Perry handed the title to Harry Broome after striking *him* illegally.

Broome possessed greater wrestling than boxing ability, though he was no slouch in the latter department. He was pretty light, never scaling more than 170lbs, but at his best gave as good as anyone; this he nicely demonstrated during his long-winded triumph over Harry Orme. Their two hour and twenty-eight minute battle (packed into thirty-one long rounds) instilled hope in the future of pugilism; currently a foul-ridden mess. Barring Caunt's rematch with Nick Ward, over the last fourteen years every single one of the eight championship bouts had been decided on a foul. Broome was known to pile on the weight in between fights but whipped himself into peak condition for this one. He then caused another period of inactivity, refusing a challenge from Perry and two from Paddock. Three years allowed plenty of time for the rust to set in and Paddock made good of his chance. Pugilism was finding it difficult to get traction but a 150lbs ace was on the way to make everything very clear.

Brighton's Tom Sayers had grown from the tough, fishing scenes of his youth to command the prize-ring. In twenty years of fighting only one man was able to beat him, the splendid Nat Langham. Nat shared his swansong with Caunt, but four years prior was busy rattling out a tune on Tom's head. This one favourably adhered to the rules, but the younger man couldn't trouble the long figure of Langham, which repeatedly thumped Sayers' peepers until blinded. Langham achieved what nobody else would but his size was thought to be something of an Achilles' heel, "Too heavy

[25] Tom Sayers, Sometime Champion of England, 1866, S.O. Beeton, p.26

for light men, and too light for real big ones."[25] Harry Orme dealt Langham his sole defeat previous to the Sayers' bout. Orme's face wasn't pretty as a result of Nat's sharpshooting but he endured the smaller man's savvy to flaunt his weight. Heavy throws had the last say. Sayers was good against larger fighters, rugged enough for technique to become the deciding factor. Perry and Paddock discovered this painful truth. A certain American begged to differ.

John Camel Heenan, the 'Benicia Boy' marked a new breed of American fighter. Self-diagnosed as "Half horse, half alligator and a bit of the snapping turtle"[26], Heenan did not allow for his physical powers to run over the essential lessons. Standing 6'2", Heenan's 190lbs frame was impeccably formed; every muscular bump stood to attention. Though his science was not lacking, evidently strength was the American's primary weapon; an English reporter once quipped that the dumbbells in his house were "about the same size as one imagines that of Hercules to have been when he tamed the nemean lion." His career included just three contests, none of which he won. As it was with John Jackson, one needed only a taster to confirm the hearsay. American champion John Morrissey first got the better of him, but that was after Heenan smashed his right hand on a stake after misdirecting a blow. After touring the States with the championship (Morrissey was stripped after refusing a rematch) Heenan caught the eye of American journalist George Wilkes.

Using Heenan as a subject for his *Spirit of the Times* newspaper, Wilkes helped to realise a super-fight with English champion Sayers. Accompanying Heenan over the Atlantic, Wilkes reported back daily. The interest aroused was unlike anything since pugilism's heyday. A couple of highly-touted international bouts had failed to materialise; first Caunt and Hyer in 1842, and then Perry and Hyer in 1850. Burke had fought Stateside but both the grounds and opponents weren't ideal. England was boxing's mecca, at least for one more fight. Despite persecution from the law which urged train tickets to have 'no destination', when Heenan arrived at the desolate field, twenty-five miles outside of London, all the ingredients were there for the original Fight of the Century. The huge crowd was clad with personalities; poets, actors and singers including Heenan's wife, actress Adah Isaacs Menken. Novelist William Makepeace Thackeray attended, as did John Hollingshead, but Charles Dickens pulled out at the last minute as his friend, archaeologist Austen Henry Layard, "had "scruples" about going to it".[27]

Opposing each other the bare basics were stark; Heenan was younger, taller, longer and heavier. It looked like a mismatch but the fight was unsurpassed in its desperation. Sayers began sharp, drawing first blood and moving nimbly. Heenan soon got near and decked the smaller man, something he would do twenty-five times. As if he didn't already have his hands full, Sayers' right arm suffered a fracture; from then on the swollen limb sought refuge by his stomach. The English champion proceeded to demonstrate amazing powers of recovery and closed Heenan's eye. The other was on

---

[26] The Times, 1860, Apr 18th, p.9

[27] The Letters of Charles Dickens, Volume 9 (1859-1861), 1997, p.235

the verge of closing when the American decided to throttle Sayers on the ropes. This led to them being cut. Knowing the police were literally battling their way through the assembly everyone closed-in, making for a temporary space to help the fight reach its end.

Two hours and twenty minutes (forty-two rounds) had elapsed when the bout was stopped and declared a draw. The undecided nature of the event sparked endless discussion. Soothsayers aside, both men came away winners, each presented with a silver championship belt. Nobody would ever forget:

> "*How through two well-spent hours and more,*
> *Through bruise, and blow, and blood,*
> *Like sturdy bulldogs, as they were,*
> *Those well-matched heroes stood*"[28]

Sayers retired while Heenan fought future champ Tom King. Approaching things very negatively, he relied solely on his throws. The tactic began to work however, nearly winning him the bout when some interference helped King gather himself to go on and win. Heenan lived on until 1873 when consumption got him while diabetes ended Sayers' life in 1865. Another chapter in the ring, a pivotal one, had closed. It wasn't the last noteworthy contest, but it *was* the final peak. Britain continued to enjoy world power for decades to come, but for all the sentiments of equality, these measures, along with America's rapidly swelling population dealt pugilism a terminal blow. Now more than ever the authorities aimed for a pugilistic lockdown.

Fist-fighting had been an identity as much as a sport, something that decorated Englishmen as resolute and noble creatures. Many authors and politicians echoed these principles, though always in the minority. Ever since Figg society was at its heels. Over the next ten years great changes would see to it that England was forever remembered as The Cradle of Boxing. Jack Broughton wouldn't have had it any other way. The ninth Marquess of Queensberry was also present for the big fight; a man whose appellation was about to sponsor a different breed of boxing.

---

[28] 'The Fight of Heenanus and Sayerius', Punch, Volume XXXVIII, 1860, Apr 28th, p.177

TOM SAYERS

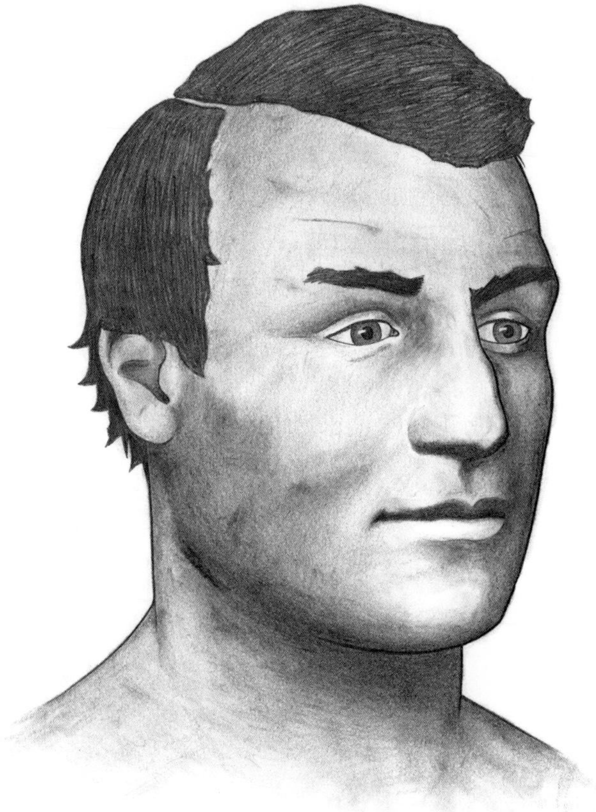

Height: 5'8"

Weight: 154lbs

Sayers was of a similar size to Mendoza but chunkier in the legs. Though no more than 160lbs he "seemed wonderfully big", broad all over and with that preferably bronzed skin which resisted abrasions. When he took his stance it was said to be "artistic and firm, yet light." His physical strength and power of punch, especially for a man of his inches was exceptional, but it was his speed of foot which proved his greatest advantage as he jumped in and out, initiating and severing contact at the drop of a hat.

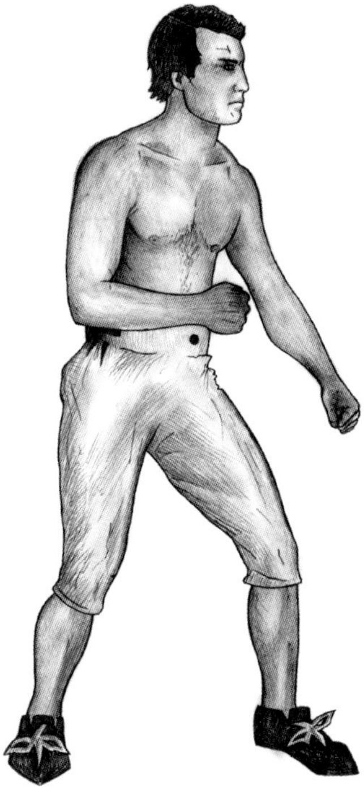

Sayers' stance was loose but considerate, barring the right over the vital mark with most of the body's weight supported under a forward left leg. The left arm draped low with deceptive intention.

Sayers could stop punches very neatly, but his preference (clearly influenced by fighting men two stone heavier) was to remove himself from range by shooting back. Sometimes it was thought he overexerted himself with this defensive tactic but it could leave opponents clueless.

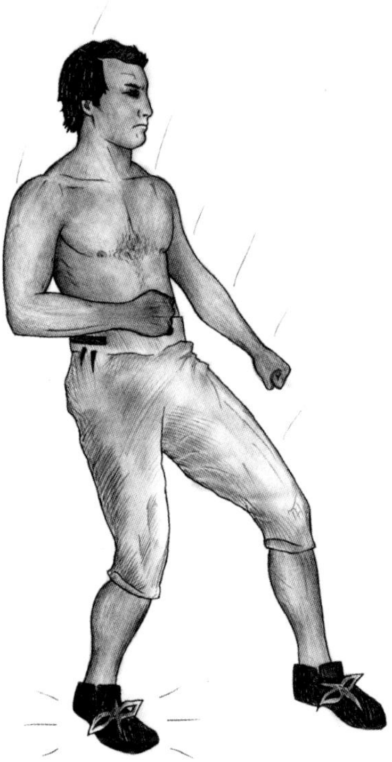

BRIDGING OBLIVION

"It is rather hard upon the patrons of this sport that they must sit up all night and steal like malefactors, amid the fog of early morning, to an out-of-the-way spot where it is only just possible that the police may be an hour or two behind them." [29]

Jem Mace

[29] The Times, 1862, Dec 1st, p.9

It was John Shoto Douglas who endorsed pugilism with its new 'Marquess of Queensberry' banner, but John Graham Chambers was the brains behind it. A sports fanatic from Cambridge, Chambers' new idea of fighting was not a facelift like the amendments of 1838 but a reconstruction. Rounds were set at three minutes, unaffected by knockdowns. Once knocked down (only by a punch) you had ten seconds to get to your feet otherwise you were deemed a beaten man. There was to be no wrestling, seconds were taken out of the ring, and wearing gloves was customary. They were officially published in 1867 and their first great representative was a lad from Norfolk called Jem Mace.

The elegant Mace, who would come to be known as 'The Gypsy', was a prize-fighter who liked the new mode of fighting. He had been competing without the gloves since the 1840s, thoroughly acquainted with being thrown on your head, but he set a new tone when the mitts hid his weathered knuckles. Jem was already promoting the use of gloves before the new rule set was in effect. He saw greater expression in gloved boxing and updated the new guard during his discoveries in the ring.

Mace was active in the game of give-and-take before puberty, and for most of his career he was no more than a big middleweight. With great strength and wrestling ability it was like entering a rose bush when the bigger man closed on him and he was a very accurate puncher; a fiend on the counter. The supreme achievement of Mace's legacy however was through increasing awareness. Beginning and ending his journey in England, Mace had a profound impact in America, Australia and New Zealand; places he inhabited for years at a time. When his ageing body prevented him from taking part in exhibitions everybody, young and old, fighter and observer, acknowledged his precious contribution.

Bob Brettle played a crucial role in making Jem into the fighter he became. In 1858 the young Gypsy had the dishonour of being knocked out in their second round. Revising his strategy he came back two years later and cleaned up. The huge Sam Hurst, going off his sole victory over Tom Paddock, had been given Sayers' championship belt. He wasn't a good boxer, light years behind someone like Mace, and the latter was now in a position to challenge him. Jem may have been giving up as much as 70lbs, and with Hurst's strength he would not be able to rush in. When time was called Mace used his powers of feinting to hoax Hurst into a slow-burning, tentative battle. In over fifty minutes (eight rounds) the big man was worn down and Mace captured the heavyweight championship of England. It was hardly a classic, and it's likely that many of the faithful left reminiscing about Sayers and Heenan. Fortunately the world of boxing was not completely void of excitement as Tom King twice fought Mace in wonderfully unpredictable bouts.

King 'The Fighting Sailor' had size on Mace. Not quite as bulky as Hurst, but taller and a better fighter. Sharp punching bloodied the champion early on and Tom looked the likely winner. For a good portion of the fight Mace was on the receiving end but he gradually slowed down the attacks until King tired. Neat counters inflicted damage, evening things up and then Mace fired a winner after sixty-eight minutes. When it came to the science, Jem was the undisputed pioneer of his day, but King made cerebral adjustments. He demanded a rematch and it occurred ten months later for the low purse of £200 a side. When things got underway it was Mace who took the initiative, happy to force the pace. The difference in skill, despite the modifications, was still blatant. In the nineteenth round Mace stepped in to finish a quality performance but he fell short. For the whole fight King had been seething to land his right, and this time it connected with an impact which had spectators comparing its sound to "a shot from an Armstrong gun." Mace slowly got to his feet, but the left side of his face blew up; not that he was aware of anything at this point. A single blow had sapped every joule of energy and the sponge was helplessly thrown up after thirty-eight minutes.

Pugilism was not a safe enterprise while Mace was fighting. Pickpockets, thugs and every kind of underhanded character that coloured a Dickens' novel were scaring away spectators to the point they were more the mob than the fancy. The patronage was drying up fast, and less interest meant less money. After the controversial win over Heenan, King retired and made his fortune where many had, at the racing track. Mace waited out the sting of defeat and got back in the mix to face Joe Goss, a fighter much more his size. They fought three times and Jem won every one. At the start of each conflict he assumed the position; "his hands well up, the left somewhat advanced, and the chief weight of his body on the right leg."[30] Technically the second time there was no fight when the police intervened before first blood. In the third Mace demanded a sixteen foot ring as opposed to the regular twenty-four and he mugged Goss, cutting his brow to the point he claimed to perceive bone. A proposed bout with Ned O' Baldwin was irritatingly undone by the authorities, convincing Mace that he was going to have to travel in order to keep his career alive. He bridged the Atlantic in 1869, touring with Heenan, hungry for American blood. Tom Allen happened to be owner of the American championship though he had lost his fair share of fights.

It was quite a gathering at Kernersville, Louisiana. That multicultural buzz which used to spiral around the English ring (presently chased back into their individual classes) had found a new release in the States, though you'd have done well to absorb the atmosphere because it wasn't much of a fight. Mace handled the English-born Allen with dastardly ease. While getting several kinds of life beaten out of him Tom still retained the decorum to beg for Jem's pardon after spiking his foot, a gesture which was "yielded gracefully, and pleasantly." In the tenth, during the forty-fourth minute, Mace finished him off with a heavy throw. The heavyweight championship of America was his. A title fight with Joe Coeburn was arranged but when they arrived they saw that the police had already taken their seats, ready to pull the plug. They fought an inconclusive affair with Mace injuring his hand. At forty years of age he had fought his last championship fight. He concentrated on touring, spreading the word while making a buck, and fighters like Goss caught the bug to do some touring of their own. That networking manuscript which Yankee Sullivan had left unfinished was on its way to completion. Gloves were used with increasing regularity, but difficult as it was, prize-fights were the only way to decide a championship fight. From 1867-76 there was not a single title fight. When the silence was broken it was drearily so with a

[30] Chicago Tribune, 1866, Jun 14th, p.0_2

disqualification win for Goss after Allen had struck him while down…sounds familiar.

Goss continued sparring. A fight was scheduled with Irish strongman Paddy Ryan but he refused when the promoter failed to produce any prize money. They made it a reality in 1880 and Ryan came away the new champion. The 'Trojan Giant' had all the form and size to draw you in. That nickname was pretty cool as well, but the big man was a rushed prospect, woefully wanting for technique. It had taken him a whopping eighty-seven minutes to get rid of the forty-two-year-old champion.

Every now and then Britain made a squeak, claiming a fight was for 'The Championship of England', but it may as well have been for the championship of the local inn. Mace's movements illustrated the emaciated state of British pugilism; the last time he had fought there was thirteen years ago. Ryan was impressive, though the majority of admiration came from wishful reporters and his manager.

In 1882, for a 'winner-takes-all' stake of $5000 ($2500 apiece), Paddy was scheduled to face "a gentleman probably as well known to the police of New York as to those of his own city."[31] A hair under 6' and with a 180lbs body, he wasn't lacking in size. A small percentage knew he was absurdly strong. At 11:45am he threw his trademark cap into ring centre, gleefully responding to a bet that Paddy would score the first knockdown. There was nothing boyish about the Bostonian, empowered by his twenty-five years but loaded with a confidence that only experience can buy. Many thousands of miles away, Jem Mace was a few hours from rising in Australia, ready to commit another day to spying rough diamonds. To be sure a couple of beauts were mined. Thirty seconds later in Mississippi City, Ryan was on his haunches from a quick right. Up he got to absorb punches that left a blotch every time they struck. The champion, apparently "afraid of his antagonist" got in a few throws, but grinning was probably not the effect he was looking for. The challenger's right hand was a wicked thing, blustering Paddy's composure whenever it twitched. In ten and a half minutes, with a swollen nose, swollen neck, and a lattice of bruising around his gut, the big Irishman was done. It was in fact John L. Sullivan's first contest minus the gloves. The influence of Jem's campaign was everywhere.

---

[31] Brooklyn Daily Eagle, 1881, Jun 14th, p.2

MARQUESS OF QUEENSBERRY RULES

INTRODUCTION

The aim behind the following seven chapters has been to represent boxing, not as a directory, but a shifting idea. It's light on statistical details, ditching a panoramic view for more personal close-ups of the fighters, tracking their deeds in accordance with their significance, be it the evolution of styles or their individual merits. The themes start off quite simply, focusing on the Queensberry's leading pioneers, but as the demography expands, the rules gradually alter, and the championship divides, themes begin to find commonalities to link key fighters; Abe Attell, Jim Driscoll and the 'No Decision' era, the Murderers' Row, upsets in the early 2000s.

1880 - 1899

OVERVIEW

John L. Sullivan penned the last great bare-knuckle chapter with his victory over Jake Kilrain. Despite the bout's infamy it was in fact only the champ's third bout under the crumbling rule set. Sullivan, regardless of his bare-fisted legend was more familiar with gloves, and his last hurrah owed just as much to a want for condition as it did of outdated weaponry. Outdone or unfit, regardless, styles were changing. 'Nonpareil' Jack Dempsey and James J. Corbett each brought individual flair to the ring, executing moves that were to be adopted by many. Four ounce and five ounce gloves still made body shots especially deadly, so hands often hovered near the waist. The huge round limits insisted on a steady pace. A little thought was necessary before boxers went pouncing in. Many discarded the slow approach with success, but starting fast in a twenty plus round fight was risky. Combinations didn't flow, but parrying and clinching became essential. You could think of the turn of the century fighters as the masterful economists.

The black man had enjoyed a period of leniency a century prior, but at the turn of the twentieth century prejudice was debilitating; the impact this would have on African boxers was immense. The wonderful Peter Jackson was the first culprit of many. Racism lived off the ideology that blacks held society back, and so it was with boxing. The enterprise of promoting also began to bud, exploding the idea of boxing as an unruly sideshow. Temporary wooden stadiums were indeed the sign of big things to come while the kinetoscope offered a new, exciting means to cover fights.

CHAPTER I

1880 - 1899

JOHN L. AND A DARK PARIAH

The last few specks of the prize ring were on the cusp of being erased by gloves and ten counts, but with one foot in each era, John L. Sullivan may be thought of as a hybrid, game under both guises of boxing. However, racking up far more gloved bouts insists on treating him more so as part of the modern clan.

"It is no disgrace for him to be whipped by me."[32]

Arriving with a bang, Sullivan set the tone for the heavyweight division for years to come when Paddy Ryan was eaten up in 1882. It was evident that the moustache wearing brute wasn't going anywhere. Far beyond the level of available competition, Sullivan rarely failed to leave his opponents in a concussed heap. The right hand was lethal to catch and fired with eye-opening speed from his thickset figure.

A British middleweight named Charlie Mitchell was to get well acquainted with Sullivan. They met in a gloved fight in 1883 and Mitchell surprised probably even himself when he dumped Sullivan on his butt. It didn't faze the bigger man though as he jumped up to thump Mitchell around the ring during the third, at which point the police intervened. A rematch was scheduled in 1884 but Sullivan's reputation for inhaling drink literally preceded him as he showed up drunk. Infuriatingly, the bout had to be called off.

A tame sparring match with three ounce gloves against Dominick McCaffery installed Sullivan as the first heavyweight champion under the MQR in 1885 and in 1888 Mitchell was granted that rematch, this time with bare fists. The champion was not in his trim of old. A few extra pounds hampered his full might and so an early finish was ideal. Through four rounds Mitchell received quite a trouncing but he hung in there to see his burly rival droop with fatigue. Further into the battle the rain began to pour which turned the floor beneath them into sludge. This didn't help Sullivan

[32] Hawke's Bay Herald, Volume XXI, Issue 6656, 1883, Sep 18th, p.3

and then the cold gripped the pair of them. Eventually the pace slowed ridiculously so and a draw was agreed upon after thirty-nine rounds of over three hours' duration. All throughout Sullivan's tenancy as a fighter, Peter Jackson could do nothing but watch the parade go by. The 'Black Prince' was exactly that, a fighter of a regal class forced into the shadows cast by a white hierarchy. Had he been allowed to shine there is a better than fair chance he would have ruled the roost. Superbly built, Jackson was around 6'2" and possessed a reach of about 77". These measurements would be adequate for today's behemoths, but back when men were smaller, the long, muscular form of this contender got hearts palpitating.

"He is undoubtedly a clever man and has a phenomenal reach. The chances are that he will give Sullivan as good a fight as any man who has ever stood up before him." [33]

Sent to Australia at the age of six, Jackson developed into a fine athlete and later used that physical prowess to thrash his opposition. The homeland championship was his in 1886 after defeating Tom Lees. It soon became apparent that a trip to the United States was required to fish the big fights. George Godfrey was another outstanding coloured fighter, but when Jackson fought him the latter cruised his way to an eighteenth round knockout. Joe McAuliffe was no joke either, but Jackson finished him in the twenty-fourth. As Peter kept himself busy, Sullivan's once attractive figure grew a little round for the ring's liking. On strength alone challenges were repelled but it was a fading force in action. Before the fat lady intervened he prepared his body for the wrath of Jake Kilrain. It was no picnic for the 'Boston Strong Boy' who had to drag himself through some hairy moments. Eventually one hundred and twenty minutes (seventy-five rounds) proved enough. A potential fight with Jackson excited anyone who knew anything about boxing but it was not to be. "I think that if he ever comes up against Sullivan, and the champion is in any kind of fix, that it will be all day with the darky."[34] was boxer Tom Allen's opinion, one more to join the gravy of speculation.

The financial whiplash from prize-fighting deterred Sullivan from seeking any more fights with bare fists. On the other hand, Jackson secured a gloved contest with a young talent who went by the alias of 'Gentleman Jim'. Taking place in 1891, James J. Corbett was hard-pressed to do anything about his large problem, but he cleverly

[33] Brooklyn Daily Eagle, 1889, Dec 22nd, p.14

[34] Brooklyn Daily Eagle, 1889, Nov 26th, p.1

moved about until the bout slowed to a crawl. In the sixty-first round a draw was rendered by referee Hiram Cook who stood between the exhausted boxers. Two years later Jackson bruised the reputation of England's Frank Paddy Slavin with a tenth round knockout. It was Jackson's last victory of merit while Sullivan was preparing, or rather, unwinding for his last fight.

THE IMMORTAL

While Sullivan did away with the big boys, a slender Irishman, some 50lbs lighter than the heavyweight king defeated his opponents, not with force but finesse. John Edward Kelly, better known as Jack Dempsey knew what it meant to be revered. They called him the 'Nonpareil' (the immortal). Similar to the heavyweight champ, Dempsey was comfortable with the gloves or bare fists. As the Queensberry rules were still finding their way almost every one of Dempsey's fights had different stipulations; four ounce gloves, two ounce, skin-tight, four rounds, ten rounds, fights to the finish, and then there was always the problem of where to stage the fight. In full trim he stood 5'8" and weighed around 150lbs. His stance was a defensive one with the rear foot so far back that he presented "almost a side view." On all occasions he was cool and never one to rush, preferring to scout bad habits, giving his work a distinct quality. He frequently called out England's Charlie Mitchell, but there was never a straight answer. He was not going to allow for Dempsey to, as a contemporary saw it, "disfigure his physiognomy."[36] Even Kilrain and Sullivan were goaded. None of these fights materialised but brief mention of them sparked hours of discussion.

"I can make more money by fighting than in any other way, and consequently I fight."[35]

As a teenager and young man he competed as a lightweight, snatching up New York's version of the title in 1884. In the same year he repelled the stalwart challenge of George Fulijames. His body quickly filled out which helped lend his blows a bit more venom. A series of knockouts were spread over 1885-86, bringing Jack to what he

[35] The Brooklyn Daily Eagle, 1886, Apr 4th, p.16

[36] The Brooklyn Daily Eagle, 1885, Dec 31st, p.4

considered his toughest assignment against Jack Fogarty; a fight he won in the twenty-seventh. Rests were minimal, and in the following month he faced the dangerous George LeBlanche. It was not easy, but Dempsey had the last say.

Exhibitions and numerous four round bouts kept him busy through most of 1887, but in December he agreed to a LPR scrap with Johnny Reagan, on a barge! Highlighting the muddled rules of the day, Reagan wore spiked shoes, much to Dempsey's displeasure. The fight went ahead but those spikes found their way into Jack's leg, creating a cut so deep that bone was visible. Unforgettable for all who bared witness, the bout moved to another location after the ring had become flooded by the rising tide. Now headed inland they opted for some shut-eye. When the time came they indifferently resumed. Even with his ghastly wound, Dempsey planted Reagan for keeps in the forty-fifth.

Challenges were issued and he was frequently pestered. If the money was right he would perform, but in 1888 a different kind of foe appeared when it was rumoured that Dempsey had been suffering from haemorrhages. His physician friend feared it was the first signs of consumption. Still only twenty-five, a ten round decision over Dominick McCaffrey showed there was still some petrol in the tank. Soon LeBlanche returned for a second crack. Due to a bizarre instance in their 1889 rematch, despite the fact Dempsey lost, he did not lose his title. LeBlanche was close to defeat when he uncorked his 'pivot punch'. "Whirling completely around" LeBlanche smashed Dempsey in the neck, leaving him in a bad way. It was easy pickings from then on as Dempsey was flogged to sleep. By 1890 a new challenger, one who had quite the reputation for punching was headed Dempsey's way. It was to be a cruel mismatch. Billy Professor McCarthy suffered the last dregs of the 'Nonpareil'.

By the 1890's great progress had been made in treating tuberculosis though it was still a major cause of death. Meanwhile New York's population exploded; reputations were easily lost. Dempsey's lawyer M.J. McMahon didn't want to see this happen and located his grave in Oregon. This desolate place of rest encouraged him to write a poem which was later put on the headstone. An exert reads:

No rose, no shamrock could I find,
No mortal here to tell
Where sleeps in this forsaken spot
The Immortal Nonpareil

Through Dempsey's elegant attitudes and conserved tactics boxing was further refined. Fighters became very conscious about getting drawn into a battle of wills and preferred to begin sparring, almost as if both combatants agreed they needed to warm up first. Though a fine prototype for the Queensberry rules, Dempsey was not its first true representative. That honour goes to an individual who took special pride in his gentlemanly conduct.

GENTLEMAN JIM

"If I ever relied much on others' opinions I wouldn't have had much confidence or strength left for the fight."[37]

There was something stimulating about James J. Corbett. Against a backdrop of mashed features and boasts of strength, Corbett's charming manner became the darling of reportage. That he frequently wrote letters (attractively so) was one of the many factors that divorced him from the rest. About the only thing he shared in common with his opponents was boxing. In keeping with his character, when it came to boxing there was individual pizzazz.

Jim was very quick for a bigger man though it was his smooth movement which really defined him. Like any smart boxer of the day everything came from the left hand, but rather than root himself to the floor he roamed the ring, utilising lateral movement to slip and lean away. He also knew how to gain the psychological edge, often delving opponents into a blind rage with his arrogance. The first opponent to put these fancy methods through their paces was Joe Choynski. He was a good deal smaller than Corbett but it would become Joe's trademark to give great heavyweights all they could handle. Choynski was a nifty operator; more impressive was his punch which could have decked a horse. The two were already acquainted but it was on a barge off the Californian shore where they would develop a deep respect for one another. Many times did Corbett get the worst of it, but a gritty core kept him going until the twenty-seventh brought him victory.

Along with studying fighting techniques, Jim also enjoyed acting. One of the people he encountered while touring theatres was the flamboyant William A. Brady. As it happened, Brady went from managing actors to managing Corbett's boxing career. The goal became to relieve Sullivan of his title, silly as that sounded. Their historic fight in 1892 was a finish fight, though under Queensberry rules; three minute rounds, one minute rest between and five ounce gloves. Police surrounded the authorized event, giving it a peculiar atmosphere as law enforcers were boxing's cancer prior to this bout. There can be no doubt that Sullivan was not his old self. He had carried unwanted flesh for his prize fight with Kilrain, but against Corbett he was fat. The challenger was younger, fitter, faster and (fully aware of this), let Sullivan chase after him. In a matter of minutes breathing became a chore and the champion was spoon-fed counters.

[37] The Book of Boxing, Heinz and Ward, 1999, p.65

Using his fresh skill set, Corbett fought Sullivan "almost exclusively with the left hand and was not a straight punch, but a sort of round-arm swing that Sullivan seemed unable to gauge at all."[38] Constantly turning and popping him, Corbett put a bit more behind his digs. By the twenty-first Sullivan was all wrapped up.

A pillar of boxing during this time was its white lineage. Respectful of this, Corbett drew the colour line to completely remove Jackson from the picture. Instead, Charlie Mitchell got another shot in 1894. Though only a middleweight it was surprising to see the man who had given Sullivan so much trouble beat within three rounds. In the same year Corbett became the second subject ever in boxing to be captured by the kinetoscope. What remains shows Corbett demonstrating his good natured mastery over a helpless Peter Courtney.

Jim was always in fine condition. He abstained from alcohol and kept himself sharp through exhibitions. He was also twenty-eight, an age in boxing when a fighter is typically at his zenith. By the time the big fight was set against the red-haired bomber, Corbett was thirty, so long had it taken to arrive at an agreement. Under a fierce Nevada sun everything was going to plan. Outboxed, bloodied, floored; the challenger was nearly done. And then it happened.*

THE FIGHTING BLACKSMITH

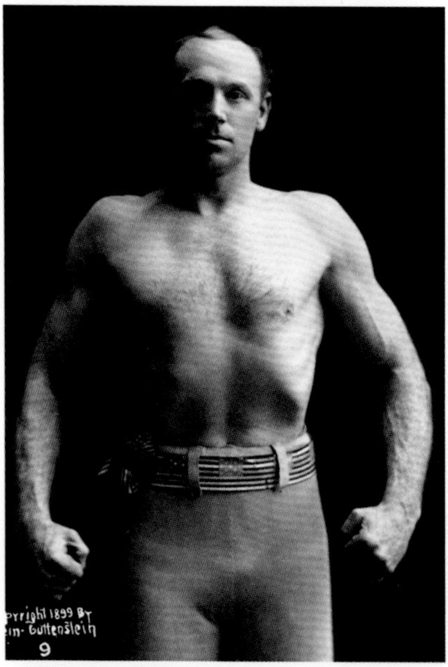

"Fitz landed that dangerous right of his on the point of the jaw and Hall fell like a dead man." [39]

When it came to breaking the mould, Robert Fitzsimmons offered a duel meaning. Receding red hair and a spindly build made for poor presentation but as a fighter he was unprecedented. The laws of physics worked differently around this Cornish middleweight. The rule states that the further up in weight you go the less effective your punch becomes. It's a rule that didn't apply to Fitzsimmons. Middleweights and, not just no-hopers, but good, durable heavyweights were destroyed. And this he did while weighing between 150-175lbs.

Moving to New Zealand at the age of nine, it's thought that Jem Mace scouted Fitzsimmons and urged him to turn professional. Joining Peter Jackson, Bob made the journey across to Australia to get things underway. Heavyweight Mick Dooley finished

[38] The Clinton Weekly Age, 1892, Sep 9th, p.1

* See Fitzsimmons – Corbett fight story page 170

[39] Warsaw Daily Times, 1893, Mar 9th, p.1

him in four rounds in 1886, but this may be put down to inexperience. Up until 1890, Fitzsimmons resided in Australia where a fierce reputation was formed. Helping to account for his devastating results were a pair of very pronounced shoulders, built from many years with the hammer and anvil. His 5'11" frame could have put on a good chunk of weight; actually it was an opinion that, "He is simply a heavy-weight sweated out and trained down to a requisite figure."[40] This is not entirely accurate, but it does help allude to his thorough training. A specialised program championed long, ten to twelve mile runs and wrestling sessions, designed to create lean muscle without sacrificing strength.

Less than a year in the U.S. and the middleweight title was his. In New Orleans, Dempsey absorbed a nasty beat-down. Stricken with tuberculosis the little marvel was powerless against Fitzsimmons who left him with a cut lip, swellings around both eyes, bruises on his ribs plus a broken nose. This bludgeoning machine was not all ice and enjoyed fooling about when the chance was there. He was also a big fan of animals. Several cats and dogs filled his home but Fitzsimmons was rumoured to have owned a large snake, a monkey and even a lion. When the latter died the eldest son recalled how their home "seemed lonesome" and so another was purchased. Despite this circus set up everyone knuckled down when need be, and the results said as much.

Sydney's Jim Hall had been in a title race against Fitzsimmons but ended up losing out. Jim was the mirror image of Bob; tall, slim and a cracking puncher. In their previous bout Fitzsimmons fell in the fourth but later swore the fix was in for a $75 bribe. When the 1893 decider was at hand the champion let a single right hand go in the fourth and that was that. The high profile victories continued in 1894. Choynski traded dynamite with Fitzsimmons but was headed for oblivion when the police stopped the bout, and Dan Creedon's title hopes crashed against Bob's fists in the second. By 1896 heavyweight Peter Maher was already a victim but welcomed a rematch. The kinetoscope was scheduled to capture the bout when poor light put a stop to that. Originally guaranteed some of the film royalties, Fitzsimmons converted his anger into a ninety-five second victory. Tom Sharkey was a tough heavyweight who had yet to taste defeat. Fitzsimmons had him up and down like a yo-yo but in the eighth the referee, the conniving Wyatt Earp ruled a body punch foul to award Sharkey the fight.

After defeating Corbett the 167lbs heavyweight champion did not defend his laurels until the summer of 1899. As one would expect there was a size deficit, but this time it was considerable. Anything over 200lbs typically meant spare tyres; on the contrary, the 206lbs of this person were wonderfully prepared. Absorbing punishment was his speciality. Anyone interested was either present or somewhere to catch the newsfeed. Boxing stopped with the heavyweights, but from Sullivan to Fitzsimmons there was a little giant who had earned the respect of everyone.

[40] The Milwaukee Journal, 1891, Jan 15th, p.8

LITTLE CHOCOLATE

"George's left hand work was the comment of all. He would bring it from the ribs to the head and back again so quickly as to almost escape the eye." [41]

George Dixon put his own spin on gloved fighting. Starting out a little more than 100lbs, his boxing was of the rapid variety. The exploits of 'Little Chocolate' were not just impressive but extensive. He became the first coloured fighter to win a world title in 1890 against Edwin Wallace and was still making successful defences ten years later. Considering how often he chose to fight his longevity is tremendous.

Four of Dixon's most memorable bouts were fought consecutively against Cal McCarthy, Nunc Wallace and Johnny Murphy, cramming one hundred and fifty rounds into thirteen months. McCarthy originally managed to hold Dixon to a draw in seventy heroic rounds but the class differential showed in their rematch. Two, four and six ounce gloves were used. By 1892 the clamour for Sullivan to tackle Corbett started to put its chokehold on boxing, but on a miniature scale Dixon enthralled with sturdy defences against Fred Johnson and Jack Skelly. The bout against Skelly was part of a program featuring Joe McAuliffe and ended with the big one at heavyweight. In the face of "considerable prejudice" Dixon made a mockery of Skelly's repute, ending his torment in eight.

Over the next few years many draws would shape Dixon's record. By the time his career was done he had incurred over fifty of them, and that wasn't excessive. During the era draws were handed out like brochures. Unless one person undeniably had the better of things it was customary to declare a stalemate. Not only did this persuade fighters to go all out, it also helped in preventing riots and discouraged gambling. Through victories and ties, Dixon kept going until 1896 when Frank Erne outpointed him in twenty competitive rounds. Though the championship was on the line it did not change hands as there was no knockout; the old last man standing tradition was still in effect to decide a bout. Dixon got his revenge the year later but then officially lost his featherweight title against Solly Smith. The title was his again the following year in 1898.

A string of defences brought the nineteenth century near its end. New talent was on the way. Taking the reins with a maniacal dash, this latest guy replaced the

[41] The Spokesman-Review, 1899, Jul 10th, p.2

cool approach of Dixon with unnerving intensity. Boxing has fashioned many curious fighters, though when it comes to oddities, there was a welterweight from Barbados who took the biscuit.

PINT-SIZED THUGS

Short for a bantamweight, how Joe Walcott ever toppled heavyweights is a good question. If any film existed it would surely make for interesting viewing; for those that witnessed the 5'1" boxer it must have been unforgettable.

Exceptionally short for his division, it was not difficult to see where he stored those 140lbs. He was spectacularly muscular, looking more like a circus strongman than a boxer with his inflated chest and bulging arms. At eighteen inches his neck was similar to a heavyweight's and went a long way in helping him absorb all those punches that rained down on his head. At the call of time there was no let-up. He is often credited to have gone all out from start to finish. Though very short his arms came from below to reach the jaws of his opponents, and his power was evenly distributed.

"When the men shook hands Creedon was almost a head taller and bigger in every way. Walcott's powerful physique, however, showed up plainly." [42]

Lightweight Kid Lavigne put an early spanner in the works. At first he won via the popular stipulation of victory unless knocked out. In the rematch Walcott lost heart and was pulled out when things got tough. It must be said, for many of Walcott's fights he probably fought with the "cuffs" on, essentially briefed not to go all out if he hoped on seeing his end of the purse. A shot at redemption presented itself with the challenge of 'Mysterious' Billy Smith in 1897. Walcott knew his opponent well having fought him twice before but the twenty round decision went against him. From then on knockouts came at a nippy rate. Bowling over a respectable collection of pins, the performance against Dan Creedon caught the most attention; despite his advantages the Aussie was drilled in the first round. This squat machine had a little while until those fearsome blows swept the 147lbs championship into his possession. When they did, it wasn't for long.

[42] The Sun, 1899, Apr 26th, p.9

"I am now ready to meet as they come, George Dixon first and the rest in their proper order." [43]

The same was true of Terry McGovern. 'Terrible' Terry was an instant problem for the bantamweight class which quickly invaded featherweight. The intensity of the man was etched into a glare, sharp and rigid. Similar to Walcott he fought a gale of a fight, storming at his opponents, but Terry took the concept of the quick assassin and put tabasco on it. In 1899 the diminutive fighter went supernova. Minutes were shaven off his average fight time, which is particularly impressive when one considers the era; the long distances and small gloves which favoured battles of attrition. It became strange for a McGovern fight to go past three rounds.

Britain's Pedlar Palmer was the man who stood between Terry and the bantamweight championship. The champion did the brave thing by travelling over to the States, but even though the odds favoured a new champion the site of Palmer grovelling in the first round was rather shocking. It was the first title fight under Queensberry rules to end in the first. There were no defences. McGovern relinquished the belt immediately to compete at featherweight. With an extra ten pounds on his frame there was a good chance of him losing his edge but the results were identical. In December of 1899 he fought four times, ending the year with a second round stoppage of Harry Forbes. Scheduled for twenty-five, a jarring right uppercut made sure the remaining twenty-three weren't necessary. You may question the standard of the era seen as McGovern was treating opponents like junk mail, but these were capable men; Forbes would dust himself off and go onto have a good stint as bantamweight champion. Dixon was now just a fight away. More was to come but it was apparent that Terry was not built for a long rule. Similar to a bullet, McGovern would come to a halt almost as readily as the trigger was pulled.

[43] The Morning Herald, 1899, Sep 13th, p.9

THE GLOVED PROFESSOR

"He will have a go at the bag, skipping rope and dumbbells this afternoon, after which he will call on some of his friends, for old acquaintance sake." [44]

If McGovern was a bullet then Tommy Ryan was a rapier, one which was brandished with an especially learned hand. The American whizz had already tamed the welterweight class. His amazingly clean record for the day helps to demonstrate how adept he was with a pair of gloves; in over one hundred fights there was just one serious blotch. The rest of the time he was supreme, and in the aftermath it was common for the papers to report that he was "without a mark on him."

Danny Needham tested Ryan probably better than anyone else. Willing to dig extra deep, the Minnesotan tried his best to upset the aspiring boxer. Seventy-six rounds were clocked but after five hours it was Needham who could do no more. It was a rare instance of difficulty. 'Mysterious' Billy Smith, the nut Walcott had trouble cracking was beaten to gain universal recognition as welterweight champion. In 1895 a bout with the 'Nonpareil' was arranged but the former middleweight champion was a shell of himself. In three easy rounds Tommy stopped his feeble opponent. The following year Ryan would incur that aforesaid blotch.

Charles 'Kid' McCoy was a regular sparring partner. He was a very capable fighter but had made a career of smearing his reputation with indecent actions. In a dastardly ploy to earn some money, so popular rumour has it, McCoy convinced Ryan that he was dying from consumption and needed a pay day. Understandably light on training, Ryan showed up to see McCoy as fit as a fiddle. From the early goings the 4-1 on favourite was punished. After a shellacking nobody would have called, Ryan was finished off in the sixteenth to cap off "one of the biggest surprises in the fistic arena for some time."[45] McCoy went on to be involved in a fixed fight with Corbett, linking him to a popular phrase; you didn't know whether you were going to see a scam or the real McCoy. Ryan wasn't about to repeat his credulous error and soon had the middleweight division by the horns. He staked his claim with wins over Bill Heffernan, George Green and Tommy West, bringing him to Jack Bonner who he comfortably outpointed.

---

[44] Brooklyn Daily Eagle, 1895, Jan 16th, p.4

[45] The Evening Telegraph, 1896, Mar 3rd, p.6

Nobody could touch him in his successive defences; Dick O'Brien had the police come to his rescue, Charley Johnson was beaten from the start, Jack Moffat was sent to bloody defeat in a fight fans were convinced that Ryan was holding back, and Frank Craig was halted in the tenth. Negating rushes, Ryan slowly introduced his moves so as not to advertise his abilities. He was strong enough to halt aggression and smart enough to gradually mould things in his favour. When it came to analysing fights and technique alike, Ryan was in a class of his own. Much could be learnt from a fighter like him and many did. One fighter in particular required his services more than anybody. Though crude, if this hefty pupil managed take on the finer points, the consequences of opposing him may be fatal.

A MAN MOUNTAIN

"He is one of the biggest-hearted, best natured, and although he doesn't appear it, one of the most discerning men one will meet in years of travel." [46]

James J. Jeffries was the fighter in question. Thanks to a head of pure concrete he managed to endure the painful preliminaries to go on and capture the heavyweight championship. Before this the big man had made a regular sparring partner for Corbett. At 6'2" and around 215lbs he appeared the destroyer yet he was predominantly a cautious fighter who jabbed his way in. He had it all as an athlete; in terms of combining speed, strength and stamina, not since John Jackson had charmed the fancy were people so captivated by physical prowess. Stints as a boilermaker and wrestler had infused his big frame with the kind of might that the public feared may kill someone. In time he would develop into the complete package but, beginning his career red raw, it was Jeffries who was almost killed.

With his paper-thin experience the young boxer challenged Hank Griffin, Gus Ruhlin and Joe Choynski; each one dangerous. Choynski created many painful memories for Jeffries, but the experience did him more good than bad. Peter Jackson made for an interesting prospect, but the once formidable pugilist was ripe with illness allowing Jeffries to stroll towards a knockout in the third. Tom Sharkey was happy to fight Jeffries. There was nothing ill about him, save perhaps for his unusual interpretation of the rules. The smaller yet explicit brawler had shaken off the effects of

[46] Daily True American, 1899, Jun 10th, p7

Fitzsimmons' cannon-balls and very much fancied his chances against the undefeated, younger man. They stuck to each other for twenty torrid rounds and though Sharkey managed to get in some of his "off-colour" work, Jeffries came out the winner. He also earned a shot at Fitzsimmons' championship.

Though a rematch with Corbett was lucrative, Fitzsimmons preferred Jeffries. The champion was use to bigger targets and confident with the huge chasm in experience. Tommy Ryan fulfilled his role as adviser for Jeffries' training. The talented middleweight, along with Bill Delaney, helped focus Jeffries' natural assets into the science of boxing. The burly contender developed an autonomous nature about him but still sometimes had "Ryan trailing along with him on a bicycle"[47] during his morning run.

Fitzsimmons' torso lost its authority when next to Jeffries who was clad in thick muscle from top to toe. The challenger fought a nimble fight and made a farce of Fitzsimmons' firepower, absorbing punches which had wrecked many. The vaunted left hand work softened the Cornishman until the eleventh when Jeffries ended matters with surprising ease. Jeffries first act as champion was to honour his promise regarding that Sharkey rematch. Back in Cooney Island, a very powerful lighting system was used to help illuminate the combatants so that they may be filmed. Unfortunately they were so hot that the rays singed their hair. Each lost the use of an arm in one of history's most desperate struggles. Though some slated the champion for fighting with what they perceived as reluctance, referee George Siler raised his hand.

Jeffries represented a new calibre of heavyweight. Even Sullivan was impressed, a man who had little business with handing out compliments. As fighters, though equally tough, it was quite clear that the changes in boxing did not stop with the rules. Things were getting quicker, more active and, more importantly, popular. Integrity had been restored back into the school of bent noses and sliced brows. The one thing that remained constant was racial prejudice. Distinguished men of colour were sometimes lucky enough to rise above, but even for the select few their position was considered no more honourable than the one Bill Richmond occupied a century ago. Times were as much changing as they were preordained.

[47] Daily True America, 1899, May 2nd, p.2

1900 - 1919

OVERVIEW

The arrival of James J. Jeffries was a breath of fresh air. If there was one thing fans, fighters and reporters were guilty of it was claiming that a big contender meant a new champion. Ninety-nine out a hundred times spectators would look on as the latest behemoth was axed by someone half their size. There was a question mark over Jeffries' head, even when defending his belt, but retiring undefeated silenced everybody. Right beside Jeffries breaking the mould was gambling man Tex Rickard. He was Dan Stuart's brilliant protégé, eager to try his hand at promoting. Wooden stadiums grew in size when Tex got going, but nobody could have fathomed how much money he would generate as New York became the new London.

The length of fights started to have its effects on the fighting. Twenty rounds were still standard, but various distances of ten, twelve and fifteen rounds encouraged a higher volume of punches. Jim Driscoll, Abe Attell and Benny Leonard were pioneers of a faster-paced boxing. The quality of gloves improved as well which made it easier to swap punches close up. Contests with big differences in weight were still common; middleweights fought heavyweights, welterweights fought light-heavyweights, and bantamweights fought lightweights.

Opportunity for the black fighter remained poor. Sam Langford and his 'Black Dynamites' performed a corrosive merry-go-round, but one man cut loose, the incorrigible Jack Johnson. He smiled that gold-toothed grin, slept with white women and generally behaved in a manner that got African Americans lynched. His actions rocked the Establishment, making life that much harder for ebony prospects. William Harrison Dempsey was quite a mixed bag when it came to race, but that didn't stop his rampage towards the heavyweight title.

CHAPTER 2

1900 - 1919

DOMINATION

The heavyweight and middleweight champion entered the twentieth century defending their titles often and in style. The furious assaults of McGovern were not far behind and soon secured the featherweight belt after crushing George Dixon. Tommy Ryan was a hard one to catch resting but McGovern made him appear lazy. Six successful defences were made in the space of fifteen months. One by one deserving challengers were hammered to the floor. Buffalo's lightweight champion, Frank Erne trained down to 128lbs to face McGovern, but things did not pan out as he had hoped. Victory was palpable when he put McGovern down but Terry was written to have "got up with a grin on his face and sailed right in with terrible force." There was no recovery. This fearlessness of McGovern engendered his demise. His attacks were too fierce for the cooler operators, but the hard-hitting Young Corbett II knew exactly what was coming his way. In Hartford, Connecticut the underdog waited for that brief window as McGovern poured it on. Corbett was actually shorter than McGovern but used this to his advantage; a clean right uppercut did the business. McGovern had put Corbett down for a moment but he arose to lose the shootout. The former champion swore revenge but their 1903 rematch repeated the result, only this time it took eleven rounds. Burned out at twenty-three, McGovern's career aimlessly stumbled over the next five years. There was to be no such thing with Ryan or Jeffries, both of whom continued to dominate.

Those fortunate enough to get Tommy on championship terms were cast aside while Jeffries looked close to invulnerable. Heavyweight Jack Finnegan wasn't a real threat; nonetheless the champion put him away inside of a minute to register the fastest ever knockout under the Queensberry rules (55 seconds). One who stood a better chance was Jim Corbett and this he demonstrated marvellously in his first attempt to regain the championship.

In a twenty-five round bout Jeffries had been playing catch-up for twenty-two of them. Jim turned and peppered his man like he used to. The crowd were bewitched by the former champion's ability. Evidently, Jeffries could be outfoxed, but discouraged… that was unlikely. He didn't let Corbett out of his sight and finally caught him with a hook. His middleweight mentor made the last defence of his crown in 1902, knocking out Kid Carter in the sixth while Jeffries resisted Fitzsimmons a second time, though he absorbed a hell of a beating in the process.

An interesting twist occurred when Ryan left Jeffries' services to come to the aid of his smiling rival. Seeing as Ryan knew Jeffries "as well as a schoolboy knows his A, B, C's"[48] devising a plan for Corbett made for a promising rematch. The dancing veteran was confident but unfortunately he met a different animal to the one he had three years ago. Clearly there wasn't much left to teach the champion as he got Corbett by the scruff. The next nine rounds weren't pretty. In the end Jim found himself gasping for air to revisit the pain of Carson City. A year later Jack Munroe attempted to do what looked increasingly impossible. It was reported that Munroe had once floored Jeffries in sparring, but when it came to it he was swatted down in the second. The champion was said to have chewed gum as he cruised through his seventh defence.

"Well, it's all over and I feel happy to-day. It went through without a hitch and we hold the world's record for attendance, purse and receipts." [49]

Admiration for Jeffries reached a new peak, and his most avid fan became a colossus in his own right. George Lewis Tex Richard, a "master of crowd psychology" had returned from the Klondike Gold Rush to thrive as a gambler. What he did for boxing cannot be understated. Under his supervision the main event developed an entirely new meaning. He wasn't afraid to make heroic investments and in doing so replaced overcrowded, obscure events with huge, fan-friendly spectacles. For the first time women decorated crowds which began to resemble military rallies. Fighters were paid several times more than was customary. There was a global significance about boxing. Tex's first promotional venture pitted the toughest of the tough against the best of the best, and few would argue with the latter being introduced as such.

---

[48] The Pittsburgh Press, 1903, Aug 9th, p.18

[49] Newburgh Daily Journal, 1910, Jul 5th, p.1

THE OLD MASTER

"The cold fact is that Gan's makes them all look cheap." [50]

That cliché of having it all preludes many great fighters, but with Joe Gan's it falls way short of a suitable tribute. The way in which he braided the essentials implied a kind of perfection. The one thing his divine abilities could not prevent was controversy.

Several years of fighting had steered Gans into the path of wily Frank Erne. This highly anticipated bout played out with the expected mix of brains and brawn, but the abrupt ending undid all that quality milling. With reports varying from a "two inch cut" to "his eye was knocked out", Gans decided that the injury sustained from a clash of heads was too severe to continue and he retired after the twelfth. Some took this as a sign of a yellow streak, but considering the racism of the day it's a worthless comment. It was disappointing, but an instance of greater controversy was on its way against Terry McGovern.

Gans became one of McGovern's many victims in 1900, though the legitimacy of his second round loss rests on shaky evidence. The film has survived and depicts Gans being dumped on the floor many times following scrappy exchanges. According to referee George Siler, "If Gan's was trying last night, I don't know much about the game."[51] Consequently Chicago banned boxing for many years. Gans carried on with his quest for the lightweight championship. Following this shady chapter Joe repeatedly demonstrated why he was deserving of his grand alias. Multiple knockouts put him at Erne's doorstep again in 1902. In less than two minutes there was a new champion. Gans executed a precise, storming fight before Erne could ready himself. It was not until six years later when illness and a gritty opponent wrested the title away. In between defending his championship Gans challenged boxing's latest welterweight champion, Joe Walcott. Their 1904 bout was a classic case of aggression trying to overcome technique, but in twenty rounds neither could overthrow the other and so a draw was issued. No titles were at stake.

Mike 'twin' Sullivan and Dave Holly were top operators but the champion couldn't put a foot wrong during this period of his fighting life. Sullivan was steadily pummelled by Gans' homing swings while the tricky Dave Holly was beaten at his own game.

---

[50] Baltimore Morning Herald, 1901, Nov 23rd, p.4

[51] The Deseret News, 1900, Dec 14th, p.6

With his eighteenth round knockout over Jimmy Britt, the 133lbs slab of granite that was Battling Nelson set his sights on the coloured champion. Against all the doubt, Richard pulled off the highly lucrative contest within Nevada's aptly named town, Goldfield. Of the $33,500 gate $11,000 went to Gans while Nelson had the pleasure of receiving $22,500.

It was a fight to the finish and Gans dealt out a beating fit for a Durable Dane. Nelson visited the canvas many times but was still trying to find a way forty-two rounds in. Unlike the neat champion, Nelson was all about questionable brawling. Several butts were committed but it was a blatant low blow which compelled referee Siler to raise Joe's hand. They fought twice more in 1908, but by then the Old Master was more reputation than reality. Nelson won and defended the title in less competitive bouts. Consumption came down hard on the ex-champion and he was dead within two years.

The lightweight division hardly fell on its face. In 1910 Ad Wolgast and Nelson delivered forty rounds of fast, bloody action. There was nothing wrong with the fighting, but a new stipulation began to hinder boxers tremendously.

NO DECISION

In response to the amount of fixed fights the Frawley Law was introduced which legalised boxing in the state of New York. Under its ruling rounds were limited to ten and no decision was given unless there was a knockout; such a clause worked both for and against fighters. For Abe Attell it worked a treat.

It remains a curious theme of the Jewish man's lively career that he purposely carried his opponents, making bouts appear competitive so that he may reap a pretty penny in the rematch. This 126lbs rogue had all the tools necessary to make a fine champion, and there can be no doubt that he used them on several occasions, but his lasting reputation is one tattered with shady deeds. Most famously he was involved in the Black Sox scandal during the 1919 World Series when members of Chicago's baseball team were banned for intentionally losing.

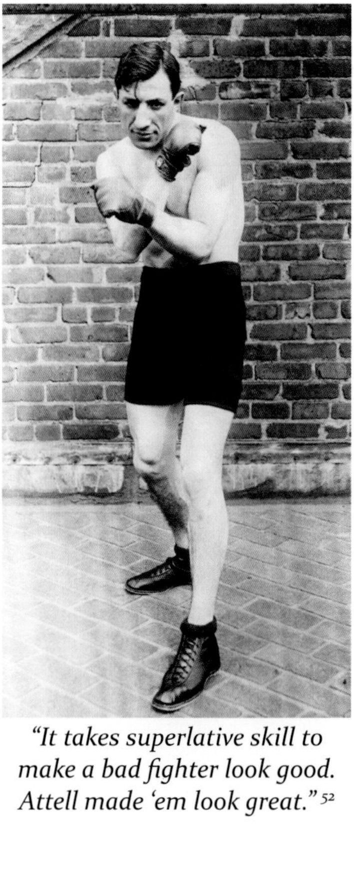

"It takes superlative skill to make a bad fighter look good. Attell made 'em look great." [52]

Underpinning the good, the bad and the ugly was a remarkably lengthy career. Attell was just sixteen when he turned professional, at nineteen he was world champion and he was still defending

[52] The Book of Boxing, 1999, Joe Williams, p.348

that honour nearly 10 years later. Beginning with flaming intentions, Abe learnt off his colleagues to fashion a style of great complexity. He was in good company from the word go. George Dixon and Harry Forbes could have squashed the bright teenager, but a close point's loss was as serious as it got. Sequential meetings fell in favour of the younger, constantly improving Little Hebrew. Abe won the featherweight title in 1903 which Young Corbett II had vacated, and though some questionable fights followed he was considered champion until Johnny Kilbane outpointed him on his birthday in 1912. From his devious call of foul against Tommy Sullivan to standard accusations that the "champion wouldn't fight hard" there was one man of whom the legend of Attell is inseparable.

"It is impossible to put a finger on any weakness in his style...like Gans, he is a type of the natural genius which practice has made perfect." [53]

From the gritty docks of Cardiff in Wales came Jim Driscoll, one of Britain's all-time elite. Curly-haired, cauliflower-eared Driscoll enrolled on his boxing apprenticeship via the boxing booths that were scattered about Welsh soil like wheat. At twenty he began a wonderfully pristine career.

Jem exemplified the British school of boxing. A straight back, a snappy left and plenty of feinting characterised his motion, but Peerless Jim removed those limitations which kept the average pugilist in a domestic rut. He led an active fight, doubling, even tripling up on his jab, though he left a good portion of weight on the back foot to inject the odd counter. Light feet did not sap his power. As the rounds passed, Driscoll continually looked for new weaknesses in his opponent, preserving his style's ambiguity. Nobody ever did figure him out.

Harry Mansfield outpointed the prototype but a ten count was in store for him in a rematch. For British recognition Jim had the demanding task of toppling Joe Bowker. The experienced bantamweight had defeated some of the very best though he couldn't keep up with the artful Welshman and dropped a decision. A rematch was set for twenty rounds. Bowker didn't hear the final bell.

America had been aware of Driscoll years before his arrival. Much was expected when he hit their shores and he didn't disappoint. Before the showdown with Attell came lightweight Leech Cross. The Fighting Dentist was no stepping stone, but in front of a heaving athletics club Jim put on a marvellous exhibition. Driscoll was

[53] The Times, 1911, Jul 29th, p.13

already twenty-nine, four years older than the featherweight champion when they touched gloves. Some reports appear guilty of exaggerating Jem's supremacy, but virtually everyone was in agreement that he deserved the nod. In fairness, more than ten rounds were required to decide a championship fight, but Attell was said to have fought hard and sustained injury which doesn't support his claim of purposely losing. There was a chance for a second shot at glory but Driscoll sailed back home to honour a promise he had made to help out at an orphanage. He temporarily retired after drawing with Owen Moran, but both he and Abe would resurface years later. Semblances of their former selves, they made their predictably sad exits.

NEW LEASE OF LIFE

"Martin Carter, of Irvington, Calif., dropped dead at ringside from excitement when Ketchel knocked out Papke." [54]

When Tommy Ryan relinquished his title in 1906, the middleweight division was left in a muddle. He had not defended since 1902, and his enduring acceptance as champion did nothing for the reputation of everyone else. He appointed Italian Hugo Kelly as champion but there were too many candidates for him to be gifted universal recognition. Mike and Jack 'Twin' Sullivan were two; Billy Papke was especially promising, but it was Stanley Ketchel who would shape a new era with his clenched mallets.

[54] Adams County News, 1908, Nov 28th, p.5

The Michigan Assassin crashed into his opponents like a drunken thug. His jagged, blusterous attack was all his own, and no amount of jabbing or blocking could resist it. It was difficult to merit Stanley as a boxer, but that's because he wasn't a boxer. As a fighter, Ketchel was 160lbs of inspired aggression. Sadly, only two films of Ketchel are known to exist. The one in which he is the victor sees him pound out a decision over Papke. It was one of his poorest performances. Peculiarities of his style may be observed but that legendary fire is absent.

Ketchel stressed the depths he was prepared to go in his thirty-two rounder with Joe Thomas. He was at the point of total collapse more than once in their 1907 battle, but ultimately handled the pace better, giving him an unofficial portion of the welterweight championship. This momentum carried into 1908 with a first round knockout of Mike Sullivan. Jack lasted nineteen rounds longer but the same fate was in store for him, establishing Ketchel as top dog. Papke, the Illinois Thunderbolt fell short in their first bout but in the rematch he got a good head start by lamping Ketchel instead of shaking hands, supposedly. Exactly how sneaky and damaging this sucker-punch isn't known for sure. Either way, the champion could not regain his strength after the initial rush and was punished until the twelfth. Overconfidence was also blamed for the defeat. They fought again within three months. This time a finely-tuned Ketchel battered Papke from start to finish, winning in the eleventh. Ketchel's valour was proven once more against 'Philadelphia' Jack O'Brien in 1909. The nifty light-heavyweight was making a mess of Ketchel's face but Stanley rallied in the dying moments to leave O'Brien senseless on the canvas; the bell saved him. In the rematch there was no escape. Following Ketchel's bout with the heavyweight champion, some believed he was burning out. To complicate matters, that urge to fight above middleweight was at war with his schedule for womanizing.

There were a couple more noteworthy scraps in 1910. In April a certain Boston Terror partook in an inconclusive six rounder, vexing reporters over who was the true master. Things were much more clear-cut against heavyweight-bound Dan 'Porky' Flynn. Few gave Flynn much of a chance. Around 15lbs heavier than Ketchel, he wasn't actually a bad fighter and the local crowd were impressed with his bravery. In the coming years only quality fighters would dispose of him but Ketchel would be the first. Come round three, pursuing his victim with those eyes "that never flinched when a battle was on",[55] Ketchel gave a fearsome reminder of his punching power, dizzying and then crippling Flynn with body shots.

Over sixty fights had already been packed into Ketchel's twenty-four years but Walter Dipley's shotgun put an end to everything. Jealousy and robbery are thought to have been the primary motives. Papke took control in the wake of Stanley's untimely exit, though while there would be middleweights just as great, never again would there be one so ruthless.

[55] The Toronto World, 1914, Jan 15th, p.3

BLACK DYNAMITE

"The biggest purse I ever got for a fight was $10,000 for fighting Ian Hague in London. The top money I ever got in this country was $3,000 for fighting Gunboat Smith. Very often I got no more than $150 or $200 for my fights." [56]

If you multiplied the number of fighters that avoided a boxer by the number of quality fighters he obliterated then Sam Langford would win by a landslide. The short man with the puffy chest and long arms came as close to terrorizing his opponents as is possible. That he was black stopped him ever entering the championship circle, consequently forcing him into a fruitless continuum where the same men fought over and over.

Two more dusky generals were part of this endless rigmarole; the sleek Joe Jeanette and the powerful Sam McVea. They were labelled Black Dynamite and all fought each other several times over, but it was Langford who was the undisputed best of the bunch. His prime weight hovered around the light-heavyweight division but from lightweight to heavyweight, from a growing teen to a blinded veteran, the Boston Terror humbled an obscene quantity of decent fighters. A healthy segment of Sam's 1913 victory against Jeanette has survived on film and clearly depicts the fighting styles of each man. More importantly the evidence is not dissimilar with the descriptions from those who saw them.

Before he was twenty-one Sam had already faced The Old Master. Dave Holly, Jack Blackburn and Joe Walcott were also at hand to aid in his advanced schooling. Many rematches transpired. Draws were revised into points victories and decisions were amended into knockouts. When Langford's body reached the middleweight limit his punching power became a plague in itself; from 1908-1914 he was insufferable. Much of this was down to that certain knack all punchers have, but Sam's broad physique was reinforced by years of manual labour. At eleven he was working at a lumber camp and so chopping wood became an essential part of training; an explosive drill which accustoms your arms to high-impact. There was also a stint as a brick layer. These activities may not strike you as exercise in the modern sense but such a lifestyle forges a type of practical strength that a gymnasium cannot. When Langford entered the ring he wasn't bulging or ripped, but he was strong as hell.

[56] The Ring, 1966, Oct-Nov, p.25

William Hague, Jim 'Fireman' Flynn and Gunboat Smith were a few of the famous white fighters Langford defeated (Gunboat even managed to outpoint Sam in 1913) but it was in his fights with McVea and Jeanette where the real battles were had. McVea's belligerent ways troubled Langford more so than Jeanette. His finest hour came in 1911 when he outperformed Sam. There was no mastery to be had however; this he bluntly discovered in latter meetings.

McVea and Jeanette were well-acquainted also and their most remarkable dispute unfolded in Paris, 1909. It was a topsy-turvy finish fight in which the fighters contested for three and a half hours. McVea had sent Jeanette to the floor at the rate of his volition, but he couldn't keep him there. By the fortieth round the slugger stared to wane. Jeanette made a superhuman comeback and McVea was retired before the fiftieth. Not since John L. Sullivan and Charley Mitchell fought their 1888 draw had France witnessed such lunacy.

"He hit Langford oftener than he did Joe, did less clinching, boxed with better judgement and made an altogether different kind of a fight against the hub heavyweight." [57]

McVea and Jeanette could have captured a championship if granted that chance while Langford is probably the best fighter in history who never won a world title. Their fates were somewhat reflective of their styles; the aggressive McVey was still a professional when pneumonia took his life at thirty-seven, long-time campaigner Langford wound up just as penniless though lived a good deal longer, maintaining good spirits for a blind man, and the smooth boxing Jeanette managed to squirrel away some of that hard earned cash, living to a respectable seventy-eight. That they were black was pivotal in their segregation, but their pigmentation, as a certain Negro had proven, was not an insoluble problem. As these dark cougars clawed at one another, a powerful and amused black man had stolen one of the key ingredients which made up the recipe of white supremacy; the heavyweight championship of the world.

[57] The Day, 1915, Jul 1st, p.12

BAD NIGGER

"Johnson liked the desert sunsets, and at the end of a days work he would stand outside the roadhouse watching the blue sky turn to amethyst and rose." [58]

John Arthur Johnson, infamous as Jack Johnson, experienced all the unpleasantness that came with being black. The difference was he returned the favour. He acted as if free from consequence, enjoying every forbidden sin, especially those for his race. The resulting attitude towards blacks was none the better for Johnson's defiance (the possibilities for black fighters perished), but as a rebel in the face of tyranny he was a hero. Jack Johnson the boxer was unique in two senses; his vaporising defence and his inclination to mock. Mind games were commonplace in boxing but Johnson *purposely* used his strength and vision to neutralise the opponent to the point of carrying them. This made for frustrating viewing but Johnson liked nothing better than to flaunt his superiority before a disapproving audience.

A life in pugilism got underway via cruel contests called Battle Royals where black youths were blindfolded and tossed into a ring. The one who managed to survive received a pot of spare change. When Johnson was old enough he didn't have to endure this kind of thing and knew what he must do in order to make the big bucks.

At twenty-two the athletic rookie bumped into Joe Choynski, a veteran ever on the prowl. Much was to be learnt on Johnson's behalf and Choynski was going to help him, though not before blasting his naivety with a terrible hook. The police weren't too happy about this interracial match and sentenced the pair to twenty-three days in jail. During this confined interlude Choynski noticed Johnson's potential and offered him some advice on how to move and defend. These lessons he soaked up and the coloured heavyweight title was his in 1902 after defeating Frank Childs.

Johnson went on to fight immature versions of his black adversaries. The rushes of McVea were repelled thrice, Joe Jeanette was outpointed and middleweight Sam Langford was soundly whipped. Johnson would never give them a title shot when champion though serious efforts were made to secure a fight against Langford in 1910. Simply, if Jack could afford to take it easy, he would. Smoking, gambling and enjoying a playboy's life were the top priorities when free of the mitts.

---

[58] Black Champion, The Life and Times of Jack Johnson, Finis Farr, 1964, p.95

By 1908, despite a loss against Marvin Hart (awarded the decision on an aggressive basis) the superiority of Johnson was such that even whites were forced to smell the coffee. Victories over an old Bob Fitzsimmons and Jim Flynn helped push his career into deep waters, edging him closer to little Tommy Burns. Getting the shortest of all heavyweight champions into the ring was no simple task. Johnson had to travel thousands of miles to Sydney, Australia for the honour but he did more than make good of his chance. In a specially constructed stadium, Johnson pummelled Burns without a moment's distress. The fourteenth round spelled the end; the most common film cut terminates with Johnson thumping Burns off balance with a hard right. After thirty long years a black man stood above. Novelist Jack London famously reported, "Fight? There was no fight."

And so began the tireless search for a Great White Hope. Tony Ross and Al Kaufman looked powerless against Johnson's sculpted 200lbs, but Stanley Ketchel, after eleven demeaning rounds, uncorked a big right which felled the champ. This one was widely rumoured to be fixed where Ketchel was to not get frisky. Clearly he got bored of this stipulation. Johnson got up a little unsteady to instantly splat Ketchel into unconsciousness. It was said that they were seen gambling together later that night, similar characters that they were.

The closest to boxing James J. Jeffries had been since retirement was through refereeing the fight between Jack Root and Marvin Hart to decide his vacated title. That was five years ago. By 1910 his return was considered a public duty but a painstaking training camp could not erase the lost years.* The title didn't change hands for another five years, but life outside the ring was far more eventful. In 1911 Jack tied the knot with his love interest for the past few years, Etta Terry Duryea, though by 1912, distraught from their shady relationship she shot herself with a revolver. Johnson quickly remarried to prostitute Lucille Cameron but was jailed due to the Mann Act which did not allow for the transportation of females across states. Rather than serve his sentence he fled to Canada and then set sail for France making two title defences.

When Johnson came back to his homeland the colossal Jess Willard was waiting for him. There wasn't much special about the man from Kansas, save for his size; 6'6" and 230lbs. The Cuban sun was in a fierce mood on the day of the fight and when Johnson's repeated tries for a knockout failed the forty-five round limit sneered at his poor conditioning. The bigger, younger and fitter man handled the pace better, absorbing Johnson's volleys to the point that "the bout was little more than a series of poses by the white and black gladiators." However, Willard's blows lost none of their steam. In the twenty-sixth a heavy cross put Johnson on his back where he shielded his eyes from the burning rays.

Willard was at first warmly accepted as champion but through a highly inactive reign shipped heavy criticism. Tremendous as that effort was in Havana, big Jess was not the saviour boxing had waited seven years for. Just one defence in four years occurred while men were risking their lives in the Great War.

---

* See Johnson – Jeffries fight story page 178

BRILLIANCE FROM DOWN UNDER

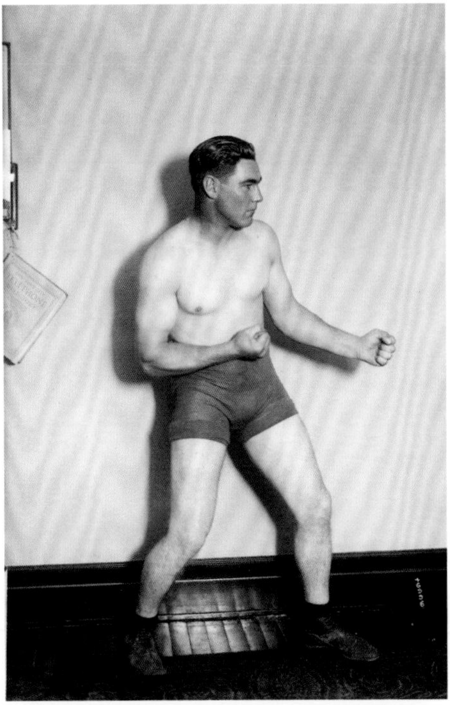

"A match between Darcy and Gibbons for the undisputed possession of the middleweight crown! It is too much to contemplate, for it would be too good to be true." [59]

Due to the United States neutral standing until 1917, WWI was not so detrimental to the careers of boxers. Actually, specifically during the war years of 1914-1918 the middleweight division was never stronger. Mike Gibbons, Jeff Smith and a maniac from Pittsburgh made up the icing of a great cake. The men directly below; the likes of George Chip, Eddie McGoorty, and Jimmy Clabby were very handy.

James Leslie Darcy wasn't just good. The handsome, physically imposing Aussie ranks as the biggest what if in history. During the winter of 1916, Tex Rickard was about to unleash the Maitland Wonder on American soil but a big future was destroyed when blood poisoning took Darcy's life. A dental injury had quietly turned septic, and with there being no adequate treatment available, the twenty-one-year-old met his dismal end. Al McCoy, Jack Dillon and even Jess Willard were mentioned as potential opponents. Instead, Darcy's body was shipped back to the country where a reputation was built that still resounds.

Like Fitzsimmons before him, Darcy hardened his body via the hammer and anvil, and from a very young age he was a sight to behold; big chest, big legs, big shoulders, though not overly massive and without a pinch of spare flesh. His family could use all the money they got so Les tried boxing to get some extra dough. There was a glint when the gloves were on and Maitland got behind their foremost athlete.

The only clear defeats Darcy ever suffered were a couple of decisions against Bob Whitelaw and Fritz Holland, both avenged. He twice fought globetrotting menace Jeff Smith, but their two fights ended in disqualification. In their first bout Darcy was disqualified when the referee disagreed with his call of foul, and in the rematch Smith deliberately hit low. Who the superior of the two was is a good question. It should be noted that Smith was the more experienced when they fought. What *was* certain about Darcy is that he learnt quickly. He checked in and out of the ring to a fast beat and cut down many of America's top fighters in a matter of months. In 1915, after the messy

[59] Evening Tribune, 1915, Nov 8th, p.16

affair with Smith, Jimmy Clabby was outpointed and Eddie McGoorty was knocked out, twice. During the same year Gibbons and Packy McFarland met in a welterweight ten rounder; this no decision bout was a treat for the purists. In Darcy's last year of fighting the Australian version of the middleweight title was frequently defended. Clabby was beaten over the distance again and in his final bout George Chip was beaten inside nine rounds. A good amount of film is left of Darcy and upon viewing it is clear that he was a very accomplished fighter. His rugby-like build suggested one mode of combat but he was a clever fighter. What's more he was amazingly nimble, taking and giving ground with minimal effort.

Australia was not best pleased when Darcy set sail for America. Many dubbed it a cowardly act to avoid induction into the Great War. Whatever may be said of that the fact was Les respected his mother's opinion more than anyone's and he had made only $35,000 in four years of fighting. The chance to triple that figure in a few bouts was too good to pass up. We all know what happened next.

THE MODERN MENDOZA

"To see him climb into the ring sporting the six-pointed Jewish star on his fighting trunks was to anticipate sweet revenge for all the bloody noses, split lips, and mocking laughter at pale little Jewish boys who had run the neighbourhood gauntlet." [60]

While tuberculosis prepared Joe Gans for the graveyard a small Jewish boxer was warming to the same bruising craft which had made him. In seven years' time he would develop into the same calibre of fighter. Since Wolgast won the 135lbs title, Willie Ritchie and Freddie Welsh had come to put their stamp on the division. Welshman Freddie was no gatekeeper, but he could only quell his successor's progress on the grounds of inexperience, for when he matured there wasn't a lot you could do with Benjamin Leiner.

Leiner, later Benny Leonard, fought at a time when boxing was reaching its peak in terms of participation. The Frawley Law was still in effect which hampered the chance to become champion, but it wasn't a problem for Leonard who knocked out Welsh in 1917. It was their third bout; in the second

[60] The Book of Boxing, 1999, p.307, Budd Schulberg, 'The Great Benny Leonard'

Welsh got the better, but Leonard sustained his aggressive advantage in the rubber match to lift a belt he would keep until retirement handed it over. As all-time greats go, Leonard suffered quite a few early knockouts, though it was a simple case of a mere boy being pitted against grizzled campaigners. He won more often than he lost, and when his body started to fill out he put together super winning streaks. New York provided the stage so Benny did not have to travel much.

In Leonard's era the modern fighter was taking form but there was still a merciless edge to the combat, a general roughness that could make even scientific bouts appear clunky. This did not hold true when Harlem's Ghetto Wizard was in action. Benny was accurate like the Old Master but far more animated. He darted around on his toes, suckering the opponent to fight at an uncomfortable pace. When the ruffians tried to do him harm he controlled them in the clinches and escaped back to ring centre. The idea of the boxer was further revised with Leonard's intelligence and grace. He was hurt badly against Ritchie Mitchell and Lew Tendler but disguised the wobbles with some dismissive backchat. When he completely outclassed Tender in a rematch it was written, "In his timing and judgement of distance, Leonard was perfection. In his boxing he was a picture."

His legend didn't need time to root itself into history. Just like Daniel Mendoza had with bare fists, Benny gave gloved boxing a new dimension, feeding the imagination. Though having publicly stated his willingness this pugilist was never called up to help the Allies over in Europe. He was free to continue with his golden career through 1918 and 1919, years in which a former hobo came to not so much feed as he did capture the imagination.

A KILLER INSTINCT

There was, as aforesaid, a different sheen to fighters during and after the Great War. With better quality gloves making it easier to concuss and ten rounds minimizing the risk of getting winded, boxing began to produce a strain of men who enjoyed the quicker method of victory, none more so than William Harrison Dempsey. The destructive Jack Dillon garnered quite the reputation as an executioner of larger men. The dimensions of his 170lbs build were put to shame against many of the lurking hulks, yet when the bell went he quickly exposed their shortcomings as fighting men. The Giant Killer was a fitting alias but the act of slaying giants for Dempsey laid the foundations for his unprecedented celebrity.

Chewing pine gum to strengthen his jaw, working as a janitor, as a farmhand, as a miner, 'riding the rods' (lying on the bars underneath a train) to get from town to town; life was one perilous hustle for young Dempsey. As an ode to the great middleweight Jack was adopted. Kid Blackie was another name by which he was known back when food was short. Indeed, Dempsey would later recall how sometimes days would pass without a square meal. This skinny appearance had him laughed out of numerous bouts, but hard times ultimately served to strengthen his will. He gorged on bread and guzzled root beer when possible. He also put weights in his shorts to legitimise bouts, but it was when the human megaphone Jack Kearns joined forces that the potential of a killer instinct was realised. Meals came in threes and the aggressive boxer was soon a lean, healthy 180lbs.

Kearns supplied meaningful fights and Dempsey responded, levelling virtually all of his opposition, the first round being a personal favourite. The talented Billy Miske and awkward Willie Meehan gave Dempsey some trouble, but the real black mark on Jack's record occurred in 1917 when an old, unsuspecting Jim Flynn scored a first round knockout. Blaming a lack of warming up, Dempsey came back to enjoy identical revenge. Jess Willard agreed to face Dempsey in 1919 and things went pear-shaped in more ways than one. Thirty-seven-year-old Jess was not the same man who had dethroned Johnson, but he was hardly given a chance to show his form when Dempsey let his hands go.*

"He's a 190 pound Stanley Ketchel, and I pity the man who makes him extend himself the full limit." [61]

Tex Rickard eyed his gloved goldmine. With the Great War safely locked in the past, America looked towards a bright, fashionable and economically strong future. The Roaring Twenties were on the way. Fuelled by promotional genius, Dempsey was about to redefine the spectacle that was boxing.

[61] Quebec Telegraph, 1918, Mar 13th, p.3

* See Willard – Dempsey fight story page 186

1920 - 1939

OVERVIEW

The pugilistic demography had been American for many years and Manhattan was its busy capital. New York's Frawley Law had meddled with boxing for an entire decade but 1920 brought about its end, finally relieving bouts of the dreaded 'No Decision'. In its place came the Walker Law which, most importantly, authorized decisions to be rendered over fifteen rounds as boxing began to find its feet.

The promotional marriage between Tex Rickard and Jack Dempsey was unimaginably successful. The combined annual salary of Babe Ruth and Charlie Chaplin was dwarfed by a single Dempsey gate. The 120,000 crowd for the first Tunney bout was unheard of for a boxing contest. This huge pot of green owed its success to the excess of the times, when the economy soared and anyone could purchase a good time. True to life, it didn't last. An extreme was reached and the stock market crashed, triggering the Great Depression which had the ring calling for the old and the unlikely. Benny Leonard was the most famed man to return as a result of the crash while many of his own began to colonise the lower weights.

Outdoor stadiums began to lose practicality once New York became enough of a metropolis. The second Madison Square Garden had housed Dempsey's 1920 fight with Bill Brennan, and the third Garden, which didn't close until 1968, welcomed all the big guns for decades to come. Fans no longer needed to concern themselves with special train journeys or sleeping in motel gangways. In the ring gloves became that bit bigger while twenty rounds was a dying concept (1939 saw the last ever championship bout scheduled for that distance). Inside fighting, often spliced with rough tactics and partial wrestling was refined into a visibly pleasing, continuous activity. Combinations were easier to appreciate, unspoilt by the mugging. Referees moved with the times and separated fighters when it got ugly.

That Henry Armstrong was black wasn't a major issue. His winning the featherweight title was accepted with minor grumbling. The real challenge was to see if America was ready to accept another black heavyweight. Joe Louis was shrewdly buttered up as the nicest coffee-coloured boy anyone could wish to meet. Once he got his chance the Brown Bomber blasted all censure with chilling performances. Come 1939 a racial debate was the least of America's worries as Adolf Hitler threatened the world with Aryan supremacy. World War II and its effects on boxing were proportionally dire.

CHAPTER 3

1920 - 1939

A MILLION DOLLAR BUSINESS

Boxing's new heavyweight champion had youth, an exciting style and good intentions. History now scowls upon the fact but part of those intentions involved honouring the old Caucasian tradition. Harry Wills ranked as the exceptional challenger for the best part of Dempsey's seven year reign but the dangerous 'Black Panther' was fenced into old territory with nothing to do but scavenge on previous kills; the blind remains of Sam Langford were frequently chewed on.

"Wills is the logical man to face the champion and the only one who is more or less generally considered to have a reasonable chance." [62]

Dempsey had two big breaks while champion but he started very actively making three defences within ten months. He first fought Billy Miske, though the bout was arranged more so to help the terminally-ill fighter out with a good pay day. Miske was suffering from Bright's disease which would take his life before turning thirty. Jack won in the third and Miske got his $25,000. In December the champion was pitted against another former opponent in Bill Brennan. Heavy-handed Bill was worked like a heavy bag in 1918 but Dempsey wasn't so sharp when they met again. It was rumoured that he had been more faithful in the bedroom than in the gym and everything nearly fell apart when zapped by a right uppercut. It was a hard fight but one in which Brennan was always fighting against a stronger current. In the twelfth Dempsey chopped away with his right hand, feeding his account a further $100,000.

There were better fighters out there than George Carpentier but nobody could challenge the Frenchman's celebrity; a fact of which Tex Rickard's instrumental mind was plainly aware. The obscurely dubbed 'Orchid Man' had fought at every weight, but he was thought too small to stand a chance.

[62] The Telegraph-Herald, 1922, Mar 7th, p.8

"Today's crowd was surprisingly orderly. It was like an ordinary theatre audience until the main bout started. Now and then a brief fuss broke out over seats, but it soon was still. During the championship bout, however, there was a constant roar from all parts of the giant saucer. Women yelled with men, but now and then there was a panic-stricken shriek as blow drew blood." [63]

Their milestone bout fell on July 2nd, 1921 and was themed as 'Draft Dodger vs. War Hero'. Dempsey was acquitted of this charge in 1920 but Rickard ingeniously used the angle to strengthen the roles of hero and villain. 80,000 spectators made a giant bowl formation over Boyle's Thirty Acres in New Jersey. Boxing had its first million dollar gate and it was also the first title bout to be broadcast on radio. A treacherous looking platform rose high near the ring for the purpose of filming. On Tex's strict instruction not to "kill boxing", Dempsey lay off Carpentier after an initial burst which caused a huge wave in the sea of straw-boaters. George managed to get that potent right of his into action, stunning Dempsey in the second, though in doing so broke his thumb. Two rounds later he was receiving the count. It was written that "Dempsey smiled for the first time as the fight ended", though who wouldn't when set to receive $300,000? That was three hundred times more than the average man made in an entire year.

James J. Corbett was a believer, admiring the fact Dempsey was a regular champion, but there was about to be a pit stop. For more than two years there would be no defences as Jack had the privilege of sitting on his throne while Rickard fussed over the perfect opponent. Harry Wills entered the equation but, "there was no mention of when they would fight, where they would fight, or what they would get."[64]

---

[63] The Gazette Times, 1921, Jul 3rd, p.6

[64] The Telegraph-Herald, 1922, Jul 12th, p.8

THE HUMAN WINDMILL

"Greb was a shadowy, flittering mark that danced all over the ring in one continuous and amazing whirligig." [65]

That no ring footage of Edward Henry Greb survives is a fact that works its way into history like a shiv, opening a wound that cannot be stitched, for it is not only a shame but makes an incomprehensible fighter even harder to comprehend. For years before and during Dempsey's patchy rule, Greb came close to making boxing his personal property. Anyone worth fighting 150lbs or more were so, sometimes so often that they were reduced to helpless fragments in his whirling cosmos. In 1919 Greb fought forty-five times; that's almost one every week, a modern career in twelve months. Fighting fringe contenders would have been hard enough; instead Greb fought and outpointed some of the best around. Former champions, champions to be and hall of famers were all treated indifferently, hammered into unanimous defeat. Most of these were rendered no decisions but the newspaper reports make no bones about who was superior. It wasn't until after the bouts got into the two hundreds that Greb achieved his most enduring victories. The big one came in 1922 against former marine Gene Tunney.*

Harry had done enough to have won world titles several times over, but he had yet to wear a single one. It was in 1923 that he made his formal introduction to the championship ranks when Johnny Wilson was relieved of his middleweight honours via uncompetitive decision. Winning the belt changed nothing as Greb continued to swarm much larger foe.

The championship is usually the apex of a fighter's career, but Greb's was already breaking down. His body was feeling it, and his eyesight, as had Langford's, began to fade. The effect was gradual and so it took a bit longer for Greb to degrade, from a phenomenon, to an earthly champion.

[65] Providence News, 1922, Mar 14th, p.14

* See Greb – Tunney fight story page 196

OUT WITH THE OLD, OUT WITH THE NEW

"Plans had been made for him to tour the states in 1913 but, because of his weight, no matches could be made and he was replaced. The ship he had been due to sail on was the Titanic!" [66]

Greb was not the only threadbare hero by 1923. There was a tiny Welshman who was wholeheartedly all in at this stage of the game.

Jimmy Wilde had rumbled the flyweight division like an eight year long tremor. He didn't even make 100lbs in many of these fights, inadvertently sparking confidence in his opponents. This only made the knockouts sting that much more. In 1916 he became the first legitimate flyweight champion of the world by dusting Young Zulu Kid, and when it suited him the 'Mighty Atom' went over to the States. Americans had hoped to see Wilde a few years earlier but he didn't arrive until the winter of 1919.

Jimmy performed well as his thirtieth year approached but bantamweight Peter Herman was too strong for him in 1921. Seventeen months of inactivity elapsed. It seemed as if Wilde had quietly slipped into retirement. Then he decided to defend.

Ecstatic about his opportunity to fight the jaded maestro, Pancho Villa prepared himself for "the greatest piece of fighting machinery ever shipped to these shores by England."[67] Villa was the Philippines answer to Terry McGovern; short, explosive and ruthless. At twenty-one he was burning with that same energy which had made Wilde's underfed exploits treasured. On the night of the fight however, for the first time in his life, Wilde was as he looked.* The new champion stormed through his first four title defences, sadly, the undoing of Les Darcy would also be the undoing of Pancho when, at twenty-three, blood poisoning ended his life.

Villa had put more excitement into an exciting era, Greb continued working on his bloody manuscript, and Leonard helped meet the varying tastes of the audience with his

"He took his fighting name at the time the Mexican bandit, Villa, was much in the public prints." [68]

[66] Boxing Outlook, May 1992, p.47

[67] The Deseret News, 1920, Apr 22nd, p.4

[68] Meriden Daily Journal, 1925, Jul 15th, p.8

* See Wilde – Villa fight story page 204

freelance ability. Regardless, the focus was unalterably on Dempsey. The 'Manassa Mauler' was ready to end a debate-filled two year and two day hiatus. Independence Day was greedily booked again to be the date for a bout with Tommy Gibbons. The decision to have the fight in Montana's quiet town of Shelby was a risk, but with Mr. Risk himself pulling the strings the odds favoured a success.

SHELBY AND A WILD BULL

Tommy Gibbons was no mug. The younger and larger brother of Mike had beaten Greb, could count his losses on one hand and had never been floored. And for all this, Dempsey was still fancied to put him away within the first half of a scheduled fifteen rounds. Not exactly what Rickard had hoped for, a mere 24,000 turned out of which only 7,000 were paying customers. Shelby was left with over a $100,000 deficit slamming their banks. Gibbons didn't receive a penny. $250,000 went to the champion but his opponent was more deserving of the pay packet. Tommy exceeded his reputation as a defensive magician, tucking away all the vital spots of his smaller body from a persistent inside attack. There was little opportunity to mount an offence but nobody expected to see him at the final bell.

"Emotionally, for Shelby, the fight was an outstanding success. The town wanted Gibbons to stay with the champion 15 rounds. They saw him do it." [69]

---

[69] The Evening Independent, 1923, Jul 5th, p.12

After the long wait it was a popular topic that twenty-eight-year-old Jack was travelling down the other side of the hill, but Rickard's next hand was to be one of his best. The problems that occurred in Shelby could be righted in two easy moves; a move to New York plus a hittable opponent. The world would see if Dempsey still had the measure of bigger men when Luis Angel Firpo was selected for a night of fireworks. Argentina's slugger stood 6'2" and threw his 215lbs about in such an unrestrained fashion that he was known as the Wild Bull of the Pampas.

"Perhaps no one will ever be able to explain accurately and consecutively what happened in the first round of that sensational fight." [70]

The Polo Grounds provided space enough for another Dempsey-Rickard epic. 85,000 helped generate over a million dollars. Three minutes and fifty-seven seconds was all they got, but in that short space the challenger crashed to the floor seven times, the champion twice; once completely out of the ring. Those nearest to the action helped Dempsey back in, but as soon as he returned Firpo charged at him. He could not find the punches to short-circuit the resilient champion however and was promptly flattened in the second. The fight was hailed as the greatest thing since the light bulb. There was no better way for Dempsey to begin his three year exile.

The champion developed a good relationship with a becoming Hollywood, enjoying the privilege of being able to sit on his success. Meanwhile the prospect of a fight with Harry Wills was again juggled and dropped. A fight for September 6th in 1924 was tentatively inked in but negotiations would go no further as the three small matters of money, location and date were never in harmony. Moreover, a sketchy

[70] The Washington Reporter, 1923, Sep 17th, p.16

fourth point was undermining this interracial clash. It may have been fifteen years ago but the race riots which followed Jack Johnson's victory over James J. Jeffries had created a serious taboo in boxing. There can be no doubt of those frightening scenes coming to Richard when he pictured the two heavyweights squaring-off.

THE TOY BULLDOG

"Sitting out there in the sun under leafy boughs watching the squatty little Irishman go through his routine of swings and scowls, his face unshaven and smeared with oils, you felt somehow that the shades of Sullivan and Dixon and Gans couldn't be far away." [71]

Had Michael Edward Walker stepped in for David and dropped Goliath, he still wouldn't have been content. The adventurous 'Toy Bulldog' was one of boxing's most brilliant daredevils; both for the extent to which he would go and the success he would enjoy. Most of these leaps of faith for which he is revered happened a decade after his first world title. Big for a welterweight, the silhouette of his squat, muscular body would take on a very rounded guise as he tried to get it to bend to his ambition.

Mickey's muscle-packed legs were surprisingly nimble and lent him a light skip. The hands went no higher than his chest as he preferred to come underneath to then, in the same motion, pounce on his opponent. He was liberal with both hands and threw wide swings, but because of his short reach they were more like mini haymakers, quick and accurate. 1922 was the year he took away Jack Britton's welterweight championship which the latter had managed to keep after a twenty-five fight series with Ted 'Kid' Lewis. He stayed champion for nearly four years when the removal of the Frawley Law worked against him in a rematch with Pete Latzo.

In 1925 Walker met middleweight champion Harry Greb. The division was looking more attractive by the day as Walker's weight became a problem. He was a little light at 152lbs but nonetheless gave Pittsburgh's superman one of his hardest. 65,000 spectators watched them go at it. The fourteenth was a bad one for Mickey but he would not fall and in the last round "the bell found them battling away at full speed." The great fight went to Greb but it also turned out to be his last as long-serving Tiger Flowers squeaked him out of a decision, and again in a rematch. A

[71] The Pittsburgh Press, 1931, Jul 27th, p.32

new champion gave the struggling welterweight incentive to try again and Walker's persistence won him his second world title. Their ten rounder was a controversial affair, just like Flowers' title victory over Greb. An eye operation then killed Flowers, and the chance of a rematch. It was good to see a fresh face at middleweight, but everyone was still reeling from what had transpired in Philadelphia.

HONEY, I FORGOT TO DUCK

"I repeat that I did go into a corner. I was behind Tunney, as the pictures will show. In spite of these things the referee made me go into still another corner." [72]

When the heavyweight ruler came back for his third stint as champion one of the few things that remained unchanged was the aura which surrounded him. Good as Gene Tunney was the clever boxer was in for a hiding. In retrospect, thirty-one years of age was not a problem for a fighter of Jack Johnson's lax style, but it was for Dempsey's. Jack's blitzing ways fed on the fountain of youth. He may have been able to iron out the creases by keeping busy, but in his three year absence he had lived like the sybarite he had become, mingling with cinema and righting his conk with plastic surgery.

Tunney possessed similar speed to Carpentier, but different to the Frenchman he had the strength to prevent Dempsey mugging him. The elegant Tommy Loughran was just the right type of fighter to ape the challenger's moves but for once it was

[72] The Evening News, 1926, Sep 22nd, p.8

Dempsey who got it rough in the sparring sessions, and it didn't get much prettier. The lone loss to Greb reassured the vast majority of Tunney's downfall, but in truth, Dempsey was thought invincible.

September 23rd, 1926. In what looked like a public announcement to the world, 120,000 people surrounded the ring in the middle of Soldiers Field which appeared as a white blot from the furthest rows. Whilst training, Tunney had spooked himself after reading about his bleak future so he abstained from newspapers and came into the ring focused. Dempsey charged at him with bad intentions for one, two, three rounds, but he could not cut his opponent down. A left hook briefly weakened Gene's knees in the fourth which proved to be the brightest moment in a one-sided contest. After ten rounds were completed there was no misunderstanding about who had won. The ex-champion's eyes were badly sliced, so bad that he needed some assistance to congratulate the victor. When asked by his wife Estelle Taylor, "What happened?" Dempsey explained, "Honey, I forgot to duck." It was a remark which endeared him to America and the sympathetic nation wanted to see the fallen idol get his title back. A rematch was likely to break every financial record; all Kearns required was a couple of signatures.

Jack Sharkey was not the best choice for a tune-up and it looked like the worst when Dempsey was on the wrong end of a pasting. Hard punches thudded against his open head, no longer the obscure target it was in Toledo. Body punches evened things up in the sixth, and again in the seventh, but a few went south of the border. Complaining wasn't a good idea and gave Dempsey, who always did like hitting on the break, the chance to stick one on him. And just like that, imminent defeat was overruled.

An astronomical sum of $2,650,000 was produced by the 1927, Chicago-based rematch of which $1,000,000 went straight to the champion. Dempsey was fitter than he had been last year, and the rounds were more competitive, but Tunney's straight-shooting and clinching tactics stopped him finding any kind of rhythm. Coming out for the seventh Jack was in need of something special. Tunney did not see the lead right, and then in came a six-punch shower which had him grasping onto the lower rope, fighting to stay conscious. What transpired was the most controversial interlude since Heenan throttled Sayers. Dempsey snarled over him, taken over by the same red mist which had destroyed Jess Willard; that was when there was no neutral corner rule. Referee Dave Barry refused to begin counting with Dempsey nearby, adamant about enforcing the new ruling. Once the excited challenger was warded off the timekeeper was ignored and a new count begun. At least fourteen seconds had elapsed when Tunney calmly rose at nine. He got back on his toes for the rest of the round, scored a flash knockdown in the next, and had Dempsey reeling in the closing seconds. Disputes over that seventh round continue to this day, but there was no disputing who was master. A third bout could have broken even more records, but, aware of Langford and Greb's ocular misfortune, the scar tissue around Dempsey's eyes made him decide against fighting again.

Tunney made just one more defence before retiring in perfect working order. Tom Heeney didn't have much business challenging for the title and was comfortably beaten over eleven rounds. Gene's exit sparked hope in the hearts of Dempsey loyalists but Jack stuck to his guns and stayed outside the ropes. It was officially the end of an era. The two biggest names in the heavyweight division traded hostility for friendship and within a year boxing's promotional mastermind fell terminally ill. You wonder if he sensed the fragile economy.

DESPERATE TIMES CALL FOR DESPERATE FIGHTERS

Appendicitis claimed the life of Tex Rickard in January of 1929 and in October the financial excess of the Roaring Twenties caught up with America. The Wall Street Crash called back billions of dollars that were previously out on loan, turning the stock market, which so many had invested in, into a trap. Dempsey lost his fortune but the former heavyweight champion bounced back with investments in real estate. Things weren't so forgiving for Benny Leonard. The once dazzling whippet was back after a seven year layoff, though only in name. His physique was closer to fat than taut and the hair that was never mussed after a fight, as he used to brag, had gone very thin.

"Well I'll fight O'Dowd, but that will be all. I go home after this fight. I get married to the best girl in Cuba, then – well, I dunno." [73]

For two years the heavyweight division was missing a champion which helped shine some light on the bigger picture. Before Richard left this world he had created a ninth 130lbs weight class under the Walker Law known as super-featherweight or junior-lightweight. Many good fighters became part of its history but its first true sponsor came after a decade of its creation. From Cuban slums to metropolis America, Eligio Sardiñas Montalvo gave up being a paperboy and restyled himself as Kid Chocolate; the most attractive fighter in a handsome era.

A crushing punch was the only thing missing from the keed's bottomless pit of ability. He still had enough at the end of his fists to lower your spirits, but so good at moving was the 'Cuban Bon Bon' that the decision to fight off the back foot was no less effective. He had a long reach for a man of his weight and used it to fire a jab Joe Gans would have

[73] Pittsburgh Post-Gazette, 1929, Nov 26th, p.21

applauded. From there hooks, looping rights, uppercuts and body punches followed, but his attack was smartly broken up with fits of elusive movement. It was his manager's assertion, Luis Gutierrez, that Chocolate studied the available film of past champions as a tool to sharpen his moves, making him one of if not the first to do so.

He left Cuba in 1928 and landed in New York where he bewildered opponent after opponent. This brought him to a fight with 1924 Olympian, Fidel LaBarba. Chocolate chose to box on the retreat which had him booed when the majority decision went his way. It was the first of a three-fight series which would end 2-1 in the Cuban's favour. More than 40,000 flooded the Polo Grounds to see Chocolate outpoint Al Singer but in 1930 he would lose all of his important fights against, in the correct order, Jack 'Kid' Berg, LaBarba and Battling Battalino. You wouldn't have guessed it but the "flashing ebony stick from Cuba" had yet to reach twenty-one. It was in his twenty second year when the culmination of youth and practice formed a peak.

The junior-lightweight crown was considered little more than a "synthetic title", but in his six championship fights Chocolate energised the crossbred weight class. Benny Bass did everything he could to keep his trim rival from taking his title but an aggressive Chocolate knocked him out in the seventh. In his first defence Joey Scalfaro found out just how aggressive the keed could be when he was done in just 39 seconds. Switching weight classes is a tricky game. You can either weaken yourself by reducing or endanger yourself by gaining. It was definitely a risk when Chocolate faced Tony Canzoneri for his lightweight title in 1931. The risk did not pay off but despite the narrow loss by split decision it remains one of the great performances against a naturally larger fighter.

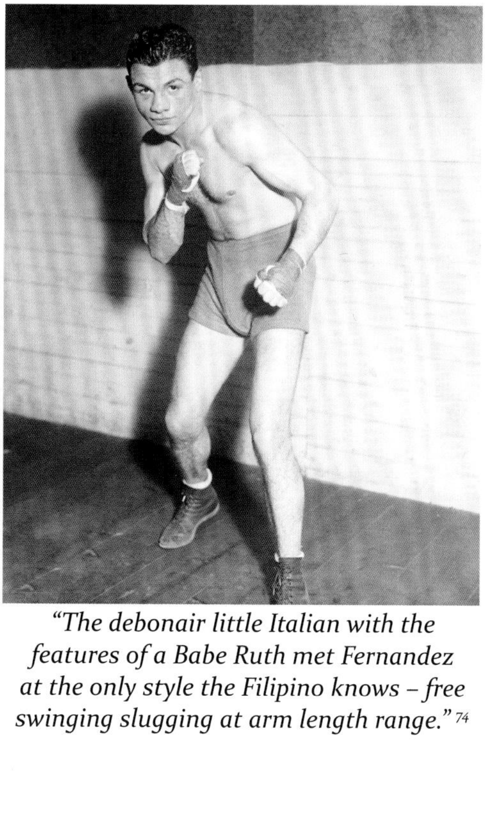

"The debonair little Italian with the features of a Babe Ruth met Fernandez at the only style the Filipino knows – free swinging slugging at arm length range." [74]

Canzoneri battled with Chocolate through "fifteen blistering rounds of unceasing action." The dark-skinned boxer never fought better; his jab was down the pipe, those flurries were tireless and his movement was picturesque. The early, and many of the middle rounds belonged to the lighter man, but a strong finish by the New Yorker won him that third vote.

Tony started out as a sixteen-year-old bantamweight but in five years' time would make a tremendous catch-weight boxer, comfortably switching

[74] The Telegraph-Herald, 1929, Jun 5th, p.1

between lightweight and junior-welterweight. A slack guard gave him the look of a careless fighter, especially next to his classically posed colleagues, and hardly shotgun delivery, punches were flung from reckless angles. These worrying habits were in fact the traits of a fighter who knew exactly what he was doing. He stayed stubbornly close to his opponent, sometimes catching avoidable punches, but by doing so encouraged a brawl where his talent for punching could come into play. The right hand was a hazardous blow and there was a persuasive left to go with it which was casually flicked into a hook.

The featherweight, lightweight and junior-welterweight titles laminated his record before the fight with Chocolate, but Johnny Jardick made him a title light. Six months later Jardick repeated the close victory, keeping the junior-welterweight title. Canzoneri's skulking ways gave him another chance, this time against brilliant Barney Ross. A Jewish boxer like Leonard, Ross twice defeated Canzoneri, first by majority decision and then by split decision. Both were excellent bouts. The junior -welterweight championship was on the line but it was the lightweight title with the colourful history; considered, next to the heavyweight division, the "most prized crown in ringdom".

Tony went on to demolish Chocolate in a rematch, got his revenge over Jardick plus outpointed young versions of Lou Ambers and Jimmy McLarnin. The latter two were major players in bloom however. With around 150 fights to his name, Tony felt more like fifty than twenty-eight. Ambers and McLarnin were not merciful in rematches as Canzoneri joined Chocolate down the winding road to retirement.

DISQUALIFICATION AND DISORDER

Long absences and poor matchmaking had been accountable for turning boxing's flagship division ugly but the current scene represented a new low. In five years there were five different champions. Jess Willard sitting on the title for four years was no better, however, many still believed in him as a fighting force; there was potential if not integrity. Nobody could seem to keep hold of the championship, and when the most promising of the bunch lost in his first defence, that to a 10-1 underdog, the hope for a new sheriff all but died. As individuals they were good competitors. As rivals they created a mess which started in 1930 when Gene Tunney's vacant title was up for grabs.

Jack Sharkey had proved himself an outstanding contender and manned one corner. In the other was a man who shared an uncanny resemblance with The Manassa Mauler, the clever German, Max Schmeling. For three rounds Sharkey had the better of it, catching Max with combinations similar to what he had shelled Dempsey with. The fourth was looking good too; that was before the 'Boston Gob' went extra low. A left uppercut went full speed into Schmeling's groin, instantly crippling him. Poor Max was helplessly carried over to his corner as confusion reigned over what should be done. The decision was Schmeling by disqualification. As an overall talent Sharkey was the best of the quintet, alas, he was unreliable. It wasn't a matter of a shaky chin but emotional instability.

"Bright and active young men who, thank heaven, read the newspapers are still marvelling at the astounding bit of referee logic which awarded the world's heavyweight championship to Jack Sharkey." [75]

A rematch with Schmeling gifted him an unpopular decision, but you need only wait a year later to see him sprawled on the floor thanks to Italy's 'Ampling Alp', Primo Carnera. Sharkey had defeated the big man before but a huge uppercut knocked him away from the title permanently. Carnera was not the bumbling glove-shy giant that history has made him out to be. It is true that many of his fights were fixed, but it was also true that he grew into, if not an accomplished, a capable boxer who could apply his 6'6" and 260lbs reasonably well. Nestled inside that manufactured career are some decent victories.

The same year Carnera became champion, Max Baer knocked the living daylights out of Schmeling in a rare glimpse of his potential. 'Madcap Maxie' had the goods to make it as a first rate heavyweight, but success forever played second fiddle to the man who, during a heart attack that ended his life, requested a people doctor when asked if he would like to be sent the house doctor. Baer the jester had the power of a tyrant. His right hand was an untamed force with a grim past. In 1930 it had ended the life of Frankie Campbell and Max was close to quitting the ring. He had the good sense to keep punching after being declared innocent of manslaughter and made slow progress. He never was a good boxer.

[75] The Vancouver Sun, 1932, Jun 23rd, p.6

Tommy Loughran, Johnny Risko and Paulie Uzcudun dealt him three defeats in five months. It didn't look like he was going to go anywhere but Baer's bad luck had ended. The big punches became harder to avoid and contenders started to drop. King Levinsky and Ernie Schaaf supplied the stepping stones for a match with Schmeling. This time the jokes were kept to a minimum and Max cornered Schmeling in the tenth to unleash an unsightly battering. Wearing the Star of David on his trunks, Baer played the role of the Jewish hero against Schemling who was portrayed as a representative of the growing Nazi regime.

Carnera's championship was now under threat and Baer did not let himself down. Floored in the first round, Primo would hit the deck a further ten times over the course of eleven rounds. For what he lacked in skill he at least demonstrated that there was a big heart in that huge body of his. The one-sided bout was called off with Carnera pitifully drowsy.

"Asked if Carnera's punches had hurt him at any time, Max wise-cracked in typical fashion, "You can't hurt a Baer." [76]

Dempsey, who was much involved with Baer's schooling, and Tunney both praised the smiling Californian. His twenty-five years put him in good stead to have a long residence as champion but he lost the championship to a very unlikely James J. Braddock. That he had never been knocked out was just about the only thing going for the Irish-American. His record was a minefield of setbacks during a life that

[76] The Milwaukee Journal, 1934, Jun 15th, p.2

personified the Great Depression. When it dawned on the clowning champion that he may lose he put together some fearsome rallies, but Braddock's ability to take it prevailed and the decision was his. Damon Runyon's knack for inventing nicknames had not left him, branding Braddock the 'Cinderella Man'. A short time ago Jim wasn't living much better than a tramp; now he had money, fame and a nice two year break before he had to defend against a mahogany gent who was doing terrible things to these former champions.

PERPETUAL MOTION

In the British Isles, Scotland was the odd one out when it came to forging world beaters. The contributions of England need not be mentioned and next door in the Welsh valleys, men such as Jim Driscoll, Jimmy Wilde and Freddie Welsh had raised the profile of the red dragon to amazing heights for such a small nation. In around seventy years of Queensberry competition Scotland had yet to produce one world champion, but in 1935 came a Glaswegian with enough energy in his miniature body to power a city.

Benny Lynch repaired the flyweight division after ten years of confusion. The suited champion looked like a schoolboy on his way to a prom when around his darling public, but the 5'3" boxer went about his business like an enraged loan shark. He was a throwback, even for his day, fighting with an uncharitable intensity and, reliving the alcoholic lifestyle of the prize-fighter, was dead at thirty-three.

Jimmy Wilde was eventually drawn to the United States but Lynch stayed put, creating a buzz on home soil where he crushed many of America's best. In 1935 Jackie Brown owned a portion of the world title and had fought Lynch to a draw in March. In their September rematch the twenty-four-year-old Scot delivered a show of aggression not seen since Pancho Villa's pitiless assaults. The distraught Mancunian was floored four times in the first and four more times in the second where Lynch was awarded the fight via technical knockout.

"By the late rounds when weariness should have set in, the pair continued at the same exhausting pace they had maintained from the first bell, bracketing the contest as one of the fastest and most skillful ever fought at that level." [77]

[77] Boxing Pictorial, Nov 1975, p.5

Shawfield Stadium (a popular football ground) was suddenly forced to accommodate boxing as Lynch attracted crowds greater than 30,000. For world recognition, a second Philippine by the name of Small Montana challenged Lynch. Villa had actually inspired him to box. He was a cut above Brown. "Lynch has proved a worthy champion over here, but there is the chance that our standards are not high enough"[78] feared a reporter. Lynch showed that he was not just a crate of TNT and outpointed his opponent with slight moves. America recognized and praised their flyweight champion but Lynch's next opponent did not need to be imported. Liverpool's Peter Kane was more than a challenge, he was a serious threat. Only nineteen he had built a striking reputation, battering grown men in front of thousands of spectators. The 40,000 turn out for their 1937 bout did not faze the challenger.

A solid right, Lynch's first punch of the right, put Kane down and got him groggy. He did well to survive and even better to fight back. For twelve rounds he bitterly resisted but the champion was much better defensively and came through in the thirteenth. It was one for the ages. It was also the last fight in which Lynch, a big drinker ever since he had the money to buy a drop, was in prime form. Alcohol was more than a problem. Bottles of whiskey were present in his dressing room before he retired. Benny drew with Kane in a rematch and knocked out Jackie Jurich. However, coming in overweight, he lost his title, on his way to complete destruction.

"They said the Los Angeles colored boy couldn't make the featherweight limit of 126 pounds and still be strong, but last night he came in at 124 pounds and almost knocked Petey Sarron's block off." [79]

[78] The Times, 1937, Jan 17th, p.5

[79] The Portsmouth Times, 1937, Oct 30th, p.6

Within two weeks of the original fight between Lynch and Kane, Petey Sarron lost his featherweight title to a fighter who, like the Scottish mite, had sussed perpetual motion. Few recall Henry Melody Jackson but Henry Armstrong resounds across the boxing fraternity. 'Homicide Hank' would have made a poor pacemaker on the track. One explanation for his unceasing assault was his heart; apparently one third larger than normal. In fights where his punching power was not a decisive factor he could always rely on literally exhausting opponents. He was tough to hit clean with his crossed-armed bobbing style. When a good one was put on him his chin did its part in resembling a rock. This amazing activity caused for a brief peak, but the achievements crammed into that period were superlative.

It is generally accepted that Armstrong was the first (and still is) the only man to have held three championships simultaneously. Barney Ross came very close to achieving this distinction but gave up the lightweight title before conquering welterweight. And even if Ross was given a pass here, Armstrong claimed his championships at three of the *original* weight classes, which is more deserving of praise. What's more he gobbled up each of these prestigious belts in an absurd order, going to welterweight after featherweight, and then back down to lightweight. Scaling a mere 133lbs for his fight with Ross, Armstrong didn't have your typical weight dilemma, chugging pints of water in an effort to lessen the weight deficit. Ross was well over 10lbs heavier than the bloated lightweight, but the size of the fight in the dog prevailed and Henry had Ross "helpless during the last half of the bout."

As a youth Armstrong had worked on the railways, preparing his muscles for the rigours of boxing. His first sample of professional fighting left a bad aftertaste when he went face first in three, but, as his blood-swallowing ploy against Lou Ambers would suggest, he wasn't the quitting type. Baby Arizmendi sampled Henry's evolution through four fights, from a budding hustler to an oppressive kingpin. Their final bout was the epitome of one-sided.

Sarron's collapse was the sixteenth in a streak of twenty-seven. Armstrong earned the Ring magazine's fighter of the year award for 1937 but it is arguable that 1938 was greater, beginning with a third round knockout of future featherweight champion, Chalky Wright. Ross was battered into retirement, though Armstrong was merciful in the last few rounds. Twenty defences would be made of the welterweight title but in his next fight Armstrong thrashed Lou Ambers, taking his lightweight title despite dropping four rounds on unintentional fouls. This harsh ruling disabled Henry in a rematch when *five* rounds were handed to Ambers, giving him the decision. Armstrong continued with his reign as welterweight champion, fighting Ceferino Garcia to a draw in a bout some recognized as being for the middleweight title; had he won Henry would have been the first man to win titles at four different weights. For the time being he jumped from state to state, chopping down the available competition at a rate of about two per month. The man who prevented Armstrong from claiming his second fighter of the year award in 1938 needed a good reason for doing so. He had two. This heavyweight was not only the saviour everyone had hoped for, there was the tender subject of him being just a few shades lighter than the scourge of Reno.

THOU SHALL NOT GLOAT

The emasculating recollection of Jack Johnson hadn't got any better. That the heavyweight division would be best served if it remained white was honoured like Aristotle himself had deemed it virtuous. Joseph Louis Barrow was as inoffensive as Negro boys came, but without his management and their carefully plotted schemes there would have been no eleven year and seven month reign as heavyweight champion. Piece by piece the legend of the sleepy looking 'Dark Destroyer' was assimilated until the 'Brown Bomber' ruled the throne with his humble, though no less iron fist.

"It will be Louis vs. Louis for years to come – Louis, the fighting man, against Louis, the young millionaire." [80]

Louis, an instant hero in the black community, and Schmeling, an emblem for Nazi Germany, got together for a politically frosty rivalry. Not everybody was comfortable with Louis taking the title from Braddock, but the not so small problem of Adolf Hitler had society re-evaluate their moral scruples. With Schmeling firmly representing evil, Louis transmuted into a symbol of liberty.*

Considering the abundance of empty pockets, boxing offered a straightforward alternative. The Jewish contribution in particular was phenomenal through the late

[80] The Milwaukee Journal, 1935, Sep 26th, p.4

* See Louis – Schmeling fight story page 212

'20s and '30s; at one point around a third of all active boxers were representative of David's six-spiked star. On the other side of the racial spectrum, Louis had helped reopen the flood gates for Africans, stirring a new generation with his dramatic rise. New York promoter Mike Jacobs had made his valiant tread in Rickard's footsteps, filling the garden on a regular basis, but no amount of inspired marketing could soften the effects of the Second World War.

1940 - 1959
OVERVIEW

The Second World War put a vice on boxing. It confiscated champions, derailed contenders and stopped careers before they'd begun. Even men like Joe Louis and Tony Zale, who were able to retain the gold after service, would have gone down very different routes had they stayed put. Which challengers would they have beaten? Would they have retired earlier? The knock-on effects are incalculable. Of course the war had its own effect, a positive one. There's a good chance we would not have seen Rocky Graziano give Zale the fight of his life if it weren't for Tony's service in the Navy. Contrary to these hypotheticals, some fighters were in and out in a jiffy. Whether you were honourably or dishonourably so, many men were discharged after a brief stint. Sugar Ray Robinson fit this category but it still took four years for him to get a shot at the welterweight title.

With the exit of New York promoter Mike Jacobs, boxing's underworld crept in. Sports tycoon Jim Norris was reputed to have fixed both of Harry Thomas' fights against Max Schmeling and Tony Galento, and he ended up bagging an all too persuasive contract with the IBC (International Boxing Club) . Mafia man Frankie Carbo threaded together a group of similarly corrupt persons who successfully bribed boxers and fixed fights. Jake LaMotta's dive against 'Tiger' Jack Fox and Ike Williams controlling management were two shady instances of many. Robinson soundly resisted this side of the ring while securing his finances with many a business venture. On the bright side Ray and featherweight Willie Pep hit standards that hadn't been hit since Harry Greb and Benny Leonard beat everybody ten times over.

Black fighters were no better for opportunity. Sandy Saddler had to suffer before he was given a shot and a collection of black fighters known as Murderers' Row essentially relived the lives of Black Dynamite twenty years on. Louis was 100% an exception. The old Bomber continued to pay off his debt, in the ring. Eventually a young Rocky Marciano plaintively sent him to defeat. You could enjoy the Rock at home with your new television set while he made history by retiring the only ever undefeated heavyweight champion.

CHAPTER 4

1940 - 1959

DUTY CALLS

By 1940 there was no confusion over who the two best fighters in the world were. Joe Louis was close to decapitating opponents and Henry Armstrong continued his impersonation of a garden strimmer. Pace dictated shelf life. Armstrong was in the ring three times more often than Louis. When he was defeated for the first time in over seventy fights it wasn't down to accidental fouling. It couldn't have been. The other guy laughed at the rules.

Fritzie Zivic took his ring philosophy of "you're not playing the piano" a little too far. He was a scholar in underhanded theory, and he enjoyed putting that theory into practice. Armstrong's eyes and mouth were prime targets for Zivic's laces and forearms. Henry didn't have the punch to turn the fight on its head, his face became smeared with blood and it bled freely. The fifteen round limit put the brakes on Henry being stopped. In the rematch it didn't go past twelve. It wasn't the end of Armstrong's journey. It wasn't even the end of his success, but after all the miles his engine wasn't so efficient and he forever departed from the championship class.

Joe Louis was at the peak of his physical capabilities, but a knockout wasn't guaranteed. Englishman Tommy Farr not only lasted the distance but gave Louis a good deal of trouble, and at the start of the new decade Chile's Arturo Godoy hustled his way to a split decision. Louis was brilliant in the rematch, brutalising Godoy with counters, but his most celebrated hardship came against Irish whippersnapper Billy Conn.

"Conn undoubtedly fought the greatest fight of his career last night. It's not difficult to understand why he made the error of slugging with Louis in the 13th. Joe had gone to his corner in a bad way." [81]

Conn was a light-heavyweight and made no attempt to stow away a few extra pounds. He scaled 174lbs with the intentions of turning that 26lbs disadvantage into a winning formula, and it very almost worked. Billy was

[81] The Miami News, 1941, Jun 19th, p.3-B

leading on two of the three cards when he decided he wanted a knockout and started to punch with the puncher. Bemused throughout, Louis was even wobbled in the twelfth but this only spurred Conn on to start trading. With two seconds left in the thirteenth, after a cascade of hooks, crosses and uppercuts, the kid with the "face of a choir boy and the fighting heart of a devil" was counted out.

By 1942 America was officially part of World War II. Many champions were snatched from their podiums and several others were robbed of their best years. The *real* challenge was to see if a fighter could retain their edge after the break, like Tony Zale. The Polish pulveriser picked up the 160lbs title in 1940. After four years of service he ran into the unforgiving Rocky Graziano. This welterweight terror had stormed his way towards middleweight and Zale was just in time for the first of a head-snapping, body-crunching trilogy.*

MURDERERS' ROW

Joe Louis was an exception to segregation; it was still umpteen times harder for the black man to make it than the white man, but in the middle of the unprofitable tail-chasing, several blacks would acquire the type of esoteric infamy not witnessed since there was Black Dynamite.

The Murderers' Row referred to a collection of doomed-to-be-contenders sprinkled between middleweight and light-heavyweight. Charley Burley, Jack Chase, Eddie Booker, Holman Williams, Cocoa Kid, Aaron Wade, Joe Carter and Bert Lytell frequently crossed paths to make for a perilous spaghetti junction.

"It's nice, it's real nice that they think so much of me, but gee, I wish somebody would give me a chance to prove it in the ring." [82]

The most revered of the lot was, naturally, the one who generally whipped the others, and that was Charley Burley. The Pennsylvanian boxer was much more than a pretty record and has left a legacy similar to that of Langford's as one of the greatest fighters never to have won a world title. In the ring he was wonderfully poised. Many fighters create static, flaunting style to veil their shortcomings. With Burley there was a near faultless substance. He could definitely punch, and he wasn't slow, but that unsung sub-genre that makes a fighter called ring generalship was what set him apart. Only on a few occasions was he justly outpointed.

* See Zale – Graziano fight story page 220

[82] Pittsburgh Post-Gazette, 1947, Dec 31st, p.13

Williams twice had the honour of pulling off this soap-clasping trick. Holman's career emerged from the Great Depression and saw the back of World War II. If one wanted to know who was fighting when Holman was then his record provided a first class reference tool, but it was his deep rivalry with Cocoa Kid which made for the most interesting feature in an extensive body of work.

The kid had the longest career out of all of them. Having begun fighting in the 1920s he was close to continuing in the 1950s. In his thirteen fight series with Williams he won eight times. A couple of those were close to going Williams' way but Holman had to make do with his three victories. The remaining two were even.

"Not even the combined counsel of the champion Louis and his two most able assistants, the famed trainer, Jack Blackburn, and his aide, Larry Amadee, who worked in William's corner, could stave off Cocoa's potent left jab which proved tantalizing to Holman all night." [83]

Jack Chase had a habit of upsetting the law. He was jailed in 1930, again in 1938, and was later involved in a shooting incident with Aaron Wade. When not behind bars he made a fine boxer. In '43 he made his stand with a victory over Eddie Booker to claim the Californian middleweight title and defeated a not-so ancient Archie Moore. He then lost to Archie before outpointing him for a second time. The following year it was as if everyone else ganged up on Chase. Cocoa Kid beat him, so did Lloyd Marshall, Williams defeated him four times and Burley knocked him out twice. Powerful competitors produced choppy waters, making it hard to stay afloat and Jack, though no small fry, was forced to the shallow end. Southpaw Bert Lytell, a fierce sparring partner, got his chin down in 1944 and raced through over 100 fights in less than eight years. Top names were beaten, memorable battles were waged; another legacy hummed the same tune.

Booker, retired at twenty-six, was the most unfortunate of the bunch. Strong and measured, eye trouble ended his flight as a boxer and his sight in general. In his last year as a fighter he knocked out Moore and outpointed Williams. He never got a fight with Burley (not that it was a sought after thing) but is said to have disclosed to a sparring partner that Charley was "just about the best there was." None were too shabby, but that was the problem.

---

[83] The Afro American, 1940, Jan 20th, p.20

PROFESSIONALISM

"Aztec assasin, Manuel Ortiz, still wears his bantamweight crown with the ease and consummate grace of a true champion." [84]

Being listed for the War did not mean you were in a queue. There was the chance you would be let off and Manual Ortiz is a beautiful example. While the Soviet Union were dismantling German forces in the Battle of Stalingrad, Ortiz was successfully, incessantly defending his bantamweight championship. In 1943 he tallied eight. From 1944-47 he made another seven. When he lost to Harold Dade he regained the belt to polish his run with another four. Some were barely contenders, others were top quality, but they were all part of a classy legacy. If the Murderers' Row were indicative of the wrongdoing in boxing, Manuel was so of the good.

At every corner Ortiz was a portrait of professionalism. There were no gimmicks, no attitude, and when that bell went "the shifty, hard-socking little Mexican" went to work. An obsession with body-punching drew Ortiz into fuming bouts. The shorter men were given some rope the way he was happy to march into range but Manuel could curl his torso over into a defensive bastion. The most important punch in boxing, the jab, Ortiz had the least use for, pressing forward while sweeping shots into the bread basket.

He perfected his rugged brand of boxing while losing to opponents he would later defeat. Jackie Jurich, Benny Goldberg, Tony Olivera and Lou Salica each relayed to Ortiz that he wasn't good enough, not yet. Olivera owned the Californian bantamweight title and it stayed that way after outpointing Ortiz. In the rematch things were different and Manuel used the victory to get a shot at champion Salica. The New York State Athletic Commission didn't accept him at first because their fight was scheduled for twelve instead of fifteen. In the rematch an eleventh round knockout silenced this ruling as well as the opponent. Goldberg had gone undefeated when he met Oritz again for the title but, after a slow start, was pummelled into the loser's bracket. Olivera was adamant on making good of his chance and "put up the best fight of his career."[85] Ortiz was again extended for the full distance but his body licks were too much.

---

[84] The Deseret News, 1943, Nov 22nd, p.12

[85] San Jose News, 1944, Apr 5th, p.16

Manuel was closer to torturing his division than dominating it. Manager Tommy Farmer liked the idea of moving him up to featherweight which he did in the summer of 1944. The goal was to fight either Phil Terranova or a rather special talent from Hartford. Two easy fights helped Ortiz adjust to the weight and then came the Hartford boxer who comfortably dealt Ortiz a blip. The urge to make his mark at 126lbs was not completely gone. Ortiz came close to winning the Californian featherweight title off Carlos Chavez in a cracking fight, ending in a draw. Losing in the rematch, it's as close as he would get. Not a lot went right for him at this point as he lost his bantamweight title to Harold Dade in his next fight. When Manuel won it back two months later most believed he wasn't entitled to the decision. In fairness to Ortiz, he had been putting on and taking off weight nearly every other fight. He only reduced for title fights.

The show was officially over in 1950 when Ortiz travelled to Johannesburg to face Vic Towel. The South African had an amazingly short career (under six years) but that was enough to become a national, commonwealth, and then world champion. Thirty-three-year-old Ortiz had not the vigour he used to and was cleanly beaten over fifteen. Five years later he retired, and just like the broken fighter he was, he didn't have a penny to show for it.

PULVERISING FOR PEANUTS

The unwholesome side of boxing evolved in the 1940s. Between managers, promoters and sketchy benefactors, hitting the big time was, now more than ever, anything but simple. Mike Jacobs was done with promoting in 1946, removing a keystone of integrity. Many fighters were bribed, even more were held back, and the majority who made it later admitted to having tanked it at least once. The lightweight scene was a microcosm of this Machiavellian trend, and Isiah 'Ike' Williams was its most brilliant victim.

If looks could kill, Williams could have slain Medusa. He had a fixed expression, one that remains unchanged in all nature of conversation. It was a face which aroused fear, and there was plenty to be scared of. Matchstick legs made for a curious foundation, but sitting atop was a torso that looked like it had been snatched from

"When I was in the sixth grade I bought a boxing record book from another kid for 15c. Boy, I read that through so many times that I memorized all the names." [86]

[86] The Milwaukee Journal, 1949, Jan 26th, p.2

middleweight; anyone you asked would tell you he hit like one too. From an early age he overwhelmed several good fighters but was lacking that classy finish and came up short against the top dogs. When experience had filled the gaps he was a refined slayer. There wasn't a moment in a fight when Williams was more dangerous than another. In the first or the tenth he could take you out. His violent barrages, while spectacular, were only one half of his fighting. When there was no knockout he could fall back on a fine jab, a real face-buster. Bob Montgomery and Beau Jack had enough talent to cripple any era so it took a very special boxer to sweep them aside the way Williams did.

In 1944 it was Montgomery who gave Ike a pasting but three years later Bob was trapped in a corner where he was subjected to a "whole barrage of high explosives", giving the lightweight division its first champion since 1942. The fate of Jack was strangely similar when he too was trapped in a corner and frighteningly clobbered. In the middle of his fury Williams stared at referee Charlie Daggart to stop the fight, which he did after another unnecessary mauling.

1948 was William's principal year. He defended the title three times, including his belting of Jack, and narrowly beat Cuban welterweight Kid Gavilan. The latter was a quality fight with Williams doing more damage inside while Gavilan had the better of it at long range. In the eighth a right dropped Gavilan for the first time in his life (something the sugar man couldn't manage) and though he made a brave stand in the ninth he certainly looked like the loser "with one eye closed, the other closing and his nose spread across his abused features."[87] Ike continued as lightweight champion as he believed there was more money there, but that did not stop him fighting bigger men. He fought Gavilan twice more but Ike could not find the punches to dent his larger rival who won closely, and then convincingly. Two more defences of the lightweight title were made but Williams' increased weight made it difficult to make 135lbs.

When you've managed Sam Langford you can expect your opinion to cause a hush. Joe Woodman had watched Ike, then nineteen, baffle various sparring partners at Stillman's Gym, and he was right to tell everyone to keep their eyes peeled. Training was more hypnotic than monotonous, but it's something Ike would develop a confused relationship with. A fan of golf like Joe Louis, there was often to time to play a few holes; preparation was more about keeping a sweat on than cutting weight. As the years rolled on trying to hit 135lbs went from comfortable to crippling. In 1951 Jimmy Carter took the title off the weakened fighter after knocking him down on four occasions. When Williams eventually left the ring he accused former manager Blinky Palermo of taking more than his share from his purses. "He robbed the hell out of me" were his exact words. He later gave away the rest of his money. "At least if you give it to them, you're not looking for it".[88]

---

[87] St. Joseph Gazette, 1948, Feb 28th, p.8

[88] In This Corner, Peter Heller, 1973, p.273

MARCEL LE MAGNIFIQUE

"Suppose the eye opens up. Do I quit? No. I keep on fighting - but I fight harder so that I will not lose because of the cut. So let's say that right now I have already fought the first round." [89]

WWII had its evil way with France's Marcel Cerdan. From 1941-46 he wasn't separated from boxing, just from meaningful fights. With no hope of crossing the Atlantic until 1946 the one they called the 'Casablanca Clouter' could do nothing but bounce around Europe and wait for the green light. And when Cerdan finally arrived at the land of opportunity his joints were already creaking. For those aware of Cerdan before his American invasion it was a common belief that the hairy slugger was a better fighter as a welterweight, which makes it all the more impressive that he made it happen as an ageing middleweight. In 115 fights Cerdan lost only four times; twice by disqualification, once on a questionable decision and the other via injury-induced retirement. Never was he beaten fair and square.

Marcel was veritable eye candy to those big on fundamentals. The attention to detail, the high hands, tucked elbows and steady footwork were evident, and then followed his bone-jarring selection of leather. Everything about him was compact and explosive, and he could keep it on you for the full fifteen.

Winning the French welterweight title in 1938, Marcel was not new to travelling and fought in Algeria, Belgium, Italy and England. A stint in the Navy put him out of action for a couple of years but when he re-emerged in 1941 there was the chance that he may be shipped to the States when their Declaration of War put a spanner in the works. Cerdan fought the best the Navy had to offer and thwarted a few Americans in the process. Before he began to knock seven shades out of star-spangled fighters, Cerdan resisted Holman Williams in France.

He made his "impressive American debut" against the endlessly rugged campaigner, Georgie Abrams. Both were cut up, battered and tired on the final bell, but Cerdan tolerated fatigue to floor Abrams in the ninth and take the decision. Harold Green was easily dispatched but Anton Raadik caused a scare in the last round, flooring an exhausted Cerdan three times. Hand trouble, dear to punchers, had niggled Cerdan throughout his mitted life, specifically the right hand which he is said to have fractured before reversing that loss against Cyrille Delannoit. All these hardships were about to pay off.

[89] The Ring, Dec 1991, p.58

There was little difference in age between Cerdan and champion Tony Zale; thirty-four to Marcel's thirty-two, but the Frenchman was sharper. Round after round they crashed into each other while Marcel delivered what Grantland Rice described as "one of the worst beatings I've seen in a long time."[90] At the close of the eleventh Zale was blasted along the ropes and the middleweight division welcomed its first champion outside of America since Bob Fitzsimmons. A scene reminiscent of royal coronations was waiting for Cerdan when he alighted on to French soil where he was dramatically escorted.

Injury stopped an interesting defence developing with Jake LaMotta. Cerdan was awkwardly thrown to the deck in the first and lost full use of his left arm. He tried to keep LaMotta at bay but fifteen rounds was a mighty long time and he retired after the tenth. A rematch was signed but in its place came one of the ring's great tragedies when Air France plummeted into the Sao Miguel mountain range in Portugal. Soon after, the Palais Des sports arena blasted out 'Les Marseillaise' in honour of Cerdan. One of the 15,000 chirping along was Georges Carpentier.

PUNCHING IN OCTAVES

"Those beautifully timed jabs kept Wright off balance most of the night." [91]

[90] Ottawa Citizen, 1948, Sep 22nd, p.20

[91] The Bulletin, 1942, Nov 21st, p.2

One time amateur fighter 'Dumb' Dan Morgan, as he was amusingly labelled, found managing to be more his niche. During his affiliation with boxing he once chose who he believed to be the three best fighters during the 1940s and '50s. Cerdan was a quirky pick, but the remaining two you could probably guess within three tries. Guglielmo Papaleo and Walker Smith Jr were empires of their divisions. The wise-cracking Papaleo and refined Smith reached for the gloves to become Willie Pep and Ray Robinson.

Pep was a seamless collage of positions, never set; moving about the canvas as if it was Kashmir. Robinson was a premier stylist, faithful to the book but infused old lore with startling finesse and power. Pep's whiteness made life much easier than it was for Robinson, capturing the title at twenty after just two years as a professional. Ray had to wait the best part of four years before he was let off the leash. Each enjoyed extraordinarily long periods of winning, both before and after tasting defeat. Initially their records were tainted by naturally heavier men; Pep by lightweight Sammy Angott, Robinson by middleweight Jake LaMotta. When interrupted for a second time it caused the biggest shockwaves in their stellar careers.*

Joseph 'Sandy' Saddler was good, but good enough to knock Pep out in four rounds? The cold answer was yes, initiating the top rivalry at 126lbs. Saddler was effectually the end of Pep but he has the added distinction of reviving the super-featherweight division after Frankie Klick vacated the title, sixteen years earlier. At featherweight Sandy made a decent champion, if a bit on the callous side. Flash Elorde had outpointed Saddler previously in a non-title bout, but when it mattered, Saddler made use of over a decade's worth of punishing wisdom to slash Elorde's optical tissue. Duly ironic, Saddler retired in 1957 due to eye trouble.

Part of what solidified Robinson as a welterweight was his career at middleweight. It was under the 160lbs weight class that Robinson lost to England's Randolph Turpin, but he reclaimed the title to thrive in a fecund division. It was commonly accepted that Robinson, at the higher weight, was a spitfire to yesteryears stealth bomber. Easing into his thirties and fighting stronger men, he was less effective than he used to be, but that was enough to recover his job as the man everyone clamours to beat. Bobo Olsen, Gene Fullmer and Carmen Basilio didn't make life much fun. Against Robinson, Olsen got the worst of it, but then he fought Ray before his first retirement. After failing to relieve Joey Maxim of his 175lbs strap due to the awful humidity, Robinson left boxing until he returned in 1955.

Fullmer and Basilio were as tough as rhinoceros hide and their respective code of conduct was to club away until you were one with the canvas. The pair would have it out in two savage encounters, but it was their fights with Robinson (the undisputed star of the era) which precede all other career highlights. There was plenty of ice at the ready after each meeting, but what stands out is how Robinson flattened Fuller with a single left hook, effortlessly delivered, for the only time in his career.

---

* See Pep – Saddler fight story page 228 and Robinson – Turpin fight story page 238

"Don't kid yourself. I was mighty glad he didn't get up." [92]

Carrying on till his 44th year, saying goodbye wasn't easy. By then it was 1965 and the sweetest personality in the business had turned a little sour, something his reputation will never do. Even today, to most people's mind, there was nobody better.

49-0

It's amazing to think you can fit the entire career of Rocky Marciano between Robinson's welterweight reign and first retirement. One reason for this is Robinson fought many times and another is that Rocky Marciano was possessed with the rare ability to know when to call it a day. The never say die battler joined Gene Tunney in heavyweight history when he retired on top, but contrary to the Fighting Marine there was not a single smudge on his 49-0 record. One may bicker that he was lucky, that a couple of his fights should have been declared even. The truth was Marciano fought like defeat was not an option, as if every round was a last resort.

"A man can win on points by clubbing the other guy's brains out." [93]

[92] Star-News, 1957, May 2nd, p.18

[93] Sarasota Journal, 1954, Jun 21st, p.7

This concrete mentality was put to the test when Marciano had three minutes to get rid of Ezzard Charles in their rematch; a stray elbow had sliced one his nostrils in half. The Rock shone under the pressure, knocking Charles down three times to protect his title. Battles of attrition were Marciano's speciality. He cut the ring up into dingy alley ways and got you on his terms, punching you into claustrophobic hell. That was precisely the plan going into his title fight with 'Jersey' Joe Walcott. The thirty-seven-year-old champion was unlikely to be able to take the heat but Rocky met an inspired opponent that night in Philadelphia, one who was out for blood.*

Six defences made for a pretty short reign but there was absolutely no filler. The only time Marciano fought somebody who wasn't ranked the number one contender was against Don Cockell who was rated number two. After Walcott made his unsatisfactory exit, Roland LaStarza was ready for his rematch. Rocky used the early rounds to warm his engine to slowly but surely destroy LaStarza's boxing, and then LaStarza himself. It was later discovered that the challenger's arms suffered partial fractures thanks to Marciano's momentous haymakers. The understated brilliance that was Ezzard Charles had taken Joe Louis' heavyweight championship in 1950. Before that he had drilled his way through wall after wall of superb opposition. His 175lbs form was version one of the 'Cincinnati Cobra', but he made a quality heavyweight, and in his first fight with Marciano gave the 47,585 audience a comprehensive demo. There is no other way to put it, but after their bout Charles looked like he had been a victim of a gang mugging, sporting huge swellings, around his cheek, his eye, and on his throat.

It wasn't one of Marciano's classic performances when he battered Don Cockell into submission. Many times he missed his overmatched rival who was eventually rendered into some kind of fleshy hitting apparatus. Thumping his kidneys, catching him behind his head, and sending a few low, Marciano was quite blasé about the rules. Cockell was put halfway through the ropes a couple of times, and in the ninth, after two more knockdowns the champion recorded a technical knockout.

The final hurrah came against the 'Old Mongoose' Archie Moore. The geriatric light-heavyweight with the turtle defence cut, bruised and floored Marciano. A little off balance, Rocky was up quickly but Moore was a scoundrel when it came catching him clean. Marciano staged some feverish rallies, sometimes missing with nearly every punch as Moore anticipated the blows, rhythmically turning at the shoulder. There was to be no tiring on the champion's behalf however. Archie was defeated in the ninth on his fifth collapse. Nino Valdez was the one contender Marciano failed to box, though it's more accurate to considerate it a lucky escape for the large Cuban. Moore had outpointed Nino in 1955. It's unlikely that he would have given Rocky much more than few scratches on his way to dreamland.

There was a waiting game until the new generation eclipsed the stubborn oldies. Marciano took heed of the unsettling quiet and left boxing with his legend secure, his pockets loaded and his faculties intact.

---

* See Marciano – Walcott fight story page 246

OLD BONES

"I'm going to try to do it in the first round. I don't want to have to work any more than necessary." [94]

'Old Bones', it was a nickname designed to connect Joe Brown to the mainstream after years of hard knocks and petite wages. Already a professional of twelve years, Brown felt strangely auspicious in 1954 when he made a helpful accomplice in Lou Viscusi. The former manager of Willie Pep also appointed the featherweight's trainer (Bill Gore) to reprogram Brown's artful style. The result was polished moves with added clout. Thirty was Joe's twenty, and to prove it the scruffy-haired globetrotter made a record eleven defences of the lightweight title.

Brown was once an unlucky victim of Sandy Saddler, but such disaster helped remind him how far he had come when it was time to challenge Wallace 'Bud' Smith for the championship in 1956. Luck was not with him on his special night either when he broke his right hand in the second. For eleven rounds Brown fought Smith with one arm. In the fourteenth he reputedly gambled and went for a knockout. "It really hurt"[95] said Brown, but Wallace found his right hand disagreeable as well, hitting the floor twice. The split decision went Brown's way, and with it, better money.

If Wallace could not beat Brown operating with one hand there was little chance with two. In the rematch Smith predictably received a beating. Joltin' Joe Brown, as he was sometimes known, was a great puncher. Underneath the pretty moves, Brown could lash out with medieval might, firing his right like a harquebus and whipping his left round like a flail. He was one of those who could maintain his guard throughout a fight, be it calm or violent. The hands were high, the elbows were best friends with his waist, and his left shoulder made a subtle defensive bump. There was a bit of Ray Robinson in his combination punching and a bit of Benny Leonard in his footwork. Many of his fights were of the off road variety, but Joe always took control in the end.

A non-title draw with Joey Lopes spilled over into a title fight but Brown upped his game and stopped him in the eleventh. As it was observed, "Lopes carried the battle to the champion during most of the scrap but he didn't carry the heavy guns."[96]

---

[94] Schenectady Gazette, 1958, May 7th, p.21

[95] The Portsmouth Times, Aug 25th, p.17

[96] The Victoria Advocate, Dec 5th, p.12

Southpaw Kenny Lane meant business and pushed Joe hard over the distance but Brown (who was slightly ahead) made sure of victory when he went for broke in the last round. Johnny Busso did the naughty and beat Joe over ten rounds, but as it was with Lopes, when it came to making it count, Brown had the answers.

True to his old man gimmick, it was not until 1961 when Brown was declared fighter of the year by Ring magazine, mainly on the strength of having beaten England's Dave Charnley who was twenty-five to the champion's thirty-five. Still, even in victory it was apparent that Brown "has to harbour his wind."[97] Old Bones became more a sad truth than an amusing identity and in 1962 Brown was dethroned by a brilliant Puerto Rican. The path that follows is usually full of journeymen, but in 1963 Brown fought Alfredo Urbina, Nicolino Locche and Carlos Hernandez, all excellent fighters. He lost to all of them and then retired in 1970 having accepted fights in South Africa, Finland, Italy and Columbia; quite the schedule for a lightweight pushing forty.

INGO'S BINGO

"I landed a left in Moore's stomach and I heard him say, 'ugh' or something like that. I knew then I had him hurt and I knew I could beat him." [98]

That unsettling quiet left by Marciano was broken by an ever-so-polite twenty-one-year-old called Floyd Patterson. Patterson had come up from middleweight and none of the extra weight slowed him down. Speed was his thing and when he got going he was a blur. Fighting out a 'peek-a-boo' style, where the hands are pinned by the cheeks

[97] The Times, 1961, Apr 19th, p.3

[98] Pittsburgh Post-Gazette, 1956, Dec 1st, p.12

so you may peep over your gloves, Floyd was the product of Constantine D'Amato, an inspired manager. Cus, as every knew him, took Patterson to Helsinki in 1952 where he won the gold. From a big middleweight to a small heavyweight he was carefully managed. Tommy Jackson was the man he beat for a shot at the vacant title with Archie Moore, and age had its way when a left hook levelled the forty-two-year-old. The youngest heavyweight champion ever, Patterson was an exciting prospect, but his worried manager stopped him fighting those who actually deserved top contender status. Pete Rademacher, a 1956 Olympian, was making his professional debut when he was given a title shot. He even knocked Floyd down in the second but was rightfully disposed of in the sixth. After two more defences Patterson had to face somebody risky. Ingemar Johansson, a broad-shouldered Swede had a right hand which the press dubbed 'The Hammer of Thor'. 'Ingo's Bingo' had a more personal touch to it and it wasn't nice. Known to train half-heartedly, undefeated Eddie Machen was fancied to hand Johansson his first defeat. Some lively sparring got things underway and then came that right which caught Machen unaware. Ingemar showed patience and dropped him again. It should have been called off as Machen was helplessly drubbed.

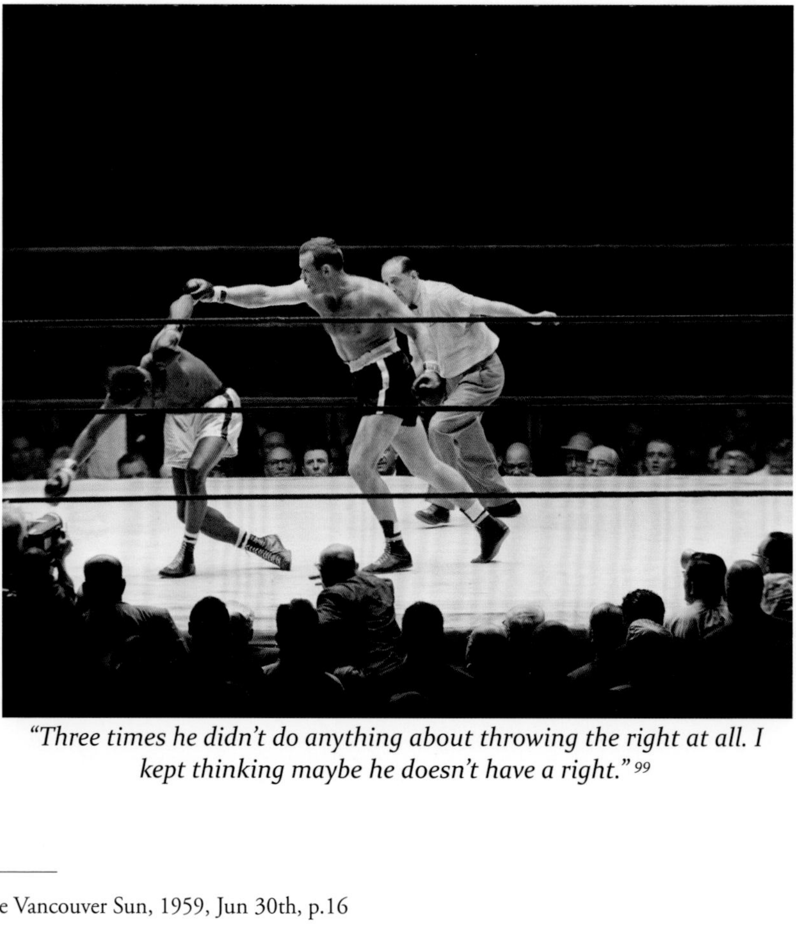

"Three times he didn't do anything about throwing the right at all. I kept thinking maybe he doesn't have a right." [99]

[99] The Vancouver Sun, 1959, Jun 30th, p.16

The upset, a sensational one at that, offered Sweden the chance of getting its first world champion against Patterson. For two rounds the fighters trod carefully, visibly wary of each other. In the third Johansson got off with his pet right which hit Patterson on the point of the chin. The dazed champion did well to right himself, but so dazed was he that he walked to a neutral corner thinking that *he* had scored the knockdown! Floyd was smacked on the back of the head for his *faux pax* and went down a further six times when the fight, and the title, went to the Swede. The decision to fight Johansson was considered the best of a thorny situation. Venomous punching Cleveland Williams was bad news and there was a former jailbird with hams for fists who was devastating contenders, Williams included. The heavyweight division was not a safe place to be but Patterson would prove that he was no paper champ. The most floored of heavyweight champions would also get up more than any other heavyweight champion.

Television, at first another curious device, became standard in every household, making it possible for fans to enjoy boxing in the quiet of their lounge. It also gave fighters the opportunity to establish themselves as personalities other than just names. In the coming years the press became a splinter of the media which magnified, for better and for worse, the theatre of fist-fighting.

1960 - 1979

OVERVIEW

In 1960 there was a pleasant revelation as Floyd Patterson ended seventy years' worth of bad luck and regained the heavyweight championship of the world. The softly spoken slugger had done good, winning back respect he never really had. Two years after this event disaster struck. The death of Benny 'Kid' Paret took the wind from everybody's sails. To see Paret bludgeoned into a coma by Emile Griffith (on national television) put boxing in a terrible light. Davey Moore died the following year at the hands of, or more accurately, due to the bottom rope when Sugar Ramos sent him down and out. Unforeseen whiplash was cited as the cause of death and, noticing how Paret had got hung up in them, three ropes were forever changed to four.

The rise of Cassius Marcellus Clay gave boxing the kind of attitude it was just about ready for. The sickeningly confident prankster had talent and guts. Or was he stupid? Challenging Sonny Liston was sure to end in tears, bruises, and possibly the hospital, but the twenty-two-year-old whizz danced like he said he would and won. Muhammad Ali is the revised name which would refer to the most famous man on the planet.

The middleweight division was in perfectly good health after Robinson had retired and Biafra's Dick Tiger walked right through the thick of it. A couple of great champions came to prominence during Ali's draft-dodging exile. Cuba's Jose Napoles and Argentina's Carlos Monzon were at once brilliant and unfortunate not to get that red carpet treatment. Unquestionably the heavyweights had it in the 1970s. With the destructive additions of Joe Frazier and George Foreman there was unrivalled drama in the division. These great matches didn't arrange themselves. A verbose chap with shocked hair had made it out of jail in once piece to become boxing's most powerful promoter. A minefield of lawsuits lay ahead as various fighters cried robbery after doing business with him, but Don King's presence meant big fights.

As the decade drew to a close the state of Nevada made the first real attempt to challenge New York as boxing's capital. Las Vegas' Caesar's Palace got the ball rolling. The end of the decade brought with it the end of The Greatest; not his swansong, just the memo that his time was up. The public were not only looking at an old fighter, but an ill fighter as the effects of Parkinson's disease ruined an already faded force. Sad as it was, his imprint could be seen in a baby-faced Olympian.

CHAPTER 5

1960 - 1979

LIFTING THE CURSE

"It was worth losing the title for this. This is easily the most gratifying moment of my life." [100]

Ingemar Johansson was no Joe Louis, but he didn't need to be. Accepting a rematch deserved respect though the likelihood of revenge was up against a backlog of history, for no man had regained the heavyweight championship under Queensberry rules. To his defence, different to Corbett, Jeffries, Dempsey and Louis, Patterson was neither old nor inactive in his quest for redemption. The twenty-five-year-old challenger realised a second consecutive loss could end his career and started assertively, forcing the champion to give ground from the opening bell.

Floyd had been classed a mechanical fighter by a portion of the public but this time he mixed up his punches seamlessly; double jabs, body hooks and looping rights. For four rounds the 8-5 underdog delivered a nifty exhibition in controlled aggression, and in the fifth Johansson was levelled with a grazing hook. Shaken but not stirred, the champion regained his form, but Patterson further tempted his hands to drop with pin-point body blows. A final hook was whipped in which Marciano thought to be "as good a punch as any heavyweight ever threw."[101] On his back again, the only part of the Swede's body which possessed any life was his left foot which adversely quivered. Floyd shared his milestone moment with various ringsiders while referee Arthur Mercante completed a needless count. After decades of failure the curse had been lifted, but the two time champion was about to have a new nightmare after their thrilling rubber match.

Upon regaining his title Patterson had said that "I feel I'm a real champion" but as much as it pained people to admit, the *real* champion was almost done with flattening every 180lbs plus fighter within arm's reach. It is not known exactly when

[100] The Windsor Star, 1960, Jun 21st, p.12

[101] The Milwaukee Sentinel, 1960, Jun 22nd, Part 2, p.3

Charles 'Sonny' Liston was born or the scoop behind his death, but when boxing threw the oversized jailbird a life raft everyone came to know his wall-denting style. With an eighty-four inch reach running horizontal across his huge torso, Liston was intimidating in general, but 'old stone face' liked to get a psychological edge with a murderous gaze. A few brave souls took the fight to Liston, Cleveland Williams in particular, but it was always a case of he who dares gets battered. A resourceful Eddie Machen extended Liston twelve but fighting cautiously did not bring him any closer to victory.

Cus knew a fight with Liston would likely separate Patterson from the title permanently, but having occupied the number one contender spot for a while he was overdue. It took some time to clear up Liston's unsavoury ties with the mob before the fight went ahead in Chicago. Floyd's speed was expected to at least perplex Liston, but the taller, heavier, and in every way larger challenger had Patterson out in two minutes and four seconds. So ashamed of his performance was Patterson that he hid behind a thick beard, glasses and a hat for a period of time. The unpopular champion looked forward to making amends with a speech upon arriving at Philadelphia airport for his public coronation but no more than a few cameramen and stray fans made the date. Sonny had hoped that the public would give him a chance, but knocking Patterson out again inside a round did nothing for his invisible fan club. And worse yet, the ex-convict looked unbeatable.

DISCREET GREATNESS

Victory over Bert Somodio brought lightweight Joe Brown's unprecedented title run to eleven defences. Six years at the top was a long time to rule and it began to show. Strength had started to leak from his muscular body, calling for less offence and more cunning. He could still charm the judges but it was apparent that Joe's star was dimming.

"I don't need the money. I'm loaded. But I would like to be the first Puerto Rican to hold three titles."[103]

Even after his shutout win over Brown, Carlos Ortiz was considered by some to be "a fighter of mediocre class."[102] It's true that the hardworking Puerto Rican was not outstanding at any one thing; his real strength lay in the fact he had

[102] Boxing Illustrated, Wrestling News, Jul 1962, p.19

[103] The Calgary Herald, 1967, Aug 17th, p.20

next to no weaknesses. The jab was solid, his power could back you up, there was no favouritism in his work and he was right at home with a blood-smeared face. Losing to Panama's slick Ismael Laguna looked like Ortiz had found his boogieman, but he put the loss down to inactivity, and he authenticated the excuse by winning the trilogy.

Before Ortiz got his mitts on the lightweight title he had a short stint as light-welterweight champion, reviving the division after thirteen years by cutting up Kenny Lane. He managed to scrape by Duilio Loi, a fantastic boxer from Italy, but in their other two contests Ortiz fell behind on the scorecards. It should be mentioned that Ortiz was one of only three people who ever managed to beat Loi in his 126 fight career. During Carlos' first and second run as 135lbs champion, Flash Elorde came up from super-featherweight to challenge him. Elorde's Philippine fans never failed to appear like spring daisies wherever he fought, and he did his utmost to please them. The southpaw stance served him well in the early goings but strength became a problem and Ortiz got the smaller man in the fourteenth. Two years later Elorde was painfully outclassed, and in the later rounds was "twisting his body in apparent agony when Ortiz sent his punches to the body." The end came in the fourteenth again when a left hook stained Elorde's KO-free career.

At the end of his reign Ortiz was just shy of equalling Brown's record at ten defences, but there were many intriguing non-title bouts like the one against Argentina's Nicolino Locche. The stumpy, un-athletic looking Locche was known as 'El intochable' (the untouchable), and you'd have to say he was as unhittable as fighters come. Almost solely concerned with making his man miss, Locche didn't offer much offence, fighting with constant restrain. This tactic resulted in many draws, and after ten rounds with Ortiz the verdict was even. To the champion's credit he fought in his opponent's homeland.

High after defeating Laguna for the second time, Ortiz warmed to the idea of taking on welterweight champion Curtis Cokes. Carlos 'Teo' Cruz was not expected to wreck his plans but that's what he did when he narrowly edged Ortiz in the last few rounds. The thirty-one-year-old loser wouldn't get another shot, but he made sure to complete the boxer's cycle with a feeble comeback. Before it was over Ortiz explained that money wasn't as important as it once was, but that's because a nice chunk had already been made. A fighter's relationship with money is a matter of gradients, not differences; whichever path yields the most bacon they'll likely go down. Carlos had made hundreds of thousands of dollars over the last few years. When those powers started to fade, no doubt having plenty of dough helped with the retirement blues.

Only when put into historical context does Ortiz's worth hit you. Making your name in boxing media was no easy thing, and the year in which Ortiz entered mainstream lingo was a year in which boxing was again charged on account of its mandatory cruelty.

PUBLIC EXECUTION

"If you didn't go out that night, chances are you had the television set tuned to CH.10 and were watching Benny (Kid) Paret defend his world welterweight title boxing championship against Emile Griffith in Madison Square Garden." [104]

The first boxing bout to be televised was back in 1938 between Eric Boon and Arthur Danaher, but it wasn't until the 1950s that television and the public were thoroughly acquainted. By the 1960s boxing was accustomed to weekly exposure. Having a ringside seat in the comfort of your living room was a revelation, but on March 24th, 1962, all the pros of broadcasted slugging morbidly backfired.

Emile Griffith's third fight with Benny 'Kid' Paret would have done well to trigger more criticism than it did. With one apiece, the two men fought in Madison Square Garden for the decider and ABC did their part in informing America. Tetchy over the homosexual slurs directed at him, Griffith was in a particularly savage mood and was instructed by trainer Gil Clancy to "keep punching" unless the referee broke a clinch. In the twelfth he followed instruction all too well, stiffening Paret with a right and then clobbered the head of his limp body. Such was Benny's posture that he couldn't fall and Griffith unmercifully poured it on. Referee Ruby Goldstein jumped in at two minutes and nine seconds of the round but the damage had already been done. For

[104] The Miami News, 1962, Apr 3rd, p.8G

ten days Paret lingered in a coma and everyone, including wife Lucy, prepared for the worst when it was stated that he had a 1 in 10,000 chance of surviving. His death delivered a cold shiver down the spine of every critic. Griffith, Goldstein, and even the fans were blamed as it was said that boxing brings out "the sadist in the spectator", and that they provide fighters with the fuel to do terrible things.

Tragedy in boxing never goes down well because it comes with the territory, not because of some freak, excusable incident. In the 1940s Ray Robinson killed Tommy Bell, and Ezzard Charles killed Sam Baroudi, but those bouts were not witnessed on a widespread medium like television. Griffith ending the life of Paret during primetime was the modern day equivalent of bare-knuckle fighter James Burke killing Simon Bryne during a sunny afternoon in Westminster. Considerable as the backlash was, boxing would not be crucified. Change was the way forward, and it came with a four-roped ring and larger gloves. Griffith had his regrets, but they did not stop him from becoming one of boxing's classic campaigners, making the ballsy leap up to middleweight where he schooled contemporaries and harassed new champions.

AN AFRICAN TIGER

The problem of having more than one champion came to light in 1960 when Paul Pender and Gene Fullmer simultaneously owned the New York and NBA titles. That there were two champions was a simple contradiction, but the real enigma was that the best 160lbs fighter in the world was without a belt.

Richard Ihetu grew up in Amaigbo, Nigeria, and he was as tough a person as his barren homeland could crop. His embossed physique went beyond descriptions of tone; each muscle had the appearance of varnished steel. At his very best, Dick Tiger was no more than a fair boxer; he played full-heartedly to his strengths, and when he did he was the archetype of a hard night's work. His high guard sported a noticeable gap, as if those broad shoulders did not allow him to bring his arms together, but he didn't need to be cute when applying constant pressure. With the spring completely removed from his step he trod heel-first, carefully but endlessly.

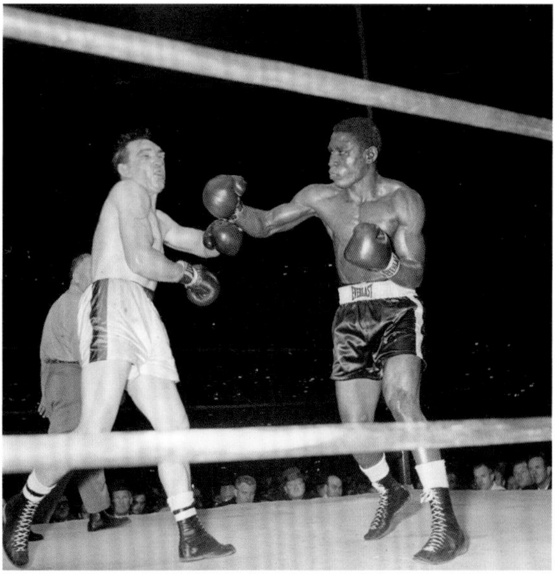

"I fight him anytime. In the kitchen, if necessary. But he tough man. He hurt me."[105]

[105] Rom News-Tribune, 1962, Oct 24th, p.8

The hook was his bread and butter (especially the left) and nobody, not a granite-jawed Gene Fullmer or herculean Rubin Carter could suffer him toe-to-toe.

The first three years of Tiger's career took their unproductive place in Nigeria, but near the end of 1955 he immigrated to Liverpool, England where his aggressive style helped fill arenas. For years he bounced around the UK, losing almost as often as he won. Nobody left without a few bruises but decisions were hard to come by. It wasn't until his thirties that he ditched the domestic scene and started to put some heat on ranked contenders.

Tiger beat then lost to Joey Giardello (who was always a problem) but stopping Wilf Greaves brought him the consolatory empire title. He had little use for the belt and gained serious consideration for a world championship fight after dismantling Florentino Fernandez and Henry Hank. Fullmer was then given the pleasure of defending against Tiger but he wasn't very happy about his underdog status. At thirty-three Dick wasn't young either, but the 5'8" slugger pummelled Gene into unanimous defeat. The Fighting Mormon was never easily rid of, and true to form he came back to hold Tiger to a draw. However, another seven rounds with the middleweight mincer was too great an ordeal and Fullmer retired on his stool. Giardello did not get a title shot until his 123rd fight, like some kind of premeditated foil. To trade with Tiger was just what he wanted you to do which is why Joey did so well against him. In 1963 the light-punching New Yorker forced the fighter to box and won the title. Two years on, after thrice flooring and generally manhandling Rubin Carter, Tiger flipped the balance between boxing and fighting to become a two-time champion. Buzzing around the middleweight landscape like a fly exploring a room, Emile Griffith jumped into the path of the 160lbs ruler. Despite conceding nine and a half pounds, Emile floored Tiger for the first time in the ninth. Surprising as that was only a small percentage felt there was a new champion. In ten of the fifteen rounds the judges were out of sync and the result of the confused scoring was a Griffith win.

At thirty-seven retirement is usually ringing in a fighter's head but Tiger, part-time rebel in the Nigerian Civil War, had more fight in him yet. A move up to light-heavyweight got him a shot with champion Jose Torres and after fifteen he got the nod. The rematch was quite controversial when Tiger won a split decision but then he too knew what it felt like to pull the shortest straw. Of all the bad decisions the one to fight a lanky grenadier called Bob Foster was surely the poorest of Tiger's career. That the champion was old was made irrelevant by the physical contrast. Tiger's block for a head was chest-level to Foster, ideal for his whistling sleepers; when a good one landed in the fourth referee Mark Conn could have counted to fifty.

Ring magazine named Dick Tiger fighter of the year in 1962 and 1965. In 1964 they stamped it on Griffith though a certain heavyweight had done as he had feverishly predicted. There was the danger of going deaf as he immodestly rambled but ignoring him was no longer an option.

HE SHOOK UP THE WORLD

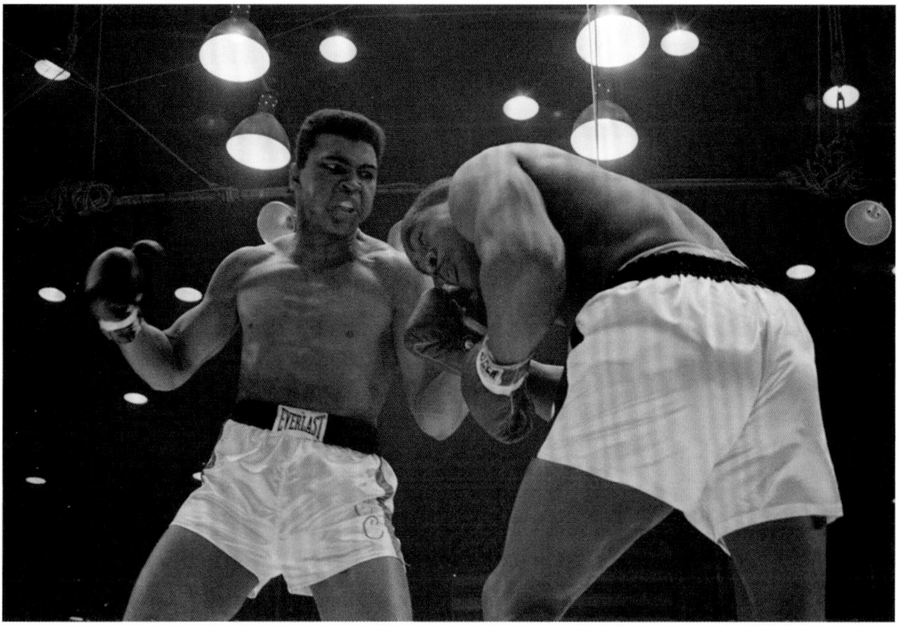

"Who was scared? I am the king. I can fight for ever. I can waste eight rounds of energy at a weigh-in and still win." [106]

Following in the arrogant footsteps of a boastful wrestler named George Wagner, Cassius Marcellus Clay went unforgettably overboard in the art of self-promotion. Winning a gold medal makes it easier to track a fighter's progress but it was his mouth that brought him international celebrity. The 'Louisville Lip' could whip them all, or so he liked to say, Sonny Liston included. Come the weigh-in Clay's mad antics raised his pulse to 120 per minute. At more than double its normal rate the vast majority were convinced the twenty-two-year-old challenger was mortally afraid of his opponent, but later that evening they watched in disbelief as the 7-1 favourite didn't come out for round seven.

It would be both unfair and untrue to suggest that Liston was simply too old or did not train adequately, but the nature of the loss remains strange. For a fighter who went the distance with a broken jaw, to see him so quickly surrender was unusual to say the least. And as if his reputation wasn't already in tatters the rematch left the once invincible champion with zero credibility. A record low attendance made its patchy appearance at St. Dominic's Hall in Maine. Restyled as Muhammad Ali, the champion made lively circles around the ponderous challenger. Ninety seconds in and Liston was on the floor where he fell about and rolled over. Had the fight not been filmed there is a better than fair chance it would have been remembered as a punchless knockout. Even with film it is immortalised as the fight of The Phantom Punch. In

[106] The Rochester Sentinel, 1964, Feb 26th, p.3

a flash, Ali threw a short right-handed 'anchor punch', dropping the shot on Liston's left temple. It would have done well to floor your average Joe, never mind Liston, but as soon as it landed he dropped with "startling and somewhat incredible suddenness." Referee 'Jersey' Joe Walcott did his part in confusing the situation when he had a word with Nat Fleischer for a time check before ending a strong candidate for the most unsatisfactory fight in history.

It took about as long as it did for the public to stop referring to Ali as Clay as it did for them to give him some credit. It was difficult to know what to make of his fights with Liston, and though dominant in his defences, none of his challengers stood out. The feather-like heavyweight was always a pleasure to watch, but with Ortiz, Griffith and Tiger fighting their guts out in the lower divisions, there were many worthy distractions. Brazil's Eder Jofre and Japan's Masahiko 'Fighting' Harada were cardinal representatives of quality fighting, and seven days before the fiasco in Maine they got together for a more stirring surprise.*

MANTEQUILLA

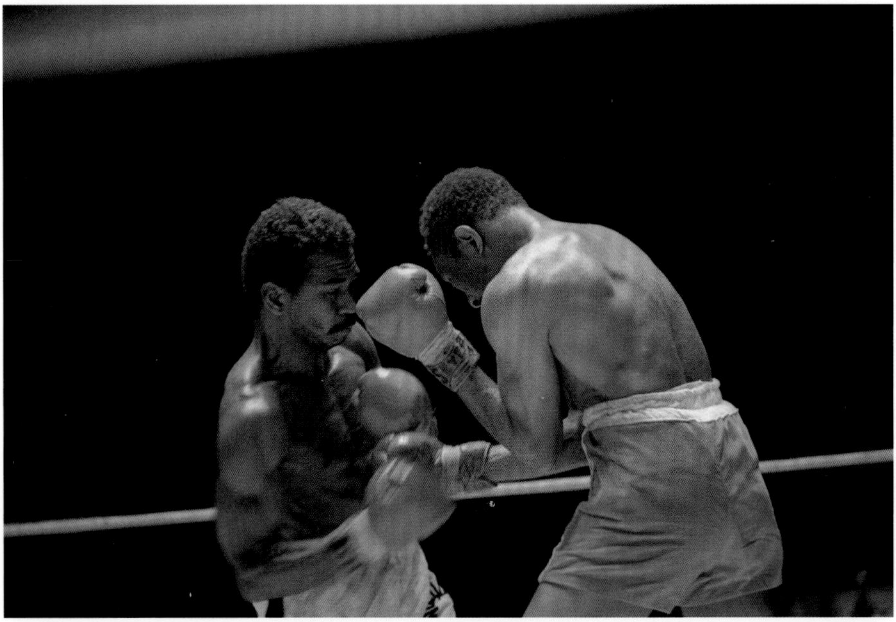

"In Mexico, I tell them I will come back the champion so I had to win or stay forever in Los Angeles." [107]

Part of the 1961 Cuban revolution recipe was the permanent ban of professional boxing. The decision largely accounted for Cuba's consequential dominance in the amateurs, but three years prior to Fidel Castro's arrival came another Cuban bon bon, though they called this guy Mantequilla (butter). The smooth moves of Jose Napoles

---

* See Jofre – Harada fight story page 256

[107] Gettysburg Times, 1971, Jun 5th, p.9

were the reason for his odd nickname. This Mexican import didn't feint in the classical sense, there was no twitching before a punch, rather he continually altered the position of his head, hands and feet, linking the individual moves to create a seamless type of motion. Curtis Cokes wasn't quite sure what happened when he "couldn't get off" as his welterweight title slipped away. The rematch would be different he assured us, but the mysterious problem reappeared at the sound of the bell. Truly, everything that is good about a combination, Napoles articulated with fascinating ease. Nobody was more creative than him when it came to putting them together making him one of the most attractive fighters to replay.

There is the revealing footnote that Jose was a better fighter at lightweight than welterweight. Before a few more pounds changed the direction of his career he defeated some of the best fighters at 135lbs with mostly dominant performances over Carlos Hernandez, Eddie Perkins and Alfredo Urbina; forgotten men who would complicate any era. There is a certain urgency which shapes a boxer's pre-title work, and it was no different here as Jose racked up the knockouts. By the time Napoles challenged Cokes, Mexico City was familiar with him and they cheered on his impressive showing in that classic "MEH-HE-CO! MEH-HE-CO!" fashion. With Cokes thumped into retirement, Emile Griffith came down from middleweight for the first time in nearly four years. He claimed to have no problem reducing to 144lbs, and there were many years of fight left in him, but through fifteen the best he could do was convince one of the judges to give him four rounds. Griffith had to dust himself off in the third, but there were no vengeful heroics and he fought utterly confused till the final bell. Again the champion looked encased in a bubble. In total Napoles defended the 147lbs title thirteen times, but his reign was interrupted by 7-1 underdog Billy Backus, who sliced him up. Unfortunately, Jose cut like butter too and Backus (nephew of Carmen Basilio) cut the champion so badly that the fight did not see the fifth. Never knocked out, virtually all of Napoles' losses were cut related. A "collective sigh" was let out when scar tissue re-opened in the rematch but it did not stop him from reclaiming his title in the eighth.

The decline of Napoles was no overnight thing. In his face and performances he was looking increasingly weary. Armando Muniz was very unfortunate when his fight with Napoles was stopped due to the latter's facial injuries. The judges decided they were caused by head-butts and Jose kept his title on a suspicious technical decision. He did however give Muniz a rematch, and in his last quality performance he bedevilled the tough Mexican for a comfortable decision. England's John H. Stracey had the honour of closing the show, though he didn't have an easy time with the ageing champion; he got himself off the floor and stopped Napoles in the sixth.

There was one itch Jose could not cure. The middleweight ranks provided bigger rewards if you were ready for the challenge. He had expressed a desire to fight Nino Benvenuti but by 1974 there was a new kid in town. When Napoles got round to making the trip up he didn't very much like what he found.

KING CARLOS

"If this were 1950, or 1938, Monzon would be a heralded figure throughout the world." [108]

Not to do the fabulous Nicolino Locche an injustice, he was more a curiosity than a fighter. The word unusual probably comes to mind before champion. Granted, the word madman probably comes to mind before champion when thinking of Carlos Monzon, but he also ticked those gladiatorial stereotypes. Tall, dark and handsome was the menacing Argentine. There was warmth in his post-fight smile, but between rounds he was a soulless ghoul, unresponsively dimming the light at the end of the tunnel with unconventional, though undeniably effective punches. You could even go as far to say Monzon looked uninspired. Assuming the classic straight-up stance he slowly moved around the ring, pushing out punches that discovered speed a few inches before impact. These peculiar blows made him very hard to read and could get opponents into all kinds of trouble. Spectacular he wasn't, but when you took a step back to absorb the full picture; how he used his reach, pressed his advantages, played it cool and shrugged off haymakers, it became apparent just how hard he was to beat.

Monzon came over to Rome in an attempt to topple their idol. 3-1 against made him a pretty big underdog. It was the first time Carlos had fought out of his place of birth. These were deep waters indeed, but the Argentinean barely lost a round coming into the twelfth, and then he dropped the champion in the manner you might imagine if all tendons were simultaneously cut. Monzon's unique selling point in challenging Benvenuti was that he had won his last sixty fights. Regardless of the pretty numbers, it was common knowledge that the majority of fighters flop after spending too much time at home. Carlos not only made an exception, but through a record fourteen defences of the 160lbs championship he never lost again, and then he retired.

Having gone abroad to win the title, Monzon caught the travelling bug and defended in France, Denmark and Monaco among other places. Only once did he defend in America. The States were more aware than familiar with Carlos as the heavyweights dominated closed-circuit television. Those in the know saluted 'Escopeta' (shotgun) as one of the greats, but it took some time for him to get universal recognition.

---

108 The Telegraph, 1977, Aug 1st, p.27

Nino got what he wished for with a rematch. During the third his corner did him a favour and threw in the towel. Four months later Emile Griffith couldn't pass up a pop at the title but for thirteen rounds he was second best, and then he was stopped for only the second time when Monzon beat him into a helpless crouch. The likes of Tom Bogs and Tony Licata weren't outstanding, but France's Jean Claude Bouttier fought like a champion when he got the chance. In the sixth they both went for the kill. Monzon floored him with a short uppercut but the Frenchman dished out some serious blows himself. It didn't look out the question that he may be in with a shout of pulling it off but he retired with three rounds to go, complaining of eye trouble. A busy 1972 was capped off with a fifteen round decision over Philadelphia's reliable steamroller 'Bad' Bennie Briscoe. The champion had to weather the storm in the ninth when Briscoe turned him ninety degrees with a right hand. Bennie, who had originally fought Monzon back in 1969, later admitted that "he is much better than last time I fought him"[109], and Carlos came back in style, cutting and shaking his durable challenger to sweeten victory.

Weight issues and bullet wounds implied that Monzon's wild side may be on the cusp of upsetting his reign. A rematch with Griffith was trickier than it should have been and though thirty was not old it wasn't young, not for a fighter with over eighty bouts. In 1974 Jose Napoles tried to better Griffith but the small welterweight was a baseball bat short of troubling the champ and got pulled out before the eighth.

Columbia's Rodrigo Valdez was a lethal nominee. He was strong, he could box and he could punch. Not to brush over the last part, he was the only man to ever stop Briscoe. He first fought Monzon in 1976 but waged a dispirited fight, attributable to the recent murder of his brother. They met once again a year later and Valdez made amends. With that dreadful right he decked Monzon in the second but the champion shot back up as if it was a slip. Valdez was soon at the end of those confusing blows and though he pushed the champion his swollen face gave late arrivals a clue as to who had won.

As an actor and a model, Monzon retired seemingly content and comfortably, but in 1988 a violent domestic with third wife Alicia Muniz ended when she fell from their second storey balcony. The middleweight legend was charged with murder and seven years into his thirteen year sentence he killed himself in a car crash. It's strange how one so collected in the ring was so volatile outside.

THREE'S A CROWD

For ten years a rivalry was what the heavyweight division had been missing. Since Patterson had the final say with Johansson, between Liston's exit and Ali's dominance, there was little to set the pulse racing. Only when the government stripped Ali for refusing induction into the Vietnam War did a Beaufort bruiser called Joe Frazier appear. Upon Muhammad's return in 1970, Frazier was the undisputed champion, a

---

[109] Ocala Star-Banner, 1972, Nov 12th, p.3D

fact of which Ali sniffed at, and not quietly. The stage was set for the two undefeated rulers, and the fight was worth the hype.*

A rematch was the logical answer but Frazier, close to taking an early retirement, was out of the ring for the best part of a year, and then he chalked up a couple of average defences. Taking on the undefeated, hard-hitting George Foreman demanded Frazier's attention, but nobody expected what they saw. The champion was ten pounds heavier than he was for Super-fight and looked soft by comparison. He was also over confident. This isn't what beat him, but it definitely put the padlock on an improbable escape route. For a fighter who fought only one way there was not much he could do as he continually walked into Foreman's gate-crashing swings, and when he got too close he was shoved back into no man's land. Six knockdowns and two rounds encapsulated the most inhumane title-winning effort since Dempsey wrecked Willard.

Foreman was not a classic case of the irresistible force. He fought more like something you'd expect to see in the cave of a Sinbad flick, grumpy about having been woken, ready to give chase with a deliberate plod. It's interesting to note young George tried to imitate Ali only for him to settle on a style the direct opposite, void of finesse but loaded with dynamite. The hugely built Texan could fight very crudely, pawing with an uncertain jab and missing by silly margins, but he was great at making the ring smaller and smaller until the only space left was between his thunderous fists. When he took his time he did not have bad fundamentals but was unquestionably more effective when being the bully.

"As you know, when I hurt a guy I have to go out and finish him - that's my job." [110]

* See Ali – Frazier fight story page 264

[110] The Montreal Gazette, 1974, Mar 27th, p.23

Foreman made only two successful defences, just one more than Liston, but his cutthroat performances had fighters looking at him, if only for a short time, with genuine fear. Knocking out Jose Roman did not deserve much praise but smashing Ken Norton did. The positive thinking boxer had slowed down Ali's comeback, breaking his jaw in a decision win, but Foreman flattened him in two rounds. The two men who had beaten Ali did not last a total of four rounds with the scowling champion, and so ten years after upsetting Liston the odds were stacked against thirty-two-year-old Muhammad.

Don King decided that the bout should take place in Kinshasa, a westernmost city in the republic of Zaire; this novel setting had the fight christened 'The Rumble in the Jungle'. Given the differences in age and recent form, there was arguably more reason to believe Foreman would win than there was with Liston, but at two minutes and fifty-eight seconds of the eighth round Ali watched referee Zach Clayton count ten over the fallen.

"He has been described as big, black and hardly beautiful." [111]

"He punched like a sissy. I stayed on the ropes. Staying on the ropes is a beautiful thing." [112]

[111] The Sydney Morning Herald, 1974, Oct 27th, p.70

[112] The Evening News, 1974, Oct 30th, p.2D

His 'rope-a-dope' tactics appeared suicidal but Foreman could barely get through a clean shot and Ali was champion again. The pleasant surprises didn't stop there as Joe Frazier put on a brutal display of heroics in 1975's 'Thrilla in Manila'. This time around Ali agreed with the public, that it would be a walk in the park, and stupidly so. Holding his hands extra high, the champion initially mocked Joe. At first outboxing him, Ali had trouble keeping him off, but the supposedly spent brawler would not stop. It was a desperate battle from then on out between two fading fighters, but Frazier was the easier to hit and got pulled out with three minutes to go.

Foreman had not fought since losing to Ali. When he came back it was against the hefty Ron Lyle and they bounced each other off the canvas in a caveman classic. Foreman came through in the fifth but his confidence was not what it was and he retired when Jimmy Young outpointed him in 1977. The year before a shaven-headed, 224lbs Joe Frazier had tried to imitate Ali in a rematch against George which, predictably, didn't go to plan.

Ali carried on as champion, unable to remove himself from the bright lights. Recycled rhymes and forced shuffles were flashed like odes to the past, but in his mind Ali may as well have been twenty-one again. It took too long, far too long for The Greatest to realise he didn't have it anymore.

CHOLO

"If I hadn't been in such bad condition, Lampkin would have been in the morgue not just the hospital." [113]

[113] Reading Eagle, 1975, Mar 3rd, p.21

It's difficult for the smaller fighter to awe the audience. A fully grown Grizzly commands more attention than a Black bear simply because it is bigger, so basic are the principles of attraction. A natural 135lbs fighter, Roberto Duran was definitely small, but he was as alluring as they came. The Panamanian was good viewing even in rare moments of calm, uncomfortably tailored for a press conference, repulsed by small talk. Reporters did not need to insert feral analogies, Duran didn't turn it on and off, what you saw was what you got. Panama loved what they saw. The dark-eyed, often bearded Latino who shared, as Joe Frazier once pointed out, a resemblance with Charles Manson was a fine specimen of a concrete jungle. The one time street fighter had fans bellowing his surname the moment he started hitting people with gloves.

As a lightweight Roberto could really dig which led to his unmistakable pseudonym, Manos De Piedra (Hands of Stone). It was a few years before opponents stopped falling over when hit solidly, but by then Duran had matured, mixing his aggression with sly feints and thoughtful combinations. He was a scrapper who fought neatly, slipping through punches while avoiding return fire with clever rolls. Ray Arcel had been a part of Benny Leonard's team way back in the 1920s and he was pushing eighty when he started to enrich Duran. As his pupil developed into the finished article, Arcel drummed it into his head that "nobody can beat you, Roberto, nobody except one man - Roberto Duran." It's scary to think how close to the truth this remark was.

Scotland's Ken Buchanan had retired Carlos Ortiz, and Duran, then twenty-one, almost did the same to him after slugging the WBA lightweight champion in the groin. Roberto was well ahead on the scorecards going into the thirteenth but a stray right after the bell, arguably intentional, produced a new champion as Ken was unable to continue. There was no rematch and Duran racked up the defences. He enjoyed fighting between title fights but Puerto Rico's Esteban De Jesus spoiled his fun one night in New York. It was a surprise to see Roberto on the floor in the first, but it didn't end there as De Jesus sustained his lead and took a ten round decision. They fought again inside of two years and again Duran was down in the first from a left hook. There was no repeat this time around however as a more measured fighter finished De Jesus in the eleventh. Edwin Viruet was the only man who lasted the distance in Duran's lightweight championship fights. Ray Lampkin and Lou Bizzarro were denied that rarity in haunting fashion.

The split championship had played its meddling part by proclaiming De Jesus WBC champion. Duran's welterweight aspirations were well known by 1978 but he decided to unify the title with a twelfth round knockout over his main rival. In his next fight Duran gladly weighed in at a comfortable 142lbs. Regardless of weight trouble the bigger fights were at welterweight. Roberto was in scintillating form when he beat Carlos Palamino, showing his worth at the new weight. Meanwhile Don King sharpened his promotional skills. There was a camera-friendly stylist who Duran was headed for.

SUGAR V.2

"I think my ambition is to retire financially independent and unharmed." [114]

Ray Charles Leonard didn't look in the least like a boxer, but he was bold enough to loan Ray Robinson's alias. Winning the gold medal at the 1976 Montreal Olympics started a financial juggernaut which was just in time for the economic boom. Leonard received $30,044 for his pro debut. Before he had even won his first world title he was a millionaire and twenty of his first twenty-five fights had been broadcasted on national television; so much for difficult beginnings. As great fighters go, Leonard possesses a meagre record having graced the ring just forty times. Much was crammed into that time of course, but it is still an unusual statistic for a man whose legacy stands shoulder-to-shoulder with men who fought in the hundreds. In a profession some spend decades waiting for an opportunity you can understand why many disliked Ray, but you couldn't deny his talent.

Speed was Leonard's forte. He was fast when passive but if the occasion called for it he could rattle off around seven punches in the space of a second. His swish moves and cheeky attitude were heavily influenced by Ali but Leonard was his own fighter. A boxer first, he was quite a finisher and carried a good punch in either hand. He knew all about mind games and did not let on if he was distressed. Things did not always go to plan, but Leonard proved to have a fighting heart to match that high-tech grace.

On the whole, things had gone smoothly on Leonard's way to Wilfred Benitez's WBC welterweight title, but it was a little generous that he was made favourite. Benitez, a defensive magician, was more experienced and undefeated as well. When they came to the champion initiated an intense stare down, neither flinched and their fight was much the same except Leonard's superior reach and fine jab put him ahead, eventually flooring Wilfred in the fifteenth. The stoppage was open to criticism but Leonard had shown himself to have some sugar in him.

Ray helped distract boxing from the fact that its most renowned professional was a sorry sight. Ali made some more history, albeit slightly pointless history, becoming a three time champion when he lost to and then beat Leon Spinks; somebody he

[114] The Sumter Daily Item, 1978, Nov 28th, p.4B

would have blitzed a few years prior. Ken Norton was briefly named champion when he received the belt without actually winning it, but Larry Holmes installed himself as Muhammad's true successor when he outhustled Norton in a classic.

Don King's greatest single fight was the one in Zaire, but he believed his greatest ever card was five years later. Holmes, Leonard, Duran and the supreme 122lbs Wilfredo Gomez all appeared on the same night at Caesar's Palace. Luckily for the promoter a huge wave of talent was about to boost his affluent monopoly. Contrary to tradition, for most of the next decade, the big money was with the little guys.

1980 - 1999
OVERVIEW

If you granted any boxing fan with the power to prevent any *one* fight from ever taking place there is a better than great chance that they'd pick Muhammad Ali vs. Larry Holmes. To see such a memorable fighter, still clinging to his theatrical routine before the first bell, get humiliated must have been pretty low on everybody's agenda. More so than Ali's defeat, 1980 was a year of champions; ambitious fighters prepared to meet their most deserving rivals. The celebrated 'Fabulous Four' (five if we count Wilfredo Benitez) gradually went through each combination over a seven year stretch, producing millions and fond memories. Salvador Sanchez and Aaron Pryor made the early 1980s brilliantly hectic.

The death of Duk Koo Kim willed the hammer and chisel back to the rule tablet. Rounds thirteen to fifteen, the ascribed 'championship rounds' were deemed too hazardous and withered into extinction before 1989. This did not stop people from shelling out. Pay-per-view had been used for the Thrilla in Manila but caught fire the following decade. The kinetoscope used to reap a pretty penny but closed-circuit television could account for over 90% of an event's total gross. For fighters like Ray Leonard who capitalised on sponsorship deals, the potential for making money was incredible.

Holmes was no joke; he could reverse certain defeat and had a left worthy of a manual, but he could escape Ali's shadow no more than he could find that all important nemesis. When Mike Tyson detonated the public were hooked. He shone extremely bright for a few years, but his initial reign was just the first phase of an addiction. In the 1990s, during much livelier times, the fascination with Tyson was discombobulating.

Oscar De La Hoya, California's 'Golden Boy', mastered pay-per-view making more than anyone outside of the heavyweight division, and eventually, more than any heavyweight. The exciting welterweight swapped pound-for-pound rankings throughout the '90s with Roy Jones Jr, a fighter of the truly captivating ilk. Similarly intriguing, an invention called CompuBox aimed to rationalise fights by converting them into numbers and percentages. This has helped to provide data otherwise unattainable, but it is by no means fool proof. At the close of the twentieth century it became apparent just how easy it is to manipulate the twelve-round fight.

CHAPTER 6

1980 - 1999

CHAMPIONSHIP CALIBRE

In 1980 boxing produced four champions we wouldn't forget in a hurry. The first of these was Mexican. At twenty-three he was no more having crashed his beloved Porsche into the back of a truck, but 10,000 funeral attendees let the world know that there was nothing common about Salvador Sanchez. Over nine defences of his WBC featherweight title the Mexican became a 126lbs legend. Toilet breaks were resisted when this guy fought. The Afro-wearing boxer had a style which delighted the aggressively-inclined American public. Somewhat enchanting, Sanchez could fight on the front foot all night without ever getting too involved. His chin was as reliable as sunny forecasts in the Middle East and he possessed incredible fitness levels, often finishing contests breathing through his nose.

"I admire his record, but he's just another challenger, nothing more. Gomez better take a picture of himself because after the fight he won't recognize himself." [115]

Danny 'Little Red' Lopez was an excellent champion when Sanchez challenged him. He had seriously heavy mitts and was even more hazardous when forced into bitter situations, the kind Sanchez would force him into. After thirteen rounds the

[115] St. Petersburg Times, 1981, Aug 21st, p.3C

title went to Mexico and easily. A few extra beads of sweat distinguished Sanchez from the first bell while Lopez was cut, swollen and stopped. The rematch went one more round when Lopez was again cut, swollen and stopped. It's doubtful there is anything he could have done to change matters. Every title fight of Salvador's was fought in America and his finest hour came when Wilfredo Gomez stopped abusing the super-bantamweight division and put on four pounds. The bigger man gave the smaller man a good thrashing, flooring him in the first and the eighth where the bout was terminated. Gomez had problems with facial swellings and looked a mess after Sanchez was through with him. The last defence came against a young Azumah Nelson when Sanchez stopped him in the last round. What Salvador would have achieved had he lived remains a cornerstone of debate.

In August of 1980, August 2nd to be precise, two champions were crowned, one in Ohio and one in Detroit. The one in Ohio was destined to stay out of the financial jacuzzi built by Leonard, but Thomas Hearns was headed right towards it after smashing Pipino Cuevas.

They didn't come any more watchable than 'The Hitman', a man whose style had a Dr. Jekyll and Mr. Hyde imbalance between the boxer and the swinging maniac. At 6'1" he was a skyscraper of a welterweight but he had the Fitzsimmons thing going on with thin arms dropping opponents like unwanted pianos. The last entrant came from Rocky Marciano's hometown of Brockton, Massachusetts and it is no lie to say he was just as tough as the undefeated heavyweight.

"His fight-by-fight record reminds me of what George Foreman's used to look like: "KO 2...KO 3...KO 1...KO 2", and on and on." [116]

Marvellous Marvin Hagler did things the hard way and he had no choice in the matter. He was once told that he had three strikes against him; he was a southpaw, he was black, and he was good. After years spent beating the same opponents Hagler listened in disbelief as a draw was the verdict of his title fight with Vito Antuofermo. That friendly motto of 'destruction and destroy' resonated more than ever and Marvin was soon in England destroying Alan Minter. Less than three rounds were necessary, but as Marvin sunk to his knees to enjoy his moment of glory a shameless audience hurled cans and bottles at the new champion. The shaven-headed boxer would get several more chances to pat himself on the back, and eventually, get his hands on those seven-figure purses.

[116] The Evening Independent, 1980, Jul 31st, p.5-C

MONTREAL AND NEW ORLEANS

"People called Leonard 'Sugar Ray'...It's difficult to live up to the name. Someday, some young Latin fighter is going to have the problem of proving he's another 'Manos De Piedra."[117]

It is those little incidents which give classic fights endless replay value; they're no longer sporting events but dramas, and everyone enjoys a bit of playacting. From Roberto Duran grabbing his crotch to calling Ray Leonard's mother a whore, 'The Brawl in Montreal' wasn't a flick for the kiddies, but after setting the scene we're again left with the bare bones of that night in Canada, and we marvel at how Duran rose to the occasion.

A tax-free $1.5 million awaited the impatient Panamanian, but Leonard, through his cut of the revenues, stood to make between $8 and $10 million making it the richest fight in history. Ray was determined to prove what happens to a good little man when he tries to tackle a good big man. The 9-5 favourite held all the key advantages. Even speed, usually the smaller man's redeeming feature was with Leonard. Duran had experience but it was difficult to see how that would tip the balance.

What the man from Panama showed 46,317 spectators was that a skilful fighter is no less dextrous than a skilful boxer. It's too vague to declare that Leonard fought the wrong fight; you didn't just beat Leonard by getting him to slug with you. A belligerent cunning swept away most of the first ten rounds. Maintaining his distance, Duran threw in tricky feints, and when he spotted a twitch punches were delivered in confusing order. A left hook hinted at the unlikely, shaking Leonard in the second, but Duran stuck to his game-plan and excelled in what was essentially an inside fight.

---

[117] The Evening Independent, 1980, Jun 21st, p. 6-C

The eleventh and thirteenth rounds were fought with unmatched intensity and the noisy crowd became deafening. To see Leonard come on strong down the home stretch spoke volumes about his courage but Duran had done enough to be made a comfortable winner. Jumping and pushing at Leonard in a jealous rage, Duran was insulted at the fact he had raised his arms. Wilfred Benitez was then provoked with a crotch-grab as he watched on from ringside. The man looked like he could not get enough but five months down the line the most bizarre thing occurred in the New Orleans rematch forever known as 'No Mas'.

Within the opening ten seconds it was obvious Leonard did not want a repeat of June. He goaded Duran to come to him, and when he did the focused challenger sneaked into a different part of the twenty foot ring. No round had been one-sided until the seventh when Leonard mocked Duran with a successful game of hit-and-run. Duran must have broiled inside when Leonard landed his bolo punch but he found it harder to make his aggression count. With sixteen seconds left in the eighth the champion threw his right arm up in a carefree manner and walked away. Renowned for his defiant behaviour, both the referee and Leonard interpreted it as Duran figuratively saying "No, you can't hurt me" but Roberto had had enough. Complaints of stomach and arm cramp did nothing to lessen the fact boxing's macho man quit. There was still some fight left in the disgraced icon, but now it was Leonard who was to face Thomas Hearns in another welterweight blockbuster.

UNIFICATION

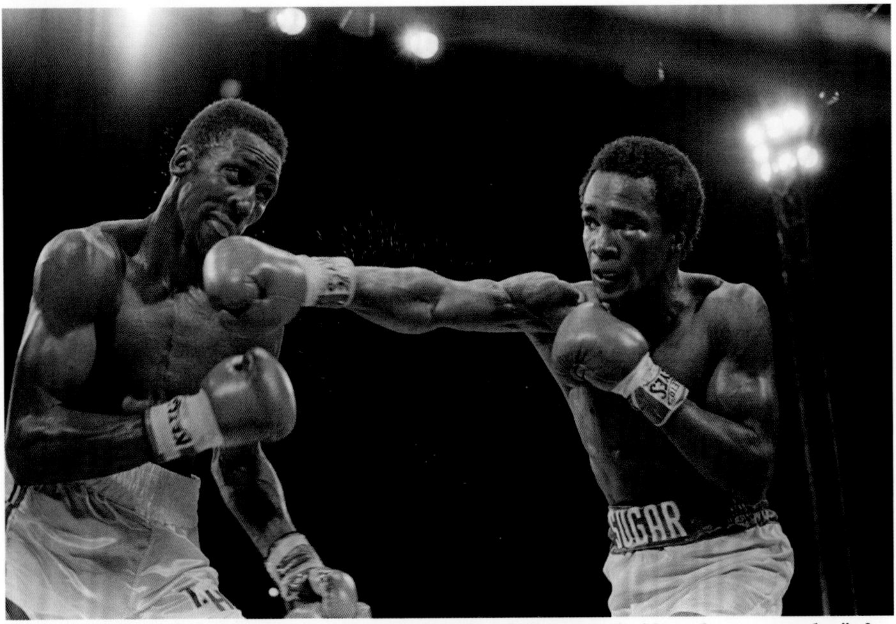

"I was very conscious of my injury. I laid back, hoping he'd make a mistake." [118]

[118] Tri City Herald, 1981, Sep 17th, p.31

The 1981 welterweight clash between Ray Leonard and Thomas Hearns did what it promised; it broke financial records and it thrilled the fans. Despite a bible's worth of gossip, you didn't know how Leonard was going to fight the WBA champion. Like Duran, Hearns was all intensity, but the similarities stopped there. Everybody had the same problem when facing Detroit's knockout artist and for Leonard it meant giving up three inches in height and four inches in reach. These advantages were put to good use in the first five rounds. The desire to go in guns-blazing could be seen in Hearns' prickly eyes but he stuck with the basics and Leonard couldn't get close.

Ray tried to be cute, making circles and leaping in with punches. By the sixth it dawned on him that he would have to create opportunities. It was take a risk or continue to be out-boxed and the solution came in the form of a left hook. It crashed into Hearns' jaw and his body wasn't good at telling lies. With both hands Leonard threw for keeps, swaying Hearns' pine tree figure after each blow only for the bell to intervene. Having survived the crises Tommy worked on that lead of his. With less zip and wider mouths the fighters continued and what was originally a mild swelling on Ray's left eye developed into an ugly bump. The eleventh and twelfth were showcases for Hearns' long jab.

Sat back in his corner, Leonard was told by Angelo Dundee that he was "blowin' it!" It was a motivational line Ray was about to make famous. The boxer was forced to be the hunter and he put Hearns through the ropes after a furious rally. With seconds to go in the round he left Tommy sagged on the ropes, taking a count. Leonard didn't need any advice on what he should do and when he got Hearns in trouble again, offering little defence, the fight was stopped. Close friend and trainer, Emmanuel Steward was upset the most. The beaten man vowed to return, but it would be as a light-middleweight. Leonard had spoken of retirement from the start, but retinal damage enforced the decision in 1982. As for Hagler, busy redesigning the middleweight décor, that meant no multi-million dollar pay check.

RETURN OF THE GREAT WHITE HOPE

The heavyweight champion was not a popular one. Battering Muhammad Ali for ten rounds was a more pathetic spectacle than Rocky Marciano sending Joe Louis through the ropes. At least that fight had been semi-competitive. As we now know Ali was a thirty-eight-year-old man suffering from the effects of Parkinson's disease. During a medical examination Ali had failed to touch his nose in a most basic coordination test. Larry Holmes shared the sympathy of the public. Reluctant to hit him, Holmes spared a tear for his boyhood hero who was pulled out before the eleventh. Understandably, the press weren't so easy on the 'Eastern Assassin'.

Once a sparring partner for Ali, Holmes forged a style quite similar; not as quick, though more tenacious. He often ditched his form for a ruckus. When he chose to box he could control a fight with his jab and his jab alone. He was not very elusive as long boxers go, but he had a great chin and powers of recovery which were put to their ultimate test when Ernie Shavers dropped him with his right hand bomb.

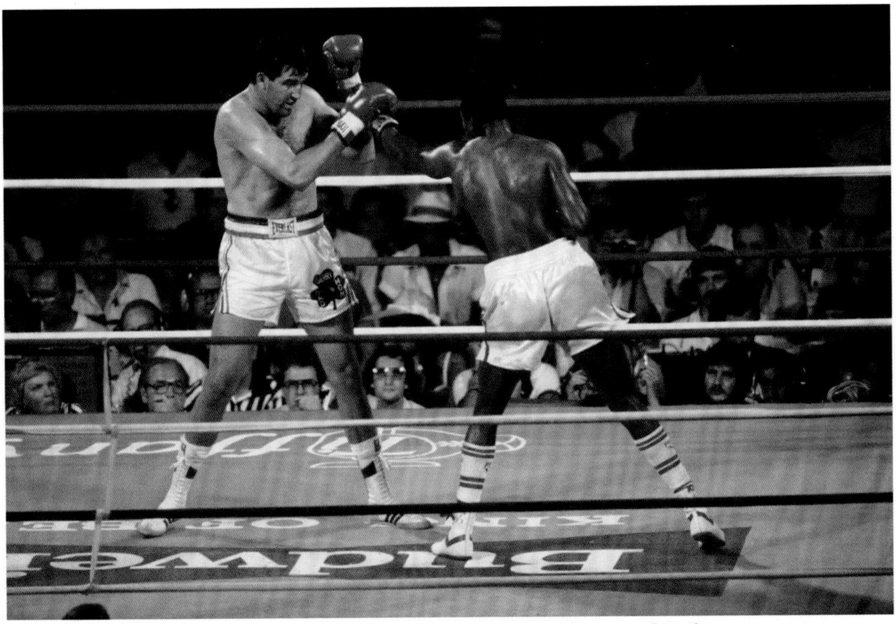

"When the fight was postponed it gave me more time and I almost got to not like him. I had to come back to my senses. My job was to outbox him."[119]

Holmes, "a worthy and, at times, noble champion"[120] was missing that exciting ambience that surrounded others. That all changed when 6'6" Gerry Cooney lurched towards his title. The pearly white giant was the perfect candidate for the media to dress-up as a monster. With his soft voice and heavy fists he had that necessary individuality to reel in your average Joe. The build-up to their summer bout verged on circus proportions but it did the trick. Closed-circuit television played its part in making it the richest bout in history, accounting for a staggering $55 million of the expected $60 million gross.

Ron Lyle and Ken Norton were diminished fighters but the way in which big Gerry annihilated them made the die-hards a little unsure. "Tick…tick…tick" whispered Cooney's rambunctious team. Caught up in the moment, most believed this new Great White Hope had an even chance of victory. Through two rounds things were fairly peaceful but Holmes landed a good right in the third. Cooney was quite happy to go to the floor, lowering expectation considerably. He was game but largely outboxed, and in the thirteenth he was rescued by the referee.

A big cancer of the 1980s heavyweight scene was the divided championships of which Holmes never unified. While Larry was rated number one, Gerrie Coetzee, John Tate, Greg Page, and Tony Tubbs played pass the parcel with the WBA title. Holmes then relinquished his WBC strap in 1983 and became champion for the newly instated IBF. You couldn't blame fans for getting nostalgic.

---

[119] Boxing Monthly, Aug 2002, p.14

[120] The Evening Independent, 1982, Jun 11th, p.C

TRAGEDY IN VEGAS

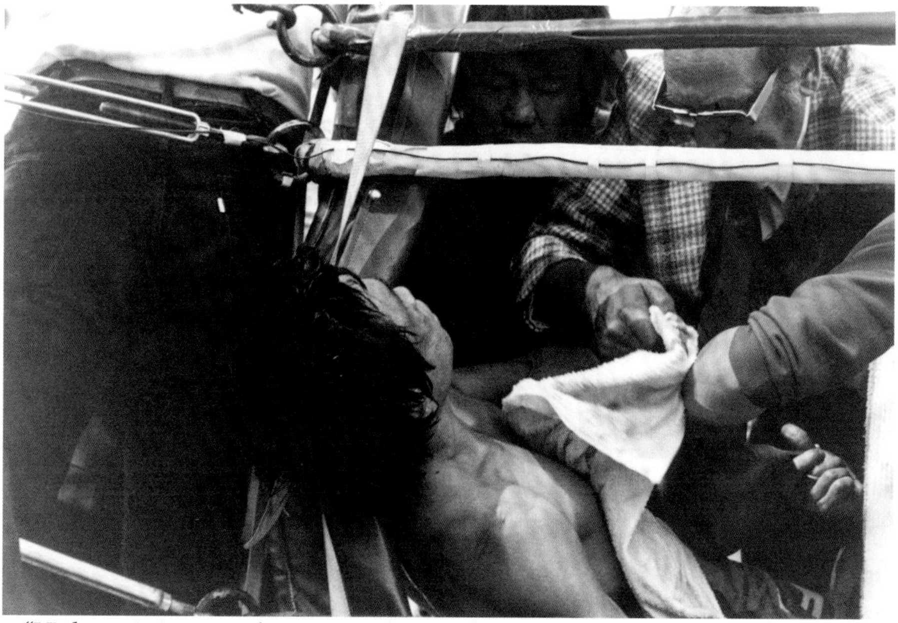

"Violence is in our culture, rooted in our bones. We are not ready to dispose of violence just as we are not prepared to outlaw war." [121]

Boxing was shaken at Leonard's retirement. The most famous pugilist on the planet was certain that his fighting days were over at twenty-eight. Later that week Ray Mancini took on Korean Duk Koo Kim and everyone quickly forgot about Leonard. A tough victory was concluded at Caesars Palace with a solid cross that drove its way through Kim's jaw, perfectly levelling him. His stiff limbs managed to prop him up awkwardly for a moment in a final show of resistance. Minutes later he was unconscious in a scene eerily familiar to the aftermath of Emile Griffith's third fight with Benny Paret twenty years earlier. It kept its eerie consistency when Kim was sent to hospital. Two and a half hours of brain surgery ended with exceedingly slim chances of survival, and sure enough the loser lost his life.

If the death of Paret caused a stir in 1962, you can imagine the backlash in a more modern world. Numerous changes had been made since gloved fighting began and still there was tragedy. That more people lost their lives horse and motor racing was inconsequential. Outside of its permanent ban the critics had a long list of suggestions to lessen the risk. Bigger gloves were an obvious idea. Some thought it best if head protection became standard. For a short time it was thought necessary if doctors were equipped with buttons that they may press to stop a fight automatically. The final say was that fifteen rounds were no more and championship fights would terminate at twelve. The reasoning was that far more damage may be done to a fighter's brain in the last nine minutes when they're most dehydrated.

---

[121] Ocala Star-Banner, 1982, Nov 16th, p.5C

Aaron Pryor's previous fight with Alexis Arguello was brought up in connection with Mancini's fight with Kim, though as one reporter rightly pointed out, "No one wanted to ban boxing after the Pryor-Arguello fight."[122] *

WAR

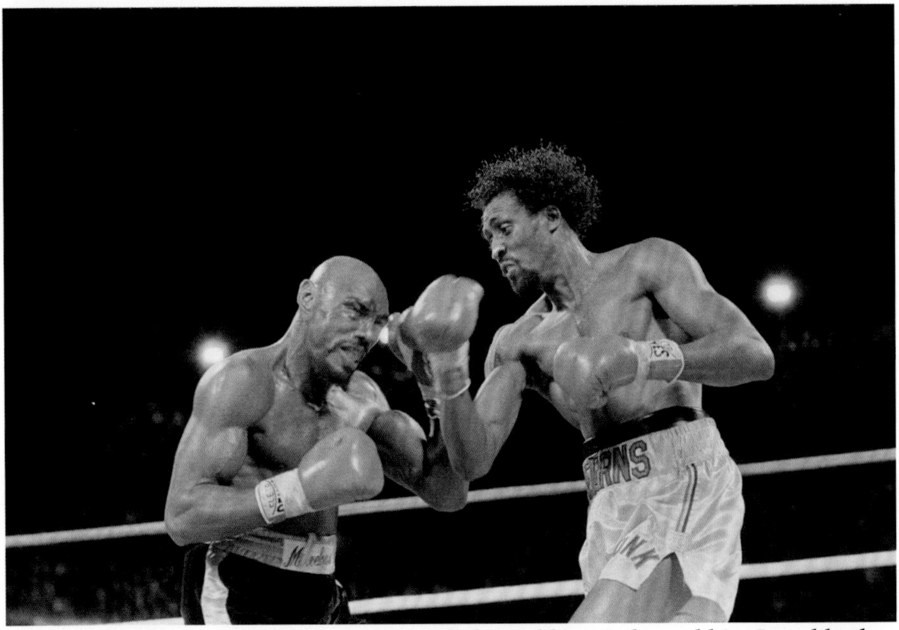

"I think he threw everything at me. But I showed him. I showed him I could take that big right hand. The rest is history now." [123]

Roberto Duran winning the WBA light-middleweight title invigorated a career that was slipping into insignificance. In 1983 he mercilessly outclassed undefeated Davey Moore and got himself a shot at Hagler's middleweight title. This was music to Marvin's ears, finally guaranteed a few million. It was a compelling fight. The Marvellous one got the decision while Duran won back a ration of the respect he had lost in New Orleans.

Hearns had confiscated Benitez's WBC version of the 154lbs title, taking it on points. Murray Sutherland and Luigi Minchillo took him the distance also. After one and a half years without a knockout the Hitman persona wasn't so fitting, but then came Roberto Duran. Had the fight come off in 1980 a fitter Duran would have fared better, back when Tommy had some filling out to do. What he got on a warm Nevada evening was 154lbs of disaster. Kissing the canvas twice in the opener, the Panamanian was done in the second by a right hand which cut through the air. The noise generated

[122] The Modesto Bee, 1982, Nov 16th, p.D-2

* See Pryor – Arguello fight story page 272

[123] Ottawa Citizen, 1985, Apr 16th, p.C3

was even more impressive. It was a performance that bought Tommy a date with the middleweight division's tough guy.

Reflecting on their seven minute and fifty-two second fight, the *Los Angeles Times* declared "a new level of violence". Officially it was given the minimal tag 'The Fight'. Hagler called it War. Marvin's tactic was to swarm his rival; not give him the time or space to function. Tommy's wild side was ignited on first aggravation and he put it all right there. A right hand turned Hagler's body sideways for a moment and he briefly took cover from the delirious punching of the challenger. For a guy who'd (at best) blinked at leather it deserved note, but Marvin fought back, trading punch-for-punch with boxing's most volatile performer.

Back in ring centre Hearns took pot-shots at Hagler, bringing blood from his head. The surprisingly hostile man from Brockton then trapped Hearns in a corner where they exchanged many blows. Tommy was sharper but the more anxious of the two. An insane round one ended with a bloody scowl from the champion. Not before time, Tommy found the space to box and worsened Hagler's cut. Marvin liked to leap in with his shots and the crowd reacted expectantly whenever one landed. Something strange was going with Hearns' legs which gave way a couple of times without a punch. "Stay away and box him" pleaded Emmanuel Steward. He did his best and a minute into the third Hagler was sent to the doctor. It was awfully early to be questioning the bout's continuation. If Marvin wasn't revved up he was now. He literally threw himself at Hearns, making him dance with a long right and chasing him to the ropes for a history-grabbing *coup de grace*. One man raised his arms, the other was ingloriously cradled. Tommy's second super-fight marked his second defeat. First Leonard's, then Hagler's key to immortality, The Hitman was again gracious, a good reminder of the difference between the boxer and the savage.

KID DYNAMITE

Cocaine shouldn't be part of any boxer's diet, but many were giving it a whirl. Aaron Pryor's career was smeared with reports of being in possession of the illegal stimulant, Ray Leonard would later admit to taking the drug, and a few heavyweights tested positive. Michael Dokes and Tony Tubbs, though capable fighters, were illustrative of the problems at heavyweight, and if you weren't on something you were having trouble staying in shape. You could never be sure if these bigger heavyweights would show up ten or twenty pound above their optimum.

Anything *but* outside the gym, on the principles of keeping on the straight and narrow, Mike Tyson was an angel. The thickly-built slugger abstained from sex and any form of liquor or recreational drug for much of his teenage years, when boys begin to flirt with adulthood. The frustration this caused, Tyson would reiterate in later interviews, but his sacrifice was fully appreciated.

Between Tyson turning professional and squashing Trevor Berbick two upsets had resounded beside his scorching trail. No sooner had welterweight's Donald Curry established himself as the best pound-for-pound fighter in the world than

Lloyd Honeyghan beat him, and light-heavyweight Michael Spinks outpointed Larry Holmes, denying him the chance to equal Rocky Marciano's immaculate record. The defeat compelled Holmes to say some nasty things about Marciano and jockstraps, but he was right to be upset when he lost a return fight in which he did much better. These disturbing revelations urged the public to invest in Tyson; he sure had looked good on the way up. Rewarding his loyal fan base, Mike's two-handed outbursts had the same effect on the world stage as they had on journeymen and boxing rejoiced.

The aura of Tyson's was soon on a par with that of Ali's, but just before the world was ready to kneel before its gloved messiah, James 'Buster' Douglas taught us to think twice about building fighters into superheroes.*

"He didn't show any respect. I was going to make him pay with his health." [124]

118-110

Fighters will claim all kinds of things when in front of a microphone. After assuring us of winning a fight the one thing you can be sure of is scrapping retirement plans. Sugar Ray Leonard had come out of his. Floored by the unspectacular Kevin Howard on his way to winning in the ninth, Leonard re-announced his retirement. It "wasn't there anymore" he declared, but a fight with Hagler stayed on his to-do list. On April 6th, 1987, Leonard finally got Hagler after a long stint of preparation. For the last twelve months Ray had been watching the tapes and talking to Angelo. For the last six months he was hitting the gym thrice a week and was quick to inform the doubters that Marvin had slowed. The details of their fight have, over the years, been broken into finer details for further examination. Controversy is one thing, but a bizarre theory of conspiracy has attempted to tarnish what Leonard did. Try to rewrite history as some may, the challenger was the underdog, and he was with good reason.

---

[124] The Milwaukee Sentinel, 1987, Oct 17th, p.1, Part 2

* See Tyson – Douglas fight story page 280

The middleweight champion eyed his thirteenth successful defence, and seeing as he hadn't lost in eleven years victory was high on the probability metre. The popular bet was Leonard doesn't hear the final bell. The distance was set at the new twelve round ruling, surely an advantage to Ray, and he exploited it. He was still there at the end.

"I think they have to change nicknames and call him Marvelous Sugar Ray Leonard. He was marvellous last night, and Hagler wasn't." [125]

Hagler decided to begin fighting right-handed. Being ambidextrous was one of his great talents but it did him few favours here. First Leonard, then Hagler occupied the driving seat, working their way towards a brilliant ninth round. It was give and take in the remainder, really a case of preference, but Leonard had definitely landed the cleaner work and the usually collected champion missed badly at times. A split decision was snatched by the thirty-year old "miracle man", though everyone was in disagreement with Jose Juan Guerra's scorecard which preposterously read 118-110 in Leonard's favour.

Hagler never fought again; positive he had run away with the fight, the injustice was too much to bear. On the prospect of a comeback, as Marvin put it, "My heart says yes, but my brain says no." Passion gave way to perspective and enjoying life became his new focus. The Sugar Ray express was officially back on track. When asked if he would return to commentating or inside the ropes the new champion replied in sitcom fashion, "depends on the contract."

[125] Lakeland Ledger, 1987, Apr 8th, p.7D

PARALLEL UNIVERSE

At the end of the 1980s began a middleweight movement in Britain. Nigel Benn, Michael Watson and Chris Eubank co-existed in unholy matrimony, producing a classic triangle rivalry starring a puncher, a boxer and a stylist. The first and last fighters accounted for most of the public buzz, but the quiet middleman, sternly labelled 'The Force', was probably the best of the bunch.

Watson and Eubank got going before Benn, but it was the former marine who barged into the public conscience, scoring knockout after knockout. The 'Dark Destroyer', rekindling a former nickname of Joe Louis, fought Watson with a record of twenty-two fights and twenty-two knockouts. In six fast rounds the difference in experience determined a domestic classic, and after punching himself out Benn was finished with a straight left.

"The American's are a big bunch of bullies. When they get bullied themselves they don't like it and start whingeing. Barkley might be able to intimidate Darrin Von Horn, but he don't intimidate me, my son!" [126]

Jamaica's body-snatching Mike McCallum was too hardy for Watson and Benn rebounded to secure the lonesome WBO title; a governing body which symbolized a lack of transatlantic mingling. Only Benn made the trip to America, but none of them fought Michael Nunn, James Toney or Roy Jones; each regarded as the best during their respective heydays.

Michael 'Second To' Nunn only held one of the four world titles floating around, but his nickname spoke the truth. In five defences the elongated middleweight defeated his opponents with that unmistakable class. He could perplex the brawlers and punish the boxers; the durable Sumbu Kalambay was comatose after eighty-eight seconds in

[126] Boxing Outlook, Mar 1992, p.6

a display of scary efficiency. It was performances like that why few gave James Toney much hope. Nothing but good old determination saw him into the tenth, way behind on the cards. Counter-punching was Toney's gift, though if need be he could uncork a big punch like the one he landed on Nunn in the eleventh. Nunn was scrambled milliseconds later, forcing the ref to save him. The defeat was more a career breaker than a bump and he never recovered his old form.

A first round knockout can crush a reputation (just ask Michaels Spinks). Kalambay is in the same basket. The Italian-based African became the first man to defeat McCallum in 1988. A shorter, more rapid jab outdid Mike's, and once Kalambay connected he smoothly backpedalled out of harm's way. McCallum had timed a beautiful hook against Donald Curry in his previous fight, but Kalambay was flawless in there and comfortably won this classy twelve rounder. Britain's clever Herol Graham had also lost his zero to Sumbu. Opponents never had it easy, save for that one damming blip.

Once Benn had come back from the States, Eubank was waiting for him and millions gathered around their televisions to watch the all-British thriller. Benn was in scorching form, ready for what he affectionately called a "tear up" and caught the posing challenger with enough to have finished off five opponents. Eubank had a strange, inconsistent style. His work rate could slump dramatically and a ridiculously telegraphed overhand right missed nearly every time, but he was deceptive and very tough. A closed left eye put Benn in a tricky situation and Eubank went for the kill in the ninth, trapping Nigel on the ropes for a stoppage. They would fight again in a controversial stalemate but it was Eubank's rivalry with Michael Watson which had a far greater impact in his career.

A majority win could have easily gone Watson's way and spawned a rematch at super-middleweight. It was a stirring affair in which Watson's constant pressure aimed to crush Eubank's funky method of boxing. As things became more desperate you could sense the denouement which detailed Eubank's first loss. The end looked certain when floored in the eleventh, but Eubank got up, and the first punch he threw, a most desperate right uppercut, cracked the unsuspecting Watson on the point of the chin. His skull perfectly concealed the fact his brain had sustained a tear and the whiplash from the bottom rope worsened the injury. From being close to death, to immobile, Watson made a slow but miraculous recovery. You can guess the reaction after the fight and Eubank became very conscious of hurting his opponents.

Toney was an active champion, if a little unstable. Reggie Johnson and Mike McCallum pushed him uncomfortably close. Satisfied with his second performance against McCallum, Toney put on eight pounds, leaving the 160lbs division to tame Roy Jones. Jones was a like something you'd imagine a kid to have come up with. He essentially played a game of tick with the customary tap on the shoulder being replaced with left hooks, big leaping lefts that went off like cannons but could thread needles. A young Bernard Hopkins was left to contemplate the raw talent which casually banked the rounds they shared together.

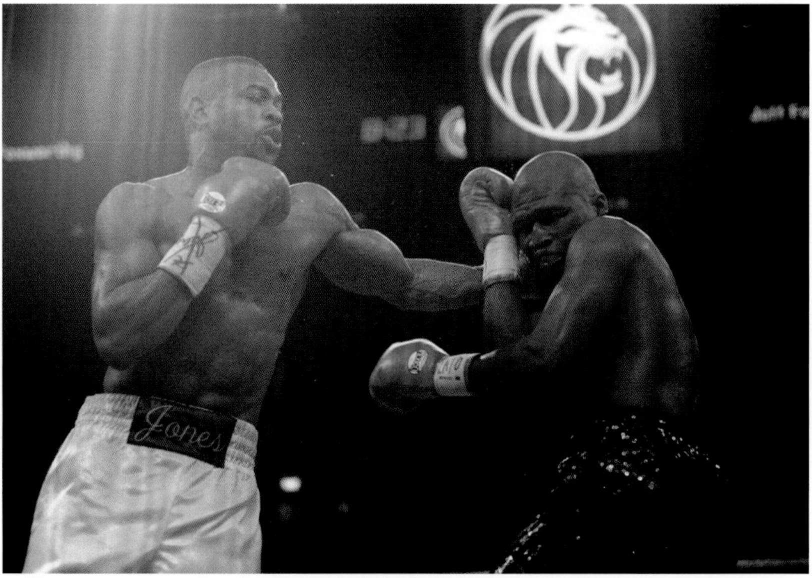

"It was supposed to be a great fight between two unbeaten champions. Roy Jones Jr. turned it into a great one-man display of boxing talent." [127]

The IBF super-middleweight title was Toney's after dismantling Iran Barkley in a reassuringly fantastic performance. He was admirably active at a time when two defences per year were becoming the norm. Leading into his 1994 fight with Jones, the big story was Toney's dramatic weight loss before the weigh-in, though the way Roy performed you wonder how much of a difference, if at all, it would have made had his weight been fine. Jones was, and would remain boxing's greatest talent for the rest of the decade.

Exploited by promoter Barry Hearn, Eubank stayed in Britain fighting contenders of dubious credibility. His 'Simply the Best' tag was officially defaced when Ireland's Steve Collins took advantage of his lazy ways. Shortly before Benn had taken on the formidable Gerald McClellan, a fighter purposely shipped over to pinch his title. The single-minded 'G-man' had a controversial, though no less genuine love for dog-fighting, and he was imbued with that same canine ferocity.

It was a helpless round one with Benn spilled through the ropes, but he got himself back in and became one with the storm. Again, he was down in the eighth but he had been getting in plenty of his own licks. For most of the fight Gerald fought with his mouthpiece half-dislodged and in the tenth he was down from nothing special, rapidly blinking. Don King yelled at his destructive toy to get back up, disgusted that he was quitting. Benn was contemptuous of the doubters but the grave reality of the situation came about when McClellan fell into a coma. Unlike Watson, McClellan remained blind with just twenty per cent of his hearing and severe memory loss. Not even four years had passed since Watson was sent to hospital and the ethical debate started over. Meanwhile, boxing continued.

[127] Lewiston Morning Tribune, 1994, Nov 19th, p.2B

CROWD PLEASING OSCILLATIONS

With the world trying to rationalise what had happened in Tokyo, light-welterweight Julio Cesar Chavez stopped Meldrick Taylor with a measly two seconds left on the clock. Had Taylor taken longer to get up, or Chavez wandered from his corner and distracted Richard Steele, the Mexican idol would have picked up his first loss. Instead, Lou Duva went berserk and everyone marvelled at boxing's unpredictability.

Mike Tyson's fallen empire created uneven reverberations for years to come. First James 'Buster' Douglas caved in at the hands of Evander Holyfield and then came Riddick Bowe. This silver Olympian, tutored by Eddie Futch, had not put a foot wrong in the professional ranks. He was refined for a bigger man and could lower the boom in a myriad of ways. Holyfield had defeated two golden oldies in George Foreman and Larry Holmes but Bowe was just the big spring chicken fans were picking to put the natural cruiserweight in his place. At 190lbs, Holyfield was unstoppable, the only man to have ever unified the titles, but as a heavyweight there were many questions to be answered. The consensus was Bowe would ask too much of him.

It was an exciting fight and Holyfield proved he was an uncommonly brave fighter, memorably taking charge in the tenth after nearly being knocked out. Bowe punished him in next round, bringing him to his knees, and there was next to no chance of the champion retaining his gold.

"Holyfield has vowed to move and box more in Saturday's fight, unlike the first in which he traded toe-to-toe punches with Bowe in a strategy that ultimately cost him the fight." [128]

[128] Star-News, 1993, Nov 3rd, p.4C

It was the end of the road for Holyfield, or at least that's what most would have you believe. Assistant trainer Lou Duva recommending he retire can't have been a confidence booster. There seemed to be no way back with this bigger, younger and talented heavyweight in the way. The public underestimated two things; Evander's will power and Bowe's disdain for the gym. They fought again in 1993, both heavier. Following a new training programme the athletic build of Holyfield inherited a heap of muscle, weighing 217lbs to its former 205lbs. Bowe put on 11lbs, every one of them unwanted. On the evidence of their first fight, Holyfield was made a 4-1 underdog. 'The Real Deal' was exactly that. Not to be a champion of the dominant breed, but only Ali could stand next to him in achieving the impossible. The better conditioned man landed the better blows, possibly benefiting from the entrance of a fan-propelled, paragliding moron which led to a twenty minute break. After a strange and entertaining fight a majority decision reinstated the bulging cruiserweight. Originally for three belts, only two were up for grabs in the rematch with Bowe having put his WBC title in the bin rather than fight Lennox Lewis, the equally large heavyweight who had stopped him at the 1988 Seoul Olympics. On the strength of demolishing Donovan 'Razor' Ruddock, Lewis was the new, second champion.

Lewis' size and power made for an intimidating tango. Attached to his 6'5" frame was an 84" reach, easily qualifying him as a super-heavyweight; a coming term to categorise the bigger big men. He fell into the good hands of Emmanuel Steward, though first came defeat. Oliver McCall, well established as a game but unspectacular fighter, hit a winner in round two. The champion got to his feet, a little shaky at that, though referee Jose Guadalupe Garcia stopped things a little early for a title fight. Previously Lennox had beaten 'True Brit' Frank Bruno, but losing allowed the thirty-three-year-old to accept his fourth title attempt. In Wembley Stadium some authoritative boxing bagged most of the rounds and Bruno managed to keep it together where he had failed in the past. It mattered not that he lost the title in his first defence; few expected him stay for long, but it was nice to see the teary-eyed giant enjoy that moment all boxers dream of.

August 19th, 1995 saw the return of Mike Tyson, and nobody, not even the aged cynics could deny the enormous appeal. A rusty, less enthused Mike Tyson was still worth $25,000,000 a pop. The opponent wasn't an essential ingredient. In less than a years' time Frank Bruno prepared for a rematch. He was not in any kind of mindset to face Tyson, crossing himself upwards of ten times on the long walk between his dressing room and the ring. In the third Tyson became heavyweight champion for the second time. It wasn't long until Lewis could add another entry into his diary of 'fighters who are avoiding me' when Tyson gave up his WBC belt rather than fight the improving former champion. He cornered the WBA crown instead, knocking Buster Mathis Jr flat in three.

Having lost his belts to an inspired Michael Moorer, Holyfield went on to lose the rubber match with Bowe to confirm the original belief that Riddick was the better man. Lewis was arguably the best heavyweight on the block, but Tyson had the public transfixed, and Holyfield was the four-limbed heavy bag to make a big pot of money.

"Tyson, though dangerous even in his cloudy state, was completely dominated by a fighter who had been, by the consensus of the boxing world, shot." [129]

If people hadn't already realised Holyfield wasn't just after a nice purse, they did the night he fought Tyson. The odds were silly at 25-1, statistics exclusive to the Iron mythology. That was put straight inside eleven rounds. 'Commander Vander' took advantage of the fact Tyson was never good at phone-booth scrapping and his degraded style was easier to solve. It was quite a dominant performance, but a good fight nonetheless. Tyson was respectably gracious in defeat and the world eagerly awaited their rematch entitled, 'The Sound and The Fury'. The street and the fury would have worked better. It was frowned upon when Jim Flynn resorted to butting Jack Johnson. Tyson was ready to put that felony to shame, eighty-five years on.

The former champion was discouraged and cut as early as round two. He brought the fight at the start of the third and had the crowd chanting his name. Fans were given a taste of the shootout they craved but it turned out to be the last act of a very frustrated fighter. In a clinch Tyson bit down on the top of Holyfield's right ear, taking away a piece of it. The bout continued after a confused interlude. He was soon going for the other one and got disqualified. Eighteen months of suspension later and Tyson was back rushing at mediocrity, losing pieces of what made him during every one. Alas, like blind love that investment refused to die. Mike Tyson probably could have, as he once proclaimed, "sold out Madison Square Garden masturbating."

---

[129] Sports Illustrated, 1996, Nov 18th

PERSONALITIES AND POLITICS

The idea of a national treasure had a very literal meaning with Julio Cesar Chavez. The long-time undefeated boxer was protected by an unspoken insurance policy, a perk that comes with being one of the most popular fighters. There wasn't a chance Pernell Whitaker would enjoy such a privilege. The Virginian southpaw didn't give the casual fan much incentive to cheer him to victory. Brilliantly and frustratingly defensive was 'Sweet Pea'. Power punching was a sore point. Taught to perform as if he had "bad breath", Whitaker used a probing right jab to lynch ring centre and a homebrew of gymnastics to avoid punches. He came close to imitating a tortoise, so low did he duck, and his self-amusing tomfoolery i.e. throwing back handed punches and grabbing under the leg lent interesting (not always well received) spice to his performances.

"In a poll of 16 ringside reporters conducted by New York Newsday, 14 of them thought Whitaker won and two called the fight a draw. Three of the writers favouring Whitaker were Mexicans." [130]

At lightweight Whitaker was a phenomenon. At welterweight he was a very hard man to beat. Chavez found this out when he was awarded a draw. Problem was Whitaker won the fight with a few rounds to spare. The 60,000 crowd were decidedly against the American which meant the judges were as well. Only one had it for Whitaker, the other two scoring it even. Way back when Wyatt Earp had flashed his gun to calm a growing disturbance. In the interest of stopping riots, one can only shrug at bad calls. Chavez lost his precious zero in due course but Whitaker remained a technical difficulty.

The one man to swap pound-for-pound rankings with Roy Jones throughout the 1990s was a masterpiece of stage conditioning. He could fight a bit too. Oscar De La Hoya was the white Ray Leonard. He wasn't as good, and he was quite different in his method of fighting, but he had that same imperial sheen, and that's why they called him The Golden Boy. Pin-up looks gave the exciting fighter universal appeal and he was inexorably pleasant, in victory and defeat. The metabolism of youth temporarily plagued the lighter weights with the natural welterweight, and Oscar's left hook did terrible things to its diminutive foes. What De La Hoya deserves full credit for was in his willingness to fight anyone. He undoubtedly benefited from that insurance policy but generally gave as good as he got.

---

[130] The Prescott Courier, 1993, Sep 15th, p.7A

Whether he liked it or not Whitaker owned the WBC welterweight title which equated to twelve rounds of frustration. The bout was very close, definite draw material, but Oscar was awarded with scores Whitaker should have got for the Chavez fight. The previous year Julio had opposed Oscar, above his best weight and past his physical peak, in event built from their individual legends than actual credibility. No reward for guessing who won there, but Ike Quartey made sure the champion worked for his jackpot purse.

During this 147lbs classic both men were down in the sixth. The classy jab of the Ghanaian had many believe he'd won but Oscar showed his fighting heart in the final round, scoring a crucial knockdown and nearly stopping Quartey. Taking his second debatable decision, it was third time unlucky for Oscar when he faced the undefeated darling of Puerto Rico, Felix Trinidad. In pay-per-view's richest fight yet with 1.4 million subscribers, De La Hoya learnt the age-old lesson not to sit on your lead. The more basic but wilful Trinidad pushed the fight in the last few rounds, clinching a split decision.

"I felt I won the fight hands down. It was my time to shine and they ripped me off." [131]

1999 was a year of abrasive politics. What happened between Oscar and Felix was one thing, but the draw rendered between Lennox Lewis and Evander Holyfield was shockingly bad. Eugenia Williams had Holyfield the winner, 115-113. Somehow she had scored round five for the outboxed warrior, Lewis' best round! Don King had no problem with rematches and they fought again in November. A closer, more entertaining fight unravelled in Vegas, but after twenty four rounds the undisputed heavyweight championship of the world belonged to Britain. It had been one hundred years since that middleweight slugged Corbett in the belly.

[131] Eugene Register-Guard, 1999, Mar 14th, p.3G

2000 - 2013

OVERVIEW

He wasn't to everybody's tastes, but Lennox Lewis had made it as the undisputed heavyweight champion of the world. Revenge over Hasim Rahman was sweet indeed, but the fact he lost to the fringe contender in the first place is an ugly black mark for a great fighter.

A bout of intoxicating hype went ahead when a sorry "I party just as hard as I train" Mike Tyson was dismally beaten over eight rounds. The timing of the two men couldn't have been worse, and Lewis' mature wine theme looked to be heading in the vinegary direction when Vitali Klitschko lost in a fight which poisoned the division due its unresolved controversy. With Lewis soon retired, Roy Jones shockingly dusted, and even Mike Tyson losing his pull, interest dropped to the little 'uns. Marco Antonio Barrera and Erik Morales' enraged bout in 2000 was the first of three, and their brilliant rivalry attracted a couple of worthy replacements in Manny Pacquiao and Juan Manual Marquez.

Undefeated Joe Calzaghe finally got a few big fights under his belt before retiring, but his impressive résumé was another left wanting for that plot-twisting antagonist. The fight against Roy Jones came ten years too late. Bernard Hopkins' economic ways did him no favours against the Welsh scrapper. With every fight fought by the forty plus Bernard you could not help but quote father time, but victories over Antonio Tarver, Kelly Pavlik and Jean Pascal took him from a physical wonder to the oldest ever champion, overtaking George Foreman. Hopkins is in a geriatric club of his own, but he is nonetheless a product of his times.

With today's long lay-offs and merciful referees boxing has paved the way for the elderly champion. This fact has been strongly linked with boxers taking performance-enhancing drugs. Many top names have been accused, and while we'd like to think a purist activity like boxing is clean the culprit list is growing. Floyd Mayweather's insistence on Olympic style drug tests is commendable, but the fact this helped dismantle a super-fight with Manny Pacquiao is a perfect example of how fighters are allowed to pull too many strings. Fortunately, as the saying goes, the only constant is change. The Klitschko era will soon be at an end, and when it does boxing's flagship division should wake up as the new power tries to establish itself. Until then, there are numerous talents to distract us.

CHAPTER 7

2000 - 2013

FOR ONE NIGHT ONLY

"Obviously you feel nervous. That always happens. If you don't feel nervous, something is wrong." [132]

The Fight of The Millennium had not gone as planned for boxing's Golden Boy but it had done nothing to affect his draw as the richest non-heavyweight. In June of 2000 another Los Angeles resident called Shane Mosley had decided it was time to stop spanking the 135lbs division and spread his wings. The quick, power-punching American did not have the experience of Oscar, certainly not on the big stage, but anyone who had seen him fight knew De La Hoya was to be given a full plate. Among those who occupied the seats in close proximity to the ring; Jack Nicholson, Sylvester Stallone, Mel Gibson, Denzel Washington, Dustin Hoffman and Arnold Schwarzenegger. It would have taken the movie buff a few minutes to name a Hollywood big shot that wasn't present. Mosley, twenty-eight, was a year older than Oscar, but you got the feeling he was the fresher of the two.

It was a fast start by the underdog, poking out his jab and trying to hurt Oscar with that right hand. He fought gamely but smartly, winning rounds with cleaner punching. Oscar's fire made for an exciting fight and there was a sustained body

[132] Today's News-Herald, 2000, Jun 17th, p.16A

attack, but one man continued to land the standout head shots. The Golden Boy had learnt his lesson not to cruise but Mosley won the last round to a standing ovation. A split decision went to the right man.

'Sugar' Shane had put his neck on the line through adopting the famous moniker; immortalized by Ray Robinson and given a fine tribute by Leonard. Tentative comparisons were made with the great man, but it was a notion which ringsiders did not totally discount. The world did not have long to wait for a reality check. Vernon Forrest, Shane's amateur boogieman beat him in back-to-back victories, and he suffered the same fate with Ronald Wright at 154lbs. A second, more lucrative, though less exciting bout with Oscar went his way again, but it was clear Mosley was closer to very good than brilliant. Oscar had mentioned retirement, but he did the fashionable thing and continued fighting. By now he had past the peak of his career. For the majority of the decade he generated huge gates while not really beating anyone of note. Golden Boy promotions helped him sustain his many millions. Mosley's original fight with Oscar was a delight, full of guts and expertise. It did however have to take a back seat to the mayhem that had occurred in February.*

THRILLS AND SPILLS

2000 was the year in which Lennox Lewis solidified his status as the undisputed heavyweight champion. The thirty-four-year-old 'pugilist specialist' got to work on his claim that he was like a fine wine. He made three defences, the first of which was a second round knockout over big American, Michael Grant. The towering, undefeated boxer had high hopes pinned on him and looked all business thirty seconds in. Lewis' rebuttal resulted in four knockdowns and a knockout. South Africa's Francois Botha kept Lewis busy while a fight with IBF contender David Tua was arranged. Botha was predictably beaten, though in style, and when the big punching Tua got his chance he was unable to cancel out the champion's huge physical advantages in a bit of a dud.

Next year came the challenge of Hasim Rahman, a drifting contender. Lewis weighed in at a career heaviest and had been preoccupied with the filming of *Ocean's Eleven*. Regardless, you'd have to have been in a very generous mood to give Rahman a shot, and high. Well in round five he took his shot and it put Lewis on his back. The upset was the biggest in a year of many. Light-welterweight Kostya Tszyu

"I felt fine in there. I was going about my work nice and comfortably, and there was no way Hasim Rahman could beat me." [133]

* See Barrera – Morales fight story page 290

[133] Pittsburgh Post-Gazette, 2001, Apr 23rd, p.C-8

outgunned Zab Judah, Marco Antonio Barrera bullied Naseem Hamed, and then Bernard Hopkins took Felix Trinidad to school. Rahman did a great job in convincing the public he was here to stay but Lewis wiped him out in their November rematch.

The coming years produced thrillers and underlined the fragility of the boxer. Shane Mosley's shocking one-sided defeat to Vernon Forrest was followed by an electric ten rounder between two of boxing's most beloved crash dummies, Arturo Gatti and Mickey Ward. The ping-pong action reached its apex in the ninth when CompuBox was in danger of breaking. Ward won the first, leading the way for two more fights which Gatti took. Typically, they weren't as good as the original, but their rivalry is rightly treasured.

Roy Jones' abusive treatment of the light-heavyweight division ended with a newfound ambition for heavyweight. Taking on John Ruiz for the WBA title was not quite the task Bob Fitzsimmons had taking on Jim Corbett, but the 193lbs former middleweight put on a great show. Having made it clear that he would not fight Lewis, who he described as the "best of the bigger heavyweights", Jones had nowhere to go but he dropped his added bulk to compete again at 175lbs. When the capable yet unspectacular Antonio Tarver arguably beat a sluggish Jones, fans put the close decision down to the loss of weight. Everybody expected a clear up in the rematch. There was just that, but it was Tarver who finished Jones in round two. One left hook dropped Roy for the first time in his career, and he has never recovered from the blow. There have been some saddening losses since but he cannot pull his withered body away from the ring.

"The only way Corrales-Castillo won't win Fight of the Year honours is if the combatants in some other showdown order their corners to pull off their gloves, cut off their handwraps, and allow them to stage a bare-knuckle brawl." [134]

In 2005 there was something spectacular to erase the sad tales. Erik Morales and Manny Pacquiao had delivered twelve pulsating rounds, but not even that belter could top the fight between Jose Luis Castillo and Diego Corrales.

The two men fought for the WBO and WBC lightweight titles at the Mandalay Bay and they left nothing to the imagination. Their styles gelled brilliantly, forming an inside battle that could have existed in a cupboard. Most of the rounds were too difficult to call with clean shots getting through by either man at every moment. As the fight raged on the

[134] The Ring, Oct 2005, p.16

sharp edges of Castillo's face became reddened and swollen while the white of Corrales' eyes disappeared behind purple lumps. There was no change of tactics in the tenth, they just kept thumping each other. Castillo's left hook cut out an unexpected angle and dropped the sorrier looking boxer to the canvas. Diego spat out his mouthpiece to buy some time, and trainer Joe Goosman took his sweet time to wash it before putting it back in. A second knockdown gave the fight the seal of inevitability and once again Corrales took out his mouthpiece for which he had a point deducted. Castillo moved in to deplete Diego's last dregs of consciousness but a big hook went through his legs. In an instant Corrales came alive, putting his punches together until it was the man on the brink of victory who was knocked into defeat.

SIXTY STITCHES

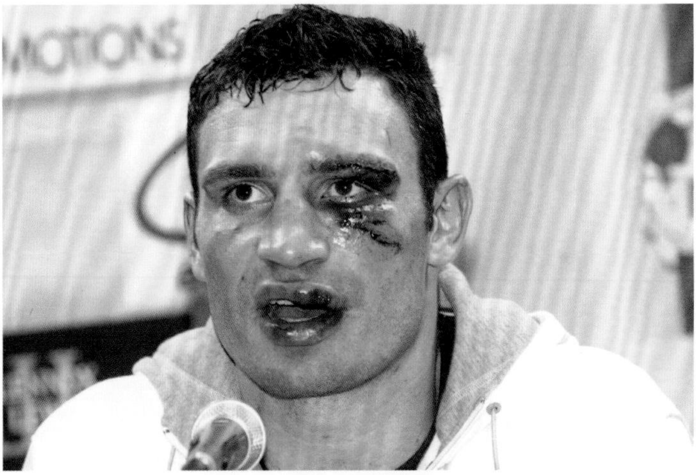

"I work so long for this fight. I believed I would be world champion. It's not a problem. I can see with these eyes. It's a simple cut. I know if this fight don't stop I win this fight on points." [135]

Directly below Lewis' undisputed rule of the heavyweight championship was a pair of Ukrainian giants, brothers to be specific. The eldest, Vitali, had transferred from kick-boxing to boxing while younger sibling Wladimir began with Olympic honours, scooping up the gold in Atlanta. The runt was looked upon as the more promising giant, to begin with. A stoppage defeat to Ross Purity flipped rank between the ceiling-scraping boxers. Vitali was way ahead against Chris Byrd but a shoulder injury forced him to pull out, opening the doors for Wladimir to gain revenge and re-establish himself as the heir apparent.

Half-retired, part-time golfer Corrie Sanders was supposed to do no more than keep Wladimir ticked over. Fans were willing to discount the fact the poorly toned southpaw was deceptively quick. The script had him suffer a beating but within two

---

[135] Philippine Daily Inquirer, 2003, Jun 23rd, p.A28

rounds he'd torn it up and Wladimir along with it. Focus again shifted to Vitali and the bigger brother got his chance to fight Lewis after Kirk Johnson pulled out. Their 256lbs and 248lbs combined to make for the heaviest ever bout for the heavyweight championship. Lewis also had the alien task of directing his punches upwards.

Klitschko's "robotic" Eastern European style was not easy to solve and the champion fought very sloppily in the first two rounds. At the start of the third Lennox put it all in his overhand right but it only landed partially, inadvertently slashing Vitali's left eye with the thumb of the glove. Blood was visible a few seconds later but the severity of the cut became apparent when treated in his corner; it was deep and split into different directions. Swabs and Vaseline were frantically stuffed into the wound. An enjoyable scrap followed with memorable scenes picturing Lewis aiding Vitali after a fall and nearly breaking his neck with an uppercut, but the fight was terminated after the sixth due to the cut; having been caused by a punch, the fight went to Lewis. On all three cards Lennox was behind but the promise of a rematch died a slow death while a disappointed Dr. Iron Fist had sixty stitches put into his face.

POPKINS

After that exquisite deconstruction of Felix Trinidad the future of Bernard Hopkins was worryingly uncertain. Roy Jones was mutually obstinate on the subject of tinkering with his weight for a rematch and James Toney was out of touch at cruiserweight. Carl Daniels, Morrade Hakker, William Joppy and Robert Allen weren't the sternest of challengers and Hopkins made a meal out of all of them. Fans were willing to hang this recent lacklustre form on the old theory that The Executioner was fighting to the level of his opposition. A big money fight with Oscar De La Hoya would surely give his career that missing limelight. Between them they were scheduled to take home a minimum of $35 million and each fought as if one wrong move would undo every penny. Everyone knew the score, the smaller man was going to have to stick 'n move, but for eight rounds it could have passed for an exhibition. In the next round Oscar was flattened by a hook to the side, a punch which appeared too cuffing a blow to cause real damage, but down went Oscar, apparently in agony.

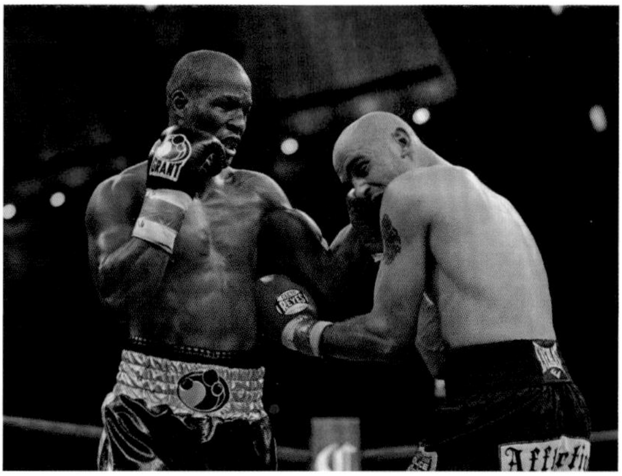

"He's outlasted and outperformed all his contemporaries, including Evander Holyfield, Oscar De La Hoya, Mike Tyson, Lennox Lewis, and Roy Jones." [136]

[136] The Ring, Apr 2005, p.67

Bernard exercised his monotonous mastery over Howard Eastman, taking the defence tally of his IBF belt to twenty, a climbing record for the division. Unbeaten Jermain Taylor was exactly the kind of talent Hopkins needed to up his game, but the young contender had far too many answers for his liking. Through twelve rounds he gave Hopkins the fight Oscar had promised to, forcing him to box at an uncomfortable pace, firing a regular jab. Bouie Fisher didn't need to rack his brain to inform Hopkins that things had gotten too close for comfort. Rounds eleven and twelve were key ones for the champion as he got Jermain in a few spots of bother. As the cards were read out Hopkins looked confident but the split decision went to Taylor. A rematch was unanimous for the new champion. At forty years of age Hopkins' options looked very limited. The solution came in going up to light-heavyweight.

Antonio Tarver had outpointed Roy Jones in their rubber match, leaving no question as to who was the best 175lbs fighter in the world. He welcomed the challenge of Hopkins who warmed to the task with his haughty quarrel. Bernard's defensive cunning got the fight on his terms and the longer 'Magic Man' couldn't overcome the gap in savvy. The big win was then tarnished somewhat when super-middleweight ruler Joe Calzaghe beat him after being floored in a fight Hopkins had more himself than his opponent to blame. Bernard's body giggled at the ageing process and got ready for another ordeal.

Gleaming after his victories over Taylor, lanky blaster Kelly Pavlik was brewing with all the confidence youth and an unbeaten record provides. The settings were very much like the Trinidad fight, only Hopkins was seven years older. Like the Trinidad fight, it wasn't competitive. Hopkins seemed to be able to read Pavlik like his trainer as each feint, spin and lead right did the business. In the final round, while sitting on an inescapable lead, Hopkins was uncharacteristically showy, reeling off bolo punches as the seconds ticked down. Naturally the following two opponents weren't as distinguished, but Hopkins should have never had a rematch with Roy Jones; in 2010 a walking corpse compared to his untouchable best. It was a messy encounter, full of melodramatics, and worse yet it went the distance. In moments like this you could easily forget Bernard's pyramid of accomplishments. The next move was much better which involved challenging 175lbs WBC champion Jean Pascal. Boring it wasn't, but Hopkins had to make do with a majority draw. A rematch went ahead, and at fourty-six years, four months and six days Hopkins became the oldest ever champion. Not a moment to be forgotten, before the start of the seventh Hopkins did a few push-ups. In 2012 Chad Dawson became the first man to clearly beat him since Roy Jones, but victory over Tarvis Cloud for the IBF light-heavyweight title improved the great man's geriatric record to forty-eight.

Since losing his pro debut in 1988, Hopkins has built quite the legacy, emulating fighters like Marvin Hagler, Ezzard Charles and Archie Moore to attain victory. Ever a student of the game, Hopkins is willed on by a unique sense of destiny. Fifty years of age sounds ridiculous for a world champion, but the ageless warrior might be falling in love with the idea. Perhaps it says more that, if he pulled it off, few would be surprised.

A FAMILY DICTATORSHIP

"That is really how the Klitschkos have run their parallel careers. One performing under the lights, the other attempting to coolly observe his brother from ringside." [137]

Pain everybody as it did, there was no rematch between Lennox Lewis and Vitali Klitschko. Amusing pay packets of $100 million were rumoured to have been offered to Lewis who officially retired in 2004. There was playful talk but the dreadlocked fighter, financially secure and eyeing-up the good life with his fiancée, was not about to do something silly. Vitali had won a great deal of sympathy from the American crowd and continued to one-sidedly thump his opponents into defeat; Kirk Johnson was target practice, Corrie Sanders was ground down to avenge Wladimir and a brave Danny Williams didn't stand a chance.

Wladimir was knocked further down the ladder by Lamon Brewster, suddenly running out of gas in the fifth. If there was any hope left after the Sanders disaster there wasn't after Brewster was through with him. None of Vitali's durability or resolve was in Wladimir. The younger brother was universally labelled as unreliable which is why he deserves kudos for how he recuperated.

When a fight with Hasim Rahman fell through Vitali went on a four year hiatus, leaving Wladimir to try and get his reputation out of intensive care. Samuel Peter was not the second coming of George Foreman as some overexcited fans had claimed, but he was armed and dangerous. He sent Wladimir to the canvas three times (more scrappy than quality knockdowns) but 'Dr. Steel Hammer' kept it together, shook Peter to his boots in the last round and won a deserved decision. This he complemented with good stoppages over Chris Byrd and Calvin Brock. He got his revenge over Brewster,

---

[137] Beautiful Brutality, Adam Smith, 2012, p.144

took the zero from the capable Ruslan Chageav and battered poor Samuel Peter in a rematch who Vitali had abused in his 2008 return.

With Vitali owning the WBC, and Wladimir the WBO, WBA and IBF they comprehensively had the division at their mercy. The biggest threat came in former cruiserweight David Haye. The insulting Brit had won the WBA title off super-giant Nikolai Valuev. Haye was quick, explosive and athletic. From creating T-shirts of him decapitating Wladimir to telling anyone with a set of ears how he was scared to be hit, Haye talked the talk several times over. When it came to walking the walk he fought a disappointingly shy fight. The Brit was not prepared to do what was needed to win and lunged to the floor at an irritating regularity. When the decision went against him a broken small toe was literally thrown into the conversation as the beaten man took off his boot.

To say the division has been poor is to put it mildly. Boxing's flagship division has never been worse as the Klitschkos loom over a batch of uninspired contenders. Admittedly they have done great things for German boxing, and Wladimir is not done with fattening his career which is notably dominant whatever may be said of his opposition. For all the criticism they have shipped for their impassionate style of fighting, they're receiving more consideration as heavyweight greats. No doubt when history has stowed them away their stock will increase.

THE CASH COW

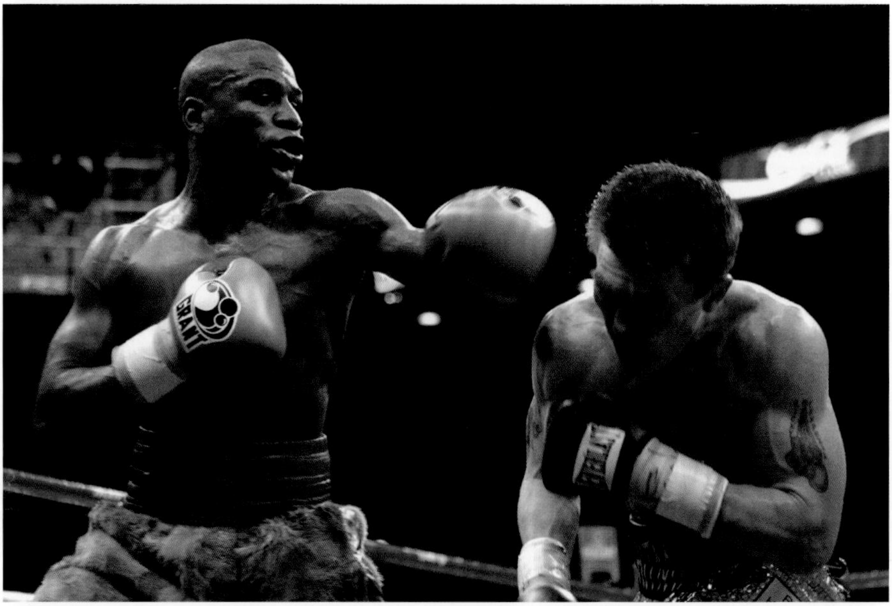

"That's the great thing about getting away from Bob Arum, I can fight when I want to and I get 100 percent of my money." [138]

[138] The Ring, Jan 2012, p.85

Lennox Lewis' retirement and Roy Jones' demise shifted the responsibility of exciting fans to welterweight and below. Weight-hopping 'Pretty Boy' Floyd Mayweather had been accused of being boring (not the first or last time he'd be called up on that one) but he broke the trend with a blistering display against Phillip N'dou. The exciting new look was again on show against DeMarcus Corley and Arturo Gatti which were preludes to a money-hoarding contest with the Golden Boy. Mayweather won his mega-fight via split decision with cleaner punching, but more impressive than the actual fight was the pay-per-view revenue which recorded 2.5 million buyers, generating over $130 million. Floyd, who would soon restyle himself as 'Money' followed the lead of Oscar and created Mayweather Promotions. To see out 2007, Floyd accepted the challenge of Manchester's Ricky Hatton who he splattered into the turn-buckle with a perfectly timed hook. The pound-for-pound number one spot was his, and with that he retired, or so he said.

Floyd put his career on hold, for twenty months he stayed in the headlines without a single fight. The big spell of inactivity was broken for a bout with Juan Manuel Marquez. The counter-punching Mexican was the designated underdog. Mayweather wasn't like Hatton and ballooned out of the ring, he kept himself in good shape and if he had decided to sign for another fight it was a move you could have 99.9% faith in. True to predictions, Floyd had a field day with the shorter, slower boxer. Eight months later old Shane Mosley had as good a chance as anyone to disturb Floyd's record. He was in everyone's good books after his destruction of Antonio Margarito and delighted the crowd when he buzzed Mayweather following a right hand, twice. With his shining moment a thing of the past, Mayweather came forward and evaporated Shane's confidence with laser-like precision. The scores were unanimous.

Keeping to his one-fight-per-year schedule, Floyd wasn't in the ring again until 2011 when Victor Ortiz was suckerpunched into oblivion. The public would have had good reason to protest had Ortiz not committed the original sin with a blatant head-butt. An interesting fight was cut short, but HBO's Larry Merchant provided the real spectacle when getting into another verbal altercation with the cash cow. "If I was fifty years younger I'd kick your ass" concluded the eighty-year-old. Miguel Cotto gave Floyd a good work out in 2012 and even managed to get his nose leaking. Seeing how Mayweather was continually backed into the ropes some entertained the idea that his legs were slowing but in 2013 an easy win over Robert Guerrero showed just how well preserved this thirty-six-year-old was.

After the win Floyd did something he hadn't since 2007 and fought again before the year was up. A young, red-headed Mexican prompted him. Undefeated Saul Alvarez was ready to give Floyd his hardest bout in a while. Scheduled to take place at light-middleweight, a catch-weight of 152lbs was agreed on; not ideal for the big-boned challenger but he looked poised in front of a ravenous media. When the bell went and the rounds began to pass, a familiar story was told. More boxer than strict attacker, Alvarez's measured style played right into Floyd's sharp-shooting hands, and to the victor went a record breaking $40,870,000 check.

With his jaw neatly flanked by his left shoulder and right arm, Floyd is amazingly difficult to hit (especially with anything meaningful) and his sharp punching has often registered 60-70 connect percentages on CompuBox, over half the average. Five more fights with Showtime and that could be it, but Floyd might be running low on respectable options. Pressure once again mounted for a fight against Pacquiao with the latter's return. Expectation remains low on that front.

Stuck in an era of very capable but unspectacular opponents, it's difficult to get excited about fights in which Floyd is the runaway favourite, especially when each cameo takes months to arrange. Championing his zero and claiming there's "no blueprint", the pound-for-pound king has made himself a target for criticism (an ingenious angle which has boosted PPV sales), but as his sparkling career winds down, it would be nice to see him take a leaf out of Hopkins' book and attempt something which has us look on in justified doubt.

PACMAN'S KRYPTONITE

"All the talk of going toe-to-toe became a reality... it was brutally entertaining."[139]

Here's hoping that Manny Pacquiao and Juan Manuel Marquez never fight again. On the 8th December, 2012 the perennial Mexican concentrated 42 rounds of frustration into a single right hand. Less than a second remained of the sixth when Pacquiao went rushing in, leaving his chin exposed. Against a lesser opponent the moment to capitalise would have come and gone. Even Marquez outdid himself. In the previous round 'Pacman' had been caught in a similar position. He managed to eat that one up, but the punch that flattened him would have finished a long list of tough men. It was the perfect conclusion to a thrilling rivalry. It also smacked a little of the Tortoise and the Hare because for many years one man appeared to be streets ahead of the other. There was a time, a very recent one when there was a bit of a Harry Greb vibe about Manny Pacquiao.

[139] Los Angeles Times, 2012, Dec 9th, p.C-1

With that 2005 loss to Erik Morales buried underneath two convincing rematches, a more refined Pacman targeted bigger game. Moving up in weight is always a concern. Morales was a diluted force outside of 122lbs, but with Pacquiao something spectacular happened. Each step up seemed to empower him. Lightweight David Diaz was no pushover but when the bell sounded Manny was, as Diaz put it in his own unique way, "too fuckin' fast man". The extent of Manny's dominance was impressive, but the single left hand which finished the job was even more so.

In retrospect, what with the strong rumours of Oscar intravenously rehydrating, victory against The Golden Boy wasn't a huge accomplishment, but all that mattered was that Pacquaio had destroyed a modern great. Exceeding expectation is a genuine rarity, but when Pacquiao blasted Ricky Hatton that is precisely what he did. Up another weight, the Philippine typhoon had Manchester's hero down twice in the first and then sent him to sleep with a wicked left in round two. Freddie Roach was the only one who didn't look surprised. An insistence on catchweight bouts gives his career a slight tinge, but Manny's superiority over naturally bigger men can't be trivialised. After brutalising Miguel Cotto the lust for a mega-fight with Floyd Mayweather made too much sense. Sadly, and never to be forgotten, boxing was robbed of this epic event.

Floyd had broken his twenty-one month hiatus with an easy victory over Marquez, but the result had more to do with size and styles than talent. The goateed Mexican was far from drifting into the shadows with lightweight victories over Joel Casamayor and Juan Diaz. Everyone may have been taken by Pacquiao's hell-raising, but it didn't get any better than Marquez's blood and guts triumph over Diaz. Manny continued to win, and his blazing fists were always a pleasure to witness, but Shane Mosley had done nothing to warrant a shot. Over twelve rounds he fought entirely negatively, losing fans as well as the fight. Meanwhile Marquez posted another stirring victory over modern day gladiator Michael Katsidis.

A third fight went ahead in 2011 and the general consensus, seeing how Pacquiao had not only adjusted but thrived at a higher weight, was that Marquez was in for a hiding. The consensus couldn't have been less accurate as all the same problems flared up like seasonal allergies. The tamest of the four bouts suited Marquez. At the final bell each man's body language reflected that; Pacquiao shaking his head, Marquez raising his arm. The judges saw things differently and a majority decision gave it to Manny. For those who believe in karma, Pacquaio's loss to Timothy Bradley may have sufficed. In reality it was criminal.

Sweeping up the vast majority of the first ten rounds, Pacquiao only needed to remain standing to keep his winning streak intact. He managed the standing part but a split decision went against him and the politics behind scoring became that bit more confusing. 2012 was a year of bad decisions, lacklustre big fights and numerous failed drug tests. A fourth fight between Pacquiao and Marquez at least promised to close the year out in style, but the shootout that followed gave boxing the electric shock treatment it so desperately needed.

Pacquiao looked razor sharp in the first two rounds, exhibiting more of that buzzsaw style which produced his alias, but choosing his moments very well. Marquez found it a little difficult to get off but a long right in the third did what it never had and dropped Manny. The fight was on. After being sent into a frenzy for the last twenty seconds, Pacquiao got back to his boxing, took the fourth and then dropped Juan in the fifth. It was more of a flash knockdown but a right hook went right through the Mexican's body. He fired back brilliantly, though perhaps with a little more care Pacquiao could have forced the stoppage he so clearly wanted. With the crowd in awe of their most unpredictable bout yet, into the sixth they went.

For 2:58 minutes it was another Pacquiao round. There had been theories of Manny having lost his touch but he'd never looked better. CompuBox would help reveal just how good he had been, outlanding Marquez in every round *and* at a better connect percentage, but at the ten second marker he craved that knockout too much and, poetically, was knocked out himself. Blood spattered and with a busted nose, Marquez saluted his fans. It was a seminal victory, and it will go on to increase Juan's sympathy vote in the series, but he only had a limited amount of time to bathe in this hard-earned limelight. Despite being one half of numerous thrillers, Marquez's counter-punching ways and subdued personality have stopped him enthralling like other Mexican greats. With his friendly smile and occasional impressions of Bruce Lee, Pacquiao's stardom (even in defeat) continues to shine that much brighter.

In the autumn of 2013, Timothy Bradley continued to mend a damaged reputation by outpointing Marquez in a lukewarm affair. The following month Pacquiao made his return against Latino tough guy, Brandon Rios, a limited opponent but many were unsure of Manny's punch resistance after his emphatic loss. After twelve rounds of target practise, Manny's hand was raised which has set up an intriguing rematch with Bradley. In the more likely event of a win, Manny could get one up over Marquez, but in these semi-retired days of the old guard there's only one fight left that needs to be made. And if the bout with Floyd Mayweather is destined for eternal speculation, we can only hope it inspires future headliners to chase each other down.

IMMATURE DIVISION GETS INTERESTING

With Roy Jones defeated Joe Calzaghe packed his bags for Cardiff. Retirement proved tougher than most opponents but he sidestepped his demons and that undefeated record of 46-0 kept its sparkle. This Welsh super-middleweight (often accused of slapping with his punches) had unquestionably slapped some of the world's best fighters into the loser's bracket. With speed, volume and intelligence, Calzaghe did the business during the last stage of his career. Universal respect was finally his, but if there is one gripe to be had it was that he didn't mingle when it mattered, facing jaded versions of his key rivals.

A year after Joe gave up his crown Showtime helped organise a tournament to produce a new ruler called Super Six World Boxing Classic. Just like its title it was long-winded and a little confusing but helped a drifting division get some traction. The cream rises to the top as they say, and the winner has proven himself to be much more than a solid champion.

"They think they're catching me at the right time. They think the layoff, the injury, I'm ripe for the picking, but they're going to have a rude awakening." [140]

Winning gold at the Olympics can be deceptive. Ever increasing its safety measures, the amateur game is very different to the professional ranks; whether you can take a good one on the chin or resist the seasoned bullies is anyone's guess while boxing three rounds and wearing head protection. Different to those who stumble at the first fence, Andre Ward looks capable of diffusing all kinds of trouble. "I was surprised Kessler didn't change up at all…" observed Andre after his breakthrough win, "…He kept doing the same thing over and over". Ward, a tactical ace, is anything but predictable. His boxing is more hurtful than flashy, and he's not the delicate type, happy to rough you up. In an age when referees can be a little fussy about heads coming together it's refreshing to see such a good inside fighter. Ward doesn't carry a dangerous punch, but judging by the results he doesn't need one.

With the initial favourite beaten, Germany's Arthur Abraham also looked dangerous but it was England's Carl Froch who reached the final, boxing Ward in Atlantic City. Two scorecards of 115-113 were obviously impressed with Carl's stubbornness because on a boxing front he was decidedly beaten. Fortunately the scoring was unanimous for Andre and in 2012 he did a number on Chad Dawson who was weakened by cutting weight. Underlining the overall rigours of boxing, it wasn't during a fight but training where Andre picked up a shoulder injury. A fight with Kelly Pavlik was scheduled for early 2013 but surgery intervened. And such is the sticky nature of negotiating that Ward wasn't back in action again until November. The man whose duty it was to flip the script, Puerto Rico's undefeated Edwin Rodriguez, was certainly not lacking spirit.

---

[140] www.mercurynews.com, 2013, Oct 15th

For twelve rounds he stood up to everything but was rendered harmless in the process. For Ward, a move up to a competitive light-heavyweight division might be the next step in a brilliant career.

Beaten but unscarred, Carl Froch soldiered on at the 168lbs weight class. Calzaghe was briefly targeted but he missed the boat there. Getting rid of Jermain Taylor in the dying seconds of their 2009 scrap is what bought Froch international respect. In 2010 he picked up his first loss to Mikkel Kessler, nothing career damming. Over in snowy Canada, Lucian Bute owned the IBF portion of the championship with nine defences to his name. Many remained suspicious of him and with good reason. When Lucian came to Froch's backyard in 2012 it was the first time he had left home since 2004. Less than five rounds were needed to demolish a reputation. There were some poor survival instincts on show but you couldn't fault Carl who walked through him. Saluting their three-time champion, Britain sensed they had a fighter to be proud of, and when Froch got his revenge over Kessler in 2013 he did so following swift tickets sales.

That fine line between enjoying your stardom and getting high on it was unclear before Carl's domestic showdown with George Groves. With not even twenty fights to his name Groves was the strict underdog, and in this age where undefeated records are babied it was difficult not to be cynical. Some expected a repeat of the Bute fight. The more measured majority predicted a competitive affair. Sure about winning, Carl was numb to the possibilities of reality.

"Normally it's very difficult getting back in the ring with someone who has beaten you but maybe Groves sees a big injustice and isn't thinking 'this man beat me'." [141]

---

[141] Boxing News, 2014, Feb 20th, p.4

Whatever nerves lay beneath the surface, Groves had them completely under control, approaching his task with a scowl. During one of their salty press-conferences he had promised to hit Froch with two right hands in the opener. As it was he outdid himself, dumping Carl hard. The consensus was similarly stunned, and from there Groves went on to control the fight, brilliantly so.

In a wild sixth round Groves' accuracy was matched only by Froch's ability to eat everything that came his way. The young gun was getting a little too involved, perhaps showing his inexperience. Both men were marked up and weary as they marched into the ninth. Froch was due his first bit of real success. A long right wobbled George as he fought his way into a clinch. Fighting back off the ropes wasn't recommended and Carl socked him with some good ones. Few would argue that Groves was fine, but then even fewer agreed with Howard Davis' decision to stop it. Apparently, incompetence was also at work on the judge's panel; two of them had split the first eight rounds.

Coming into boos and leaving to cheers, Groves' world class credentials are no longer a mystery. To the delight of everyone, Froch has agreed to a blockbuster of a rematch; a fact of which both men deserve credit...perhaps there's still hope for Floyd Mayweather and Manny Pacquiao. On the positive side, boxing is not as reliant on this super-fight as it once was. Discounting the heavyweight division, which has dragged its feet for over a decade, there are outstanding (non-American) talents grilling the opposition. Kazakhstan's Gennady Golovkin looks impervious at middleweight, super-bantamweight Guillermo Rigondeaux is a boxer of startling efficiency, and Russia's Sergey Kovalev might just bring the light-heavyweight division to its knees. Even in this more merciful climate, none of these guys have lost that spite which makes this, quite possibly, the toughest of all professions.

Things are looking rather different since James Figg entertained a bunch of unhygienic Cockneys. "How times have changed" many would say. On the contrary, what is noteworthy is the fact boxing continues to be defined by its chaotic simplicity. Hundreds of years all bound by a timeless ingredient. It's only natural that era's will forever be held dearly by their generation, but if we take a step back to admire the journey, you'll see that it's boxing itself which has earned our rose-tinted respect; dancing around threats of abolishment before slugging its way back into the public's heart. From gripping and bitter memories comes a reassuring thought. The greatest thing about boxing might not be the characters, fights or inspirational stories, but the promise that more are on the way.

FIGHT STORIES

INTRODUCTION

The following fifteen fight stories are a considered collection of some of boxing's most celebrated and infamous bouts under Queensberry rules. Various aspects and controversies are highlighted, but a basic structure is present in all, including the general feeling before, promotional hurdles, progress in training, atmosphere on the night and the aftermath. You will find many of the usual suspects: Jack Johnson vs. James J. Jeffries, Tony Zale vs. Rocky Graziano, Muhammad Ali vs. Joe Frazier, but a couple of screwballs have been thrown in; Alexis Arguello vs. Aaron Pryor was chosen over every 'Fabulous Four' fight and Masahiko 'Fighting' Harada vs. Eder Jofre comes as an advertisement for the little guys.

BOB FITZSIMMONS
VS.
JAMES J. CORBETT

March 13th, 1897
World Heavyweight Title
Carson City, Nevada

At 5:00am he begins to stir. Aroused by the filtering rays, a fine product of routine is summoned to strengthen body and mind. There is not a drop of liquor nearby. Solely for the purpose of alleviating the sniffles a few hot scotches have been necked. His preparatory hideaway has escaped everything but the rain and recent downpours have turned the sand from the nearby beach into a muddy slush. This is still good to run on; for upwards of ten to fifteen miles he will walk, jog and sprint in cunning intervals. A bicycle is at hand to complement the endurance-focused programme. In a newly constructed gymnasium there is "every modern appliance known";[142] rowing machines, punching bags, Indian clubs, lifting machines and skipping ropes. There is the general assistance of a training camp, providing in ways in which one cannot on their lonesome i.e. rubs-downs and a clockwork diet, but save for the bare necessities he is a wonderfully autonomous fighter. There will be no over-indulgences, no scrimping, and he does not need anyone to steer him away from either extreme. With the shoulders of a swimmer, each enwrapped in wiry fibre, Robert Fitzsimmons had no trouble causing bystanders to slow their walk and take note. From the neck up and waist down Bob was a contradiction, but that he could fight was only the first of several revelations.

"Boxing is one of the best exercises that a young man can take up. The art of self-defense, as it is called, brings into play so many qualities and helps to develop so many traits of character which figure in one's daily life that it furnishes quite a moral training in itself."[143] In an excerpt from Fitzsimmons' 1902 book, *Physical Culture and Self-Defense*, the fighter articulates the principles of boxing, not just for safety-sake but the greater good. The boxer was "fearless, mild-tempered, and lovable." That professorship one may acquire while punching for pay, the kind Daniel Mendoza had stressed was inherited by Fitzsimmons. Prejudice may have rejected the books conclusions, but for the liberal reader it aided in the understanding of a fighter, rightfully or wrongfully, who had fist-fighting down to a terrible science. If one was attacked on the street but possessed a basic mastery of boxing he may keep cool and send in a well-directed blow. "Ten to one Mr. Ruffian goes down"[144] if the victim follows instruction. A single punch was the chance to end a fight. Even when synchronized in the rhythm of battle, this truth echoed in his sub-conscious. It was an inelegant style with shuffling feet and staggered contributions, but he could turn a trivial mistake into defeat. The ability to punch hard with either hand was a prime feature of his, but while two-handed punchers typically have one hand a little stronger than the other, Fitzsimmons' power was expertly distributed. Be it a left under the ribs, or a right to the jaw, the effects were indiscriminatingly awful.

In a career which spanned three decades, Fitzsimmons was rarely more than 170lbs. The Cornishman's ideal weight resided somewhere between 155 and 167, making him a large middleweight at best, and as a middleweight he liquidized heavyweights. Physical measurements can only go so far in supplying a reason as to

[142] Brooklyn Daily Eagle, 1895, Jul 18th, p.5

[143] Physical Culture and Self-Defense, Robert Fitzsimmons, 1901, p.61

[144] Physical Culture and Self-Defense, Robert Fitzsimmons, 1901, p.64

why he was able to knock out opponents sometimes 100lbs heavier than himself. Since clobbering 'Nonpareil' Jack Dempsey for the middleweight title, Fitzsimmons had been hunting bigger game. Peter Maher was tough, powerful and respected. After twelve rounds with Bob he was bloody pulp. Lasting five rounds with the Fighting Blacksmith was too demanding a feat for virtually all of his competition. When Maher got a second chance he was knocked cold in ninety-five seconds. This performance led to a bout with Tom 'Sailor' Sharkey who was as sturdy as the iron columns which support a dock. Greater resistance only meant that instead of getting blasted he was repetitively floored. Fitzsimmons was wrongfully disqualified to safeguard some heavy betting, but everybody was aware of the heavyweight division's number one contender. Training for the championship got underway with that methodical thoroughness. Previously scheduled to fight at Dallas in 1895, the authorities voted against it. Fitzsimmons was now a distinguished veteran at thirty-three. Lightly reddened hair made a case of premature balding more blatant, but his camp assured the public that 'Ruby Robert' was in glistening form. He wasn't too fond of his opponent, and during an afternoon he bumped into him a mile from his camp.

A full set of dark hair covered the tip of his figure. Every strand was swished back with brylcreem, creating a bump which arrogantly soared above his forehead. Thick eyebrows drew your attention to a face unspoilt by alcohol or tobacco. A cigar would later become part of his foppish repertoire, but there was to be nothing of the sort while fighting. That searching gaze of his agitated Bob but he was pleasantly surprised to see James J. Corbett extend his arm. This show of respect didn't last long when Corbett slyly retracted his hand. Fitzsimmons picked up his frown and Corbett vowed to shake his hand *after* he had licked him. Mind games were a speciality of Corbett's and he had no problem getting Bob to threaten him.

It was by no accident that Corbett was involved with the theatre and his ability to bluff gave him an edge when the gloves were on. The seemingly opposing professions were smartly linked by Corbett, so well that he virtually lived a double life. John L. Sullivan had exploited another form of income by performing for Vaudeville, a theatrical setting where actors, sportsmen, comedians and dancers entertained the masses. Once the name Jim Corbett registered with the public he held exhibitions whenever and wherever possible. The handsome boxer smiled and played inside the ring. There was none of Fitzsimmons' austerity, but he adhered just as strongly to the rule book. Corbett's relationship to boxing was the same as that of Michelangelo's to marble. Everything was scrutinized. There was a faithful troupe of sparring partners while touring and trainer Jim Daly helped organize his daily choirs, but like Fitzsimmons he was an oracle on the science.

There were many parallels in Corbett's style with the British-mode of boxing. He was straight-up and tripled his left, but from there the old moves were varnished with daring intuition. He performed like a ballet dancer who had just been pushed into a ring, but it was crazy enough to work. And it was this elusive grace which drove the larger and much stronger Peter Jackson to exhaustion. Corbett wasn't in the best of shape either, but who would be after sixty-one rounds? The chief activity to sharpen his inspired movement was handball; a form of exercise he regarded as highly as Fitzsimmons did running. Years later fighters played handball to improve their footwork, coordination and reaction times. Not every gym has the space to play a game but since being introduced few training regimes (right up to today) have been without some sort of tennis or rubber ball. To improve his accuracy, Fitzsimmons belted a specialised punching bag; an oval, oversized speed ball which hung down to around head height. Corbett ripped into the heavy bag when it took his fancy, but for speed, concentration and to spark a competitive spirit, handball could not be beaten.

Try as they may to please everyone, no champion escapes the wild slander of the public, and with Corbett they called into question his bravery. Fighting as he did after the decapitating swings of Sullivan, many felt cheated. Young men who had witnessed Tom Sayers fight till the sorry end would have grown up to see prize-fighting disappear; and then for someone like Corbett to replace those iron-willed pawns was enough to sicken the diehards. Hard evidence would suggest otherwise on the subject of courage. To have outlasted Joe Choynski, held Jackson to a draw, and left his dressing room knowing that John L. Sullivan was moments away from trying to blast him were not the acts of a coward, quite the opposite. You could believe Corbett that he was not afraid of Bob, and in Carson City, Nevada, out on a racing track is where he was assigned to prove it.

Construction of the arena which would take up three hundred square feet of space began on February 17th, giving the carpenters exactly a month to have it completed. Designed to seat 17,000 people the big collection of timber was to be "temporary, as the race track people would not allow a permanent structure to be put up on the track."[145] Dan Stuart, a native of Texas, had failed to make the fight a reality two years ago. Though that venture was undone by external forces the lasting feeling was that "there had to be a place in the States where the two men could fight unmolested by politicians or preachers."[146] He gained as much support from various cities as he could and challenged Nevada's anti-fighting law. They would at least hear him out but his ace-in-the-hole was the fact their economy had taken a dive. More people meant more business. They were soon seeing things his way and Stuart forever changed the relationship between boxing and the public.

Reno, Carson City and Virginia City helped support the event, hollowing out barns, sheds and any place one may lodge for the many men (and women) who managed to catch a train. Seat prices ranged from $5 to $40 but on the day of the fight only 7,000 showed up, a good 10,000 short of capacity. A lack of middle class citizens created a big gulf between the ringside and cheap seats. It looked semi-successful, but in certain parts of New York and Chicago thousands of fans congregated for the big telegram. Their rustic training headquarters were separated by about fifteen miles with Corbett staying at a resort known as Shaw Springs, and Bob at the more ascetic Cooks Ranch.

---

[145] Baltimore American, 1897, Feb 16th, p.3

[146] Dan Stuart's Fistic Carnival by Leo N. Miletich, 1994, p.193

Corbett's last fight was an inconclusive four rounder with Tom Sharkey. The fight before that he beat Charlie Mitchell in what was thought to be a fix. The last time he had been in a credible fight was against Sullivan in 1892. The younger champion was possibly on the slide but nobody co-signed with that theory after watching him go about his training camp. A young Jim Jeffries was instructed to go at him full pelt which Corbett responded to masterfully. There was lots of handball of course, once going sixteen rounds against four different opponents with no rest. For two days Corbett's wife joined his manly entourage, slowing things down a little. The champion would not have allowed such a thing if it was at all surmised to burden his progress, and he enjoyed the calculated downtime. The only moment when it was thought Jim showed any effects of his rigorous timetable was during a rubdown when fussy reporters perceived his face as gaunt.

Bob took to the road daily before a growing audience. Following the trail was Yarrum, an amber-eyed Great Dane. His four-legged companion made sure no stranger got too close to their pad. One of Fitzsimmons' knuckles was still sore from the beating Sharkey's head had given his hands, though it was a minor concern. A good deal of wrestling was completed to disturb Corbett in the clinches. Up to ten rounds on the bag intervened between the challengers' less artistic but promising sparring sessions. Snow storms threatened those delicate sinuses, but as training eased off Fitzsimmons was beaming with health. Bob was sure that if he managed to get just one good shot on his opponent that it would be the "end of the gentleman who has no manners and only pretensions."[147]

On the penultimate day the only part of Corbett's body which got exercise was his ears as his men needlessly assured him of victory, distracting him from the morning print. Fitzsimmons ran a single mile up to the local penitentiary before coming back to enjoy his lazy day. They certainly weren't lacking in confidence over at Cooks Ranch either but none were too happy about referee George Siler who had made it crystal that he was going to be firm with a breakaway rule in the clinches; a tactic which better suited Corbett. They were to receive two pairs of gloves each, just over five ounces in weight and made "of the finest velvet tanned dog skin, and stuffed with selected curled hairs."[148]

March 17th, 'St. Patrick's Day'. On the day of the fight both boxers were up at 7:00am. Rose Fitzsimmons whipped up a breakfast which made sure her husband wasn't going to be hungry for a while; half a chicken, two slices of toast, one cup of coffee and a bowl of stewed fruit. When asked how Corbett felt he replied, "Fine as silk." Fans had to be quick out of bed to catch breakfast. The overcrowded hotels could not cater for everyone, and with the fight set for 11:00am it would likely be their only meal of the day. The schedule slipped when Corbett's carriage arrived a bit later at 10:00am. With the two mile journey to the arena almost up word spread that Corbett had entered and random cheers multiplied for a warm reception. One more rub down and the calm champion threw on his chequered fighting robe.

---

[147] Brooklyn Daily Eagle, 1897, Mar 17th, p.2

[148] The Morning Herald, 1897, Feb 27th, p.8

Kissing his wife goodbye, Fitzsimmons began the three mile trip to the scene. There was less of a commotion when he was identified, Bob was the least popular to match his underdog status. Most of the Cornishman's support came from the local mining fraternity. Not until noon did the 167lbs challenger enter the ring. Somewhere between 170 and 180 had been hinted as a possibility, but with Corbett at 184lbs there was a seventeen pound difference. A few strides from the ring stood a specially made enclosure for the kinetoscope. The clear weather provided ideal conditions for the strange filming device of which Stuart was to recover every penny it generated when later shown in novel 'peep-hole' cinema. Corbett inspected the device from inside the ropes, visibly excited. Much of the twelve-sided arena was disappointingly empty though Stuart had come too far to express regret, cheerfully declaring "it is the best we can do." Siler reiterated the way in which he was going to handle the fight. All that was left was for the bell to be dinged.

The first act of Corbett was to try and shake hands, but Bob's manager Martin Julian cried "No, no!" remembering the childish quarrel outside of his camp. Rose had gone one better than arriving at the fight and positioned herself behind her husband's corner. The champion was wearing his revealing trunks, cut halfway up the buttocks to not restrict any possible manoeuvre his gifted legs might attempt. Each held their hands low to feint and ward off body punches. To stop head shots they raised their forearms in the prize-fighter style, or pulled back their heads to watch them brush past their nose. Lots of nervous gesturing featured in the opener.

The form of Corbett was something to admire, a charming oddity. Fitzsimmons' boxing brain was just as efficient but he was definitely last on point of grace; a functionless trait though appreciated. A jab threatened to touch Fitzsimmons as Corbett observed his reactions. Fitzsimmons replied by making some rather wild swings before pulling back. Neither wanted to lead. Through the second and third, Corbett improved his scared boxing to a lively spar. A jab and hook to the body caused Fitzsimmons to think more so than react. He had confidently asserted that five rounds would be enough to grab victory but trying to jaw Corbett was a sight more difficult than catching Sharkey.

The aggressive challenger was unabashed with his haymakers which Corbett either blocked or smoothly skipped away from, widening their arc. Shots to the body proved a safer bet. After three rounds the champion was marginally the better of a tame, though intriguing bout. John L. Sullivan watched on from ringside, reporting for tomorrow's headlines. Save for the clinching and misses he believed it to be "one of the prettiest fights I ever saw for two big men, but no harm has befallen either man yet."[149] Fitzsimmons broke out with a smile at the start of the fourth having blocked a couple of punches. No advantage was taken. When an opening was created the chance was lost through hesitancy. Bob's two-handed rushes took a back seat to a counter-punching style that lacked timing. A quick hook, a favoured punch for Corbett, stung Fitz for the first time and right body punch left his fair skin with a little sunburn.

---

[149] Chicago Tribune, 1897, Mar 17th, p.4

None of these punches were deadly. It was a push to call them solid. Sullivan, a former knockout king, was wholly unimpressed with Corbett's punching ability, but in the fifth the ambitious middleweight received a split lip. Moments later it could be seen that blood was coming from his right ear; a result of the coarse gloves overshooting their mark. The first signs of distress came from the Cornishman as Corbett attempted to reverse his vision of an early victory. Though the half-inch wound on Fitzsimmons' lip produced lots of the red stuff it may as well have not been there the way he sat on his stool, still and content. After his homerun contest with Choynski, Bob had developed a reputation for his recuperative powers and he came out for the sixth swinging freely.

Corbett's right was a superior blow and scalded its opponent's head. The knock-kneed legs of Bob (stilts as Sullivan called them) were firmly underneath him, but he grimaced and Corbett was again the attacker. A smart clinch interrupted the effort, but Corbett wrestled out of it. Decent right hands creased Fitzsimmons' neck and a clever uppercut kept his head in a bad position. Another right hit home causing a fall which he tried to prevent. The Corbett bet looked pretty good with Bob on one knee. Some of the fans showed their depreciation for Jim standing so close to his downed rival. Boxing was thirty years away from instating the neutral corner rule but Siler enforced some kind of fair play and instructed him to back up. Sixty seconds were left on the clock and Bob survived every one of them. Corbett could not finish his man. Rose was a worried lady on the walk back to the corner. Her husband looked particularly pleased.

Following this crescendo was a repeat of the bout's tentative beginnings. With Corbett tiring and Fitzsimmons adjusting they revived their awkward, unproductive waltz, like a chess match in which moves are made but mean nothing. Sullivan aired his disdain, claiming to have "never seen so much clinching" though the momentum had definitely shifted. Corbett expertly demonstrated how to make one miss, if little else. It could also have been termed artful running. Fitzsimmons continued hunting.

A handful of even, uneventful rounds merged together to reach the eleventh. The first good collection of punches from the challenger connected with a snap. Ramrod jabs and a stylishly tripled hook could be measured by Corbett's tense expression. The twelfth continued with the incoming threat. In retaliation Corbett flung out a right uppercut; a punch so far off target it must have made the perfectionist inside cringe. The champion looked awfully tired. Re-watching the old footage, their low hands make them appear leaden with fatigue. They were there for a reason, as you may remember. Rose had been bellowing at her husband to "hit him in the ribs!" which was poison with those gloves. Instead the former blacksmith mimed an anvil to Corbett's head, cracking him with a left. A few reports declared to have seen a tooth eject from Jim's gaping mouth, and Sullivan strengthened the story; "I saw his mouth twitch or chew around after receiving that blow." Totally robbed of optimism, Corbett walked towards Fitzsimmons for the fourteenth. It had gone longer than nearly everyone thought, but it didn't look like going much further. Bob was childlike giddy to see Corbett's jab troubled by the wind resistance. The challenger was numb to the blood dripping down from his mouth and he shoved Corbett out of the clinches to muster a finishing blow.

'The Shift' was the base of the 'Solar-Plexus Punch'. In a move far too innovative for the tired champion to spot, Fitzsimmons stepped forth with his right leg, briefly turning southpaw. With his left now his strong hand he threw in a short hook just below the sternum with the kind of force which made those gloves obsolete. Corbett's body was repulsed on impact. Fitzsimmons watched him tentatively with his arms down, like a doctor performing an on-the-spot diagnosis. Corbett held his glove around the area of pain, helping the far-seated drunks with the plot. He was in a position fit to rise but stayed on his hands and knees for ten, crawling in agony.

Rose peered over the top rope to meet Bob's crimson lips with her own. Sullivan didn't agree with this growing idea of women in the crowd, but he had to admit how essential a factor she had been in keeping her man focused. The ring became a scene of confusion as it filled up with unwanted people while cries of 'foul!', jokingly or seriously intended, were thrown in there. Corbett had previously said that he would do his talking "after the fight" and he didn't break his promise. "You've got to fight me again!" yelled Gentleman Jim. The new champion extended his arm, no funny business, but the defeated boxer refused and threatened to lamp him if they ever met again on the street. Fitzsimmons was deadly serious when he replied that if he should ever try such a thing, he would kill him.

In thirty minutes Stuart's odd arena was empty and ready for demolition. What he had set out to do, he had achieved. The moderate success and ethical backlash may as well have been part of the plan; the determined Texan proved to himself that if you persue something enough you can make it happen. Better still he became the leading light for future promoters.

Corbett underestimated the potential of his sparring partner. Everybody did. If he gains some speed the big lug might be useful was the general opinion. In two years Fitzsimmons was defending his championship against the twenty-four-year-old contender. The weight difference was severe this time at 39lbs. Sure, Fitzsimmons had levelled men close to 300lbs, but Jeffries could take a punch better than Sharkey. He moved with speed, precision and knocked Bob out in the eleventh round. A year later the protégé defended against the maestro where he failed to tame him. Two years on there was a rematch, and while Corbett had aged Jeffries had developed some science to go with his raw talent. Corbett hadn't a prayer. Fitzsimmons failed in a rematch as well, but three months after Corbett had fought his last fight his forty-year-old conqueror was doing what came miraculously natural, outpointing twenty-six-year old George Gardiner for the light-heavyweight title. "Realizing he must foster his strength, there was not a moment when he was not careful."[150] At the final bell it was the record books that were left gasping for air. Boxing's first triple champion had also become its oldest.

[150] The Baltimore Sun, 1903, Nov 26th, p.1

JACK JOHNSON
VS.
JAMES J. JEFFRIES

July 10th, 1910
World Heavyweight Title
Reno, Nevada

The strain was felt the moment training began. His joints creaked, limbering up was stressful. With all the huffing n' puffing it was difficult to catch him sigh, but this wasn't fun, the opposite of life at Burbank ranch. Initially purchased in 1904 it was to prove a lucrative sanctuary; the perfect epilogue to a life in the ring. There were no niggling health problems, everyone within telegram distance respected the owner, and when the Californian sun rose it lit up 200 acres of land. Never was retirement so promising. Well removed from any kind of bustle, the calming sound bites of nature made work that bit more therapeutic. Tommy Ryan was envious. The big man needed to block it all out; reminiscing was only going to make this harder.

James J. Jeffries, one time boilermaker, was called upon to make his triumphant return to the ring. The 'great white hope' was not a fad but a plan, and it was time for serious action. Things had gotten desperate as of late with the last four opponents having left the ring empty handed, often humiliated. Jim Crow America was confident of victory on this occasion. Money was dismissed as bait.

Standing in the way of justice was Jack Johnson, the sly Negro whose strength and smarts had melted away all that dared. From the gold-capped grinning to relations with white women to carrying the opponent, Johnson riled most Americans to the bone. For Jeffries, this comeback grew off the racial bigotry of which Johnson suffered daily. On the day before the fight Jeffries would recite that he was going through with this for "that portion of the white race which has been looking to me to defend its athletic supremacy."[151] And this agenda was not just to do with how skin tone denoted social rank, but how your ethnic background determined your intelligence down to your moral decency. Scoring one-up over the Negroes in famed professions was key in supporting the theory of ethical superiority. And Johnson, well, he was White America's worst nightmare.

Jeffries did not appear to carry any racial motives; long time black contender Bob Armstrong commonly played a part in his training, but it was in respecting the white lineage that he appeased the prejudice masses. Jeffries' fists were to confirm their beliefs. The beliefs concerning Johnson were almost always to do with his speculated lack of heart; the detractors were still looking to sniff him out as it were. Former victim Tommy Burns and veteran James J. Corbett vehemently claimed Johnson to have a yellow streak; that he was fearful of a real challenge and would cave in at the first sign of trouble. "Every Negro, when the test comes, is apt to fall a victim to that form of nerve-storm which is called panic" wrote an imaginative fellow. Ironically this was Burns' view before he defended his title against Johnson in 1908 when he was punished in degrading fashion. However, this was old news. The real champion was back to prevail. The importance of being right on the 4th July, 1910 was vital.

Through adopting a "systematic course of training" Jeffries thought himself able to boil off the weight he had gained and come back to mirror his unbreakable best. Scaling in at almost 300lbs, Jeffries began thc oncrous task of getting back into the same condition that saw him conquer every man he had fought. Yet it had been nearly five years since Jeffries had his last bout, his face cracked a little and the thinning of

[151] Los Angeles Times, 1910, Jul 4th, p.1

hair took away from that champion image which everyone still applied. Rehabilitation was going to be slow and painful.

Preparation was not taken with a pinch of salt; no in fact Jeff was already in some kind of shape early in 1909. Shortly after Johnson had whipped Stanley Ketchel in October, Jeffries proclaimed that, "I am in better physical condition than at any time since my retirement from the ring."[152] Not even Jeffries' manager Sam Berger had known of his secret training. Shortly after the title changed hands, Jeffries put his hefty body through its paces. He got back to weigh in the 220lbs range thanks to a thorough regime of ten miles roadwork every day followed by the gymnasium. Burning off the blubber proved straightforward, but the long exile had made the art of boxing foreign to him. For nearly four years he was reluctant to even apply the gloves. It's second nature for many boxers to retain their work ethic once retired. In Jim's case he was completely out of touch with that which he was once an authority.

Later on in the year, old rival and friend James J. Corbett offered his services to assist in the re-making of a monster. At forty-four Corbett had gone away to get into fine working order so that he would not be a hindrance as they turned up the heat during training. He emphasized hard sparring and fast paced activities that would get Jeffries back on his toes, like handball. Many more would join team Jeffries including former opponent Joe Choynski, middleweight Billy Papke, and Farmer Burns who was there for the wrestling sessions. Yet even before the real labour commenced the physical presentation of Jeffries stood out. Those huge shoulders, tree-trunk legs and armoured mid-section had re-emerged to the permanent fixation of the press. Some pugs looked sturdy with their sunken eyes and heavy brows, but Jeffries had this posture about him that dissected the very meaning of tough. In a nutshell, the silhouette of Jeffries was not unlike that of a brick wall. The terming a "physical marvel" continually married any column that spoke of him. Nevertheless, the problems were on the inside. Looks were not going to win the day.

Training, as expected, was a shock. He requested that his headquarters have the roof removed; all his activities were to be close to the outdoors where he was at ease. Fishing trips helped break things up, and he would go great distances through the wilderness for trout. Fishing gave Jeffries reason to get up as early as 3:00am on occasion and the mountainous jaunts provided great exercise as a nosey reporter attested. Every one of Jeffries' movements was studied. Sparring sessions were sometimes accompanied by numbers in the thousands as Corbett, Choynski and Berger alternated rounds against the steadily improving student. Diehard Jeffries' supporters would often wait hours under the blaze of the sun only to catch a glimpse of their hero making a trip to the local river. Encouragement was certainly not missing, but Jeffries' mood could waver. Was he really in as good shape as everyone insisted?

There are periods which can unsettle a fighter in between the rigours of training that must have held Jeffries at times. Any newspaper that he picked up would tell him that no man could stand up to his full power when unleashed. Jeffries was no fool. The pressure was punishing in itself. He would later speak again to the *New*

[152] New York Times, 1909, Oct 23rd, p.12

York Times without the hyperbole two days before the fight, "I don't think the betting odds should favour me. Even money is nearer right." He continued, "How do people know that I can come back successfully after being out of the ring so long?" These episodes would then swing back into streaks of confidence. After one good day of sparring Jeffries declared optimistically that "I am going to be faster in this fight than in any other I have had in the ring." Corbett had been focusing on trying the right uppercut, Johnson's best blow, to which Jeffries was reportedly catching every time. The consensus was that if Jeffries was anywhere near the shape he used to be in then the Negro didn't stand a chance.

Over at Chicago, Johnson completed the initial stages of his training. The April weather could be a little nippy and so the long trip to San Francisco was a welcome one. At Seals Rock House (a coastal site), the champion began a schedule which would chisel his 226lbs figure into a svelte 208lbs. As was the trend, Johnson and his retinue took to the road fully dressed. Running in your trousers and hat got the sweat pouring. Back at his spacious headquarters there was plenty of work to be done. A reluctant sparring team had to rev each other up, especially during the hotter days, as Johnson would always leap into the ring full of energy. For publicity he would partake in racial bloopers like melon devouring and chicken chasing, but you would be wrong in thinking this black was on a white leash. One muggy afternoon, during a slow day, Johnson decided to launch a medicine ball at ringsiders. Getting them to flinch before throwing it in another direction, there was no question as to who was in charge. Famed cartoonist Rube Goldberg had trouble getting out of the way.

The fight was planned to take place in San Francisco but government disagreements left the event to inhabit the unwholesome town of Reno, Nevada. The great stadium had little time to be reconstructed in its new location and the result was a loss of 10,000 places. Soon-to-be-great promoter, Tex Rickard had been so stressed by the organization that he let out a noteworthy statement that he was getting out of the fight game, "From now on I am a miner after this fight comes off on the fourth of July. I will never mix into the pugilistic game again."[153]

Time determined the strength of the human magnet as each passing week brought forth larger human freight. The dingy little town of Reno was gradually becoming the nation's hotspot as its specially designated train stations packed in men of every profession and creed to be a part of 'The Fight of The Century'. One writer described it as having a carnival atmosphere, day and night, and that it was "one of the strangest assemblages imaginable." Police saw this as an opportunity to do some fishing of their own as inspectors were sent in and arrested twenty men who had committed crimes in different parts of the city. Despite the huge clash of people the police did a great job instilling order. Disturbances and quarrels were virtually non-existent.

Reno's base population of around 5,000 had been forced to contend with over 20,000 visitors. General houses were converted into temporary hotels, cots were shoved into the aisles and tents were set up outside for the great excess. The vast majority of the visitors were excursionists who had been driving all night to make the

[153] New York Times, 1910, Jun 23rd, p.9

final cut. Some vehicles bore the sign 'RENO OR BUST'. When the fight was within 48 hours the tension appeared to be niggling Jeffries who sought some last minute advice from featherweight champion Abe Attell.

Attell had been in the corner of Philadelphia Jack O' Brien during his crack at Johnson. For a moment the tank-built man was anxious as he listened with muted interest on how he should tackle the champion. Training came to a halt for the two men so they were to relax before the big day. In Jeffries' camp he was approached by Stanley Ketchel who smiled over him as he spoke to friends. Ketchel had been playing cards with Johnson the night before and Jeffries got up to tell him, "I don't want you here. You have been fooling about with that Negro, and I don't think you belong here at all."[154] Farmer Burns quietly escorted Ketchel to the gate by the shoulder and gave him a light push. Ketchel left in his motor. John L. Sullivan had been doing special reports for the *New York Times* and explained that he didn't know of any other fighter who had gone through the "strenuous grind" that Jeff had just done. He was particularly impressed with Jeffries' capacity to tolerate that amount of training. Some had clocked that the total time of preparation was as high as sixteen months. Over a year later and 80lbs down, Jeffries had to be ready.

On the day of the fight the big man awoke to some fruit, tea and toast. Not to be outdone Johnson got up and demanded a double helping of lamb cutlets, three scrambled eggs, several slices of rare steak and potatoes. Jeffries issued a firm message, "I think I will surely beat Johnson. I would not have signed to fight at all unless I was reasonably certain of victory." Johnson was as cocksure as ever, "When I go into the ring on the fourth of July to fight Mr Jeffries, I will do so with full confidence that I am able to defeat him at the game of give and take." Most tellingly in the statements was the difference regarding a fight plan. Jeffries said that, "It is impossible for me to say just how I will fight this coloured man. My method of fighting will develop as the actual scraping is on." Johnson was far more convinced, "I honestly believe that in pugilism I am Jeffries master, and it is my purpose to demonstrate this in the most decisive way possible. I think I know thoroughly Jeffries as a fighter and with this knowledge reassuring me, I am more than willing to defend the title of champion against him." All kinds of rumours had been circulated about Jeffries by over-excited fans; he had broken his left arm, ruptured a blood vessel in his elbow and even undergone surgery for appendicitis.

The great stadium at Reno waited for the onslaught of humanity that was foaming from town. For the past two days the wood had been hosed down for fear of it catching fire through the sun's rays. In town there had been food shortages, house shortages and most were short on change. Many had not eaten nor slept over the last day and a good bunch were nursing hangovers as everyone squashed their way down the one and a half mile road to the arena. Japanese, Chinese, Germans, miners, men of sport, men of construction, manufacturers, millionaires and criminals all rubbing shoulders in unison, getting nearer to having the great question answered, 'WHITE OR BLACK? Who will win the great fight today?' On the road there were button designs to buy;

[154] New York Times, 1910, Jul 4th, p.14

the most common had the inscription, "*Oh, you Jeff!*" At the entrance were designated policemen. If they found anyone suspicious one would grab their legs, the other would grab their arms and the third would search them for guns, knives or clubs. The culprits were then sternly pushed back into the crowd and told to "keep quiet". It worked rather well. There had been threats of shooting Johnson so all guns, which could be purchased for as cheap as $1.50 before WWI, were safely removed.

On top of the mass of wood were two individuals who would act out the fight to the thousands who could not get in. Tickets were from $50 and down. Nobody under ten years of age was to be allowed in unless accompanied by an adult. When ready the crowd poured in through the six entrances and quickly filled up to the 16,000 capacity. The curiously dressed foreigners were jeered by natives every time a new group came in. Anticipation levels had everyone, once fatigued, absolutely wired for the combatants to appear.

Not so far away, Johnson had made a quick trip to a casino where he put a little on black on the roulette table. As it landed on black Johnson, in full character bellowed, "Gentlemen, there's another black a-goin to win this afternoon." Meanwhile Jeffries had found a small dog and chose the lucky stranger to be his mascot for the day. The champion arrived an hour later than the set time and Jeffries made his appearance within the next ten minutes. The crowd had been kept entertained by a band and after they finished up a slew of former greats took to the elevated ring to receive their praise. Battling Nelson, Tommy Burns, Abe Attell, Tom Sharkey, Jake Kilrain and Bob Fitzsimmons were cheered but the biggest was reserved for the old American hero, John L. Sullivan who revelled in his momentary spotlight. After the band had made their exit the motion-picture devices were put into place, a sure sign that the big moment was just minutes away. And without further ado, with the clock at 2:25pm, Jack Johnson made his merry way to centre stage.

An accommodating ovation greeted Johnson, but scattered insults were clearly audible. "Cold feet Johnson!", "Now you will get it you black coward!" were a couple of the reported digs from the hundreds of journalists who mashed their typewriters at ringside. The presumed calculating nature of Johnson was as natural as can be. The wide grin on his face reflected his morning thoughts on feeling "like a two year old at Christmas". Nothing had bothered the dusky giant, not in training, and not now. Four minutes later and Jeffries made his entrance to a booming reception. The herculean man was all smiles and kept it on as he stepped inside the ropes. The removing of the robes revealed that Johnson was in impeccable shape but when Jeffries saw it to exhibit a year's graft there was a moment of quiet admiration. His muscles were as broad as they were thick, and his chest was matted with the animalistic hair that offered writers that indulgent chance to romanticize the strict difference between the average man and a beast like this.

A coin toss was to decide which corner the men would occupy. Johnson was not fussed and gave Jeffries the southwest corner, which was slightly better guarded from the sun. Jeffries had said before that, "I want those to know who fancy my chances this much: If I had so much as a slight pain, a sore finger, or the most trivial thing imaginable that might annoy me, I would immediately insist on a postponement." He also refused to shake hands.

Everything was in place, and as the thirty-five foot high mass of wood quivered, the opening bell clanged. They left their corners slowly to assume their fighting postures; Jeffries with a partial crouch and an extended left, Johnson leaning on his right rear foot, circling his arms, ready to defend the want for an early victory. Jeffries feinted the delivery of many punches as Johnson felt his way around the ring. There was an initial air of respect which is to be expected when so much is at stake. Johnson was the first to land a light left on Jeffries' face. Falling into a clinch they both laughed; an old school trait as if to appease the crowd. There was much missing and blocking in a nervous opener.

Johnson's mouth was bleeding in the second; an old wound from sparring had re-opened. The blood came out quickly and spurred Jeffries on to continue with his steady pounces. Johnson never seemed troubled and jokingly patted Jeffries on the back at the end of the third. The fourth round was with Jeffries as he breached Johnson's famed defence, bringing more blood from his mouth, but Johnson remained still. His face was glum in deep thought, his boxing brain ticked along with the noisy typewriters. Every move was economical, safe, and as soon as his nimble body ensured Jeffries missed again he would erupt into this heartfelt laughter. Whatever Jeffries was trying for, it was not working.

The chance for a knockout would surely reside in the early rounds. Jeffries own words of being able to see a full forty-five round fight now looked to be crucial as the science of this Negro was getting the better of him. Johnson who had characteristically opted to sit back appeared to feed off Jeffries' failed efforts. At the end of round six, Jeffries' right eye had begun to close due to Johnson's accurate jolts. The great strength of boxing's saviour was apparently wilting as Johnson pushed him about in the clinches, keeping him off balance and then ripping in his right uppercut. As the bell clanged to end round seven Johnson may have spoken on behalf of the quieting crowd when he uttered, "Jeffries has come back in to the game too late." Those originally crude advances were getting cruder and easier to spot. Jeffries' huge mass now looked like a burden to his creaking joints. The heavyweight champion was landing with more regularity. Short left hooks with right uppercuts were there for the thirty-five-year-old on the inside as he became a prisoner of Johnson's trickery. In what must have been one of Corbett's fears before the bout started the younger, fresher fighter looked in total command. Acting as a desperate aid to Jeffries, Corbett began to goad Johnson and get him to fight to which Johnson irritatingly replied, "I'm just fighting the way you did, Jim!"

The undefeated iron man of the ring suddenly did not look fit to box as blood from his broken nose coursed down and splattered his body. He was breathing heavily and rubbed his injured right eye; there was a hint of self-pity. Try as he might, the further the fight went, the more it took out of him. The many faithful who thought it imminent that Jeffries fabled strength would have the last say grew sick of the reality, the collective feeling of hopelessness, because hopeless is what it was. "Don't drip your blood all over me" Jeff was told during a painful fourteenth round. Thirty one were remaining, but the fifteenth round brought forth the merciful end. Johnson followed up a right uppercut with a few hooks that put Jeffries down. For a moment he glanced at referee Tex Rickard as if he would offer some miracle advice. With no neutral corner rule, Johnson hovered over Jeffries. Tex attempted to give the former champion some space by halting Johnson before he was sent out on the apron, legs straddling the bottom rope. Helped back in, Jeffries' seconds were climbing in to stop the fight when he was chased around the ring and dropped one last time. Johnson signalled to hit him again as he ruffled about for a moment.

The champion was, one might say, generously congratulated as the largely white crowd began to leave as quickly as they had entered the arena. Jeffries, obviously upset to have let his men down, solemnly retired to the quiet of his changing room. Of a $101,000 purse Johnson, as winner, received 75%. The remaining 25% was left for Jeffries, although Jeff was entitled to two thirds of the motion pictures' revenue. The biggest pugilistic spectacle ever known had turned into a sad exhibition. "I never knew any fighter to leave the game and then come back again and regain his old laurels," said an insightful John L. Sullivan beforehand, and he never would. Not until fifty years later would a man who had previously held the heavyweight championship of the world reclaim it. Jeffries let out a statement that was as big as his heart, that Johnson was better than he ever was and that he "could never have beaten him." Johnson's chief-second, William Delaney had insisted that Jeffries "is not a fighter who loves the game." It's hard to dispute the last point. Even in Jeffries' prime he disliked training which gives you an idea of what he went through, mentally as well as physically. The man who knew nothing of defeat had been selfishly conscripted back into the ring, aimed to restore some kind of natural order. Instead all that prejudice, concentrated through the press, lit the fuse for race riots and many deaths across America. The repercussions for the black boxer were awful, but if Jack Johnson really was a bad egg he didn't let it spoil his fun. Leaving Reno with over $65,000 in his pocket, the champagne began to flow.

JESS WILLARD
VS.
JACK DEMPSEY

July 4th, 1919
World Heavyweight Title
Toledo, Ohio

It only makes sense that the man who enjoys his job should get the promotion. Jess Willard had never cared for his. To him, boxing was an unnecessarily brutal and callous business. During a bout he had no desire to hunt his opponent, no killer instinct. So long as he won then he had once again successfully "cashed in on his size", therein explaining why he entered an otherwise loathed profession. "I like to fight; it seems to be inborn" were the words of Jack Dempsey, Willard's next challenger to his heavyweight title. And that was the beginning of the differences between these two men. Every little bit of the twenty-four-year-old Dempsey was dissimilar to his mature rival. It's the old cliché, but you'd be hard pressed to find two so opposing fighters.

For starters, Dempsey was active having tallied twenty-one contests in 1918 alone. Willard had gladly defended his title just once within the last four years. Inside the ring, Dempsey was a speedy, marauding type of a fighter, hunched over and trigger-happy. Willard was stiff and upright with a basic style of steadily thumping the target. Outside the ring, Dempsey was a restless prankster, always cracking smiles, looking for new things to get involved in, gelling with the public. Willard was a shy, awkward man, not particularly cheerful and content with secluding himself back to Kansas.

'The Pottawatomie Giant' as Willard was known could not have been blamed for wanting to hang up the gloves either. Having taken care of Jack Johnson he was to be made a figure of ridicule, hounded by most writers. An "accidental champion" Willard was labelled. Starting his professional career late at twenty-nine, he was just another 'white hope'. It's doubtful that big Jess ever thought he was going to climb as high as he did, but when Jack Johnson fell before his right he obtained the unforgiving role of heavyweight champion of the world. The man who openly claimed to hate violence now occupied the position of the most revered man this side of male testosterone. It didn't add up. Being the one who had removed Jack Johnson gave Willard a privileged lifestyle of which he was to take full advantage. After a single title defence over Frank Moran, Jess went into hibernation, but it did not take long before fighters started knocking on his door. The most worthy challenger to Willard's title was Minnesotan plasterer, Fred Fulton. Now when Willard said that he fought so he could cash in on his size he did not explain the policies behind it. If you were around the same size as him there might be a problem. Scraping 6'6" this giant was not just big though, he was good. Tall and rangy, Fulton could box and punch a ton. The advantages that Willard held over all of his opponents were practically levelled against Fred.

Willard had a way of cuffing and smothering the smaller opponents; a kind of safety measure after his defences had been breached. This gave him an opportunity to wreak havoc with his rabbit punch and generally wear the opponent out as they got trapped in his hulk. But there may have been more to it than a fear of physical equality. Mike Collins, Fulton's manager, claimed the pair had fought an exhibition bout in 1915 in which Willard was manhandled. Regardless of the validity of this event, Willard *did* display an apprehensive attitude towards Fulton; one report had big Jess warily avoiding eye contact with Fred at a meeting. On numerous occasions they were scheduled to collide only for Willard to persistently find the arrangements to be unsatisfactory. Collins had been pulling his hair out trying to lure Willard into the ring; purses of $30,000, $45,000 and $50,000 were put up only for the champion to keep flaking. It got to the point Collins felt he had no other choice but forfeit Willard's title and proclaim Fulton to be the new champion. It was a sad state of affairs, but boxing was not to suffer too much longer. Fireworks were going off in other parts of the country.

Dempsey, the much slighter man had been knocking fighters cold, out of the ring and even broke an ankle along the way. If three minutes had passed you were likely meat, and if not then plenty of lumps were on the menu. Ranked fighters were succumbing at such a rate that it was soon determined that Dempsey should meet Fulton to see who ultimately deserved the title shot more. Fulton's big chance was then cruelly disintegrated in twenty-three seconds when Dempsey swatted his weak jaw. It proved an easy $9,000. With Willard's boogieman out of the way this Dempsey fellow made for a much more attractive proposition. He was smaller, lighter and surely vulnerable to his considerable advantages. The challenger had slipped into the fast lane, but being a top fighter required having a top manager, a fierce character to pull strings, make deals and never take no for an answer. Jack 'Doc' Kearns was probably overqualified for the position. He'd been selling stories to reporters, making important contacts and filtering all publicity towards Dempsey in typical whirlwind fashion. "Just look at that scowl" roared Kearns. This was ballyhoo at its best.

Kearns' nous for networking had amassed an army of Dempsey supporters as quickly as his fighter had burst on to the scene. It really was quite something because, not too long ago, Dempsey had been fighting purely out of necessity. He later recalled after the Fulton fight, "I was mobbed by enthusiastic fans - for the first time in my life. They tore at everything, just wanting to take a little piece of me home. They even trailed me to the Treat Hotel where I was staying. Fans. Up to now I never thought myself as having any fans."[155] By May next year these fans were to saturate the roads that Dempsey ran down for his Toledo training. The atmosphere from the offset was one of tense excitement. Debate on who was going to win played like a stuck record. Training headquarters resided at The Overland Club on the shore of Maumee Bay. The weather was hot and getting hotter still. A slight breeze off the coast helped to reduce the humidity which tried tempers daily. A minimum of six weeks' training was compulsory and part of Dempsey's schedule was to alternate every week between training and resting. This seemed unnecessary to him but both Kearns and trainer Jimmy DeForrest were aware of the potential to over train and 'go stale'.

"Day after day I trained, up at six, then seven to ten miles of jogging followed by a hot and cold shower and a rubdown until breakfast, which consisted of meat and vegetables. After breakfast, a quick nap and then off again sprinting a few miles."[156] Standard exercises and sparring accompanied the afternoon then another dose of sprinting for the evening. As a youth Dempsey ran alongside horses to improve his wind. Speed had always been one of his best assets so sprinting figured to enhance that explosive style. Following an afternoon spar one of the reporters wrote that, "It is

---

[155] Dempsey, Jack Dempsey, 1977, p.85

[156] Dempsey, Jack Dempsey, 1977, p.105

doubtful if there has ever been a heavyweight boxer who could move around as quickly as the challenger."[157]

DeForrest, cigar chompin' as ever, watched Dempsey like a cat at all stages of the day. "An incredible dynamo" is how his pupil later described him. The Jamaica kid and 'Big' Bill Tate were Dempsey's appointed sparring partners; the first to work on speed, and the second to get Dempsey weaving under the bigger man's reach. When it was time to relax, Dempsey would mingle with the press, tell kids old tales as they sat around him and play baseball on the beach. When reporters left to recharge their interrogation batteries Max Kaplan appointed himself camp comedian; songs were sung, the kazoo was played and Kearns and Tex Rickard were uncharacteristically at peace with each other. A holiday it wasn't but morale was favourably high in the challenger's camp.

Just a half mile from festivities was Willard and co. It was a quieter gathering there, much better equipped to the champion's taste, but there was an important omission. Jess arrived without manager Ray Archer, seeing it as a point of personal judgement that having a physical supervisor would not provide him with anything he did not already know. Close friend Walter Monaghan worked him hard, but the quality of sparring was questionable. Whether or not Willard was sharpening up or just imposing his size was hard to tell. Anything considered a factor was so widely interpreted that it became impossible to get an objective overview of the bout. To some, Willard's superfluous flesh was not a problem, "No matter how finely drawn he was, Willard would look oversized" while others said that he had barely trained and found it hard to breathe. For weeks on end the stifling heat had been confiscating everyone's optimism and bringing on the arguments, many nonsensical. The truth was that Willard's preparation was not going too bad; he was doing his rounds and miles as they came, though his temperament was one of perplexing ease. "There is a supreme confidence about him while he is in the ring which gives one the impression that he regards this coming fight as a mere canter. There is an undeniable impression that he feels that he has nothing to worry about."[158]

Dempsey had won the popularity vote, but the size of Willard still persuaded the backbone of newspaper opinion to side with him to the point slacking was looked upon as hiding his power. He didn't go all out because perhaps "he considers their jaws too brittle." Willard was not going to be facing his sparring partners though and the Toledo boxing commission enforced style impeding rules. There was not going to be any smothering, a clean break was to be obliged when clinching, the rabbit punch (a favourite of Willard's) was banned, as was the kidney punch (a favourite of Dempsey's) and the length of the fight was cut short at twelve rounds.

In order to accommodate for the incoming numbers a stadium of milestone proportions had been assembled once again by promoter Tex Rickard. This huge octagon of wood was four times bigger than the one constructed in Reno. It was 600 feet across, the equivalent of 24 miles of seats and 1,750,000 feet of lumber.

[157] New York Times, 1919, Jul 1st, p.23

[158] New York Times, 1919, Jun 27th, p.23

The Roman Coliseum sprung to mind. Rickard was said to have been spotted daily walking around the great stadium in admiration, even having it scrutinized by a building inspector. Tex could feel the vibe of what was scheduled to be boxing's first million dollar gate. Toledo's original population of 225,000 was sharply doubled as the glamour for the big fight began to put its squeeze on the town. An initial 25,000 cots and beds had been reserved for people who arrived at the dawn of July; the plentiful excess were left to contend over office space. Soon billiards tables were considered fair game and rented as sleeping devices. When indoors was no longer an option the shores of Lake Erie became inhabited by a plethora of automobiles and tents. The event began to prevail over the taxing atmosphere.

Dempsey got cut in sparring and needed six stitches. Naturally the opinion of it re-opening varied from improbable to a certainty. Willard had sustained a very minor cut in sparring and a cracked lip due to a cold sore. Other than these little blips the contestants were both fit and confident. The betting had evened out as the days passed, but Willard was still the slight favourite with the majority finding it hard to see Dempsey getting at the big man. "The few bets that have been recorded are long shots that Dempsey will crack huge Jess on the jaw in the first or second round and send him snoring. Naturally, the odds on this interesting turn of affairs are very long."[159] At 10-1 the odds of a signature Dempsey win were long indeed, but an opportunity to make money was not to escape Kearns who contacted a gambler dubbed John 'get rich quick' Ryan for a bet of $10,000 on a first round victory.

Having just turned twenty-four, Dempsey was the essence of youth in all its restless glory. He was edgy, borderline impatient. The prospect of fighting for the title had caffeinated his very blood. Many sleepless nights followed a hard day's work as he felt the weight of July 4th bear down on him. When Independence Day landed the challenger was on his toes as early as 6:30am. After some oranges, poached eggs and coffee, Dempsey ran through his exercises at full speed; medicine ball throwing, hitting the bag, pulling the weights and a few rounds of sparring were completed to keep him peaked until the big moment. This perpetual movement from day one was part of Dempsey's ethos; "I was seldom inactive-inactivity led to laziness, and laziness lead to a dead end. No thanks."

The weigh-in whipped around in no time. Dempsey kept his eyes locked on his feet, nervous as hell, trying not to sweat in front of a hungry press. Willard casually waltzed up to the scales and sniggered at his small rival; training had been easy, and this was to be a snip as well. 180lbs to 245lbs, it was some margin. The official odds for a Willard victory had stabilized at 5-4. The champion had expressed concern for the challenger's life and even Dempsey's father, Hyrum had predicted Willard to come away the winner. So sure of victory, Willard reserved a space for his wife to witness the beating. "I wouldn't dream of asking her to be present if I thought I would be defeated."

The weather was getting fierce. Temperature readings were comfortably over 100 degrees; at 1:30pm one thermometer read 120. Another summer day in Toledo

[159] New York Times, 1919, Jun 27th, p.23

brought forth the kind of boiling atmosphere which had singed Dempsey's white skin to bronze. An escalating crowd raided any available drinks within an hour; you were lucky if you got a scoop of ice cream and the sandwich stands had been heated to an inedible, sticky mess. To top it off there is the tale of the great lightweight, Battling Nelson who mistook a tub of lemonade for a bath. Reporting for the *Chicago Daily News*, Nelson did his bit in contaminating the last of the refreshments.

$60 for a ringside seat was pricey. General admission was at $10, the equivalent of a week's wages. Not a cheap day out, but the problems for Rickard did not stop there. Just before the main event was set to pop, reported statistics had the arena at about 45,000, approximately half the capacity. Reason being the roads had got choked up during rush hour. Things had not quite gone as planned but there was no time to stall as the fighters arrived. Attention zoomed in on Dempsey's hands as DeForrest applied the wrapping. Two of Willard's colleagues had come into the challenger's dressing room to ensure nothing funny was going on. For one and a half hours Dempsey had been cooped up during the preliminaries with no alternative but to absorb the tension. And if the echo of the thousands roaring for action was not enough pressure already, Kearns informed his fighter of the bet on a first round knockout. With no time to argue it was good luck and out you go!

Bolting out of his temporary prison, Dempsey was enveloped by an army of men wearing straw hats and a few hundred women who gave his entrance a warm applause. Willard strolled towards his corner to a lesser cheer, looking disinterested in the whole event, grumpy that he actually had to fight to receive his $100,000. Instinctively, Dempsey pulled at the ropes and tried his feet for grip. His head continually bowed in apparent doubt. Every now and then he would wear a scowl and bare his teeth. It was imperative to look mean. The two men were called to the centre of the ring to have their pictures taken. A meaningless handshake was captured as the championship belt was presented. Willard sneered and let out sighs; his vague expression scanned the crowd, slowly looking in different directions as if he was in a shop and could not find what he wanted. Dempsey worked a groove in the canvas with his persistent foot scraping; he primed his shorts and kept bowing his head as Pecord shot through the instructions. The huge, half-filled wooden stadium oozed sap under the sun, making everyone as uncomfortable as possible. Damon Runyon was said to have been unable to keep still for more than five seconds as he sweated buckets. 110 degrees was recorded at ringside.

Back inside the ropes, hair sharply cropped, pug-nosed and three days without a razor, Dempsey did well to live up to his image of the savage wild man. Another canvas had been placed before the main event, but one of the ropes holding it down went over the bell, muffling its sound. The initial clang was not heard causing Willard, still looking lost, to peer over the ropes. Dempsey had gotten himself so worked up that Willard's lack of reception in turn annoyed him. A second attempt was audible and Dempsey skipped out of his corner, right arm crossed near his chin, left armed hanging lower but moving in little circles as he assumed the crouch. Willard was straight like a pole, lifting his hands from his waist and tried a jab on Jack's sweeping head.

The champion woke up a bit, suspicious of the little speedster, but he remained square in front of him, hands very low, defiant of this supposed punch. The smaller man steadily shuffled around the huge champion, feigning punches, changing direction, never still. Soon came the first pounce; a left hook that fell short of the mark. Willard sarcastically spread his arms out to disengage the rough stuff. A smile slowly replaced that vacant look. Dempsey's quick feet searched different avenues, arms twitching for the opening, chin neatly pinned away. The concentration within Dempsey was palpable, underlining the contrasts between the giant who longed for home and the hungry contender. The challenger moved around with an educated smoothness, turning off his shoulder and trying on a variety of punches. Willard attempted to batter Dempsey following his surges but could only manage to cuff the top of his head as it bore in. A solid punch had not landed just yet. A hard right hand body blow sunk in, but Willard barely moved and was content to let Dempsey do his worst. Jack eased himself out of the clinches to compose another attack. $127,500 and the chance to win the heavyweight championship of the world were at hand, and the first sixty seconds had expired. Willard was known for his stamina and had fended off Jack Johnson's repeated tries for a knockout in rough conditions. Time was not a virtue.

Patiently, the challenger made a quarter-circle to Willard's left. Dempsey's projected head tempted another jab, but no sooner was it thrown than he let both fists go. A right, left and right fired into Willard's midriff, driving him off balance for a left hook that pulverized his exposed jaw. When Willard's backside slammed to the canvas it triggered row after row to stand to attention. The big man was not too big after all. For the first time in his fighting life, the champion had been decked. He smiled as he struggled getting up, but if it was supposed to unnerve Dempsey it was to spectacularly fail. Moments of calm then again erupted into extreme aggression. Moving into the nearest corner, Dempsey keenly analysed the next angle of attack. He made his way around Pecord to get at Willard the moment his hands left the floor. With no neutral corner rule in effect, things were about to get ugly.

Left foot forward, left arm out, right arm…WHAP! Before Willard could even get into his stance the challenger was all over him. Digging his toes into the canvas, Dempsey's punches flung Willard into the ropes, turned him 180 degrees and had him on all fours. Some were upset, a few more were celebrating, but the vast majority of the crowd just stood there, amazed. Willard's obligation to rise only put him back in the path of Dempsey's endless milling. Every punch was hurtful, no fancy flurries or counter punches, just wrecking balls. For a sixth time Willard arose, supporting his cumbersome body with the aid of the ropes. Absolutely defenceless, Dempsey took a couple of free shots to dump Jess for keeps. Pecord started counting over him again and reached ten. That was it, there was a new champion! The winded Dempsey tentatively walked away from Jess to greet his elated cornermen. Kearns made sure he was first in there, instructing Dempsey to get out of the ring, itching to clarify victory. Officials and spectators entered the ring. Willard was lifted back up while Walter Monaghan stuck ammonia under his nose to help revive him. The post-fight ring bustle then changed from excited to puzzled. There was doubt as to the exact time the round had ended. DeForrest was also confused as to why the three minutes had not corresponded with his watch. "Shut up!" Kearns snapped, "For $100,000 who the hell cares if there's something wrong with the bell!" The time keeper decided that the bell had failed again in being heard. After a spot of math, he concluded that the bell had gone off when Willard's count was at seven. He was still the champion. Kearns had to get his fighter back or he was disqualified. Dempsey, who had made his way alongside the press seats, was called to return. Back he ran. To the displeasure of both fighters it was time for round two.

Dempsey had to get his game head on again and Willard was sent back to the front line. The energy levels of both men had dwindled leaving Jess with virtually none. Dempsey did not carry the same zip, but the remorseless attack continued. Overhand rights and hooks were thrown in great volume. Willard's tall frame staggered at every effort but stayed vertical. In the clinches there were moments of pause as Dempsey tired. Willard managed to land a few uppercuts which stung but they couldn't make an impression.

The damage sustained by Willard did not look like it had occurred in a boxing ring. With the standard five ounce gloves, Dempsey had punched the right side of his face to a sorry state. Blood gushed from his face, on to his chest, down to his leg, and all over Dempsey. There looked to be a fracture of the cheekbone, the jaw and possibly the ribs. In the third Willard showed tremendous stubbornness, but he was so weak that an attempted jab almost tipped him over. Dempsey sucked in big gulps of air as he poured it on. His arms had grown heavy, but the damage inflicted was such that Willard no longer resembled a fighter. Cries of "Stop it!" were heard, but by this time much of Willard's support had got behind the one who was to inevitably replace him as top dog. The bell called Jess back to his corner. His condition transfixed Dempsey as he struggled to hold his gory head up. "I felt sick. I hadn't realized that my inner fury could do so much damage."

It was unanimously decided that Willard should pull out. Shouts of "quitter!" were shamefully aired. The ex-champion sportingly got off his stool to shake the hands of his conqueror before Dempsey was given a straw hat and hoisted up by his rapidly growing fan base. In an unforgettable passing of the torch, Toledo saluted their new hero. The young champion and the weary old giant went their opposing ways. The fight was over, but the legend the 'Massacre under the sun' was to become a story of controversy. Years later Kearns, and bitterly so, would go on to claim that Dempsey had in fact encased his hands in 'Plaster of Paris' (somehow without his knowing) to inflict the injuries Willard received which history would exaggerate.

Dempsey's electrifying style captured the spirit of the Roaring Twenties, and with Rickard's talent for delivering the big gate they truly did make the heavyweight championship the richest prize in sport. Willard waited until his swollen right eye had sufficiently reduced to make the long trip back to Kansas. Four years later he would have two more fights, but as far as him making headlines this was the end. And a welcome end it was as he gladly shunned the sport that had mocked his presence. The world lapped up Dempsey, but amongst the superficial stories of the man behind the gloves, Willard was given his dues by the victor.

"He is a brave man and a tough one to beat. He took a lot of punishment and stood up under it until he couldn't stand any longer. He's no quitter."[160] Manager Ray Archer was refreshingly straight about it. "Jess was beaten, and we have no excuses to offer. He was game to the core." Yes, he really was.

[160] New York Times, 1919, Jul 6th, p.20

HARRY GREB
VS.
GENE TUNNEY

Harry Greb vs. Gene Tunney
Old Madison Sq. Garden ~ Referee Kid McPartland

May 23rd, 1922
Light-Heavyweight Title
New York, New York

Pittsburgh, USA, known to some as The Iron City; a thriving, wedge-shaped metropolis painted with steam boats, factories and mills, all geared towards churning out steel. The man born Edward Henry Greb, a.k.a. the 'Iron City Express' was made of something just as sturdy.

Emulating his hometown's bustle, Greb's alias pertained to the idea that he had climbed out of a welding pot, to quickly cool, unbreakable and unfeeling. Now Harry was not the villain, but if boxing is an art form then Greb was its Picasso, sniffing at convention and distorting reality. Bouncing about like a loon, elbows spiked outwards, arms continually making different shapes, Greb's style was hard to decipher. Everything was executed at such breakneck speed that he could fiendishly bury fouls underneath his blurring movements. A hook was just as easily a forearm, pawing was transitioned into thumbing, and kneeing…nope, no idea how that was done. Yet Greb's notoriety as a dirty fighter may have been exaggerated to go with the bad man image. "So far as I know, there is nothing foul in Greb's boxing style. If there were he would have been disqualified long ago" said William Muldoon, president of the New York State Athletic Commission.

The type of fight served up by Greb was like an incurable disease. Opponents, no matter how big or good were defeated by the natural middleweight. This may have happened more than once, twice, three times, and it may have occurred all in the same month. The trademark activity of Greb reached its zenith in 1919 when an incomprehensible forty-five appearances against the talented likes of Billy Miske, Bill Brennan, Battling Levinsky and Mike Gibbons concluded without a scratch. Even the heavyweight champion of the world wasn't spared. In 1920, the recently crowned Manassa Mauler, undisputedly at the top of his slugging powers was sentenced to look daft when Greb popped in. With all the critical newspapermen there, each on stand-by to type pro-Dempsey adjectives, Greb made headlines.

"Dempsey hasn't seen so many gloves in a long time as Greb showed him. Greb was all over him and kept forcing him around the ring throughout the session. Dempsey could do but little with the speedy light-heavyweight, while Greb seemed to be able to hit Dempsey almost at will."[161] Greb got swiftly ejected from the team. It was never to be, but a speculated match between Dempsey and Greb excited people for a while. A few months later and 80,000 spectators celebrated boxing's first million dollar gate between Dempsey and Georges Carpentier. It was barely noticeable, but also performing was a young contender from Greenwich, Connecticut called Gene Tunney.

Tunney's preliminary fight against Soldier Jones did little to merit attention, but the erudite 'Fighting Marine' was on his way to the top, and that also meant he had it in for the gambler's wallet. Tunney had this crazy thought, this developing obsession that he would one day whip Dempsey. This belief was not of blind hope or insincere friends; Tunney was his own man, a man of science, a believer in the deep study of an opponent's capabilities in order to forge the right weaponry. So far so good, but the manipulative cunning of Gene gave his career the Mendoza effect, alienating him from

[161] New York Times, 1920, Sep 20th, p.10

a bloodthirsty public. Pulling out various Shakespearean quotes in conversation did not help his cause either. With the gloves off and his sharp tongue flapping, Tunney could have easily been a politician or a doctor. His well-proportioned face and shrewd glares did not look to be a product of the ring. In many ways he wasn't. Boxing was not on the young lad's agenda as he made his daily jaunt to St Veronica's school; he was to make a fine priest for his mother. Enter a pair of gloves for his tenth birthday, and what was originally designed to aid in self-defence suddenly led to a change of career.

Tunney did not explode on to the scene as was the case with many of the greats, he just existed, blossoming so slowly that his presence never registered. If he did not look convincing or made a few mistakes then he would brood over the fight, replay it numerous times in his head as he fell asleep, and then again during breakfast. His objectivity would search for the reasons; he would ask fellow pugilists, apply different techniques in sparring. To every problem there was a solution. American's light-heavyweight title soon came his way against the old war horse, Battling Levinsky. The wily campaigner, now a veteran of over 300 bouts was easily handled by Tunney who was even said to have "plunged in recklessly", sensing his opponent's worn state. Every one of the twelve rounds went to the new champion from Greenwich Village. Levinsky would pester the ring with unwelcome returns until he eventually called it a day. "A fighter is a bum when he starts and a bum when he finishes"[162] he morbidly declared.

The last comment was not at a loss for examples, but Tunney lived safe in the knowledge that he was not going to crash n' burn. While a milestone achievement, it was only a paper title in the grand scheme, merely serving to edge him closer to destiny. Greb did not have a title. He remained content with milling away at anything that moved. Chuck Wiggins, Hugh Walker and Jeff Smith were reported to be at the brunt of newspaper decisions. The theory of Greb never needing to train due to his schedule made sense (fighting as often as he did), but he did not despise the pre-fight graft. When Harry could manage a pit stop he would take to his exercises happily, drawing off the huge crowds he created. He was also quite the self-indulged character, a victim of the Roaring Twenties' urge for fashion if you will. Rarely was Harry seen without his hair flawlessly parted, soaked with Vaseline, and he even applied talcum power to his face. Winning was at the top of the list, but if looking good helped satiate a big appetite for women then he was all for grooming.

Tommy Gibbons, the skilful brother of Mike liked the sound of America's light-heavyweight championship, but first up was Greb who itched from their last bout. It quickly went into Tunney's noggin that he was a marked man wearing that diamond-encrusted belt. Gene knew all too well about Gibbons, the shifty boxer from St Paul. He had licked the vast majority from middle to heavy; he was a vaunted tactician, and ultimately, a fighter Tunney would prefer to avoid. Gibbons was a boxer that Tunney could appreciate infinitely more than Greb. One of his father's heroes was the dexterous James J. Corbett, someone who Tunney would later develop a man crush for as they traded tactics. He was accustomed to studying fighting styles that

[162] The Miami News, 1929, Jan 16th, p.8

were much like his own. Consequently, Tunney feared Gibbons' honed techniques, specifically his double-feinted hook to the liver. The fate of Tunney depended upon the defeat of Gibbons, or so his scientific brain had sliced it.

Madison Square Garden was forced to stretch its wings for around 14,000, one of whom was Dempsey. The event was something of a double whammy as everybody was eager, not only for a good fight, but to see who would meet the champion. Gibbons was favoured to emerge the winner which was no doubt a statistic that had cool Gene cool and pensive. A 3-1 on favourite Gibbons was made in certain areas. How hindsight is a wonderful thing. When the underdog leapt into action he clearly fancied the role of victor and begun to run circles around Gibbons. The frequently tagged 'Pittsburgh Windmill' went about his usual business, manically hopping about and trying on every punch, every second. Greb worked his style a treat, rushing into a clinches to smother the uppercut and then jumping out of range. The rounds went by and saw him sustain his mastery. Whatever game he decided to initiate he got the better of and was described to be "stepping around the ring with all the agility of a Benny Leonard." Greb's speed discouraged Gibbons whose feet started sticking to the canvas; it turned from easy to effortless, or at least Greb gave off the impression. When the fifteen rounds ended Gibbons was entitled to three. It had been a carbon-copy of about another 200 of Greb's fights; bewildering to watch, dominating in the outcome. And yes, this also meant Tunney's stack had flopped nicely. It was impressive, but Greb was the softer touch. Tunney remained confident that he knew what to do when the Windmill closed on him.

The fans rejoiced, but Tex Richard was more interested in baiting Georges Carpentier back to the States with astronomical pay packets. Carpentier was not the cream of the crop, but he put bums on seats, many of which were females, good looking chap that he was. The huge audiences that the Frenchman could produce were precisely what came to mind when Richard thought promotion.

Although Greb had this habit of making his fights look as easy as it was to press a light switch, things were getting harder. After losing your arms, losing your sight must rank as one of the worst ailments for a fighter and Harry's was failing him. The capable Negro Kid Norfolk was said to have poked Greb in his right eye, likely resulting in a retinal tear. Only a few select friends were aware of Greb's injury and he wanted to keep it that way. At a dairy farm in Red Bank, N.J. Tunney trained to the level he thought adequate, apart from one problem, his hands were giving him trouble again. To try and combat this he went through a routine of clasping and unclasping them on metal springs. While Tunney was tucked away in the wilderness, working hard on his blueprints, Greb was filling in the downtime with drinking and dancing.

The contest was confined to, where else, but Madison Square Garden. This was the second Garden, originally built in 1890 and actually located at Madison Square Park, unlike today's. The large indoor arena could put up 8,000 seats and offered plenty more space for the extra thousands who tailed the big events. Distinctive arcs went around the base of the building and an unmistakable tower, which was then New York's second largest structure, shot up thirty-two storeys high. As citizens took their daily stroll through the park they were able to consider their evening entertainment via large posters that were slapped on the brickwork. On the day of the fight the arena was cleaned and customized, ready for business.

At 2pm the fighters weighed-in. Tunney registered 174.5lbs with Greb marginally over 162lbs. He was heavier, as was expected being the bigger man, but it did not stop there. Greb was done for height by nearly five inches, reach by over six and age by almost four years. Tunney was undefeated champion to boot, but, despite all these advantages, he was expected to lose. Soon enough the two men were fixed on each other, all the preliminary moments having been filed away. For such a handicapped fighter, Greb looked generously embellished. The terming 'put together' is appropriate here. You could see his muscled legs set to begin their incalculable juddering on the canvas and his chunky arms promised never to stop. Tunney looked fit and calm as referee Kid McPartland seemed to be bracing for something grizzly, sleeves rolled up, tie tucked in.

Greb treated the first gong of the bell like a gunshot for a 100 yard dash, diving into the champion's personal space. Tunney mixed it, ready to take Greb by the scruff when disaster, literally, struck. The man from Pittsburgh, dubbed a 'pitter-patter' puncher, swooped in an overhand left that landed square. Less than a minute in and Greb was two fractures up. Tunney convulsed under the impact. That quick-fire, bullet-point style of the papers reported the wallop to have "drew blood", failing to capture its exploding qualities; splat it went on to Greb. Taking Harry's measure required at least a few rounds, but here was Tunney, already fumbling about and breathing awkwardly as the red stuff poured out of his nose and down his throat. Greb charged in and ripped at the body, forcing his man to the ropes. The champion bravely landed some good ones, making it known he wasn't going anywhere. A stray head also came into play, slicing open a wound Tunney had incurred during training. Before the fight he had an injection of adrenaline chloride to stem the flow of blood for when the cut was likely to re-open. Gene later recalled, "I am convinced that the adrenalin solution that had been injected so softened the tissue that the first blow or butt I received cut the flesh right to the bone."[163]

The bell went with the two men in a pushy clinch. Doc Bagley, Tunney's chief-second, now had a very poorly patient on his hands, getting to work as soon as his butt touched the stool. He applied the adrenaline to Tunney's leaking face and rubbed it into to his hands to then have Gene sniff it up. Rather than have the desired effect, Tunney started to ingest his new plasma cocktail. The second round showed Greb threatening with the same fury, but Tunney did very well in matching it and pushed the smaller man back. Sparring would start the rounds with Tunney distracted by his condition, Greb throwing his body about, in-and-out, side-to-side, waiting for that opening. When Tunney faulted, Greb would go storming in with his jagged attack. He was described as "aimless and without accurate direction, in the strict analysis" yet "steady, consistent and active".

---

[163] A Man Must Fight, Gene Tunney, 1932, Chapter 5

Carrying the worst luck in the world, Tunney picked up another cut over the right eye in the third. In the fourth round both men went at it, not wasting an instance, Tunney with his gladiatorial blood mask. Every now and then he found Greb's body under wide elbows. Some of the punches were even credited to have lifted Greb off the floor, but there was no stopping him. A furious exchange took the crowd of their seats and called for referee McPartland to separate them after the bell; the original colour of his shirt was disappearing. Gene at least appeared to be holding his own, picking up a few of those broken pieces. Harry was cautioned in the fifth for holding and Tunney worked this advantage by driving him against the ropes with that strenuous body attack. In the sixth, Greb's irrepressible drives almost sent the pair out of the ring. Gene's valour caused the hundreds who claimed him to be a fancy Dan to take notice, but in terms of winning, he seemed powerless.

The crowd may have been guilty in developing a soft spot for the courageous champion as Greb was booed for hitting on the break in the seventh. Back in the corner, Bagley's occupation was given the acid test after every round. Tunney's mouth became chockfull of gore, so there were four serious wounds to nurse. The blood trickled out at the start of each round and was gushing at the bell. Greb made the patch-up job seem futile. When the bell started the ninth round, Tunney was bleeding from both eyes. Bagley could only do so much as an adrenaline shortage had occurred. From this point onwards Tunney went on to say that Greb came across as "a red-filmed phantom". Still fighting with belief, Tunney did what he could in there, but Greb, clearly unmarked, looked unstoppable.

A further measure that Tunney had taken, which would also backfire, was the inclusion of a brandy and orange juice concoction, "At the end of the twelfth round, I believed it was a good time to take a swallow of the brandy and orange juice. It had hardly got to my stomach when the ring started whirling around. The bell rang for the thirteenth round; the seconds pushed me from my chair. I actually saw two red opponents." A straw hat sailed into the ring that could be interpreted in no other way but to have the fight stopped. Greb "tore into Tunney leading with both hands to the face and stomach." There was no explanation for it, but Tunney survived. Blood would not stop seeping from his wounds, splattering the canvas. Never one at a loss for introducing new deceitful schemes, Greb pinned Tunney's arm against his body and thumped away. In an over-eager launch he slipped to the canvas, then up again immediately to haunt his blood-drenched victim. If victory was to come Tunney's way something miraculous was in order. Last round was up.

A customary handshake was exchanged between the challenger and half-dead champion. Tunney's feet were still there, but he was woefully uncoordinated. A few weak swings were made to miss. Some steady jabbing ensued, which Greb used as an opportunity to summon his strength. In one final rush Greb put his signature on the round. Tunney remained standing, not much else. Harry was taken back to his corner after insightfully telling Gene he had won. Tunney prophetically claimed Greb the winner, "To-night". While getting seven lumps belted out of him, somehow, Tunney saw a route to victory. Greb could be beat; "the way Harry dropped his shoulder at times, the move he made when he threw a right hook."[164] Revenge would come, but, in no condition to theorize, Gene gave into his torrid state and crumbled. Two quarts of blood is the common statistic. If it was anywhere near that then Tunney must have set a record for blood loss in the gloved era. The-ex champion evaded his parents after they got word of his loss, not wanting to distress them with his shredded mug. He had not won a single round, being given a share of three. Whilst Tunney took to bed, Greb instinctively slapped on his best clothes and danced until the sun came up in a rented-out club. The next day Rickard was tempting Carpentier again, this time with the prospect of fighting Greb, but he was now talking to deaf ears. Georges concluded that there's being brave and then there's being stupid.

The principal combatants would clash another four times. Tunney is often likened to have tamed Greb through their five fights, but it wasn't so. Their second encounter, one which Grantland Rice thought Greb won, was very close, as was their fourth. Suffice to say, the word robbery was let loose more than once. Of course, going blind never helps either. Trying to accurately summarise the rivalry proves something of a catch twenty-two situation. As Greb relapsed, Tunney improved. He did not just improve, but grew, continually finding it harder to meet the 175lbs limit as his 6' frame filled into that desired heavyweight region. Greb's best asset, his speed, began to slump, unravelling his style, ridding it of all its unpredictability. In their last bout in 1925, Tunney was positively numbed against Greb and punished the fading fighter, after which Harry insisted on never fighting Tunney again.

Despite how callously Greb had handled Tunney, it had not been easy, taking in big gulps at the final bell. Tunney had shown he had what it takes, and Greb knew it. He too would have a giggle at the bookies when Tunney boxed the ears off Gibbons and then, unimaginably, Dempsey in front of a 120,000 strong audience. Greb had watched Dempsey prepare for his fateful bout. Whenever a sparring partner hit the deck an ever-willing commotion went up; fans saw the young Mauler again, casuals joined in with the cheers. Harry was unmoved. Dempsey needs "more rugged" sparring partners was his lasting thought. He remained on the public side of things, predicting. The hype was enough to sway astute observers but Greb, just as he had inside the ring, chipped away at fiction until all that remained was bloody reality. Who'd have thought the owner of that unhinged style was a top analyst?

Brilliantly and sadly, the two men went their separate ways. Tunney repeated his defeat of Dempsey one year later, save for a famous Long Count. He retired champion, thrived as a millionaire, watched one of his sons enter Congress, made lifelong friends with the Mauler and ripened to the distinguished age of eighty-one. Greb's lust for battle dug his own grave, controversially departing him from the middleweight crown, crippling his sight and put him on an operating table where he lapsed into an anesthetised-induced coma for good. Straightening that nose would have delighted Harry in a way you could never have guessed from watching him torment his prey. Instead he was administered the cruellest blow.

---

[164] The Long Count, Mel Heimer, 1969, p.47

On the 27th October, 1926 Tunney acted as one of the pallbearers at Greb's funeral to personally see his old friend off. Out of all the lessons he had learnt from men like George Bernard Shaw, his loving parents and the Great War, Greb was the one who inspired him to study harder, to be a success. Hundreds of men gathered to pay their respects to the fallen warrior, a great many of them boxers; that is to say victims of the Human Windmill.

JIMMY WILDE
VS.
PANCHO VILLA

June 18th, 1923
World Flyweight Title
New York, New York

Pride defines fighters. It reaffirms the idea of warriors as opposed to humans, naturally estranged from terms like quit or stay down. In boxing there is nothing more laudable than giving your all which often involves losing. Those last futile efforts to keep the flame alive are what turn statistics into stories. For reasons stated, Jimmy Wilde's curtain call gave a gleaming career the badge of honour. Losing with style is a rare talent, but Wilde went one further, insisting that collapsing was as important as winning. Eight years ago pictured Jimmy, then bedridden with a heavy flu, climbing out to face Tancy Lee. Inevitably losing his corner decided to throw in the towel during round seventeen, and boy did they get it! "Never, never throw the towel in for me again. If the other fellow can put me down and out, let him have the credit for it."[165]

Pride; to take one look at Wilde was to know he was full of it. Custom-made threads decked out the little man immaculately. A select bowler hat and pocket watch round off the sophisticated look. Laughter had followed him for that minute stature belied his occupation, yet a fiery belly insisted the naysayers to take a second look. Wilde is "boyish and almost insignificant until he begins to box."[166] Once reluctantly allowed inside a ring, Wilde would demonstrate just how lethal a 100lbs man could be. The arms lay on top of the thighs, the heels rooted to the canvas, and from there he began to punch, just how many weights above his own we're still not sure. There was not much bouncing about, Wilde styled himself over a conserved fitness, relaxing his stance so that the strength of his attacks would not wane. Wilde's friend and representative, David Hughes explained, "When we first came to this country, we were surprised to see that the boxers skip to their corners very quickly after each round. Wilde always had shuffled to his corner as if he were a little, old man."[167] This attention to detail was further reflected in Wilde's training habits of which the highlight was a calisthenics routine. The foreign spectators gathered to witness the champion's well-schooled drills. Relaxing after each push, Wilde eased himself in and out of every exercise as you would a hot bath to acclimatize his muscles, reducing the chance of potential strains and injury.

"For a little man Wilde trains very hard. He goes out on the road every morning, covering about eight miles in West Side park. Then he rests until the afternoon. At 3 o' clock he has tea and begins his gymnasium work an hour later." Cool as a cucumber, Wilde picked up where he left off, but not before his traditional afternoon tea would he exhibit the grounding which had helped secure world honours for seven long years. Nothing but old fashioned dedication had amassed healthy numbers in his win bracket, but the aura surrounding the creatively dubbed 'Mighty Atom' was not built off pretty wrapping.

Of fights in the hundreds, Wilde had faulted only twice, but the momentum which propelled him to such heights was dying. A patented choice of many fighters known as the lay-off was creeping up with all its harmful side effects. Over two years

---

165 Old Holborn Book of Boxing, Peter Wilson, 1969, p.71

166 The Times, 1919, Apr 1st, p.13

167 New York Times, 1923, Jun 8th, p.24

of idleness was more than enough time to blunt Wilde's slashing fists and turning thirty-one did not help either. Being on the wrong side of thirty did not come into the equation when flyweights were concerned, simply they should be well within their third decade of life. The general rule in boxing is the smaller you are the shorter you last as if there were less coal to burn. This wasn't a problem for twenty-one-year-old Pancho Villa, a dynamic Philippine who had recently gatecrashed America. It was customary for all the best fighters to try their luck in the States, but it's doubtful whether they were ready for this 5'1" bull terrier.

Thriving off his wild schedule, Villa trained to get into the ring as often as possible. The Americans were suckers for drama and Villa gave it to them by the bucket load. A few lapses did little to dent the Philippine's confidence. His ballistic style swooned all. The Filipino "was unceasing and untiring in action", plus he could "absorb punishment like a sponge absorbs water". These talents of Pancho, pretty accurate in their description, went a long way in keeping his dream alive. Twice had the tricky Frankie Genaro repelled him, but the stormy efforts for victory had left audiences buzzed and wanting more. And wherever there was money there was Tex Rickard. Plans for Wilde's next opponent were still awaiting a long-winded confirmation before Villa rushed into the picture. Suddenly it all clicked and Tex saw himself looking at a flyweight match-up for the ages. The agreeable styles and popularity of both men ensured interest far beyond the realms of the discerning fan.

How little Pancho "a pugnacious individual if there ever was one" had earned the right. Manual labour in the tropical humidity of Ilog, a town or 'Bayan' in Negroes Occidental, Philippines instilled the young mite with a truckload of independence. Helping his mother raise goats kick-started a lifetime's worth of slogging, developing the body and hardening the mind. Whatever was to come Villa's way, he was taught to prevail. Boxing proved an agreeable outlet. Fewer than five years was sufficient for him to partake in 88 bouts, averaging out at nearly twenty a year. Wilde was not shy in this department either, but Villa had managed to record thirty-nine more bouts in half the time. Comparisons between the meteoric rise of Villa and current heavyweight champion Jack Dempsey were popular.

In 1922 the eternal bliss that came with the flyweight title beckoned Villa to the lights and bustle of New York, over eight and a half thousand miles overseas away from sunny home. As the Great War faded into the back of memories, an economically prosperous era synonymous with jazz music and prohibition supplied ideal grounds for a wealthy party animal like Pancho. Banging the snare drum whilst drinking like a fish till all hours, Villa got his kicks by behaving like a disobedient child. He was generous beyond his means, rumoured to have once littered the streets of Manhattan with green as he motored by. And if America had fallen for Pancho it might have given you an idea of what his country felt for their sporting hero. No less than President Quezon of the Philippine Senate and President Rozas of the Assembly sent their representative a cablegram to wish him luck before the big event. The highest patronage tailed Villa and likewise, Royalty followed the champion.

Edward VIII, the Prince of Wales would often make an appearance, underlining the importance of a Jimmy Wilde fight. Another customarily larger opponent named Joe Lynch was defeated and in response Edward climbed inside the ropes to personally congratulate the victor. So too did Wilde have a fan base to match any, but lest we forget, two years without boxing was an ugly statistic. Comebacks had a poor history, and it looked as if, while not entirely losing faith, observers were frowning in educated doubt. The last outing saw bruising bantamweight Pete Herman (a good 15lbs heavier) overcome Wilde's piercing assaults to wear him down. It was another drawn-out beating like the Tancy Lee episode, but what this meant was that the Welshman had not won a fight in a long while.

Jimmy's training headquarters were found at a building known as 'Peoples Palace' in Jersey City, first constructed with the idea of being "a hippodrome where every man could ride his hobby." Pancho's activities could be located at Pompton lakes, N.J. which would later be put to good use by Joe Louis. The West had not seen anything like Wilde before, nobody who could punch like him anyway as he put the heat on unfortunate sparring partners. "His handlers are hard pressed to find bantamweights and featherweights who are willing to work out with him."[168] The champion's camp quickly recruited the talented locals Al Fox (117lbs) and Mickey Taylor (121lbs) to force Wilde into the hellish depths Villa was capable of. Many good rounds of sparring followed though the apprehension held for Wilde surfaced with Taylor, "It was during this workout that it became quite evident that Wilde is not hard to hit. Perhaps he was a little careless because they were wearing the big "pillows" and did not attempt to defend himself." Villa was not the most elusive fighter either, and that is what was set to make this fight very watchable.

On the highly anticipated day it was declared, "There have been championship contests that still linger in the memories of those who have witnessed them, but few of them have held as much promise of action as the one that will begin at 10 o' clock this evening."[169] A week beforehand, the odd news came in that Wilde had quit sparring, bearing no intention of throwing any more leather until the first bell. Continuing to perplex the American people with strange customs, "He claims, or rather it is claimed for him, that, being a natural boxer, he does not need much sparring." If Wilde had reached just half of his alleged 800 plus contests then it could be conceived that sparring was nothing but a superficial tweak. Villa raced till the end, training his upmost every day. By now a month's preparation had been completed.

The Polo Grounds in New York, immortalized by baseball's New York Giants, was groomed to welcome the matched fighters. Under Coogan's Bluff (a promontory which rose above the Harlem River) provided the battle zone. The ring was assembled over the pitchers square on the day of the fight. A snazzy new lighting system was installed promising "as plain a view of the fight as if it were held in daylight". As the stadium neared completion Jimmy and Pancho stripped down for the 2pm weigh-in. Wilde had often saw it fit to hop on fully clothed to max out his poundage. Philadelphia Jack

[168] New York Times, 1923, Jun 8th, p.24

[169] New York Times, 1923, Jun 18th, p.10

O' Brien's gym housed the affair. A stuffy room of smartly dressed officials crowded around the scale, towering over the mini-fighters. 109lbs and a half was announced for Wilde. Villa registered in slightly heavier at 110lbs which was another peculiar statistic for it was thought he would surely be lighter conceding height. One aspect that did ring true was both men had agreed to make the flyweight limit of 112bs (8 stone). It is common for the odds to abruptly swing one way before a big fight but the doubt surrounding Wilde sealed Villa as the 6-5 on favourite.

Matchmaker Tom O' Rourke predicted the bout would generate huge interest, expecting more than 60,000. Tickets ranged from the affordable prices of $2.20 - $16.50 to assist in baiting lowly city slickers towards 25,000 unreserved seats. Despite this ploy fans were noticeably slow in arriving. Following the opening of the gates at 5pm left the initial small mob peering over at the entrances, hoping for everyone's sake that more would come. Time burnt on and with it the crowd found the funny side of things, cynically cheering each new arrival. A poor performance by the pre-fight band sent the spectators on to new heights. Newspapers were scrunched up and used as summer snowballs. Random victims were then singled out and pelted in an attempt to alleviate boredom. It was a clear night with a gentle breeze, but efforts to self-amuse had brought on dehydration. All the lemonade and ice cream was predictably blitzed. Luckily, before everyone lost their marbles, Jack Snyder and Al Beder produced a decent scrap, warming folk to the main event. A small group of dedicated Philippines were particularly edgy.

10pm. The sun had disappeared leaving the dazzling lights to intensify the white of the canvas. Initial rows of straw hats reflected the rays and then dithered from sight like buoys on a night sea. At ringside cigar smoke eerily climbed into the atmosphere as tens of thousands pricked their ears for any commotion. Cheers started to spread amongst the dark; there was Pancho Villa, wrapped in a black Japanese robe, taking his short speedy steps to the ring. Wilde entered just after to another big cheer, looking sleepy as ever, thought accompanying each meticulous step. Joe Humphries the great ring announcer first introduced champion Jimmy Wilde to the Polo Grounds. He sat still in the corner, head partially slanted, acknowledging nothing as he focused his strength in the time permitted. Villa shot up and saluted his fans. Wilde had the novel experience of looking over his opponent's head. Villa contrasted nicely with his brown skin and muscled body; no matter distant it would not be difficult to distinguish champion from challenger.

Ding went the bell. They slowly closed on each other, no need to rush with fifteen rounds available although Villa had made it a point that he was not there to cruise, expecting to "beat him before the fifteenth round". Wilde went to his man, throwing punches in numbers that suggested he was confident of hurting his opponent, but Wilde had always been an enigma. "Wilde does not attack in the generally understood meaning of the word. He almost invariably draws the opponent's leads and counters so fast as to make "fans" think that his returns are leads." Villa would rush in and then scurry off to find better footing. Wilde kept close. The challenger negated most of the blows with his crossed right arm and easily soaked up the few that landed. He seemed to eye the champion warily, waiting for the chance to surprise him. Wilde plodded after him, leaning forward, arms circling in "Why I Oughta" fashion. Out of his shield-like stance Villa suddenly pounced on Wilde with quick flurries. These punches were substantially faster, cruelly intended. Wilde coped well, but it was advisable to avoid them. One of the left hooks crunched into the Welshman's body, causing him to gasp and hold on tightly. First round went to the challenger. Wilde was not taking any back steps.

They came out again in the same vein as the first, careful but serious. Wilde tried to apply his mischievous leading tactic, but for all of Villa's renowned aggression he was adamant on uncoiling at the right times. Wilde used his superior reach, distancing himself from the impulsive challenger. Maybe the punches Wilde absorbed did not concern him, but many hit home, validating the claim of him not being hard to catch. The bell to end round two clanged, and depending on who you asked, Wilde was walloped with a right hook either on or after the bell. After is the most frequent take, and the crowd testified with a huge roar. With his arms down poor Jimmy ate a wicked shot and crashed to the floor. It was rendered as no foul by referee Patsy Haley, which left Wilde in the dubious position, currently getting carried back to his corner, of attempting a rematch in sixty seconds. The champion's corner rallied to restore him as best they could but out Wilde came for the third round, visibly inebriated by the last punch. Slugging away in a daze, Wilde went at it. Pancho got the better of his weakened foe but had his hands full nonetheless. The champion was punched about. Again he did not wilt.

Villa's punches lacked the placement and technique of Jimmy's, guilty of flinging his arms out straight like a bat, but the frantic manner in which he operated implied that they were not going to stop. Wilde trumped Villa with a knockout percentage three times higher than his, but these revered blasts lacked snap. They were more pushy than punishing. He could find the mark, just not make one. He refused to stop trying and in the fourth, setting his feet just right, planted Villa with a right that staggered him to the ropes. Instinctively he rushed towards the retreating prey and pressed only to be obliged.

Jimmy's right eye was closing up and blood leaked from his nose. In round five he fought back as if his life depended on it but Villa attacked and attacked, hitting at anything within the rules. Not much was known about these rules though. What was OK with Wilde and what was OK with the referee were two different things. The champion, a man from the British school of clean contests was mugged by Villa's unruly backhand chops. As Pancho missed a hook he would relay it back, often striking with the angular side of the glove which can poke the eye. In a debilitating round six Wilde found the time to complain but he was bluntly overruled. Another referee may have felt the need to atone for what had happened at the end of the second, but Haley was not in a giving mood. A distressed corner pleaded with him to pack it in. The right eye was completely closed, badly gashed and the left eye was closing fast; injuries which leapt out against his pale complexion. Virtually blind, the once unbeatable terror now stared at defeat. The brash youngster who had to yell from his toes to be let inside a ring was now forced to do the same to stay inside. Father Time was not looking kindly on Jimmy Wilde, but he was to function until he couldn't. America writer Robert Edgren reported Wilde to have shook his head with "British bulldog grit" when asked to pull out at the end of the round.

Wilde crept away from his seconds as the seventh round begun. His sight was so badly impaired that it was said that he "often did not know which way to turn to face his foe". Villa worked him on the ropes and threw a fair right that landed flush. Better punches had landed but Jimmy could do no more. His whole body fell over face-first like an unhinged door. At one minute and forty-six seconds of the round the bell sounded for the end of the fight. There was no count. Wilde was once again carried back to his corner as Pancho Villa bathed in the applause he so rightly deserved; it had not been easy. Later, the Philippine was said to have shed a tear for the ex-champion. Wilde received a healthy $65,000, Villa significantly less at about $12,000. 40,000 spectators had witnessed the fight, not the 60,000 as hoped. More disturbing was the fact the fight had only generated $94,590, later found out to be the result of 17,000 having not paid!

The beating was such that Wilde was unable to recognize people for a good while after. Nonetheless, remembering the Tancy Lee drama, the decision to fight on was far more preferable. Many hailed Wilde as the best flyweight that had ever laced 'em up, but there was a controversial undertone to the big event. Edgren had also written that "If the rules of boxing has been strictly followed, Villa would have been disqualified, and the fight given to Wilde." Certainly if Wilde hadn't been socked at the end of the second it would have put him in better stead to be victorious, but the signs of ageing could not be denied. It was just so that boxing in America worked differently than it did in Britain. Back in 1919 when Wilde beat Joe Lynch, in direct response to the American's holding it was written, "There is little doubt in my mind that the referee extended a leniency to the American which he would not of given to a fellow countryman. But that is the British way."

Villa spent the next day contemplating being champion at Pompton Lakes. He looked forward to heading back east to see his bride when Tom O' Rourke proposed a return bout with nemesis Frankie Genaro. Nothing needed to be reiterated, Pancho's burning gaze said it all. Jimmy wisely stayed put until his face deflated. A physician summed him up as "Painfully but not seriously injured." On the 4th July he made his unperturbed way back to Britain. Boarding the Aquitania, an ocean liner destined to survive both world wars, Wilde looked prosperously towards a cinema business with David Hughes.

That was it for Wilde as a fighter, instantly swatting down rumours of a comeback. It had been one helluva journey that turned into a one-of-a-kind legend, sporting a warped "the smaller they are, the harder they punch" thesis. Pedlar Palmer immortalized him as "The ghost with the hammer in his hand". The title which Wilde had so brilliantly worn undeniably fell into the right hands. Legends are all too often taken to the trash by unspectacular fighters when age blows a gasket. Villa though is often right behind Wilde in a list of the greatest flyweights; at two that is.

The fans at the Polo Grounds were a noisy bunch, but the constant cheering hit its deafening climax when an incoherent Welshman was broadcast by Humphries as "The gamest loser pugilism has ever seen." Jimmy smiled on receiving his new title. Pride had won the day.

JOE LOUIS
VS.
MAX SCHMELING

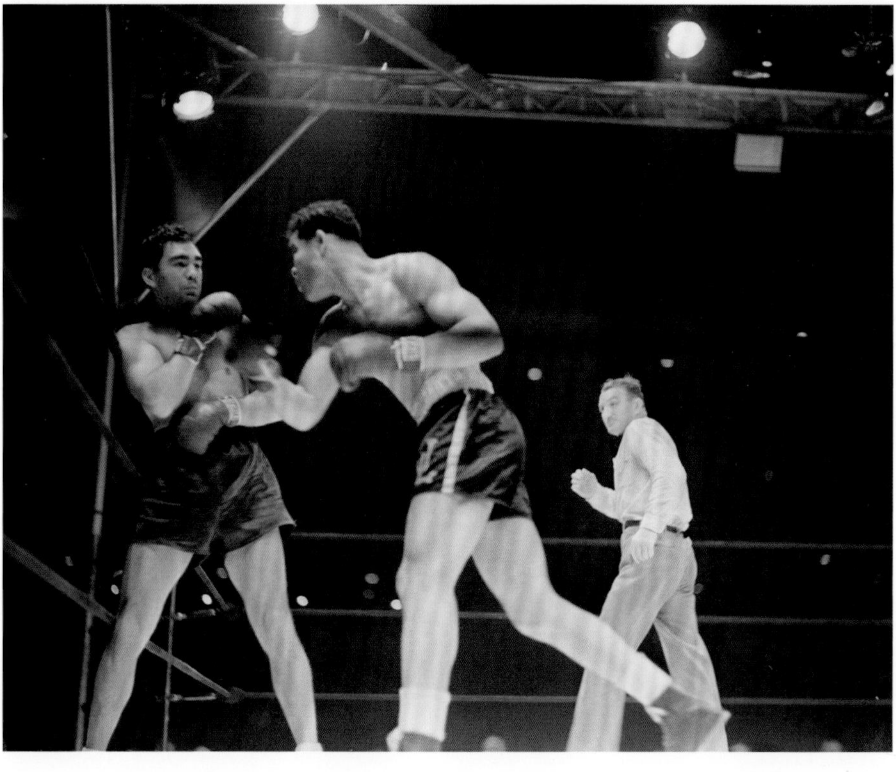

June 22nd, 1938
World Heavyweight Title
New York, New York

Using his knee as a crutch, Max Baer did the right thing and stayed put. Not even four rounds were needed. Out of these targeted former champs, Baer was neither old nor damaged goods, but he was up against Joe Louis. In 1935 that spelt disaster. Madcap Maxie did manage to hit home with his life-taking right hand. Sweet as the shot was the young man from Detroit stayed put, depreciative of its impact. Louis took aim amongst the cross-fire to bludgeon his opponent.

You could be safe in the knowledge that the Brown Bomber was sure to perform white hot at every bell, but it was Jack Blackburn, a former lightweight guru, who educated those triple hooks and fierce crosses. A year prior, the critical Blackburn could not complain about his generous training induction salary of $35 per week, but he remained unsure of his new pupil, raw and uncoordinated as he was. Jack had previously been working with the silky-smooth 'Jersey' Joe Walcott, so this transition to the plodding Louis had Blackburn approach with mixed feelings. Not before long did Louis begin to take on these fighting philosophies with great speed. It turned out that the twenty-year-old was of the right icy temperament to learn, practice and convey all of Blackburn's knowhow with deadly accuracy. He was taught how to use his feet to sucker his man in, time his counters and pace himself; up to twenty rounds if need be. Louis was sharply transformed into an economical assassin, and as he gathered momentum opponents were rattled before the first ding.

It was not inside, but outside the ropes where the coffee-coloured boxer encountered resistance. If memory served correctly then it would appear that the unruly Jack Johnson was the last black heavyweight champion and Louis was heading in that same sensitive direction. Eleven years earlier a fight between then champion Jack Dempsey and top ranked black contender Harry Wills was partly undone on the premise of what had happened when Johnson fought Jeffries. Much time had passed but it lingered in the conscience that a fighter of African heritage should not have the chance to become champion. Louis was effectively forced to walk on egg shells as he strived to get the public thumbs-up, but he was in good hands. A capable team of backers were at hand to ensure Louis got a fair shake.

John Roxborough, a seasoned local black bookmaker, acted as the catalyst. He delivered meaningful bouts and joined forces with promoter Julian Black who finalized proceedings upon hiring Blackburn. They all worked together to cleanse the Louis image of any potential, ugly stereotypes. The sporting world was not prepared to accommodate any more 'fresh Negroes', so Louis was designed to be the exact opposite. His apparent personality was diluted to the point one could not be detected as knee-jerk, short sentences answered the media. "Interviewing Joe Louis…is a laborious task"[170] was the conclusion after an interview comprised entirely of yes and no answers. Two of the most striking rules of these commandments assigned to Louis were that he was not to have his picture taken with a white woman and that he must not gloat (Johnson style) over his fallen opponent.

Louis, originally from rural Alabama, had struggled with a speech impediment from an early age, resulting in a shyness that did not always make for comfortable

---

[170] Chicago Tribune, 1938, Jun 14th, p.15

situations. A little more introspective than your average man, he had been made all too aware of how whites still looked to take advantage of black folk, so while he was not ever going to charm the nation with star charisma, Joe was far from a clueless lurch. "You gotta let your right hand be your referee" inculcated Blackburn. It was in the ring where Louis was at ease.

At fifty-seven Jack Johnson was an elderly ex-boxer, but he hadn't lost his touch. Still dressed to perfection and forgetful of road laws, the invasive Johnson craved publicity and eyed Joe's career as a way in. He had barely acquainted himself, hoping to slip into the group, when he was told to beat it. "I'm gonna do everything possible to get you a fight for the championship" promised John Roxborough, and not one speck of that plan included Jack Johnson who, naturally, responded with a public vendetta. The knack for verbally punishing his enemies had not left Johnson, but the old pug was rendered a meagre threat. Louis on the other hand was terribly hazardous. Pauline Uzcudun and Charley Retzlaff shared five rounds between them before the inevitable curtain call lifting Louis' undefeated record to an attractive 20 KOs in 24 fights. For the next bout it was decided that Germany's Max Schmeling provided respectable fodder; coming in as the 10-1 underdog he captured the very essence of the phrase. For Louis this was easy pickings. To Schmeling it presented a golden opportunity.

Max had recently gotten the best of Uzcudun but brought with him a tiring past. He'd been through the mill once. Observers fancied the German to bite the dust, and quickly. In his last big showdown Schmeling survived until the tenth when Max Baer knocked him silly. Proudly wearing the Star of David on his trunks, Baer let Schmeling have it, fulfilling his racially-driven assignment. Baer was only half-Jewish from his father but it gave morale to the country to have beaten a 'Nazi'. Portrayed as a representative of Aryan supremacy, Schmeling might as well have been one. Historians are not sold on Schmeling's incarnation as the anti-Nazi having never openly refuted his position as a supporter of the regime, but well known deeds like his rescue of two Jewish children emphasize the compassion he is remembered for. At this time WWII was coming to the boil, but Schmeling first had to prepare for his own personal war. Dead-pan Joe was not going to feel compassionate come fight night.

It was at this juncture where Jack Johnson's haunting babble hit a rare, informative tone. Choosing Schmeling as the victor was not surprising, explaining *how* he would win merited attention. As Johnson perceived, Louis was guilty of letting his left hand sink after jabbing and that would be his undoing. Schmeling, also a scholar in the art of observation, had an identical thought, later signalling to the American people when he cheerfully quipped, "I zee zomething…but I won't tell!"

So Baer had beaten Schmeling and Louis annihilated Baer. In that case, Schmeling was as good as dead. Popular stories of the German being thirty years worn encouraged Joe to take in a few more rounds of golf than standard. He got into shape but was wanting for condition. And as for a plan, Schmeling had a jaw. The betting for a Bomber KO was emphatic, but the only thing that hit home was reality, and it pictured Louis off his feet. Biding his time and spotting the error, Schmeling synced his cross, generally cited as a sucker punch, over Louis' lazy left. Johnson was destined to exist outside of Louis' world, but right now he was very much in it, reaping genuine gratification. Down in the fourth, rattled at the end of the fifth and thumped all the way up to the twelfth, Schmeling put the finishing touches on a senseless Louis with one more right.

The swollen left eye Schmeling later wore was more superficial than telling; he was the overwhelming winner. As for Louis, "his invincibility as a fighter a shattered myth, his vulnerability convincingly established, and his claims to heavyweight title distinction knocked into the discard."[171] The real question now was not "Will Joe Louis return?" but "Can Max Schmeling become the first man to regain the heavyweight title?" Germany had previously held reserves about Schmeling, Jewish manager Joe Jacobs and all. It mattered not. Standing as a prime example to validate the propaganda, his country embraced the victor. Fans deep in the thousands covered the grounds of Frankfurt where Schmeling landed to a hero's welcoming. All the pre-doubt and frowning faces were mended with broad smiles and scenes of jubilation. It was not a title fight but the reaction implied global significance. For the melancholy loser, he was forced to endure the burdens of an ill-fated preparation. Public opinion turned sour, supporters lost faith. The shine had been removed from Joe's fearsome fists.

From a boxing perspective, the stirring affair at Yankee Stadium came through as a ray of light. Jack Sharkey, Primo Carnera, Max Baer and current title-holder James J. Braddock rounded off a list of handy fighters who doubled as unreliable champions. This unlikely outcome knocked the combatants on to different routes. Schmeling took over a year out, enjoying his celebrity status but failed to bag the title shot he thought himself worthy. Louis demonstrated no gun-shy tendencies, a widely dispersed theory after losing as former champ Jack Sharkey was dismantled in three rounds. Many more victims were chewed up with minimal fuss, putting Louis within reach of tearing the title out of the champion's fragile hands. James' obligation to give Louis the shot did not occur after flipping a coin. A highly lucrative deal was cooked up with a $300,000 purse and a further percentage on Mike Jacob fights for the next decade. Having only recently left behind his gritty days on the docks, and with the coloured boy in no position to call the shots, Braddock got what he wanted. After an impressive hustle, the Irishman succumbed in the eighth when Louis' big right cracked his jaw. A new champion, a black champion stood at the top of the heap.

This victory initiated a new dawn for coloured athletes, but not in Louis' or the people's minds had he confirmed total superiority. Schmeling's shadow loomed, only to grow larger with time. Regular defences could not escape lasting sentiments of the opponent not being German, or called Max Schmeling. "Louis Victory Fails to Settle Burning Issue" was a headline that did not need an explanation. International qualms and their brotherhood with sporting events pulled the fighters closer as the glaring logic of a rematch eventually drove promoter Mike Jacobs to set the date, June 22nd, 1938. All over the announcement like a rash, Philadelphia, Chicago, Detroit and Cleveland bid for the honours, but it was Yankee Stadium that won the race. To keep

[171] New York Times, 1936, Jun 20th, p.1

active Schmeling defeated Steve Dudas while Louis defeated Harry Thomas before packing the bare necessities and heading off back to Pompton Lakes for "the most intensive training campaign in his four year professional career." Max secluded himself further away from Manhattan, 200 miles north-west of skyscrapers for the peaceful lakes and greenery of Speculator village. He was just as focused as Joe and aimed for physical excellence. To ease the nerves and keep the fighters relatively protected these isolated camps were a top choice for preparation but they did not deter the press from getting in their motors. With its air of adverse discrimination the contest guaranteed to take the American and German out of boxing, restyling their professional roles as gloved politicians. "This heavyweight championship bout between Joe Louis and Max Schmeling is a desperate grudge fight. Neither can afford to lose."[172] Doing what they do best, the papers made sure to stir the pot.

Six mile runs and spots of rowing occupied Louis on the days when he wasn't thumping his sparring partners about. Sometimes over 7,000 watched him work on his revised methods which resulted in plenty of worry. A popular thought came in that Louis had failed to correct his low left. "Rights bounce off Louis' chin" headlined a column. If unable to correct the flaw, Louis was in for a very short reign. James J. Braddock had little fear of losing his 10% cut, favouring Joe to end matters in seven rounds or less. Schmeling likewise commanded a big reception where many believed him to be well on his way to regaining the title he held nearly six years ago. Scattered around the walls of a quaint pad were streams of barbed wire and four State troopers escorted Max to the ring in order to spar. Printed as the spawn of Hitler, Schmeling's security measures were not excessive by any means. Lake Pleasant was nearby and he would occasionally go there to work on his balance and patented moves. On his two day breaks, Max took advantage of the surrounding waters and fished.

Gene Tunney assigned himself to cover the fighter's progress. Whilst very impressed with the power and delivery of Schmeling's vaunted right hand, Gene went on to say after watching Joe one day, "If Joe Louis will set a pace like he did today, he will whip Max." Jack Dempsey was the other big voice in the press and added fuel to fire, "Max Schmeling will knock out Joe Louis in a short, fast fight." In the lighter weights a swarming dynamo named Henry Armstrong was squashing all his opposition with a non-stop barrage. "Bomber Needs A Style Like Armstrong's" was a thought, figuring that Louis would have to bore in and seek shelter from the right hand. Despite the fact Louis was again the betting favourite, Schmeling was set to threaten with a potentially unavoidable punch.

Training typically ended with about forty-eight hours to spare before the first bell. Demonstrating his confidence, Schmeling piloted an aircraft on his way back to the noise and madness of New York City which contained 30,000 more visitors than usual. Back in Germany, Hitler had seized supreme control of the armed forces and was one year away from invading Poland. With intentions made clear, Schmeling came across as a lone Messerschmitt, diving into enemy territory. At the midday weigh-in around seven hundred reporters scurried into Madison Square Garden to post the

[172] Chicago Tribune, 1938, Jun 16th, p.2

weights, and look for any needle between the two. Schmeling was one pound more than he was last time at 193lbs. Louis had added three quarters of a pound on to his previous 198lbs. There wasn't a crease on either body, nor did they say anything, giving reporters the chance to make something up; never a problem.

Boxing got out the red carpet for its seventh million dollar gate. Mike Jacobs was pretty confident of the fight surpassing that magical seven digit sum. Big money meant big crowds and 80,000 were scheduled to spill into Yankee Stadium. Up till the first bell Louis was the favourite, but the general outlook was undecided; that didn't stop celebration parties being arranged in Harlem and across Germany. Schmeling was positive his "seventeen days of boxing for a total of 109 rounds" had worked him into peak condition. Louis was silently confident as ever, but a little sharper. In response to those who thought he did not look so great in training he countered, "did anyone ever win a title against spar mates?"[173]

At 8:30pm the champion and challenger got into their dressing rooms and at 10pm they were in the ring. The long walk up was an uncomfortable experience; at least it would be for anyone else. The butterflies must have been fluttering but their faces did not twitch. In front of and behind the fighters lived a swamp of trainers, managers and policemen which occasionally expanded as random spectators tested their powers of camouflage. The closer to the ring they got the slimmer the groups became until all that remained was recognized officials. The arena kicked out a noisy, disruptive din. Officially the attendance was in the 72,000's of which 66,227 were paying customers to deliver a $1,015,096 gate. Max made the effort to go over to Louis who was currently smearing his soles with resin. You had to feel for Max, the handshake seemed intended more so for the public in the hope he may yet rescue his reputation. Introduced first, he got off his stool to sincerely bow in different directions. The bell clanged twice. At the end of his introduction Louis rose briefly, letting out a suppressed flurry at the corner post. A little pivot and Max could be seen walking to the centre of the ring. Chappie walked with his star pupil, briefly straightening that robe. Referee Arthur Donavon was given the microphone and began the instructions. "And may the best man win" made a welcome conclusion to the spiel.

Louis bounced on the spot, shutting out anything that was unlikely to be distracting him. Schmeling was still to absorb some parting tips. Joe was out quickly with an exemplar guard, each arm held very straight and steady. Schmeling opposed him with an extended left and cocked his right like an archer. Detroit's Bomber had promised a fast start and was off first with two lefts and a short hook. Not hurtful but accurate punches, Louis backed off without stepping out of range; a stylistic nicety drummed in by Chappie. He was eager and got off first again with both hands. Short hooks got the German a bit flustered and a wonderful cameo ended with a brisk jab.

There was a do-or-die feeling in the atmosphere as they stood right in front of each other, total faith in their equalizers. Schmeling was forced to make a decision and let go with his right. The punch reached Louis' head but he was already in retreat which reduced his principal weapon to a tap. An attempt to crowd the champion was scalded

---

[173] The Evening Independent, 1938, Jun 22nd, p.8

with a hook. Louis was strangely hostile. He put more into his next effort, a double jab-cross which sent a ripple down the opponent's body. Max was formally shoved off before he could compose himself. Louis stayed very close, disabling the danger punch. A big cross took Max's feet away from him but he received help from the ropes. He would have been better served to fall.

The ropes then turned into a trap when Louis pitched a right to his turned body, fracturing two of his vertebrae. An awful scream was let out which was audible on Germany's radio broadcast during the wee hours. One of them receiving the adverse shriek was Adolf Hitler, then at his Bavarian mountain retreat. A left hook came next, whipping that six ounce Everlast glove into the solar-plexus. Schmeling wanted to fall, but, crippled by the pain he couldn't. Louis was given an open target and a couple of rights spun Schmeling 180 degrees while the ropes continued to be about as helpful as scaffolding on a demolition site. Donavon hesitated to count and instructed them to box on.

Germany's plight to regain the heavyweight championship was looking rather suspect. Max was given zero time to recover and was a helpless target for Louis' one-two. Just enough punching room was left for the champion to blindside him which he did with a six-inch blast. Max rolled in the motion his senses were churning. He leapt up but his legs appeared different to the rubbery kind, more damaged, twitching like a busted robot. In Joe went again, knocking his target on to its gloves. Max extended his left once more, trying to create space that Louis could take away with despotic ease. The shy boy from Alabama threw a crunching right body slug and finished with the same punch, square on the jaw. The "fiercest fusillade I've ever seen" typed Grantland Rice. For a third time Max went down. The white towel of surrender was thrown in by Schmeling's corner, but only Donavon could stop the fight and he threw it away where it caught the rope to mirror the folded challenger. Donavon helped Schmeling find his feet as his men came rushing in to escort the wreckage. It had taken 124 seconds to turn a perfectly fit fighter into a hospital patient.

He was sent to the nearby Polyclinic infirmary while Harlem began its merry marathon. Whichever way you cut it, Joe Louis had proven himself a modern great, taking all the doubts, not to mention unbelievable pressure and delivered the most decisive performance in heavyweight history. There was just enough left in the tank for another twenty-one defences, smashing previous reigns to create a record that remains in pole position to the present day. Schmeling had a long future ahead of him, but not as a fighter. Germany soon had him suited and booted as a paratrooper. In 1941 he was wrongfully reported to be dead during the Nazis' invasion of Crete. He married but never had any children. A lasting friendship with Louis ended with the death of Joe and Schmeling took it upon himself to help pay for the funeral. He lived up to the extra ripe age of ninety-nine, remaining a fan of boxing till the end, even catching the odd Klitschko fight, though the man just shy of a century admitted that he was beginning to find it difficult to stay awake.

Louis came out of the war to squeeze past 'Jersey' Joe Walcott (not without some help from the judges) and then retired. Lots of golf was on the agenda but outstanding tax bills left him with no choice but to reapply the gloves. He only received around one fifth of what his fists had generated in the ring and he wasn't frugal. That long stint in the war was no alibi and the interest piled on. When Rocky Marciano flattened the aged Bomber there was still lots of debt to be paid off.

For many years Louis was associated with professional wrestling, but when tumbling began to get the better of his joints he found himself unglamorously appointed as a Vegas doorman. Close friends helped regulate his financial woes, but Louis' health began to suffer, and as is customary, he suffered in silence. Cocaine abuse was strongly linked with episodes of paranoia. The universally respected ex-boxer began to live in a very lonely world in which it is rumoured he unscrewed light bulbs to subside an inexplicable feeling of a doom. Joe was sixty-six when a heart attack ended his life. Schmeling was one of the pallbearers who carried Louis' casket into Arlington National Cemetery. Jersey Joe, Muhammad Ali, Joe Frazier, Michael Spinks, Ray Leonard; a long list of everybody was present at Joe's funeral.

Above all a day of remembrance, those closest to Joe may have drifted off to 1930s Detroit. The reason being obvious; few things in life got the blood pumping like a Brown Bomber fight. In those early days, holding himself in a manner which could be mistaken as defeatist, Joe blasted his way through opponents while parrying the racial libel. Each knockout inspired black communities, like mini conquests in the march for equality. Less forgiving African-American's may have dreamt of Louis' cross flattening their superiors…a fantasy worth replaying…that's not to say Joe's fists didn't have their own effect outside of stinking concussions. After 69 bouts there was more to be said about tolerance than division. One of those sly white reporters agreed. In the definitive words of Jimmy Cannon, "He was a credit to his race, the human race."

TONY ZALE
VS.
ROCKY GRAZIANO

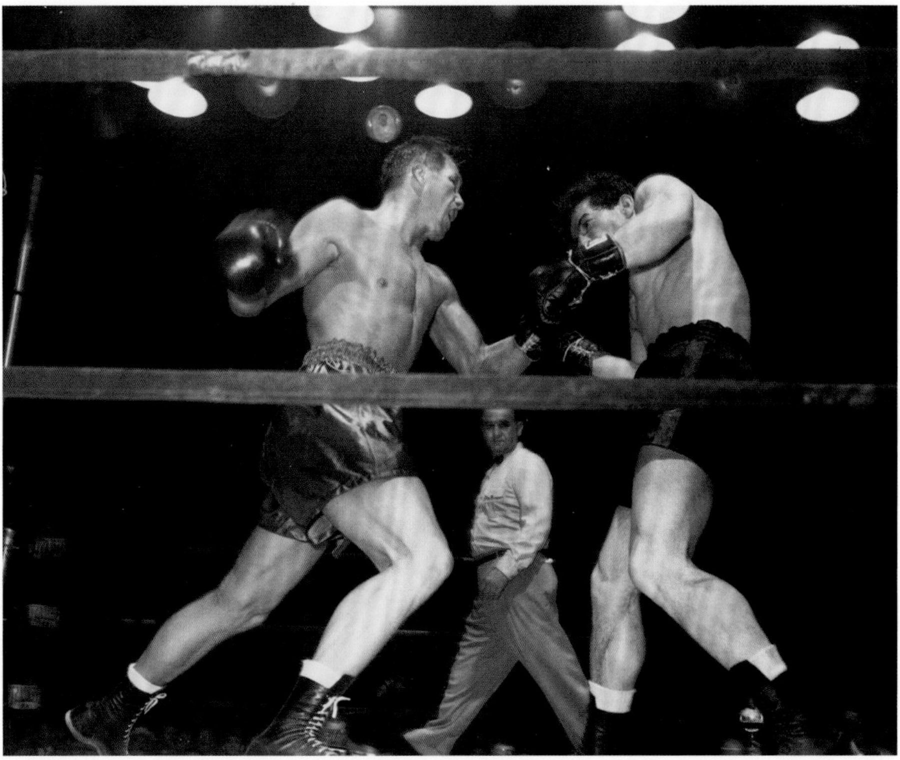

September 27th, 1946
World Middleweight Title
New York, New York

Tony Zale and Rocky Graziano took very different paths en route to collision. Lacing them up the best part of a decade before his rival, Zale's brief stint as middleweight champion ended with the United States introduction into World War II. Swapping his shorts for naval uniform, the Polish boy from the steel mills of Gary, Indiana suddenly found himself with a baby daughter and no choice but to put everything on hold. Like so many other fighters, his career began to receive the count. Swiftly drafted not long after turning professional, Thomas Rocco Barbella insisted on his own route when he directed what the press would later dub his 'rockabye baby' at an officer. As a result he was dishonourably discharged having boxed under the title of Rocky Graziano.

An instance of such recklessness would usually entail a graver penalty, but instead Rocky was admitted the luxury to carry on with his crude ways in the ring. From 1942-45 each successive swing drew more New Yorkers while Zale's new maritime lifestyle discovered necessity in exhibitions and fitness drills. Hitting thirty only made the likelihood of returning that bit slimmer, and even more marginal was the chance of him retaining the kind of blistering form that had tenderised Georgie Abrams. No doubt when Rocky begun to smash, a few recalled a time when Tony Zale issued body blows that stole both the opponent's, and the crowd's breath. Nothing had come easily. After racking up nine victories Tony suffered consecutive losses. He would incur four more defeats during his first year and back-to-back stoppages awaited in his next. Reflecting on these setbacks, only three bouts were fought over the next two years, leading Tony into an unfruitful 1937. In '38 a first round knockout at the hands of Jimmy Clark destroyed whatever concepts of success he was unlikely to have entertained. Managed by Sam Pain and Art Winch, the same men who'd handled Barney Ross, Zale's abilities were slow to flourish.

Billy Celebron, a fellow resident of Illinois knew a little too much for Zale, earning a draw and claiming the return bout, but these were productive encounters for "Chicago's bruising title threat". Tony received a rematch with the man who had given him his bleakest hour to stop Clark in the second after flooring him eleven, yes eleven times. Having become numb to the fear of losing, Zale bulldozed his way into contention. Reigning National Association boxing champion Al Hostak (characterized by an iron jaw and a pair of weak hands) was outpointed in a non-title fight. Securing a rematch with his apparent mastery, the immortal Benny Leonard was the third man in the ring and got a good eyeful of Zale's crippling body attack. A terribly measured right hook repeatedly caught Hostak in the twelfth to bring about his first introduction to the canvas. This rarity occurred twice more in the thirteenth, forcing a stoppage.

The middleweight scene in 1940 was a distinguished mess. Virginia's Ken Overlin disputed Zale's stake, being recognized as champion in New York and other states; then came Billy Soose. This quality boxer from Pennsylvania disturbed whatever order existed between the co-champions by outpointing the pair of them. Winning the first two rounds, Zale started well only to fall victim to Billy's educated left. The loss was decisive. This neighbouring talent was top draw, but Zale was ready to give credence to the opinion that he was "every bit as tough as the finest steel ever turned out at the mills around his home in Gary, Ind."[174] Traipsing through the boxing landscape like an undertaker, contenders were systematically buried. From Fred Apostoli, to Steve Mamakos, and back to Al Hostak, the "blonde buster" put a hurtin' on everyone. When it came to mashing Billy Pryor, quite fittingly, Jack Dempsey refereed the largest ever attendance for a boxing match (135,000). Zale disposed of him in nine rounds in Juneau Park, Milwaukee; a free-entry event organised by a local brewery. Just about anybody worth mentioning was clobbered; *just* about anybody. Georgie Abrams wasn't half bad when it came to bloody disputes, and having thrice got the better of Zale's master in Billy Soose the Washington bruiser had plenty of reason to be confident as he entered the Garden.

Experience, talent, grit; it all came together for Zale on this night. After each volley Abrams' legs were filled with lead. A knockdown in the opener got the alarm bells going. Nothing out of the ordinary, Zale proceeded to take charge and rupture a blood vessel in Abrams' right eye, leaving him visually impaired from the sixth onwards. Another dilemma was in store for Tony in the eighth, but his heavy artillery produced unanimous scores.

Mickey Walker, the crowd-pleasing 'Toy Bulldog' marked the last man to have undisputed possession over the 160lbs title. Now Zale could consider himself part of that prestigious ancestry. The handsome champion was well acquainted with warfare, but mayhem was to extend far beyond the confines of the ring as Japanese pilots targeted Pearl Harbour. Shortly before Zale made that leap from the ring to the sea, a match was arranged against Irish light-heavyweight general, Billy Conn. That courage which had insured Zale during his climb up the mountain wasn't missing, but little could be done about his larger and better schooled opponent running away with the fight. The general impression was one of disappointment as Conn failed to show any real power in his decision win. It was an ambitious task for any middleweight. Bound for Great Lakes naval training base in Illinois, Tony left for his new profession in the spring of 1942. He wouldn't fight again for three years and eleven months.

The newly styled, twenty-two-year-old Rocky Graziano was already on his way back after his little mishap. Born into a life that considered street fighting and theft top priorities, Rocky focused his energies to light up Manhattan with leather-clad violence. Put through a more merciful regime, nothing like the speed bumps Zale suffered came between Rocky's slugging. The odd decision was dropped but he was too busy for doubt to creep in.

Graziano was not a big middleweight. Customarily weighing in a whole ten pounds under the limit he was closer to welterweight, but that right hand had enough on it to trouble a heavyweight; for men of similar size it was pure hell. Poor technique allowed Brooklyn's Harold Green to carve out a victory, but in the last round Rocky needed only a moment to knock Green insensible when the final bell intervened. There was nothing of the Benny Leonard on show; it was difficult to perceive shades of Mickey

---

[174] The Vancouver Sun, 1940, Jan 30th, p.11

Walker. Graziano didn't possess rhythm, much less a game plan. Each outrageous period of milling splattered the chances of the word style ever entering a report. A man reputed for chaos deserved chaotic reportage. Writer Jack Cuddy had the beat when he identified Rocky as "a hammer-slayer on the loose."[175] It wasn't pretty, but Rocky showed the benefits of his savagery, defeating those with style and often.

Harold Green came again to win another decision, but only via a majority this time. Improvements, while not evident in his fighting were so in the results. The public welcomed Rocky like a brother, and the Garden began to act as a second home. 10,000 fans arrived for his bouts with Green. Danger was around the next corner in the shape of Billy Arnold, a nineteen-year-old slugger from Pennsylvania, owner of a KO record that could make any puncher blush. One loss, one draw and one points win put the hiccups in twenty-eight straight stoppages. Arnold was made a big 5-1 favourite. Over 14,000 were present for a night of haymakers in which the underdog got through to floor Arnold three times, compelling the referee to step in during the third. The crowd was speckled with shock, but it was just the beginning of a rip-roaring 1945. Out on the ocean, Zale looked towards another year in uniform as the boxing world grew increasingly sceptical of its middleweight king. Al 'Bummy' Davis, Freddie Cochrane, and once more, Harold Green, all told of a familiar story; you could trouble Rocky, but before the announcer called for the score cards some wild swinging was on its way to render them obsolete. The first encounter with Cochrane perfectly captured this theme of doom when, after leading by no small margin, the roof spectacularly fell in during the last round. Ring magazine rewarded it with a fight of the year stamp. Their less dramatic rematch, ending again in the tenth, raked in over 18,000 spectators and $100,000 at the gate. Graziano had developed into more of a happening than a draw. Thick waves of fans marched from the slums of the East-end for a slice of gory theatre, and to the joy of their barbarous palates, Graziano only fought one way.

While Rocky had been hitting homeruns, Adolf Hitler had perished and Berlin was captured by Soviet troops to bring an end to WWII. During the fall of 1945 it was announced by the National Boxing Association that all drafted boxers were required to defend their titles. Keeping his promise of four years past, Zale set his sights on returning with the gold. Waiting for him was a man who resurrected notions of Stanley Ketchel.

A good deal of rust was to be expected and so Zale enjoyed a string of sub-par competition to help warm his engine. Bobby Giles had the honour of welcoming him back into the ring and said his goodbyes in the fourth. A further five opponents took him into May of 1946 and none of them made it past the fifth at which point the champion was looking at a July 25th date with the New York sensation. Rocky's punches lacked their usual narcotic powers against the tough Sonny Horne, but his powers of attraction were in full flow as the unanimous decision recorded his third $100,000 gate in a row. Marty Servo had the distinction of twice giving the great Ray

[175] Greensburg Daily Tribune, 1946, Mar 30th, p.8

Robinson lots to think about and was considered fair game to come out the winner. An oxygen-taxing assembly of 19,088 generated $173,103, but Rocky was rightly psychotic, achieving a KO in the second.

The prospect of fighting Zale had the potential to eclipse everything on Rocky's quaking campaign. Younger and probably fresher, Graziano was made the slight favourite. Zale felt confident, happy with how training had gone when pains in his side and back sent him to hospital. Lower grade pneumonia was the diagnosis. Disappointment surged its way through boxing but nothing could be done except postpone the showdown until the 27th September became its new date. This minor interlude was not likely to make an impression on Zale, but for Graziano the six month gap presented an unwelcome chasm, a potential black hole for anxiety. Financially the postponement was to prove something of a blessing, allowing Mike Jacobs to extract every gram of marketability. Uncle Mike, an exponent of thinking big, was a little sour that not enough time was available to switch Graziano's fight with Servo to the spacious settings of a ball park, maximizing profit. Things were about to look up though, and no promotional trickery was required. The rematch between Joe Louis and Billy Conn, 1946s supposed super-fight went down like profanity during a sermon. The rematch that promised all the excitement of the original died after eight cringeworthy rounds. A poorly conditioned, once brilliant light-heavyweight was there for the taking.

The hospital released Zale by August 9th giving him plenty of time to prepare. Izzy Klein and Ray Arcel, both renowned for cropping winners got to work on the battle plan. The principles shared their place of training in the unmistakably stuffy confines of Lou Stillman's gym. A place of serenity it wasn't as gym rats, no-hopers and contenders all buzzed about to their own tune, causing the dust to fly and heat to swell. Every time there was a spar the press pushed against the edges of the ring in a mad dash. Catching a rest was a skill.

The thirty-two-year-old champion failed to impress; that steady manner of doing his homework was often perceived as sloppy. Impassive as ever, manager Sam Winch firmly relayed that "I have never seen the day when he was a good gymnasium fighter. He will be all right in the Yankee stadium ring Friday night, and that's where it counts."[176] Rocky did as he did, indifferently hunting men down which included a sprinkle of featherweights to sharpen a frequent want for accuracy. Primary handler, Whitey Bimstein fussed about his person constantly. Food, exercise, sleep; everything was moderated. Rocky looked like the world's worst bully getting ready for school. At the day of the weigh-in Zale took to the scales where it read bang-on the 160lbs limit. Expected to come in a portion lighter, Graziano's 154lbs was no cause for fuss. Medical examinations had also proclaimed them to be in tip-top condition. The odds believed that the younger, more active man had a better shot of coming out the victor, but there was a theory that the 7-5 draw in favour of Rocky was slightly influenced by East-enders chiming in with phantom bets. Whatever the vibe, Arch Ward of the Chicago press service wrapped up nine months' worth of predicting nicely; "Graziano

[176] Chicago Daily Tribune, 1946, Sep 25th, p.33

is rated one of the hottest glove throwers who has come along in years, but before we join his ballyhoo wagon we want to see how he takes a battering in the ribs."

When the place of fighting had reached capacity, 39,827 produced $342,497, topping Joe Louis' recent blasting of Tami Mauriello. Uncle Mike could switch off. That heavy mixture of society that fights create included Zale's four brothers, everyone a fighter; they were sure to make up for mother's disapproval. Any outdoor setting brings with it the fear of bad weather, but as the evening drew in the famed Polo Grounds suffered not a chill or splash of rain; it wasn't ideal but warm enough. Zale wore a pair of black trunks while Graziano went for something a little more imaginative in purple. When each man took to their corners a "joy-crazed, wildly yelling mob" exercised their vocal cords, ready to pay tribute to the impending bedlam. The ring was the one place in which Graziano could relive a lifestyle that no amount of hand-shaking or blazer wearing could erase. Tony Zale was cut from, if not any less soft, smoother cloth. That aged template of greased hair and big smiles fitted him perfectly, but on the call for seconds out his happy mug washed away. Ding went the bell.

Chasing didn't figure as punches erupted from either side; Rocky crouched a little with waving arms, Tony straight-up, elbows tucked in and high with the hands. A contest for highlighting technical nuances this wasn't as hard punches flew in, each one with fight-ending properties. Catching a short hook, Rocky hit the deck. Just as the crowd were discovering their seats everyone went wild. Rising in reassuring fashion at the count of four, Rocky shook off the resin to hound Zale all over the ring, guided by a fearsome spirit. The bell sounded to rescue the champion from his new predicament between Rocky's fists and the ropes. The action started to align with the odds as Graziano's thunder crashed all over the champion. In the second Graziano mashed the target wherever the momentum of his heavy swipes relocated it. During Zale's retaliation he chipped a bone in his right thumb. The whirling activity of the New Yorker acted like a tornado, sucking Zale in before pelting him from every angle. A series of right hands put Zale on the floor; a punch which was in danger of being accurate. Tony bested Rocky, getting his feet under him at three, but then came the wobbles and a very concerned corner to assist the champion back to his stool. A split lip was trivial. A damaged fist wasn't.

If new tactics were disclosed during the one minute break, nobody was listening. At the bell both men came to with about as much restraint as mistreated pit bulls. Rocky carried the honours for a second time in a wearisome third, but Zale continued to dig for gold. In the fourth Rocky's honey punch lost its way and those shots to the abdomen got the younger man wheezing out in pain to which over sixty others could relate. The fifth heat, while the slowest of the bout "was far from tame".[177] The winded challenger needed a moment, and while he took it Zale sunk in blows that could puncture a lung.

The champion seemed to be working his way towards something decisive when, quite incredibly, Graziano fired himself back up to repeat the scenes of the second. Lefts and rights got Zale retreating as they scuffed his face. The bell gently chimed

[177] Chicago Daily Tribune, 1946, Sep 28th, p.17

against the wall of noise. Tony sat down in another state of doubt. Those thirty-two-years, four of which had left his instincts to dull, were ominously close to headlining tomorrow's list of excuses. Down but not out as is often said, but Tony left the shelter of his corner in no better state than he was upon arriving; a sure sign that the end was near. Rocky ignored the lactic acid and went for it. A fight with multiple plot twists, one which had done its best to exorcise the ghosts of war looked to be preparing its epilogue. The advantage was pressed and then some when a further episode of belly blasting churned Rocky's insides. The man who knew only one gear was slammed into reverse.

It was as if Graziano had finally satisfied a four year craving when Zale later explained that "I knew what I was doing all the time from the start of the third on."[178] Zale called upon those supreme powers of resolve to plant Rocky with a leg-stiffening right to the gut. The effect was ugly and then, as he was accustomed, Zale switched the attack to the head. Down went Rocky. Former welterweight Ruby Goldstein assumed the position amid a clutter of whistles and jeers. Beginning to count, Rocky slowly evolved into a squatting position. He would later applaud that preceding body slug but "it was plain that he didn't know what had hit him."[178] At "five" his head started to clear and at "eight" he looked good to go. Goldstein did his best to penetrate the din with "nine". Ready for more, Rocky achieved vertical only to hear "ten" at the 1:43 mark. Confused then angry, Rocky's embers were still blazing, but as the ring filled with officials the beaten fighter held his tongue. The underdog, the one hit with "everything but the ring post"[179] kept his title.

Having the means to continue with your career after WWII marked one of the biggest obstacles in gloved history. Tony had confronted a man eight years his junior, no less with a style designed to mash your bones to rubble. Absorbing it all to give better, the Man of Steel embraced his alias. The Edward J. Neil memorial trophy and Ring magazine's fighter of the year distinctions went to Zale. As a consolation prize, Rocky shared his second consecutive fight of the year award. Gene Tunney could not recall better. Sixty-six-year-old Uncle Mike, improving in hospital after a cerebral haemorrhage and heart attack, received second place for his undying commitment to sculpting events.

Tough times were overdue for Graziano and came in the form of bribery. Scheduled to fight Ruben Shank, he was presented with \$100,000 to throw the fight; something he seriously considered before feigning a back injury. Legal squabble delayed the rematch from March of 1947 to July, but Rocky made good of his success in the first encounter to have the referee stop the contest in the sixth with Zale doubled over the ropes in another fight of the year. His post-fight declaration that "somebody up there likes me!" led the way for Paul Newman to replay his story on the big screen. Their third bout, the decider occurred the year later, but more controversy was on its way. That 'incident' from the forces came back to dirty Rocky's name that bit more. The state of Illinois banned him from fighting there while America let out a patriotic sigh.

178 Chicago Daily Tribune, 1946, Sep 28th, p.17

179 Oxnard Press-Courier, 1946, Sep 28th, p.2

New Jersey became the fight's new home. Zale, a big thirty-four-year-old underdog turned heads again as he put on the most clinical display of the three fights, finishing up in the third. When Rocky's body fell limp, a chapter had officially closed. The spiky-haired brawler would fight on after Marcel Cerdan had pulverised Zale in 1948, but that savage joy had consumed itself.

"When Graziano threw straight lefts and brought around his rights, Tony weaved in under him, according to our plans"[180] explained Art Winch following the rubber match. Once his head had stopped spinning, Rocky let out the embarrassing truth that he had actually tried to think his way through this one, something which caused him to stutter his way to defeat. Fortunately, the thrashing brought him back to his senses. You could say a discovery had been made. "Every time I try to think, I take a hell of a licking."

[180] The Milwaukee Journal, 1948, Jun 11th, p.10

WILLIE PEP
VS.
SANDY SADDLER

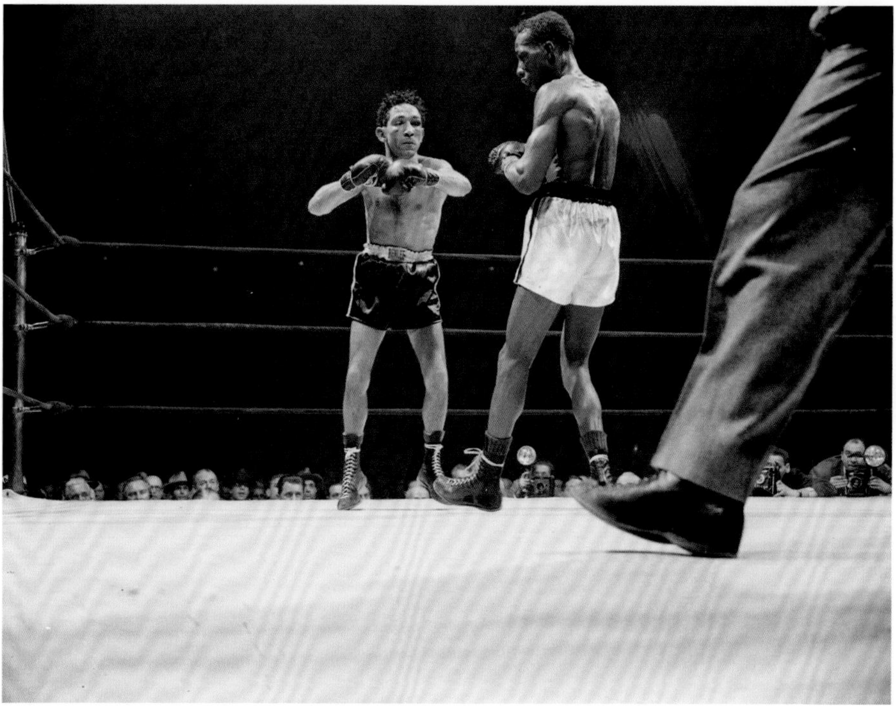

February 11th, 1949
World Featherweight Title
New York, New York

To be great you need to beat great fighters. It's not the rule, but it's the most common factor. After viewing Willie Pep float to victory everyone knew he was nothing less than special, but when crunch time came in the form of Sandy Saddler the ring knighted the pair with four fights of disorderly brilliance. This went beyond a rivalry. Trying to mention one without the other is impossible. In a 1940's featherweight division the swift movement of Pep bagged the decisions while the violent ambushes of Saddler beat his man to the floor. When united they merged their differences plus fouling, lots of fouling. "I never boxed rough or tough with anyone except Sandy Saddler…he made me lose my head."[181]

Fighting dirty is an unspoken skill. It's not just about disguising single fouls but setting a tone that leaves the referee confused as to what's legal. Saddler routinely stepped outside of the rule book with deceptive expertise. He'd hit you and then use the rest of his arm to swell your face up, maybe a lace to slit it, resourceful person he was. Even in his twilight years Saddler's efficient ploys ruined a wonderful effort from the talented 'Flash' Elorde after his eyes were hammered shut. Saddler was willing to go to dark lengths for the win but it was skin colour, not the vigilante attitude, which would again make things difficult. For years Sandy would be left to chew on the pond dwellers while his infinitely whiter adversary reaped the benefits of a milky complexion. Joe Louis had done much but the basic agenda against Negroes remained corrosive. "The black man in this country, he have to do twice as hard as the white man to gain anything"[182] recalled Saddler. It would take a gruelling total of ninety-four fights before playing second fiddle ended and the name Sandy Saddler struck fear into anyone who made a pass near 130lbs. Until then, the lanky fighter had to suffer the waiting game.

"He delivered his left jab with sharpness and precision and actually outgeneraled Bartolo, whose forte was supposed to be his boxing ability."[183] First successful defence for Pep spelt another whitewash. A year prior, hard-punching Chalky Wright had done his utmost to stop Willie from taking his 126lbs title which amounted to clutching on to three rounds. In the other twelve Pep had Wright on the slippery slope, overreaching and crossing legs. Barely over twenty and he already looked invincible. There had been that one blip against Sammy Angott, a natural lightweight, interrupting a 63-0 winning streak, but now at the right weight all opposition got lost in his box of tricks.

Pep executed sequences of movements uncommon to boxing. "He who fights and runs away lives to fight another day" became the motto, but never had using the ring been so seductive. With an open guard and wide swings it could look a bit scrappy at first glance, but then his dazzling ability to read the opponent became apparent. Catching him was like trying to seize a feather in a gale. The favourite story to highlight his 'Will o' the Wisp' legend occurred in 1946. During the third round of his bout with Jackie Graves it had been reported that Pep had tipped a few officials off that he was going to win the said round without throwing a punch. Technically,

[181] In This Corner, Peter Heller, 1973, p.254

[182] In This Corner, Peter Heller, 1973, p.293

[183] Hartford Courant, 1946, Jun 8th, p.1

Pep admitted to have "jabbed him a few times"[184] but there was plenty of eye-catching ducking, slipping and spinning.

Supported by the savvy abilities of manager Lou Viscusi and trainer Bill Gore, Pep fought often and continued winning, skating towards what would accumulate into another astounding unbeaten streak of 73-0. In numerous towns he re-matched, tormented and conquered all fighters who were willing to chase him around the ring. New York resident, Phil Terranova represented some of the better competition around but he only managed to claim a third of the fifteen rounds. When newspapers reported that Pep had won another lopsided decision they did not print so hesitantly. Systematic illusions were cast, fight after fight, round after round. If being boxer-proof was such a thing, Pep was it. A fighter of the year award was stamped on him in 1945, taking him up to 1946 where he whipped up 18-0 in seven months. Twenty-three years young, world champion and without a scratch; life could only get worse.

Trouble must have seemed distant as Pep fell asleep on a plane trip from Miami to Newark. It was to be a disastrous journey. The aircraft, later found out to have been operating on a dangerously low fuel supply, got caught in a snowstorm. The crew did their best to circle some farmland before the left wing was ripped off causing an emergency landing. A crushed nose saw to it that the co-pilot and two of the passengers did not escape. The other nineteen survived, Pep being one of them; that at the expense of two cracked vertebrae, a broken left leg and chest injuries. His battered body was hospitalized. Three whole months, from casts to crutches, Pep, as expected, made a full recovery. Six months later he was back in the ring. Doctors A.W. Brannon, John W. Larrabee and Mauriee M. Pike seated themselves in the Hartford Auditorium to watch their former patient. A mix of expectation and doubt surrounded the champion but did nothing to stop him from having a field day with Mexican, Victor Flores. Two knockdowns put a few sparkles on a performance that involved (you guessed it) taking every round.

The Hartford Courant reported that "It was the concensus of those who had seen Pep's first return to the ring after previous layoffs of eight and nine months duration while he served in two branches of the armed services that Willie's performance last night was infinitely better than either of the other two."[185] Bill Gore kept a wary eye on that back for fear of potential strain but Pep was certainly not limping about the ring. The crash had not, at least noticeably, affected his ability, though this opinion may have been tainted with a little hometown bias, eager to coronate their hero's return. Saddler on the other hand couldn't be better; a spritely twenty-two, never anything less than in optimal trim and continually handling opponents as if aspirations were blasphemous. Future lightweight guru Joe Brown suffered a second round blowout when he got in the way of Sandy's busy, concussive schedule. Save the odd points defeat, everyone was getting mugged. Chico Rosa managed to put one of those black dots on Saddler's record in a disputed split decision, but it did nothing to slow the Harlem puncher who proceeded to trounce Kid Zefine and Aquiliono Allen in two

[184] In This Corner, Peter Heller, 1973, p.253

[185] Hartford Courant, 1947, Jun 18th, p.1

rounds apiece. By now the fight count had reached ninety-two without a mere glimpse at a world title. Such a career could have easily slipped into the doomed continuum where every other talented black was held hostage. Fortunately, the end was about to justify the means.

On the 11th September discussion of Pep's next defence got underway; a choice between Rosa and Saddler which soon went in the latter's favour. The big date was set for the 29th October. To Saddler, a fighter whose lifestyle did not secrete an iota of smoke or booze, this meant everything, all the setbacks, all the waiting he had had to endure, he was determined to take these niggles and let his fists hammer them into something agreeable. The champion had plenty of reason to be concerned on this occasion, but pre-fight remarks such as "Saddler's record, although impressive, does not compare with Pep's"[186] were tainting his focus. In preparation Pep sparred with former bane of Saddler, Humberto Sierra. Feeling their way around a routine session, Sierra later removed every last crumb of pressure. "You win, you win easy."[187]

Bang on 124lbs, Saddler conceded one and a half pounds to his celebrated opponent. Reporter Pat Robinson observed of the elongated challenger that it "looks as if a strong wind would blow him over"[188] but he was about to receive a most dramatic reminder that looks can be deceiving. When the bell went and they came to Saddler's slender body trudged forward with arms that looked heavy and dense, contemptuous of any strong wind Pep may try to invoke. The champion moved about to his usual, arbitrary jig, but Sandy marched inside to get his nose leaking in the opener. Nothing out of the norm, save for the challenger's tenacity, Pep found his rhythm a little better in the second, landing with a few clever counters. In the third, Saddler, whom throughout the first two periods seemed to be agitated with excess energy lashed out. Three uppercuts were funnelled in between Pep's guard, numbing the senses. He followed up his advantage with a left hook, bringing Pep to his knees. Up at the count of nine, another left, this time to the stomach, put him down again. The bell then came in to offer the dazed champion a paltry minute rest. Indifferently it sounded again to push Pep back into the bleakest situation of his career. The fired-up man from Harlem blocked all exits on the possibility of a comeback. Pep was hounded all around the ring until Saddler, again whipping in his favoured left hand, rendered him prostrate. Feebly rolling on to his front, referee Ruby Goldstein counted the brave little man out before he got his shaky pins under him.

Those close to the scene took a moment to absorb what had just happened while the majority of the distant 14,685 began a steady chorus of booing. The odds, originally locked at 14-5, had fluctuated some to fuel the ever-willing rumour of a fix. Defeated just once in 137 contests, there was certainly reason to raise an eyebrow or two but the following day, Eddie Egan, chairman for New York's boxing commission, concluded that "The bout appeared honestly contested. Pep just didn't seem to have his former legs after he was nailed in the third round."[189] Was Saddler all wrong for

[186] Sarasota Herald-Tribune, 1948, Oct 29th, p.9

[187] The Milwaukee Journal, 1949, Feb 8th, p.2

[188] The Miami News, 1948, Oct 30th, p.4

Hartford's finest or was there something else to it? No doubt the former idea was vented as everyone began to file out of the arena, but a few men began a delicate counter-argument; perhaps Pep *hadn't* fully recovered from last year's crash.

Pep "no longer has the amazing leg-speed that made him a phantom before the New Jersey crash" reflected writer Jack Cuddy.[190] Another harmonized, explaining that "Peps lack of foot-speed last night indicated that he had not regained the lightening elusiveness...in his pre-accident days."[191] At twenty-six years of age you'd be hard-pressed to claim to have seen anything of the geriatric in Pep's performance, but Saddler's manager Charley Johnston perceived just that, "Pep has nothing left to threaten Saddler with. It's my opinion that he's burned out after 137 professional bouts."[191] Around the boxing fraternity, Pep's misfortune stood out as the one major blip. Every other contemporary headliner had prevailed; Ray Robinson over Kid Gavilan, Ezzard Charles over Jimmy Bivins, Ike Williams over Beau Jack and Marcel Cerdan over Tony Zale. And worse yet the road back to redemption looked dubious. Charged with a wicked confidence, Saddler blazed through another four bodies with only one being able to endure the full ten. Pep stepped back inside the ring within two months, consoling his year of calamity with an easy decision over Hermie Freeman.

The start of 1949 enlisted the fallen with one priority and one priority only; to get back what was once his. Everything that Pep was known for, the captivating movement, the impeccable record and wisecracking was driven into the ground compliments of a single man and his dreaded left hand. The topic used to revolve around how many times Willie would make his opponent miss. Now it was if boxing would ever see that magic strut again. History was also against the little boxer. No man had ever regained the 126lbs title during its sixty year lifespan. As early as 1943 Pep was received as the best thing since Abe Attell, but this was unknown territory. True to his manager's word, that he'd "be glad to fight Pep at any time",[191] Saddler arranged a rematch well within the six months allotted for a champion to defend his property.

The rematch, set for February 11th unearthed great interest. Intended for Madison Square Garden, the famous arena was still recovering from the whirlwinds of leather served up by Rocky Graziano. The last time the Garden was filled to capacity was to watch Rockabye Rocky make short work of Marty Servo in 1946. In preparation for the rematch both fighters opted for a January tune-up in over-the-weight contests. First Saddler got his claws on Panamanian Young Finnegan on the 16th. Finnegan came back strong after a poor start, cutting Saddler and briefly giving as good as he got, but the stand was short lived as the champion steamrolled him in the fifth. Pep fought the following day to iron out some more creases with a decision over native boxer Teddy Davis. Strangely, the odds during the build-up were almost dead even. People questioned Saddler's ability to repeat last October's carnage. Much had been postulated in the aftermath of Pep's quick demise but a popular theory insisted that the former champion had simply, as he admitted himself, underestimated the spindly

---

[189] The Milwaukee Journal, 1948, Oct 30th, p.2

[190] The Montreal Gazette, 1948, Oct 29th, p.8

[191] The Pittsburgh Press, 1948, Oct 30th, p.7

slugger. The biggest advocates of this belief were, naturally, his loyal fans. A motley of support from all over Connecticut; from Hartford, New Haven and Bridgeport, towns were supplied with special trains to efficiently channel 6,000 New England fans into an arena which was racing to capacity. Pulling out the stops to attend, people stood willing to pay $30 for $10 seats. $1.50 got you a variety seat, designed to squeeze in as many casuals as possible.

To get that 5' 8" frame into perfect working order, Saddler prepared at his training camp in Summit, N.J., the same place where he had honed those title-snatching moves. Sandy was just as diligent as he had been first time around; a few days before the big event he was declared to be in that "same magnificent physical condition."[192] Pep secluded himself to his hometown in an attempt to eliminate whatever was thought to be encroaching on his genius. Sport columnist Frank K. Corkin, Jr offered that "If the Will O' the wisp wants his crown back…he'll have to be the Pep of old."[193] Exactly what version of Pep would appear, boxing would have to wait and see, but things had gone swimmingly enough for *The Hartford Courant* to state that Pep is "ready for the most important test of his brilliant ring career." The big night was to headline a program featuring welterweight phenomenon Sugar Ray Robinson and light-heavyweight kingpin Ezzard Charles. This time the featherweight division was to take boxing's mantle. Saddler was most journalists' pick to win, sooner rather than later, but through a tangled route Pep winded up the 5-6 on favourite. Regardless, the odds weren't going to protect the challenger.

The noise produced inside the famed arena was quite unlike anything else. Almost half of the ticket holders vouched for the former champion, desperate to witness his reprisal. Escaping the delirium proved hard for the officials. Instructions were overcome by the din which hummed through each tier like surges of electricity. It was no exaggeration when Bob Zaiman reported from ringside that Pep's introduction unleashed "a roar that rocked the Garden."[194] Saddler's sleek body looked awesome. The crowd, if not entirely against him, was certainly not behind the champion, but for the man about to compete in his 100th professional bout the atmosphere couldn't spark any concern. Pep was very still as his mind searched for that detached clarity which all combative arts treasure. A good start was vital. If another early night was on the cards Sandy wouldn't hesitate.

When the bell went one thing seemed to bubble inside the challenger's head, "must be fast out of the blocks!" Carrying out that instruction in style, Pep engaged his dark menace firmly but cautiously. Four, five, six jabs were streamed out in rapid sequence before dashing to the side, backwards, anywhere out of the taller man's range. The challenger was not free from nerves. This timidity did more good than harm as Pep snatched the opener with his feverish pelting. The second round showed them no less fresh than they were three minutes ago, each anticipating distress signals. Saddler managed to get inside Pep's guard, but, remembering how he'd fallen victim,

[192] The Hartford Courant, 1949, Feb 8th, p.13

[193] The Meriden Daily Journal, 1949, Feb 7th, p.4

[194] The Hartford Courant, 1949, Feb 13th, p.6

the challenger clamped down on Sandy's left arm with his right. When referee Eddie Joseph managed to separate the boxers, not without some difficulty, Pep stepped on Saddler's foot causing him to trip. Taking the honours for a second time, the predominantly New England crowd let their idol know how they felt about it with rapturous applause. There was a cinematic quality to the evening.

The third round presented Sandy with the same irritable dodger. Pep was actually sent back to his corner for excessive application of Vaseline on his left arm and neck, designed to foil Saddler's urge to hold n' hit. He continued to measure the challenger with unblinking eyes but things weren't going to plan. Sandy dropped another session, though not without leaving his mark as Pep walked back to his corner, blood seeping from his right cheek. Focusing on the red stuff Saddler made the superficial wound his target. A few swings managed to scuff Pep's head, disturbing those boyish curls. It was enough to get the judges' attention, and in the fifth Saddler scarred his left cheek with another swipe. Hartford's little wonder started to look like he was in a fight. The blood harmlessly trickled down his face, but the pace was such it was a challenge in itself for reporters to exaggerate. Big gulps of air were needed in between Willie's lunges and endless scurrying. Great sequences of ducking, slipping and weaving were carried out, often leaving Sandy staring out into the crowd. Growing in confidence with every passing round, Pep stepped into his punches and complemented that jab with an accurate cross.

Rounds six to nine were very close, arguably a couple belonged to Saddler, but the momentum was with his agile foe who caused a shiver in the eighth. Many thought to have Pep sussed; "the former champion, at 26 definitely is not the fighter he used to be",[195] but right now Sandy was slowly drowning. The tenth whipped around, firing Pep back into ring centre. The champion, avidly stalking since the first gong, looked no closer to solving the problems when the unlikely weapon, his right hand, thudded home. Steadying his aim, Saddler ruined Pep's silky movement with a single punch. An instant hush cast over the event as legs quivered. What was a slight blemish now came out like a small egg under Pep's right eye as he used Saddler's chest for cover. Snapping out of the daze, Pep got Saddler back on to his terms. Things were getting rough.

In the eleventh the pair fell through the ropes as they each tried to foul the other. Taking round ten as a stiff reminder to keep moving, Pep fought Sandy all over the ring, getting him in such a state of fatigue that "his long arms and skinny legs flopped about as if he was coming apart."[196] Clasping on to the driver's seat Willie refused to budge, leading the way in the eleventh, twelfth and thirteenth rounds. Catching a few, a slash over the right brow improved the challenger's injuries into a bloody mess. Round fourteen revived this nasty game of cat and mouse when Saddler tagged Pep's chin again with "the same kind of bombs that had dumped him last time." Using every scrap of his dwindling strength, Saddler came at Pep with "everything except broken beer bottles." Dripping on the canvas, looking decidedly beat, Pep managed to

[195] Edmonton Journal, 1949, Feb 11th, p.10

[196] The Newburgh News, 1949, Feb 12th, p.11

shake some tension back into those rubbery legs; they needed as much spring as they could muster for the last three minutes. Saddler came out for the fifteenth with all the realisation of a man who probably wouldn't get a second chance.

Pep skidded around the ring like a car about to total. Cuts over both brows did their best to cover as much of his white mug; distorting the youthful portrait into a lump of flesh. For a third time Saddler separated opponent from senses. Pep winced under the vicious incoming. It was all getting a bit too much. Ominously the champion pressed forward, his body instinctively drawn towards wounded prey. Pep indeed looked, as many newspapers would later echo, that he was fighting for his life. The dying moments were set to have a very literal meaning. Instead a mesmeric turning of the tide brought the Garden to its feet. Spinning his man, Pep leapt in with both fists, plastering any target. Most of the crowd sprung up in jubilation to see their idol resist defeat. The final bell clanged sending the fighters back into the care of their trainers. A moment of relative quiet received the decision when "wild turmoil broke out in the Garden" as Pep was awarded a unanimous decision. Scores of 9-5, 9-6 and 10-5 crowned the new champion.

The opportunity to bask under the limelight was short-lived as the winner was taken to the refuge of his cloak room. Ice was applied to his angry swelling and then it was into the shower, though the new champion was so tired that Bill Gore had to wash him. When the time came for the press to obtain the champion's secret blueprints, Willie casually offered, "He didn't catch me off guard this time."[197] In the other room Sandy sat, oblivious to cuts worn over each eye as a deep melancholy held him. The manner in which referee Eddie Joseph handled the rough stuff was scrutinised; something which Johnston championed as having jeopardised their chances. Sore loser or a fair complaint, victory was not to be dampened and the spiel lost credibility in a few days. 30% of the $87,563 gate was claimed by each fighter, but nothing could put a sparkle in Saddler's teary eyes. Red Smith from *The Washington Post* gave Pep his dues but concluded on a vengeful note, "Sandy will get the title back...he'll catch Willie sooner or later and belt him out."[198] He was right about the catching part. Twice more the odd couple would pair up, once in 1950 and once in 1951 during which time Saddler relieved Orlando Zulueta of his junior-lightweight title. In the rubber match at Yankee stadium, Pep moved about well. All the tricks were on display and the judges were back on his side. He couldn't, however, steer clear of the rough stuff and ended up retiring after round eight with a dislocated shoulder. The final encounter transpired at the Polo Grounds with every intention to deliver a conclusion. Instead, boxing was served one of its dirtiest episodes.

It was written that referee Ray Miller's hair "stayed combed about 10 seconds after giving instructions"[199] as he tried to reason with two men insistent on fouling. Only for imagination could points have been awarded as they thumbed, laced, tripped and even throttled with such blatancy it was as if they'd never received a single warning in

[197] The Evening Independent, 1949, Feb 12th, p.8

[198] The Washington Post, 1949, Feb 13th, p.C3

[199] The Telegraph-Herald, 1951, Sep 27th, p.12

their eighteen years of fighting. The clutch n' thump technique returned to deck Pep in the second. For a third time he came off the worst, retiring after the ninth with a deep cut above his right eye. Saddler didn't lose his title and neither had their purse withheld, but both licences were revoked on the trifling basis that the fight "violated every rule in the book."[200]

Pep fought on, mainly against fringe contenders to bring home the bacon. Flashes of brilliance brought grins from ringside but Willie slowly regressed into the second stage of a fighter's life, when nothing is left to learn but everything is hard to do. Quite incredibly, he carried on a good nineteen years after his near fatal accident, not retiring until 1966. The younger man from Harlem kept punching in good company. He retired two fights later in 1957, faced with the prospect of total blindness if he continued.

Perusing over the last six decades, the featherweight division has been more waterlogged than starved of talent; men like Jim Driscoll, Vincente Saldivar, Salvador Sanchez and Marco Antonio Barrera each helped to shape their eras, yet nothing quite like the anarchy that Willie Pep and Sandy Saddler whipped up has been seen since. From brutal beginnings things transgressed, almost into the realms of comedy. When enough time had passed to reminisce, the one thing that nobody forgot was how the vanquished came back to reclaim his throne. "They introduce Pep, Pep and I would be at a fight at the Garden, and they'll say, "One of the greatest featherweights, Willie Pep. Here's another retired champ, Sandy Saddler."[201] Weary from the racial divide in his country, Saddler was forced to take a back seat every time his pearly nemesis slipped into conversation. Nobody could ever doubt Pep's brilliance, it's just so that his finest hour came against a man who had his number.

Pulling himself together after his famous defeat, "Everything's all right"[202] said the coloured fighter, ready for that icy breeze whistling down Eighth Avenue, "...it's one of those things."

---

[200] The Milwaukee Sentinal, 1951, Oct 6th, p.5 (Robert Christenbury)

[201] Peter Heller, In This Corner, 1973, p.293

[202] The Washington Post, 1949, Feb 12th, p.3

'SUGAR' RAY ROBINSON
VS.
RANDOLPH TURPIN

July 10th, 1951
World Middleweight Title
London, England

May 17, 1966. Out in the leafy repose of Leamington Spa, the four walls of his room at Gwen's Transport Cafe are the first to witness Randy Turpin's dead body. In the chest and just above the eye are fresh bullet wounds. A revolver sits next to the lifeless body as does Randy's seventeen month old daughter Carmen; she's in critical condition. A soon-to-be-discovered suicide note proclaims his love to wife Gwyneth. Two Lonsdale belts and that glorious world championship belt remain in his possession after attempting to sell them for more than twenty thousand dollars. By any means necessary was the ex-boxer willing to assuage a haunting streak of debt, even if it meant pawning his pride n' joy. Driven to the scrapyard after being declared bankrupt in 1962, a $560,000 career, built of blood, sweat and tears allowed carelessness to undo it all quicker than that 48 second knockout of Luc Van Damme. Five houses, eight cars and one divorce later, Randy's pocket had developed a hole.

There were echoes of Joe Louis as he tried his hand at professional wrestling but compared to the bright lights of Earl's Court it made for a poor substitute. Helping his wife supply the passers-by of everyday life began to disturb Randy's sense of identity. No boxer takes retirement in their stride and very few successfully mourn. For many it is a difficult process where nature condemns the ageing fighter long into the winter of life. A year had not passed since fellow Brit Freddie Mills was found slumped over the wheel of his car with a rifle by his side. Like Turpin, Mills had become captive to dark thoughts.

Police are not long for the scene and the following day promoter Andrew Griffith's sentiments are printed that Randy "was down in the dumps of late."[203] Common with suicides, nobody could see it coming. As nostalgia goes few British men have experienced anything like the rapturous scenes of Leamington Spa as residents huddled around the town hall to salute their new middleweight champion. Having grown accustomed to shifting sandwiches and coffee, it is a memory that must have felt like it belonged to another life. The overnight sensation to which all others are measured, Randy was the one who had licked Sugar Ray Robinson before 18,000. It registered as the biggest upset in boxing history since Max Schmeling let Joe Louis have it with his right hand, sixteen years earlier. Just why it was such a momentous occasion requires something to be said about the loser born Walker Smith Jr.

Whenever the dark, slender figure of Mr Smith took its residence in the opposing corner, the aficionados were on mute. His performances carried an exhibitive air about them which could perfume a knockout. The ease of his movements captured the showmanship of a man who enjoyed tap-dancing in his spare time. This restless flair of his worked its way into everyday gym chores like jumping rope and drumming the speed ball, doubling as alternate forms of entertainment.

Raised in Detroit, Walker rounded off a trio of children. As a juvenile he had that indefatigable zest for life, for all sports, anything that came his way he sought to command. Boxing swiftly took top priority and his family watched on in intrigue as the small kid bounced off the walls with unannounced instances of shadow boxing. His assortment of talents kept pace with his confidence which got him off to a golden

---

[203] The Spokesman Review, 1966, May 18th, p.14

start inside the ropes during 1938. Indulging in a little bit of trickery as had idol Joe Louis, Walker hid behind the stage name of Ray Robinson, originally appointed by manager George Gainford, enabling the unlicensed Walker to join a card that was one fighter down. Ray Robinson was actually another fighter, but after a few bouts there seemed no sense in changing it and so Walker Smith Jr became Ray Robinson. This was later amended to 'Sugar' Ray Robinson when Gainford responded to an admirer that he was "as sweet as".

Robinson would later inform author Peter Heller, "I was very poor all my life… until I got started fighting."[204] And so began an amazing string of success. Capturing various Golden Gloves titles with plenty to spare, Robinson enjoyed a stellar amateur career which reads 85 wins, 2 defeats, 69 knockouts (40 of which transpired in the first round). The Harlem 'string-bean' did not miss a beat, turning pro less than a year after his final amateur victory against Tony Ancona. Already accustomed to the big crowds, there was plenty of familiarity in the surroundings, and so to in the outcomes. Frazzled by Robinson's lightening, Puerto Rica's Joe Echevarria set the example when he fell in two. From October 1940 to the end of 1942, Robinson competed in forty bouts, averaging out at nearly three bouts per month, many during the same week. In every one he was the master. A spindly lightweight grew into a well-muscled welterweight, one who must be champion. For the longest time Robinson ranked as the best fighter at 147lbs minus the belt. Attractively moving about the ring before pulling the plug, the superiority was Brown-Bomberesque.

Bout 41 welcomed bulletproof middleweight, Jake LaMotta. The 'Bronx Bull' returned again after dropping a decision; a 16lbs advantage was used to send Robinson through the ropes. The knockdown paid dividends, giving LaMotta the nod and Robinson a strange blemish on his otherwise faultless crusade. In their four remaining battles Robinson prevailed. Here as is often though, the final tally fails to convey the competitiveness of their rivalry. Jesting about their sixty-five rounds, Robinson later chimed, "we almost got married."

Nearing the end of 1943, Robinson entered the war along with Joe Louis to boost morale with exhibitions. The stay was not for long however as Ray got honourably discharged under suspicious circumstances. Patriotic scruples aside, in October 1944, Izzy Jannazzo was done in two, launching a second winning binge. A few trips to the canvas recited the fact that no man has everything, but save the occasional referee interruption, Robinson blurred that fantastical line between man and a force of nature. From 147-160lbs, opponents were dismantled in perfectly cued scenes. Noteworthy debris included Ohio's aspiring Tommy Bell and Cincinnati's own Sugar man, George Costner. When Costner came to fight in front of more than 20,000 at Chicago stadium, it was as if there was a secondary challenge for Robinson to see who the real 'Sugar' was. No prizes for guessing who won. Another close shave came thanks to Jose Basora. A 7-1 underdog, the body-snatching Puerto Rican came "within an

---

[204] In This Corner, Peter Heller, 1973, p.278

eyelash"[205] of defeating the 'uncrowned welterweight king', fighting him to a draw. There were no more blips for the next six years.

LaMotta made his second stand of 1945 against Robinson, dropping a split decision over twelve rounds. Again it was a thrilling encounter with late rallies tilting things in the lighter man's favour. 1946 was the most vital year yet. Fourteen straight wins, from January to November put Robinson at the doorstep of Tommy Bell's title, vacated by Marty Servo in September. The only person left to prevent what appeared to be a foregone conclusion shook boxing, if only for an instance. In a handicap match, middleweight Artie Levine planned on using his extra bulk to pull the upset. The venerable Ray Arcel proposed beforehand that "He (Artie) will weigh-in at 160 at noon-but he's going to put away two healthy meals before the fight, which may raise his weight to 164. That extra poundage could be the difference."[206] The chance to utilise this victual scheme came in the fourth when Artie wound up every muscle of his stocky build and hooked Robinson's jaw. The effects were near disastrous, but Robinson arose to suck it all up and exhibit some equally impressive powers of resolve. The only way in which Levine could win passed leaving Robinson to infuse his fencing with fire. The bout had 12,000 screaming in approval which Robinson concluded with nineteen seconds left. Scratched but unscathed, Ray's smooth face kept its cheeky optimism as he locked both eyes on Bell. Hardly a body, Tommy fought defiantly, flooring Robinson in the second and forcing the fight at every turn. Indeed, installed with the routinely daunting odds of 5-1, Bell contested with such intensity it was written that, "Never before has a welterweight dared to take such liberties."[207] Gallantry does not always thrive in the ring however; a precept which paved the way for Bell's unanimous defeat.

Robinson used his latest injection of Franklin to feed that quirk for the finer things. Conscious to make sure nothing was missing he employed a personal barber, masseur and valet, all of whom split chores to bring out the movie star in the champion. To put an exclamation mark on this swagger of his, Robinson would drive his band of merry men, or entourage, around in an incredibly pink, pink Cadillac. He looked to be heading towards financial ruin, but there was a vigilance to match Ray's flamboyance. He was nobody's man but his own, and if the circumstances weren't right, be it gate receipts, profit from the film, or he did not think himself to be 100% ready, he'd pull out without a pause. This unmovable hustle of his came to in the wake of a tragic encounter with Jimmy Doyle.

Ray would recall how the night before their bout he dreamt about killing Doyle. His superstitions ordered that he confer with priests and other men of theology to put him at ease. His reserve to cancel the fight remained but it went ahead. Robinson lapped up the rounds as was expected, and then followed the curtain call; a pinpoint left hook that zipped its way through Doyle's jaw, rendering his body limp. His head bounced off the floor. Referee Jackie Davis reached nine at the bell but Doyle remained

205 The Telegraph-Herald, 1945, May 15th, p.9

206 Spokane Daily Chronicle, 1946, Nov 5th, p.11

207 The Calgary Herald, 1946, Dec 21st, p.21

on his back. Just fifteen months ago Jimmy was making his way to the hospital after losing to Levine. He wasn't to get another chance and died shortly after arrival. He was twenty-two. Every boxer is liable to lose their edge after witnessing an opponent die by their hand. Ezzard Charles' nasty side went into hibernation after killing Sam Baroudi. Fortunately, Robinson's ability to get rid of his man did not depart, but memories from Cleveland gave the coming months an eerie quality. A brave face was put on and he continued to cut down the hard workers and rising talents. All of Ray's talents were needed to overcome the super-resistant, bolo-punching Kid Gavilan. Twice they fought, once in a non-title bout in '48 and again in '49 for the belt; each time Robinson needed that extra gear to outshine his gifted rival. They never met again but Gavilan's tenure as 147lbs champion was just around the corner. 3000 miles over the Atlantic, clubbing his way into contention, the quaint Randolph Turpin took his first steps into Robinson's universe.

Whenever the bell sounded you could be sure of Turpin's unsuspecting fury to make more than a cameo. Though certainly not wanting for gunpowder he wasn't a real blaster, more of a thumper who swatted you about. There were shadows of Scotland's great Benny Lynch in his preference for wide swings, but there was a pinch of awkwardness; back very straight and plenty of curious dipping. While not the darkest of coloured folk, Randy was ultimately a Negro. A few years ago that would have denied him the opportunity to gain ownership to a British title but the colour bar officially collapsed when older brother Dick outpointed Vince Hawkins in 1948. Gaining the British middleweight title, coloured fighters were no longer secluded to juggle the racially-appointed Empire belt. Dick kept the title until Albert Finch turned the tables in 1950. Randy had refused to face his brother while champion, now the gates were open for the twenty-two-year-old to let his fists fly. Finch's boxing ability hoped to numb those early assaults but failed when a right hand put him out in the fifth. The younger, more promising Turpin received his first taste of glory.

Randy didn't look like a world-beater; there was a general inaccuracy and greenness about him which reporters were not shy in noting. Britain were more impressed with the results and got behind their man. When it was time to dance his hair was shaved around the sides, creating that marine look. A well-muscled body with broad shoulders caught the eye, but he often had the look of a timid child, as if that impressive figure was painted on. Observations aside, it was Randy's punches that continued to have a negative effect. The logical leap for European honours was scintillatingly completed with a first round knockout over Netherlands' Luc Van Damme. Luc had also fallen before Robinson during his campaign in Europe; a well-planned jaunt which made him $45,000 better off.

On his return in 1950, Robinson was pushing thirty and those 147lbs were finding it easier to stabilise at 160. Meanwhile LaMotta had wrested the middleweight championship off Marcel Cerdan. Their sixth fight, fondly remembered as the 'St Valentine's Day Massacre' captured widespread interest. The last time they had fought was nearly six years ago, but their rivalry was well known. This heavier version of

Robinson was not considered quite as brilliant as the welterweight edition, but LaMotta's body was put through a grinder in order to make the weight; game to the core but gassing badly, Robinson forced referee Frank Sikora to intervene during the thirteenth. Ray collected his second title, but the real story was that, for all his scything combinations, LaMotta stayed upright. The new champion entertained the idea of fighting for the light-heavyweight title, but before that became a reality off he went again to dazzle Europe. It was smooth sailing in France, Switzerland and Belgium, but in Germany bottles were propelled at Robinson after he crippled Gerhard Hecht with a kidney blow, later rendered a no contest. Eighteen days prior Robinson had added one more casualty to his Euro-tour; that being Britain's finest. Rereading the small print as had become customary, Robinson made sure a rematch was compulsory, if he lost. He wasn't genuinely concerned about Turpin getting the better of him, but the potential to lose out due to a foul was a cause for worry; if one of his kidney specials did a mischief the expected 18,000 weren't likely to exercise their powers of forgiveness.

Turpin had never fought outside of England. This did not do much for his reputation in the West, but enough Englishmen were behind the 'Leamington Licker' to give this fight global significance. Three days sufficed for it to sell out and Robinson was scheduled to receive his biggest purse yet at $84,000. Though manager George Middleton thought the fight was more of a "50/50 affair" it didn't change the fact Randy was a 3-1 underdog. Many preferred 4-1. The champion had gone undefeated for the last eight years through a whopping ninety-three fights. Robinson's latest effort came against Cyril Delanoit who after failing to take the heat declared "no other middleweight in the world can."[208]

The challenger completed his training among the old stones and vegetation of Gwrych castle in North Wales. On the day before the fight he made his way down to London were a brass band and a sizeable mob gave him a warm welcome. Robinson took in some golf at Windsor on his day of rest. Weighing in on the afternoon of the big day, Robinson scaled 154lbs and a half to Turpin's 159. He was shorter than Ray but those shoulders more than made up for that. Later at Earls Court that prefight air whooshed through the corridors to try the nerve of the men having their hands taped, both aware that the distant rumbling was reserved for them. Robinson had seen it all, two, three times over. For twenty-three-year-old Randy Turpin this was a big unknown. "Robinson has got only two fists, same as me."[209] He sure didn't sound spooked.

Save for Turpin and his manager, any other picks for the Brit must have contained a good portion of blind hope. Some amended the odds to 5-1. In the popularity contest Turpin won via a total whitewash. In the customary English way the foreigner received a decent reception, but when the announcer turned his attention 180 degrees it sparked a low humming which climaxed in unrestrained applause at, "RAN-DEE... TUR-PIN!"

---

[208] The Dispatch, 1951, Jul 3rd, p.8

[209] The News-Sentinel, 1951, Jul 11th, p.5

Coming together for the first they eased themselves into that familiar pantomime, suggesting movements. Robinson shot out a few short jabs. Holding himself very square next to the champion's sleeker stance, the boulder-like muscles of Turpin made Ray look a little wiry. Taking a few risks early on, Turpin fought like a man out of sorts but a couple of hard shots demonstrated the method in the madness. Robinson moved around the ring like he always did, attractively, harmonising rhythm and poise. The bell ended a rather even first session, arguably Turpin's. The second round revisited the pensive disorder of the opener. Robinson got fresh with a few right hands but failed to land on his strange target. Turpin, at once looking to press, shifted his weight on to his back leg and then shot forward with a counter hook. His guard was nowhere during this manoeuvre but it worked. It also marked the highlight of a scrappy round. Too seasoned to be thrown off his game, Robinson switched-up his attack to get off with a combination in the third. Turpin was quick with the retort. A wide left hook drove the champion towards the ropes which got the crowd lively. Ray came out for the fourth to try and see what he was dealing with, so bizarre was Turpin's collection of movements. Most bizarre of all was a vertical dip that made him look like he was exercising mid-fight. While lowering, his knee almost touched down. Though not forward, he did shoot up in the clinches which confused to no end.

Robinson's slow gait back to Gainford and co bared the look of a man realising he had a full night's works ahead of him. Through leaping backwards, lunging in after the break and kneeling down, Turpin had created a stylistic loophole. A sweeping hook flew at him with good effect. Robinson targeted the body, an area many thought to be Turpin's main weakness but he took it to force the action. From the sixth to the eighth little changed bar Robinson's left eye which was leaking from a clash of heads. He was not catching that many punches but barely landing any of his own. He was "being made to miss an amazing number of times."[210] Turpin acted like quicksand; the more Robinson tried, the more he was countered. Many fell short on the challenger's behalf, but when they connected an accommodating roar of approval lent them added spice. Randy grew conscious about his progress and concluded most rounds with a little run back to his corner. Once there the legs were stretched out and his sad brown eyes scanned the big event. There was a great independence about him, and on the referee's signal he used his clumsy glove to insert the mouthpiece himself. Ray received good treatment but that sliced lid didn't figure. Beforehand a knockout was expected. Alas it was the challenger who looked to be banking most of the rounds with an "unforeseen steadiness" guiding his attack.

In the ninth Robinson finally caught Turpin with his first clean shot in many rounds. A solid right cross buzzed his chin but Turpin ate it as if the pound-for-pound king's knockout record was a fake. The champion had a good spell in the round but a lot more was needed. A lot more was vital. As the fight reached double figures both men welcomed a slower pace, saving their arms for the remainder. Moments of obliged slugging were very rare but Randy put the full stop on each scuffle. Robinson's ability to dictate was nowhere in Turpin's world and a big swing in the eleventh missed

[210] The Times, 1951, Jul 11th, p.6

by some margin, causing many an Englishman to sarcastically jeer. Punches to Turpin's midriff, hooks to his head; the 160lbs ruler implemented various tactics, all of them poorly so. Turpin came back stronger, and often with better. An element of distress took away from whatever punches Robinson landed. To Turpin's credit he opted against cruising and had Robinson in a genuine spot of bother nearing the close of the fourteenth.

The last round called for Robinson to achieve what was expected of him nine rounds earlier. From round one Turpin had tuned himself into an undetectable frequency. The Leamington boxer walked Robinson back to his corner before referee Eugene Henderson raised his arm in unimaginable triumph. Demonstrating his mastery of sportsmanship, Robinson declared, "I have no alibis. I was beaten by a better man."[211] On the subject of the rematch in September, his teary-eyed wife firmly asserted, "He'll get the title back, just you see."[212] It was a sound prediction, but too soon do we move. Hoisted above an army of support, Earl's Court erupted to serenade the new champion with a hearty rendition of 'For's he's a golly good fellow'. Though a little hard of hearing there was not a chance Turpin didn't catch the chanting of a proud nation. That passive expression was liberated with ear-to-ear grinning. When a slight lapse opened amidst the bedlam, Britain's new middleweight champion softly announced, "I hope I'm able to keep this for you for a long time."[213] Robinson made good of his rematch clause in New York, severing Turpin's sixty-four day reign during the tenth. Maintaining that signature manner, Turpin's post-fight statement proclaimed the loss trivial as he was taking with him "the good wishes of a thousand American people." Sadly those wishes expired along with the handsome pay-packet, leaving him with a memory which soured upon each revisit. Fifteen years later he met his grim destiny.

Through years gone by much has been made of Robinson having never seen his British nemesis until the first bell. The stress of his European tour, those "charity fights and the gay life of the continent"[214] may have provoked his downfall, but the difficult rematch banishes the idea of an off night. Whatever the lasting squabble, it pales next to the stone-cold facts; how a boxer, who'd never gone more than eight rounds, who'd never fought out of his own country, and whose slim chance of victory rested on a knockout, outpointed the great Sugar Ray Robinson.

---

211 Pittsburgh Post-Gazette, 1951, Jul 11th, p.15

212 The News-Sentinel, 1951, Jul 11th, p.5

213 The Washington Post, 1951, Jul 11th, p.17

214 Lewiston Evening Journal, 1951, Jul 11th p.10

ROCKY MARCIANO VS. 'JERSEY' JOE WALCOTT

September 23rd, 1952
World Heavyweight Title
Philadelphia, Pennsylvania

Delighted about his new relationship with Jack Blackburn, Arnold Cream foresaw a rosy future as 'Jersey' Joe Walcott. An ode to welterweight's Barbados Demon, the change of name was no caprice. As a fighter not much was missing. Plenty was eye-popping. The side-step, the shuffle, the pivot, all the moves came naturally. Walcott was the kind of fighter who could replenish the desire to teach, gradually lost through those who refute discipline. For the man who knew his craft he was a treat.

A steely lightweight from steely times, Blackburn had made the common transition from fighter to tutor. Knowing peepers glimmered out of his flattened mug, though run-ins with the likes of Jack O' Brien, Dave Holly and Joe Gans ensured there was nothing pretentious behind the worn exterior. Pinning Walcott down after his first dispatch, Blackburn secured a deadly alliance. In 1934 Walcott's grooming was to continue over at Chicago. The tale of Joseph Louis Barrow was taking form and his murderous fists needed the finest money could buy. Money not being a problem, Blackburn was readily employed. He would have been quite mad to pass on the opportunity but, respectively, was obliged to continue with Arnold's development.

Chewing over the benefits of joining a world class stable, Walcott grew restless. And then, with everything set, his high hopes were ruled hasty with the intervention of typhoid. To his enduring pain he was left with the sole option of cancelling his journey. The sole ultimatum laid the tracks for many years penniless and hungry. Continuing on his lonesome, Walcott was punished by Al Ettore in 1936. Despite the setback a trip to camp Louis took place soon after in order to help prepare Detroit's sensation for Max Schmeling. Reputed to have floored Louis during sparring a $25 handout was offered. Walcott packed his things. And after Schmeling was through with battering Jack's new protégé it was sour grapes all round. Disappointment came often and hit hard. Light-heavyweight 'Tiger' Jack Fox repeated Ettore's eighth round knockout the year later, tainting what meagre progress had been made. This patchy trend persisted until 1940 when the hulking Abe Simon delivered 'Jersey' Joe his third knockout in a professional career already a decade old. Coming home bruised and tired Walcott's duties were no less than sustaining a wife and six children. The imminent financial pressures forced the luckless boxer to get on a relief role. For 18 months, $9.50 weekly checks were handed out while he doggedly applied for life's less glamorous professions. Through sweat and grime, from mixing cement to hoisting trash over his shoulder, his faith in the Lord could not be shaken. Hopeless as everything seemed a pious spirit helped him endure.

Acting like a counterweight to Walcott's hardships, Louis used his college's darkest hour to establish himself as the greatest fighting machine since Jack Dempsey. Undoubtedly, the 1938 rematch against Schmeling was the most significant and on one end of the millions enjoying a radio feed was fourteen-year-old Rocco Francis Marchegiano. The captivated Italian-American would become better known as Rocky Marciano.

Different to your generic story, it was not love at first sight. Baseball came first in Rocco's list of passions. On the sketchy streets of Brockton, Massachusetts there were many occasions to enjoy a scuffle, but after the poor kid had been knocked senseless it felt more natural to pick up the bat again. Pain him as it did, Rocco was deemed unfit for the school team and got relegated. The knee-jerk reaction was to ditch education and start anew. Menial work sufficed for a time and then at twenty Rocco was drafted into the army where boxing reappeared to improve whatever skills had emerged from slugging away at a customized mail bag. A few spots of amateur success encouraged him to fight the seasoned Henry Lester which ended in disqualification. Clearly fouling out to avoid a pasting, it didn't look like plan B held much promise for the stumpy Italian, but that didn't stop him turning professional. Marchegiano being rather difficult to pronounce, "Marciano!" was blurted out by the announcer. Undeniably catchier it stuck. By 1947's clock twenty-three was a little old for one to begin punching for pay. And while not a serious flaw, Rocky was noticeably small for a heavyweight; short, short arms and light. Coordination was a bit of an issue also. Unlike the showy Walcott it was going to take a certain kind of trainer to discover the bright side.

There to the rescue, another aged fellow whose petite body appeared to have stored every little incident of a physical past. Charley Goldman had been a fighter one time. A mere four hundred times he credited himself with having squared-off. Not dissimilar to Blackburn, Goldman knew something good when his gaze fell upon it. That initial disbelief took hold whenever anyone noticed Marciano, but unlike an army of critics who echoed throughout his career, Goldman saw through the negatives to see one big positive. One of Charlie's key doctrines was in getting a fighter to play to his strengths. This sounds elementary but with Rocky it was to prove a most devious principle. The short man was to fight shorter still, exploding the idea of utilising range to insist on the opposite; close-quartered warfare. Numerous lessons were required before the end product. Fortunately, Rocky's punches were awful to catch.

As Rocco lived his amateur days the name of 'Jersey' Joe Walcott reappeared in print. Not one reporter had expected to cover anything else about a fighter four years in exile, but back came the thirty-year-old with a vengeance. An opportunist from Camden called Felix Bocchicchio perceived untapped magic in his muscular limbs. After improving his outlook he made sure of his family's accommodation and renewed that boxing licence. Passionate about his children's education, and not completely rid of that craving for pole-position, Walcott began to enter the ring well-trained, well-fed, and as if that wasn't enough, conscious of the fact each punch was building that rosy future he had foreseen ten years ago.

Victory over Joe Baski caught attention and then a couple of common opponents in Lee Q. Murray and Curtis Sheppard each left the ring with another black mark. 1946 improved on '45s success, bagging the big fights and doing the business, though Walcott was sometimes guilty of stepping off the gas. He could delve into periods of disenchantment as if reflecting on how on earth he managed to pull off those avant-garde manoeuvres. This fight-endangering habit redirected two decisions, but he returned to correct this against Joey Maxim and Elmer Ray. Within two years Walcott had gone from a hazy recollection to the leading contender, and while Marciano was etching his first entries into the record books the leading contender had signed to fight Rocky's boyhood hero.

Most were in agreement that the post-war incarnation of the Brown Bomber was not the assassin of years prior. Even the casual fan could see the rust taking hold, yet nobody had taken his championship. Walcott, a 7-1 underdog had fun with the odds, flooring Louis in the opener and heavily in the fourth. Taking advantage of a regressed ability to pull the trigger, Walcott "used a dance step with a feint that ended in slamming home hard rights."[215] Round for round it was difficult to offer Louis a draw; however, not fully recognising his duty as challenger, Walcott's poor decision to switch off in the closing moments gifted the champion a split decision. Those bedevilling ways upset Louis' radar again in the rematch, but Goldman hit on a shared theory when he later observed of Louis, "If he made a mistake in the first fight he never repeated it in the second."[216] An eleventh round knockout ended Walcott's second title challenge. It was defence 25 for Louis, a statistic that remains to this day.

Though still champion, the rust between Louis' joints refused to leave and after vacating Ezzard Charles officially terminated his long rule in 1950. A year before Charles had comfortably handled Walcott over the distance. Lacking inspiration, 'Jersey' Joe fought a weak fight, standing off Charles who easily dictated from the outside. Wife Lydia concluded, "I hope he quits now."[217] Those thirty-five years were highlighted with amnesic regularity. Walcott the 'pappy guy' couldn't help but impress as not a lot was expected. 1950 went well enough until Rex Layne, a boxer assuredly not of his class, caught Walcott sleeping and earned a decision. This did not stop a return bout with Charles from transpiring where unanimous scores caused a good deal of booing from the audience. Walcott picked up his 16th loss but a valiant effort secured a rubber match. A third fight, which would give Walcott his *fifth* shot at the title, was set for July 18th, 1951. The eight year advantage and 2-0 score in favour of Ezzard had some reporters up in arms about the fact it was going ahead. Go ahead it did though, and Walcott was more focused than ever which convinced him to lead an unusually aggressive fight. Landing more through six rounds than he often did through fifteen, Walcott pulled away on two of the scorecards. Nobody anticipated it but they weren't needed as the seventh produced a knockout for the ages; one exquisitely delivered left, half way between a hook and an uppercut. Charles' head violently twisted on impact leaving him perfectly horizontal, face first. A gutsy effort to rise merely resulted in a change of position, falling in a manner one would if the ring was jacked-up at one end. As insensible as one can be minus being unconscious, referee Buck McTiernan reached ten. Thirty-seven be damned, the "heroic veteran" became the oldest heavyweight champion in history.

In the life of Goldman's young thumper, this was all very insignificant. Rocky did not need to concern himself with the headlines. The delicate task of finding opposition relative to his development had been the topic for the last three busy years. Save for Don Mogard and Ted Lowry, a knack for punching had left opponents with two options; to be scraped off the floor or saved by the referee. The alternative for

[215] The Evening Independent, 1947, May 21st, p.18

[216] The Pittsburgh Press, 1951, Oct 24th, p.37

[217] The Milwaukee Journal, 1949, Jun 23rd, p.12

Carmine Vingo was much gloomier as he slipped into a coma. Thankfully, a 50/50 chance of survival ended in the green. At the start of 1950, Goldman hypothesized that what he originally surmised to be "one of the crudest fighters he had ever seen"[218] may be ready for a world title fight. Any statement released to the press is liable to a bit of ballyhoo. Elaborating, Goldman explained, "I know Rocky isn't ready for Ezzard Charles right now. He needs a little more experience to teach him pace."[219] New York's Roland LaStarza was to provide that considerate test; something to get the sweat going but no alarm bells. A looping right in the fourth put LaStarza in an expected rut but he corrected himself to give Rocky no quarter. After ten rounds the 13,658 jury was split right down the middle. Under the faintest wind the decision could have gone the other way, but Marciano claimed the split decision. Al Weill, savvy matchmaker and manager of Rocky was not shy about making big statements, but Roland had underlined an unavoidable fact; a few extra coats of paint were in order.

The calibre of opposition was reduced, allowing Rocky to mature. Fighters who lost as often as they won were thoroughly clobbered. Ted Lowry returned to last the distance again, an achievement that would give him cult status. Four consecutive knockouts were reeled out and then the unlikely Willis Applegate joined that elite group when the final bell tolled to see him upright. Since LaStarza nine opponents had fallen improving Marciano to 34-0. His record still glossy, and, being a touch wiser, Rex Layne was next. That victory against Walcott was far better than anything Marciano's fists had mashed. The risk had to be taken, which it was, concussively so. Odds of 13-5 favoured Layne to repel the puncher but he was unable to cope with a style which denied him "an opening for a clean shot",[220] and then came that right hand. Layne paused at first. A second later he assumed a foetal position fit for a medical billboard.

By 1951 Joe Louis was perhaps 40% of the fighter he used to be, but in terms of a celebrity he was still big business. The taxman did his part in prompting his return to the ring. The other name on the contract read 'Rocky Marciano'. Rocky wasn't high on the idea of fighting him, but no fighter will ditch their livelihood if they can help it. Louis was, as Goldman had noted, poison in rematches. Problem was this was no rematch, and, "the difference is he can no longer do what he wants."[221]

One of the great, sad instances in boxing portrays Joe Louis' limp body leaving the ring through the bottom rope. With his back on the apron and arms uncontrollably flung out a few men, including a security guard, offered their hands for support like they were tending to some victim in a motorbike accident. While tragic for the fans it was no more than another day in the office for Joe. He never did lose that ability to bring about a quiet with his straightshooting way. "I saw the right hand coming but I couldn't do anything about it...I'm too old I guess."[222] Later Marciano gave some

[218] St. Petersburg Times, 1950, May 25th, p.22

[219] Spokane Daily Chronicle, 1950, Jan 12th, p.36

[220] The Free Lance-Star, 1951, Jul 13th, p.9

[221] The Pittsburgh Press, 1951, Oct 24th, p.37

[222] Spokane Daily Chronicle, 1951, Oct 27th, p.8

first-person perspective on the nature of a fight; "there's nothing personal about it and you don't carry this over outside the ring. You get rid of it in there."[223] And with that ugly junction out of the way Marciano made a beeline for the top.

A bloodied Lee Savold was retired after the sixth before an unimpressed audience. Despite winning every round the critics fell hard on Marciano who failed to floor someone ancient Louis had stopped. Citing four months of inactivity as the culprit, Rocky slogged on. Gino Buonvino and Bernie Reynolds shared less than five rounds between them. As for the championship, it was only fair that Charles got his rematch against Walcott, which he did on June 5th, 1952. It was a slow and comparatively tame affair that again went the distance. Charles rallied in the final round but narrowly lost out on all three cards, leaving their series at two apiece. Rocky's following looked to be losing hope until Harry 'Kid' Matthews was spectacularly dismissed. A toxic puncher, Matthews had not suffered defeat for almost nine years. He started well, but a pair of scorching hooks came in the second to show there was a decent left to go with that belting right. Comparisons with the great Dempsey made for a popular choice of banter, but more notable was September 23rd. This was the date with Walcott.

Two weeks into August and they got down to serious preparation. Crossinger, N.Y., inside of a converted airplane hangar was where Marciano stripped his form of any unwanted flesh. Morning fuel came in the form of oatmeal, two soft-boiled eggs, two lamb chops, dry toast and a cup of tea. Once that had been demolished Rocky set off for four miles of roadwork. In the afternoon, six rounds of sparring provided the highlight of regular gym protocol. Atlantic City, N.J. was where Walcott nested. Having witnessed the relentless energy of the twenty-eight-year-old's camp reporters must have expected a comparatively lax tempo to suit the older champion. As it happened there was nothing lax about 'Jersey' Joe. "Usually he just sharpens his reflexes, practices his shuffle off to Buffalo"[224] but towards his sparring partners there was no charity and little mercy. Perceiving Rocky in his team mates, no three minute session was pleasurable. Taken by that rare aggressive whim, seven men hit the deck, one so often that a writer quipped "he must have canvas burns." Wary about his fighter 'going stale' Goldman instructed Marciano to reduce four miles to three and six rounds to three. The remaining time left the challenger a bit fidgety, but there was no questioning the engineer behind that 42-0 record.

Bocchiochio was denied a manger's licence in the state of New York due to his criminal past which included connections with murder and robbery. This was one of the factors in changing an early venue suggestion for Yankee to Municipal stadium in Philadelphia. This hallowed ground was where Jack Dempsey had lost his crown against Gene Tunney, however, this time the slugger was the younger man. On the penultimate day light rain aroused recollections of that drizzly event twenty-six years ago. Another feature contrary to Dempsey's loss was in the odds which favoured Marciano. Heavy betting from his New England fans was the reason. Only a slight

---

223 'How it Feels to be Champ', The book of boxing, W.C. Heinz and Nathan Ward, p.224

224 St Petersburg Times, 1952, Sep 22nd, p.10

favourite, observers forecast a bloody struggle. Come nightfall, 40,379 uniformly arranged themselves around the ring, filling the box office with $504,645.

At the sound of the first bell it was no surprise to see the rugged challenger close in, but so did the champion with a knowing strut. Simultaneous jabs flew over each man's shoulder as a phone-booth brawl started to crystallise. Utilising his ice-skating feet did not seem to figure for Walcott who let go with the heavy stuff. It was no secret that 'Jersey' Joe was rather contemptuous of his opponent's ability as a boxer, and with a question mark still looming over Rocky, the veteran smelt a knockout. The decision to bully Marciano, a tactic most would have grilled, was perhaps not such a bad idea. Next to his slighter rival, the bulging torso of Walcott's 196 and a half pound frame looked every inch bigger than Marciano's who was a touch over 184. The often negative champion dived in with both hands. And then, just as he had with Charles, Walcott came from a corner to sink Rocky with a short left hook.

As a precautionary Goldman had instructed Rocky to stay down for a count of eight if Walcott managed to deck him. Shooting up before the count had reached five, Rocky reflected, "I guess I'm only half smart."[225] In the established mid-range spot for trading, Walcott chopped away with concussive intentions. Breaking free from his grasp, Rocky got in his own licks whenever the opportunity presented itself, and even when it didn't. Slithering under big swings he retired into his imaginary cave to re-emerge with heavy punches. Whether they landed clean, scuffed the arms or missed, each one breathed an air of defiance. Throughout the second there was no change. In Walcott's desire for an early night and Marciano's refusal to succumb there founded a vicious stalemate. A sharp cross stunned Marciano but somehow intensified his charge. Rocky's fight lacked that pleasing aspect that a Walcott twist could produce, though there was plenty of method as the challenger mixed up his attack and found new angles. Shirley Povich neatly separated the wheat from the chaff, "He was crude, but crude compared only to Walcott the master stylist."[226]

The desire to box didn't appear in the third. In the middle of the round Marciano's right hand bounced off Walcott's head. The punch seemed to die on impact but the Massachusetts fraternity let their approval be known. After taking it in turns to pelt one another, simultaneous thumping ended the session. There was no hesitancy on Rocky's behalf, happy only when going forward, throwing his body into every shot. The big right came again for Marciano which spiked the atmosphere. The champion still possessed snappier punches. It dawned on Walcott that his opponent was not going to vanish as easily as he had wished and slipped on to the back foot. Far from waging a fleeting fight, 'Jersey' Joe was mild with his movement, keeping his feet grounded for power. Marciano's accuracy was lacking but he kept Walcott on the ropes with a two-handed assault as the fifth closed.

Knitting together his swings with moments of study, Marciano's attack was high-risk but learned. Walcott's gut was forced to endure the type of punches that had cracked ribs, but he moved well and countered hard. In the breaks preceding rounds six

[225] The New York Times, 1952, Sep 25th, p.40

[226] The Washington Post, 1952, Sep 25th, p.2

and seven Marciano grunted to his little mentor that his eyes were burning. Goldman later said of Walcott's corner, "They were rubbing liniment on his legs between rounds and he would sit with his gloves on his knees and some of the liniment got on his gloves."[227] Appealing to the referee wasn't an option in the 1950s. Not to worry, Marciano carried on as if the liniment was moisturiser.

A showcase of jabbing distinguished the eighth. Walcott was less eager to trade but won the round comfortably. Come round nine and Walcott's lungs were creating little vacuums in the air. Marciano's intentions were generally read but a few uppercuts to the body made Walcott fight slightly ragged for the first time. Flipping his attack cleverly the challenger went upstairs, downstairs and vice versa. Walcott summoned his own right hand for the two men to swap their honey punches. Just before the bell sounded a Marciano right landed which went off like the kick of bass drum. There was a pinch of reluctance as Walcott began moving around. Finding it easier to land, Marciano gained momentum. Out of nowhere, Walcott offered a right body hook which crippled his target. The champion pushed his advantage and all of a sudden it looked like Marciano had reached his limit for absorbing punishment. Round eleven was all Walcott's.

His legs still sturdy, there was a glow about the champion. The quality of Marciano's chin was no longer a mystery, but victory was flaking with each miss. The twelfth tallied thirty-six damaging minutes. During the last three the old man had perfectly illustrated how to fight a bull. Sure about his revised tactics, the fight was Walcott's to lose. For the first thirty seconds of the thirteenth Walcott moved away. Making a big circle he drifted back towards the ropes with Rocky in hot pursuit. Setting himself, Marciano seized the attention of Walcott who began to devise an appropriate counter. There was no counter and Rocky didn't miss. Some called it a hook, some a cross, Rocky called it his Suzie-Q. Whatever its name, its effect was dreadful. It was an instance in which all previous criticisms came flooding back.

"He is like a powerful hitter in golf who slices to bunkers or hooks to ponds...He can't call his shots"[228] insisted Grantland Rice. Compounding many years of doubt into one blast, Marciano's stubby right arm could not have landed any sweeter. The champion had been ahead on all three score cards, but down he slid comatose, left arm slumped over the bottom rope, the top of his head resting on the canvas in a most awkward manner. Referee Charlie Daggert counted over his oblivious recipient. Rocky signalled to the crowd, raising his arms and mingling with his corner while Walcott was tipped on to his back. A few more minutes showed him to have no serious injury however, observing how "pathetic" he had looked, Bocchicchio thought retirement the only option. At first Walcott agreed, citing how good Felix had been for him over the years to then change his mind in a matter of days. Now owner to the shortest retirement in history the rematch went ahead. Sadly, the one similarity it shared with the original was the result. Walcott may have misheard the count as he shot up at ten, but, evidently, it was not the same man who had waged war last year. The fight did

[227] The Miami News, 1953, May 13th, p.17

[228] Pittsburgh Press, 1952, Feb 25th, p.17

not reach round two. He withdrew back into family life to watch Marciano bludgeon his most worthy contemporaries. Five defences later and Rocky retired at the age of thirty-three. "I never spent more than two weeks at home in a row"[229] he explained. A niggling back injury had also encouraged the decision. With no draws a record of 49-0 (43 knockouts) was left intact. Marciano was not to be a casualty of the comeback as were Jeffries and Louis. Instead he became the casualty of a plane crash. Travelling on the eve of his 46th birthday to Des Moines, Iowa, all three passengers were killed.

Despite a life which had once forced him to cover up the broken windows of his dingy house with burlap bags, Walcott lived on until the age of eighty having been a professional wrestler, referee and chairman for the New Jersey State Athletic Commission. In past times Joe had quipped that he had been training with a billy goat as it would help accustom him to Marciano's style. Far removed from days of ticket-selling banter, Walcott could attest to Rocky's claim that he "got rid of it in there".

"Inside the ring he was a lion, outside a lamb."[230]

[229] Lewiston Morning Tribune, 1956, Apr 18th, p.8

[230] The Windsor Star, 1969, Sep 2nd, p.6

EDER JOFRE
VS.
MASAHIKO 'FIGHTING' HARADA

May 18th, 1965
World Bantamweight Title
Nagoya, Japan

Whenever the little boxers hit the headlines you can be sure they've earned it. Heavyweights have this ugly habit of representing boxing as a whole, and when this sin occurs it has an exponential effect; the lower in weight you are the more chance there is of going unnoticed. The bantamweight division is located in the deep south of weight categories at 118lbs, but it's one of the original eight weight divisions, and as such, it hasn't been at a loss for talent. In 1899 'Terrible' Terry McGovern left his sizzling imprint, the impossibly long figure of 'Panama' Al Brown carved out a fine legacy from 1929-35, and punishing Latino Manual Ortiz was splendid throughout the 1940s. There have been bantamweights worthy of having their faces pressed into their national flag and yet you'd do well to find a poster of one.

Eder Jofre still gleams, ever so slightly, and not just because he was Brazil's first world champion. He could box, which he did beautifully to his own samba jig, and on the point of punching, with either hand, he was a killer. From an early age there was this captivating maturity about him. That he was only three years of age when father Jose helped him into his first pair of gloves gives us a clue. The Jofres were knee deep in gloves. Following his brother's death, Jose continued to run a long-standing boxing academy and all six brothers of wife Senora were professional fighters. Little Eder received the star treatment from day one and he responded brilliantly. As an amateur he faulted only twice, the other forty-eight times he won, twenty via the cataleptic route. Part of the Olympic squad for the 1956 Games, Jofre arrived with all the alacrity expected to be seen in one representing his country. His proud moment was terminated in the quarter-finals but much time was needed to allow such talent to flower. And where better for the Brazilian belter to come into bloom than Sao Paulo; the country's largest city. Carefully listening to dad, Jofre sanitised the domestic scene, improving at such a rate that subtle differences could be seen through the course of a fight. The more he fought the more impenetrable he became. A trio of draws were as close to calamity as it got, and those who shared honours were later dismissed with new bruising intelligence.

Ernesto Miranda had twice halved the scores and met Jofre a third time in 1960 for the South American bantamweight title. The decision was only going to go one way but Miranda wanted another try. That maturity of Jofre's was close to entering its final stage, something which Miranda discovered during the third round. Victory against Miranda had brought another accolade to the Jofre mantle, but the proceeding bout meant far more than any trophy or belt. No title was at stake when Jofre faced Claudio Barrientos, but pride certainly was. It was Barrientos who had pushed the ejector button on Jofre's Olympic dreams. The desire for redemption was strong, but rash behaviour wasn't to come into the equation. With a pleasing mix of patience, variety and power, an unpleasant conclusion was reached in the eighth. Big paydays were just around the corner and Eder sensed it. Swiftly drafted into a title eliminator for Jose Beccara's world title, Brazil's finest polished his fists and got to work. He couldn't afford any slip-ups against a fighter with similar aspirations.

Mexico's Jose Medel was anything but a soft touch. A man of experience, he had the tools and the temperament to make a dent in anyone. Different to Jofre's light tufts, Medel's black hair was shocked to attention, lending him a severe portrait. Unfortunately for his opponents, he fought as he looked. Come fight time he refused to be oppressed by Jofre's cunning and went flying in. In the third he applied a ravenous body attack, in the fifth he swapped heavily and in the ninth he had the muscles in Jofre's legs fighting to keep him erect. Happily leaving his mouthpiece to gather dust, Medel continued as if protective gear was a nuisance, catching Jofre with both hands. The attack died however on account of a quick hook, a punch which took everything away from the aggressor. The tenth offered nothing but a beating and saw Jofre come through his sternest test.

While shooting up the ranks there had been one man on Jofre's mind, Mexico's Joe Beccara. Victory against Medel had undeniably put him at the front of the queue but Beccara was days away from announcing his retirement. The National Boxing Association title was made vacant and so keeping it from Jofre was now the duty of Eloy Sanchez. In a non-title bout Sanchez had stopped Beccara over eight rounds which convinced him to leave. There wasn't the pretty packaging you got with Jofre but a stepping-stone he wasn't. For the first four rounds Eder's versatility had Sanchez in that common muddle. Casting shadows with his fists, the tempo was his to alter. By the fifth Sanchez had grown restless and stung Jofre with a left hook. Not taking too kindly to this, Jofre threw the chess board out of the ring and turned hunter. Capping off a strong rally, a long right hand put Sanchez down. A championship spirit picked Sanchez from the floor and positioned him back in front of Jofre, driving his arms into him like a static bag. Fans were quick on the uptake that if there was one thing Jofre could do as well as box it was fight. As Medel had come to understand, Eder was a man as tranquil in chaos as he was during a spot of afternoon painting; an unlikely hobby of his alongside playing the trumpet. The sixth was non-stop, but it was Jofre who applied the full-stop at the 1:30 mark. How often do you see a bantamweight end a fight with a single punch, off the ropes? Jofre's style was more than textbook, it was perfection strutting. His fiancée was present to share the big moment and police had to be at the ready for the small percentage of Brazilians that made up the crowd rushed at the new champion. Security safely delivered the twenty-four-year-old sensation back to his dressing room, and so began a stellar reign.

Jofre wasn't back in America for a while during which time he gained worldwide recognition as the leading bantamweight. In 1961 Piero Rollo was forced to retire along with his severed face before the tenth. So impressed with the showing were Ring magazine that Jofre inherited their belt. Another couple of knockouts kept him sharp and then Venezuela's Ramon Arias was finished in the seventh. Everything had gone to plan inside the ring, but outside Jofre recalled how people had thoughtfully offered "to cut my head off or run over me with a car."[231]

There was little debate when it came to the topic of who was the best 118lbs fighter in the world; nevertheless, Ireland's Johnny Caldwell held the last piece of the jigsaw in the form of the European title. Ten rounds later and Jofre was the undisputed champion. Caldwell was down briefly in the fifth and nearly out in the ninth. In the

[231] The Milwaukee Sentinel, 1961, Aug 25th, p.30

tenth Jofre's punches left Caldwell with his arms by his waist and his corner stepped in. A trip to America presented another gopher called Herman Marques and then back in Sao Paulo a rematch with Medel only made it to the sixth. Japan was next.

The scales provided more of a challenge than Katsutoshi Aoki. Reducing to 118lbs was becoming an increasingly difficult task. "What can you do when you only eat vegetables and fruit?"[232] reasoned a member of the Jofre entourage. In fairness, Aoki's three round showing was not a fair depiction of Japan's pedigree. There were better fighters out in the Orient like Masahiko 'Fighting' Harada. This squat little warmonger had captured the flyweight title in his nineteenth year with a showcase in sustained aggression to become the first ever Oriental champion. Thailand's Pone Kingpetch was a hero to his native people. He was the fighter to end the celebrated run of the deadly Pascual Perez, first outpointing him and then knocking him out. This made him the firm favourite against Harada, but it did not prevent him from being suffocated under a torrent of swinging arms. The rematch was going much the same way but Harada failed to press his advantage and dropped the decision. He had yet to turn twenty. Curious to see how well slightly larger men would handle his fury, Harada entered the 118lbs division though taking on Medel so soon was a little boisterous. He led the way for five rounds when in the sixth everything went to ruin. Three knock downs not only signalled for the referee to end matters but blasted the idea of scaling this new mountain. In the ring two months later, Harada needed little incentive to try again.

1600 miles north, Jofre had once again illustrated the gulf between top spot and second place. In the Philippines it was the usual story against Johnny Jamito with a healthy points lead preparing a stoppage. It was May of 1963, but Jofre would not fight again until November of 1964. No injury was sustained; something more serious plagued the champion. Twenty pounds removed from his fighting weight, the tender subject of retirement played on the Brazilian's mind. Between his career earnings, national celebrity and affiliation with a dry goods store, the real world didn't look so bad. Eder was also a skilled designer of cloth which promised a worthwhile existence minus the bruises and general sacrifice. It certainly wasn't the worst idea, but, naturally, the ring took precedence. And with no visible cracks in the paintwork, why not? Standing to receive a tax-free $50,000 against Columbia's Bernardo Caraballo had Jofre licking his chops. In keeping with his meticulous ethos he trained well and performed brilliantly. During the seventh Caraballo greeted the canvas for the first time in 40 bouts. The referee did the rest.

There wasn't long until the clock struck 1965. The last twelve months had given plenty to chew over. Undoubtedly the big news was how Cassius Clay had dethroned Sonny Liston. Clay had this ability to turn small conferences into political debates or comedic rants depending on his mood. Now champion, his opinions spread far and wide and it was the job of the newspapers to print all the treasures of his motor mouth. The name of 'Fighting' Harada would do well to cause a twitch in the countenance of the Western world. If a bell rung it was solely because he was listed as Jofre's next opponent. When the eve of the fight came Eder took it upon himself to discuss the

---

232 St. Joseph Gazette, 1963, Apr 2nd, p.9

details about his next defence. The notion of Harada winning was as foreign as the idea of the heavyweight champion turning modest.

Britain's Walter McGowan was penned in for September and some believed he had a fair shout of winning, if not entirely on his own merits; "Eder needs the heat to sweat off that last two or three pounds"[233] was offered on the point of England's chilly weather. After this Mexico's destructive Jesus Pimentel would make a fine opponent. The future looked good whatever the route. Coming into this fight Harada had outpointed Manila's Ray Asis in a lively ten rounder. Jofre sat at ringside but expressed more interest in tackling Pimentel. Chipping away in hope for the big bucks, Harada faced countryman Katsutoshi Aoki and did as had Jofre, winning in the third. A respectable body of work had been built which, of course, paled next to Jofre's conglomerate of achievements. Whether Harada truly deserved a shot was up for debate, circumstances just happened to favour him.

The fight went ahead though not without trouble. Jofre's manager, Abraham Katzenelson was not happy about the prescribed six ounce Japanese gloves. He ruled them unsafe and liable to cause serious facial injuries and so he had Mexican gloves ordered at the last minute. An agreement was reached and that feeling of no escape resumed. The weigh-in, something that Jofre had come to dislike, instructed that he strip naked in order to make the 118lbs limit. More alarmingly it was reported that in order to do so he had "not eaten since yesterday."[234] Harada was perfect on first attempt, just a quarter pound under. Jofre could switch-off again, and as he did it was back to Harada's chances, or lack thereof. The last seventeen fights of the Brazilian's had ended before a decision could be rendered. A popular forecast was that Harada would be smelling salt before the ninth. Further illustrating the disparity in prestige, $30,000 was headed Jofre's way while Harada would receive only $2,500. This was nothing new for the underdog who, in his first fight with Kingpetch, took away a mere $2,000 next to Pone's $45,000. Scheduled for Japan, the one thing Harada was not on the short end of was crowd support. The recently built Aichi Prefectural Gym housed 10,000 excited fans, perfectly arranged in rows that gradually escaped the overhead lights.

As soon as the rules permitted him, Harada literally ran from his corner to crash into the composed champion. The younger boxer was all energy, throwing punches of every type, bouncing around. It was agreed that he would need to take risks, but the approach was insolent; a dangerous game to play against such a formidable opponent. Peering out of his guard, Jofre didn't make much form, perhaps amused. Though voluminous, Harada's punches did not carry much steam and many were blocked. You got the feeling the champion was making notes, jotting down mistakes to be punished later. On the bell Jofre patted the head of the enthused pretender. For most of the fight he curiously stood between rounds with his back to his opponent. The second started as did the first with Harada running at the other corner as if it was some secret means of scoring points. He hammered a left hook into Jofre's elbow several

233 Evening Times, 1965, May 4th, p.26

234 The Times, 1965, May 19th, p.5

times. No damage was done but it didn't matter to the crowd who responded loudly. Jofre's jab made further enquiries. Compensating for his lesser reach, Harada fired his jab in spurts to keep Eder in a state of analysis. In the remaining twenty seconds the big punches were flashed, though better accuracy was needed. The third found Jofre in an aggressive mood, closing in for a chin-checker.

Harada's defence was his offence, giving you a target only to remove or smother it to safety. More jabbing from him suited the pace and whenever a clean one got through there was an acoustic boom. None of this fazed the champion. The fighter making his ninth defence of the 118lbs title comfortably let his left hook go which caught Harada on the cheek. A few more got through during Jofre's first good spell. The champion prepared to knuckle down, but something unexpected awaited him in the fourth. Harada made his rushing entrance but soon followed a right uppercut which displaced Jofre's mouthpiece. It was a sickening shot, one in which there is no head-snap. As Eder went into a defensive shell ringside photographers came close to slithering their whole bodies under the bottom rope as they tried to capture the drama. Jofre was well enough to exchange pleasantries at the bell, but one thing was clear; the pest had become a problem.

It was time for a rethink. The opening thirty seconds went well but that pitter-patter jab coaxed Jofre into fighting shy. Luckily he broke free from his tactical plight to slam Harada's head with venomous blows. They lacked the desired effect, though they must have had some as Harada was convinced that Jofre's corner had become his. The confused challenger was pulled back to his rightful spot amidst plenty of laughter. Things slowed in the sixth. Harada peppered the body while Jofre swung for keeps but a cut appeared above the left eye of the champion, apparently "the first time the Brazilian had been cut in 50 professional fights."[235] It was not serious. Desperate he wasn't but Jofre's awareness of the problem was visible in his willingness to try new things. Bolo-like uppercuts came at Harada in the seventh. One missed wildly, causing amusement. The weak yet repetitious left hand kept Jofre off balance and though he cunningly slipped out of Harada's clinches the retort either missed or fell into another clinch.

Mutual weariness made the rounds very difficult to score. Jofre's intentions were transparent, but when a solid one landed there was no capitalising, no consistency. Harada's early lead was potential insurance. The action kept a healthy pace but neither could take control. Jofre eventually made use of his seat though he stayed facing the other way. In the twelfth his inactivity was a disservice even to sparring; it was difficult to tell if he was running out of gas or had lost that mental notebook. Harada's efforts were minimal, but as the champion did next to nothing the round could only go one way. Eder needed something big. Every resourceful trick of Japan's little hero was doing its part in dissolving that chance. A full-blooded hook made its case in the thirteenth. Harada's durability said just as much. The fourteenth re-wed the two men with no sign of change; the steady taps of Harada hoping to overrule Jofre's powerful, though erratic contributions.

---

[235] The Hartford Courant, 1965, May 19th, p.19A

Suddenly Jofre's posture tensed up. He let his right hand go for it to bounce Harada's head back. Another one clipped his chin, momentarily sending shivers down his legs. Courageously and smartly, Harada flurried himself into a clinch. Though not as accurate as he had been in past defences, the momentum was, finally, with Jofre. It was time to stick him but tired arms stopped making it anything more than his round. Harada played it safe, seizing the champion in close which brought cheers from the Easterly audience, expressing a rare admiration for survival techniques. The arms of Jofre's were shaken vigorously in an old attempt to restore strength; his back still obscurely turned. On the other side Harada's chunky legs were treated as he lazed on his stool looking winded. A building cheer lifted the spirits of the miniature combatants. More kind gestures were exchanged.

Jofre again tried to spear his jittery target. Quantity came from the Oriental but he was always the first to catch a break. Still boxing in spots, clinches had become as frequent and irritating as traffic jams in Sao Paulo. Throughout the whole fight Jofre had appeared weak and bemused. The knockout he evidently sought was nowhere and the bell clanged to end a fight far too close for comfort. Quickly into his robe, Jofre looked to be readying himself for bad news. Judge Jay Edison gave it to Harada by 72-71 while Judge Masao Kato gave it to Jofre by 72-70. The once great fighter, now busy referee Barney Ross cast the deciding vote which read 71-69 and went to Harada. He was now the first Oriental fighter to win world titles at *two* weight classes. The ecstatic new champion skipped towards one of his corner men but was cut off by Jofre who hoisted the better man into the air. At twenty-nine Jofre's unbeaten days had come to an end. Retirement played on the ex-champion's mind but he decided on a rematch. The very beatable Manny Elias was picked for the tune-up but he was able to take everything Jofre threw at him. Harada remained busier, outdoing Britain's Alan Rudkin for his first defence.

Coming in two pounds lighter, Jofre had revenge written all over him. For a second time however Harada's hand was raised. Like the original there were no knockdowns, Jofre's eye was cut, and Harada was a nose ahead. Close unanimous scores were read out and the thirty years of Eder Jofre stood out like sore thumbs. He had been favoured to regain the belt but a new power in the 118lbs class had established itself. With confidence to burn Harada threw down the gauntlet to Medel of whom he had a score to settle. Now a true bantamweight, a sturdier Harada fought his fight and outpointed the man who had sacked him with something to spare. Just like his style there was no let-up in his schedule and another victim of Jofre, Bernardo Caraballo, got what you could call the Harada treatment. There was plenty left in the tank when Harada met Lionel Rose but the slick Aborigine severed his run as champion with a majority decision. Reacting in the same manner as he did when outpointed by Kingpetch, Harada entered the weight division above. After a handful of bouts a title shot against Ray Famechon was his.

Referee Willie Pep rendered the decision but not without difficulty. The former featherweight announced a draw but as the crowd booed the card was re-examined and one point went to Famechon to give him the win. Harada did his best in a rematch but was stopped for the second time in his career. Unlike Jofre, his decision to retire at the particularly young age of twenty-six was concrete. He stayed close to the ring and made cameos as a guest commentator for Fuji's television station.

While removed from the picture, Jofre had been nursing his ego. After three years of exile, surely it was the end. In actuality he was again close to swapping his civilised life for the uncivilised life of the ring. The thirty-three-year-old former bantamweight tried his hand as a featherweight in August, 1969. As comebacks go, this one looked set for total disaster. Three years of executing mediocre competition nabbed Jofre a title shot against Jose Legra. Thirty-seven years of age was an ominous statistic, but it did not stop him taking the 126lbs championship via majority decision. It was a most special accolade to etch into that long list of achievements, but he wasn't done yet. The WBC champion successfully defended his new jewel against brilliant southpaw, Vincente Saldivar. For the celebrated Mexican this was his first bout in over two years. He had undoubtedly seen better days, but his opponent was not exactly in his prime either. A volley of jabs and crosses left him "hung dazed on the lower rope"[236] as Saldivar became KO victim 47 before the fight was even four rounds old. Refusal to fight Vietnam's Alfredo Marcano had the World Boxing Council strip Jofre of his belt, forever knocking him from that summit he was so well acquainted with. Once burning bright with every prerequisite, Jose's star pupil continued to exercise his blunted moves. Departing from the ring, the gloves and the cheers was testing, but the fall of 1976 saw this become a permanent reality. The years rolled on, the light tufts became lighter still, but the pull of the ring was loosened by keeping active. At seventy-eight Eder still looks like he could walk an upstart onto a counter.

It was a shock to witness Japan's buzz-saw cut through Brazil's Golden Rooster but it did not compare to how shockingly poor next weeks heavyweight title rematch was between Sonny Liston and Muhammad Ali. Months of training and speculation were rewarded with a very poor excuse for a title fight. Years prior to the infamous debacle, while Sonny Liston was almost in danger of getting a sweat on as he squashed Floyd Patterson, the bantamweight king was busy turning away challengers in mesmerising fashion. There was everything you could want in Jofre and yet he never (as was the case with Al Brown, Ortiz and Perez) received universal acclaim. Ring magazine did not offer any of them a single fighter of the year award. For a fighter who is often rated as one of the best ever pound-for-pound, the neglect is strange.

Harada wasn't one to expect any favours. Moments after taking Jofre's title the new champion could scarcely believe it. "I was only fighting hard"[237] confessed the kid from Tokyo.

---

[236] Tri City Herald, 1965, Oct 21st, p.12

[237] The Hartford Courant, 1965, May 19th, p.19A

MUHAMMAD ALI
VS.
JOE FRAZIER

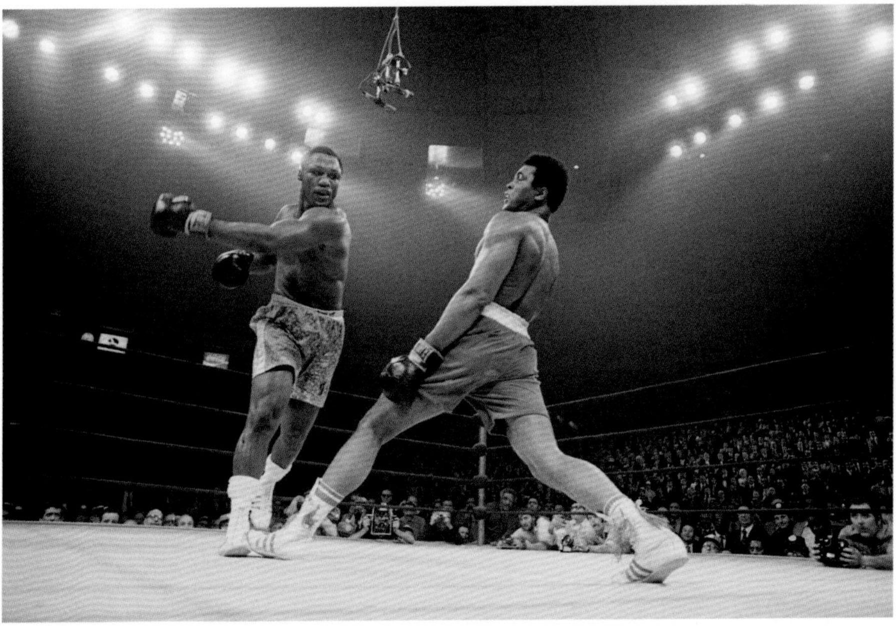

March 8th, 1971
World Heavyweight Title
New York, New York

Hyperbole is a necessary evil. More often than not the action will find it hard to keep pace with the publicity, never mind live up to it. The fight which occurred on March 8th, 1971 managed to justify expectation, somehow. It was, and in many ways still is, the most important heavyweight fight of all time. Not since Jack Dempsey had tried to regain his heavyweight crown against Gene Tunney did a fight gross more money. That was forty-seven years ago. Both boxers were set to receive a record $2.5 million apiece, neither had tasted defeat, and their contrasting styles and personalities created a unique divide among spectators.

In one corner was the champion Joe Frazier, a very approachable, easy mannered man from the farms of South Carolina and the closest thing you will get to a 200lbs Henry Armstrong. In the other was the challenger and former champion Muhammad Ali, a fleet-footed, highly opinionated man whose sharp tongue was as guilty of shocking as it was of amusing. Frazier never entertained Ali's claims of him being a white man's black man, but the constant slander wore thin. At first laughing, then brooding, Frazier grew to dislike the man.

Joe certainly wasn't the first to suffer the caustic quips of the self-proclaimed greatest. Insults came naturally to one time Cassius Clay, and defeat was foretold in playful rhyme. A mischievous grin broke up the howling, but the act wasn't some charade to hide a lack of ability. You needed only to get a glance at Clay boxing to see he was the rarest of species, but the outrageous commentary helped no end. Having won the light-heavyweight gold in Rome, Cassius joined the professionals as a thin heavyweight, though there was potential in that long frame. With dangling arms Clay seemed to put himself in unnecessary danger but incredible reflexes allowed him to evade and counter in a split second. When properly filled out at 210lbs Cassius was no small man, but he moved around as if he was made of some light synthetic material. He was fast as well; amazingly so. The long-retired figure of Jack Dempsey had turned his cobbled fists to writing and even the great mauler had to admit, "he may be the fastest heavyweight ever - and I never thought I'd see anyone as fast as Gene Tunney."[238]

Progress was smooth until Sonny Banks caused a scare in 1962. Sweeping his left over Clay's low right, Banks exposed a fundamental weakness in the brash boxer. It would remain throughout his career. A useful left hook was fired from the ropes and down he went. Nothing more than buzzed, Cassius got back up and even managed to stick to his fourth round curtain call; a trick he claimed made him the double greatest. Under the supervision of Angelo Dundee and lyrical worship of Drew Bundini Brown, Clay racked up the victories. Archie Moore slumped in the third along with his advanced years, but Doug Jones was contemptuous of Clay's forecasting. The New Yorker was expected to fall in the fourth, a favourite round for Cassius; instead he made the fight close enough for a small portion to cry "robbery!" Jones was not entitled to the win, but he at least proved that Clay did not always win on his terms. Next was Britain's Henry Cooper. The Englishman's skin tore like wet paper but he possessed a punch which could make any fight interesting. The five said rounds it would take for Clay to win were honoured, but not before a slight hiccup. As the fourth neared

[238] True's Boxing Yearbook, 1966, p.7

completion a left hook struck again. The ropes helped to cushion his fall, but the effects were plain to see. The bell did its part in resuscitating the big favourite and smelling salts were at the ready. A great deal of commotion unfolded in Clay's corner during this famous interval, but the myth of his corner splitting the glove is just that. True to his word, Clay "jived in five", slicing Cooper's left brow. A few more aggravations and the trickle of claret began to gush. In the shortest space of time Cooper's left eye was, as Harry Carpenter put it, "in an absolutely appalling state" and referee Tommy Little had no choice but to send the game Brit back to his corner. Clay's slashing blows put him at the front of that reluctant queue which led to Sonny Liston. Cassius was psyched about facing the menacing champion, but 7-1 odds in favour of Sonny painted a bleak picture. Cassius called eight. Most sided with the champion's version of the fight; no more than two. At the stare down Liston's collection of towels helped to make his cartoon torso stand out even more, but, regardless of the scare tactics, he was the shorter man.

Using his range, speed and that charming movement, Clay made Liston lunge with his primary weapon. In fact, he could hardly lay a glove on Cassius, let alone prepare him for the kill. Falling behind he took the fifth after Clay had vented to Angelo that he couldn't see, supposedly the dastardly work of some corrosive substance Liston's corner had put on his gloves. Fortunately the effect subsided and the challenger took control again to cause an angry swelling under the champion's right eye. At times the champion desperately took cover from Clay's combinations. Ringsiders may have recalled Liston digesting Cleveland Williams' Sunday best, but he retired in his corner blaming a shoulder injury. Clay went ballistic.

In later defences, not counting Liston's abysmal showing in the rematch, Canada's George Chuvalo provided a glimpse on how to, if not defeat, at least approach Ali. The scorecards did not tell of any success, but every now and then, when not eating a stream of jabs, the incredibly rugged Chuvalo drove the champion back to rip short arcs into his gut; an ambitious hook sometimes found the kisser. The attack was too basic but there was hope for one better inaugurated in trench warfare. And if Joe Frazier wasn't that man then there can be nobody else. The 'black Marciano' was a decent pseudonym, no doubt there were similarities with Brockton's Blockbuster, but as the fights rolled on Joe shed all generalisations to unveil his warrior signature. Addictively bobbing forward, delivering his hooks like a bullwhip, Frazier's agitated, grunting manner was all his own. The idea was non-stop aggression, but it didn't explode from the offset, rather the temperature rose with each passing minute, going from uncomfortably warm to a furnace in the space of fifteen rounds. Reporters noted this rising hostility and Smokin' Joe was born.

With his Olympic conquest and an unbeaten record, Frazier's progress was the stuff of golden boys, yet his career was improbably littered with hardships. That he was partially blind before he knew how to position his hands was the start of them. Boxing was originally a remedy for Joe's spare flesh. He wasn't half bad and so the gym-rat turned fighter. The 1964 Tokyo Olympic Games reserved a space for him and Joe recalled how he sneakily alternated hands to pass the optical examinations. It would be near impossible to pull of such trickery today, but Frazier succeeded in duping the officials and won a gold medal. Keen to escort him into the professional ranks was an institution known as Cloverlay. Yancey Durham was the man hired to enhance Frazier's strong points and erase his weak ones. A contract was signed and the kid from Beaufort was soon climbing in and out of the ring at a healthy pulse.

Mike Bruce attained his fifteen seconds of fame when he floored Frazier in his second bout. It was a tense moment when he touched down, but fortunately he was only a shade dizzy and won in the third. There was a nice rapidity to Frazier's early career but it nearly undid him against Argentinean Oscar Bonevena. It was rather ambitious to face this strong, bull of a fighter in only his second year as a pro. The first round was lively enough. In the second Frazier got caught square with a chopping right which put him down. When he managed to reconstruct his stance a left dumped him again. He rose and Bonevena needed just one more for the three-knockdown rule to intervene. There was over a minute left but Frazier stayed on his feet and brought the fight to Oscar for the remaining eight rounds, squeezing through on a majority decision. The finished article was a still few fights away. Joe fought too upright which left him exposed. Encounters with Eddie Machen and Doug Jones helped sharpen that bobbing movement. By 1967 Chuvalo was just the right kind of iron bear to test him. A long night was expected but a left hook gravely sliced Chuvalo's eye in the fourth. Interpreted as a bad cut, Frazier had actually fractured the right orbital bone and, in doing so, became the first man to stop the granite Canadian.

A heavyweight tournament was proposed for one man to eventually meet the outspoken champion. Initially Cloverlay did not figure they should play ball as they had the hottest contender out there. Eventually they agreed. Ali's most recent effort involved flattening Zora Folley, but his next opponent was entirely different. As had Detroit's favourite son, Ali was expected to fall in line regarding conscription. In 1966 he was reclassified to '1A' but when called before the Houston induction board the answer was no. The punishment was five years imprisonment. Through appeals and good behaviour he lessened the sentence, but his absence gave Frazier's arched clubs all the room they needed to level the division.

The Garden had grown accustomed to Joe and was eager to see how he would handle his amateur boogieman. Buster Mathis had got the better of Joe back in Tokyo but a broken thumb passed national responsibility. Mathis' fleshy midriff wasn't pretty but he could fight. The big man was quite the mover and used his surprising mobility to get Frazier on even terms; at least for a brief period. The fight went on and Frazier got closer. The hooks that initially whistled past started to scuff Buster's head and in the eleventh a compact left dropped him hard. Arthur Mercante fulfilled his duty and New York appointed Frazier as heavyweight champion. Bonevena was equally stubborn in their rematch but Frazier controlled the inside battle, showing up stronger, flaunting superior firepower. He had no problem absorbing the cross this time and ran away with unanimous scores. The next step in the hunt for worldwide acclaim spelt Jerry Quarry.

The twenty-four-year-old 'Bellflower Belter' had been denied the gold once before and was ready to go through a brick wall for the win. Frazier, though a fan favourite, had nothing like the relationship Quarry did with the crowd. From the opening bell the blond underdog attacked Joe with a ferocious confidence and the 16,570 capacity sounded their delight. If there was one weakness in Frazier it was that he was rather slow out of the blocks. Quarry evidently sensed this and repeatedly smashed Frazier's head with short punches as Joe searched for his rhythm. Few men could have suffered Quarry in that form but Frazier was one of them. The second round wasn't too pretty either but Joe didn't budge as he began to warm up. Jerry's belief didn't fade. His condition did. The pace dropped and was then picked up again by Frazier who concentrated his attack on the body. Quarry grit his teeth, trying to punch with his bulldozing foe but even the clean blows were swallowed whole. A deep cut was opening in the third and by the seventh both eyes were wounded. Jerry retired before the eighth. "He's just too much fighter"[239] acknowledged the loser.

To gain complete ownership of the heavyweight title, World Boxing Association champion Jimmy Ellis needed tending to. The possibility of a fight with Ali figured in every conversation, but nothing could be guaranteed given his exile. The unification fight against Ellis ended the longest absence of Frazier's fighting life. Seven months away from the gym had not been kind; "it was gruelling work to get back down from 232 pounds to 205"[240] said Joe. In the ring it was the same old song and dance. Jimmy stuck Frazier with long punches in the early goings but Joe just fixed his greedy leer on him. It wasn't hard for punches to reach Frazier's head but so much jittering and slipping was going on that effective punches were always an inch or two off target. It was Ellis who looked uncomfortable and in the third that uncompromising left landed flush. There was no light at the end of the tunnel and in the fifth Frazier twice decked Jimmy, the last time with a hook which he described as feeling like "when you hit a baseball that rides out on the open field." Boxing had itself a new, official heavyweight champion. Five hard years of slugging had come to replace the memory of Louisville's estranged luminary. That was until the state of Georgia granted him his boxing licence.

The ex-champion was hungry for his return as were the many faithful who had supported his political stance. Jerry Quarry was the man to welcome Ali back into the ring. The big question was; what would be left? In three rounds Ali showed there was still lightning in his arms, cutting Jerry up for the stoppage. It was a touch creakier than fans remembered, but three years was a long time for a fighter to twiddle his thumbs. It didn't take long to deduce what fight topped everyone's wish list though the number one contender needed to further oil his joints. Frazier took his preliminary the month prior against light-heavyweight champion Bob Foster. The gangly blaster never could cure his heavyweight itch but Frazier did his best to permanently discourage him in the second round when his senses were sandwiched between the ropes and a speeding hook. Things were not so simple for Ali when Bonavena made his stubborn reappearance. The wide bruiser was insistent on referring to Muhammad

[239] The Milwaukee Journal, 1969, Jun 24th, p.13

[240] The Spokesman-Review, 1970, Feb 18th, p.10

as Clay before the fight and wasn't too friendly during the fight either. Coming into the fifteenth round it had not been the most convincing display but a left floored Oscar and two more signalled for the automatic stoppage making Ali the first, and eventually, only man to stop him. Boxing's super fight was fast approaching. A brief rest could be taken by the two men before morning jaunts and early nights governed their existence for the coming weeks.

The intensity of Ali's workouts fluctuated daily inside Miami's "steamy" fifth street gym. The press couldn't decide which one it was, whether he thought "so much of himself or so little of Joe Frazier."[241] As far as Ali was concerned about his opponent he had him sussed every which way. He was too easy to hit, too predictable, and of course, too ugly. Flirting with his various exercises Ali gave reporters plenty of material. It was going to be "no-contest" he vented, more serious than tongue-in-cheek. The champ's training digs were originally in New York but the frosty weather had team Frazier relocate to Philadelphia. Joe was no less vocal than his rival while limbering up, but the closer it got to the fight that welcoming manner of his all but dissolved to leave a pensive, easily irritated grouch. Ali was convinced that the change in mood was a sure sign of doubt but there had been times when even he was hit by the possibilities of reality; "this fight is going all the way. I'm training for 15 rounds"[242] said the challenger, his opinions cooling during the harder graft. When the bickering gave way for the official weights of the men they read 215lbs for Ali and 205lbs for Frazier. Not only in weight, but in height and reach the challenger had the champion outdone. The notable statistic for Frazier was that he was the younger man by two years; twenty-seven to Ali's twenty-nine.

At 10:30pm, in front of a record 20,455 attendance, the combatants burrowed their way into the middle of the garden, first Ali, then Frazier. A brief glance near ringside revealed a vast collection of some of the world's best known personalities. Betty Davis, Burt Lancaster, vice president Hubert Humphrey and Frank Sinatra (who got his ringside view via taking pictures for Life magazine) were a handful of the celebrities present. Ali made his graceful entrance into the ring. He wore a red robe with white trim which, when removed, unveiled his chiselled form. There was no delay and Frazier slid between the ropes in a bright green robe with gold trim. His physique never was flattered with definition but it was all solid. Those thick legs and bull neck weren't for show. Arthur Mercante did his professional best to divert their attention but they couldn't resist a verbal tussle. Though his mood had changed whilst training, Ali's prediction stabilised in the sixth.

Frazier shot out of his corner much faster than the norm, bobbing up and down, his guard fluttering around his head. Ali quickly adjusted to get his range and then in came the jab. The left hand of the challenger was there to do damage. A lead right and hook collided with the champion's moving head more than once and the punches weren't soft. That dreaded left skimmed past. Ali shook his head at its ineffectiveness. It was a quick start to the second as well, hard punches from either

[241] The Evening Independent, 1971, Feb 24th, p.3-C

[242] The Palm Beach Post, 1971, Feb 16th, p.C-2

man. "The Muhammad Ali we remember three and a half years ago was a dancer… he's not dancing tonight" observed Don Dunphy. In place of the twenty-two-year-old kid who glided around Sonny Liston was a flat-footed attacker, and he was about to do some damage. Ali found Frazier easy to track and each punch landed with a thud, not that it seemed to bother him. Every time Ali sensed danger he yanked his head back. Frazier got close and dug into the mid-section. As was habitual he switched the attack upstairs and got there quicker than Ali could remove his head. The bell dinged with the champion on top.

The fourth opened with heavy assaults from both sides. The pace was blistering. Ali created favourable space and got back to jabbing. His left lashed out at Frazier like a foot trying to stamp out a fire but it had the effect of kerosene. He was landing the cleaner punches when Frazier swatted his jaw. A second hook landed as he backed away, getting a deep "Ooooooh!" from the crowd. There was a good deal of ghetto talk to go with the boxing and Mercante warned them again to cut it out. There was another battle to be won beyond the gloves. In the fifth, after eating a right hand Frazier dropped his arms and goaded Ali to hit him. Many punches were made to miss as he bent at the waist, imitating his persecutor. When the round ended he took a dismissive swipe at Ali's head. It was back to business in the sixth, the round in which Ali had foreseen victory. He seemed to have forgotten all about the prediction however. The new priority was to try and stop Joe from reshaping his organs. With every breath Frazier went forward, and while it was common knowledge he didn't fight any other way his sheer refusal to even acknowledge the incoming hail was a marvel on its own. Forward he went, "apparently oblivious to any blows he absorbed."[243]

The first signs of fatigue began to show. Ali tried to frustrate Joe, leaving his extended left in his face. Frazier slapped it out of his vision in that grunting manner. Again he took a battering around the brow and cheek bones. Ali turned the tables and goaded Joe as he lounged on the ropes. In the eighth the crowd got on the challenger for lazing, but in a move which brought great cheers Frazier grabbed both arms and pulled him off. Returning to his corner, Ali knew it was time to get serious. From the offset in round nine he tagged Joe with hard shots. They bounced off him like always but his face was officially getting ugly. With thirty seconds to go Muhammad socked him with a crisp one-two. Pushing him off the combination was repeated and he concluded the good spell by smashing two left uppercuts into Frazier's bowed head. No more than a blink, until now. For the first time Joe buckled and the bell went. Another close round brought them to the eleventh.

Ali was happy enough countering from one of the corners when a hook smashed his jaw. His knees quivered and one more made him sag. As if the champion wasn't already all over him, Frazier went wild. The drowsy challenger ate a couple more head-snappers and some cold water was at the ready when he stumbled back to his corner. Things didn't look any rosier in the twelfth. Ali had gone from scrapping his prediction to trying to survive. The reddened scowl made for a strange sight, so used to smiles and boasts of invincibility was everybody. The thirteenth round was a candidate

[243] The Washington Post, 1971, Mar 9th, p.D1

for the most torrid, and that was saying something. The conflict nestled in another corner where they made brilliant exchanges. Something Ali had neglected the whole way, his legs, got moving and helped him get the better of the penultimate round. Frazier pursued in a, by his standards, casual manner, probably saving himself for a big finish. Ali too knew the importance of a big finish.

At the call of time Mercante insisted on them extending their failing arms to touch gloves. The noise flooded through from the furthest tiers and the undefeated ex-champion set his feet for maximum leverage. Joe responded furiously. His charge fixed them in a clinch. Mercante broke them up but Frazier was about to deal the greatest a great disservice. A hook was motioned to the body when, in a violent change of pace, a second was sent to Ali's unprotected jaw. The punch travelled spectacularly through its destination and Ali hit the deck. The tassels of his boots flailed into the air, his body lay horizontal. After forty-three minutes it looked a done deal, yet before the count had reached four he was up. Coming out like some kind of compensation to reason, the right side of Ali's jaw suddenly stood out. It was horribly inflamed. Joe didn't look so hot either with nasty swellings all over the left side of his face. That didn't stop him from firing his honey punch with absolute contempt for both his and his opponent's wellbeing. Halfway through Ali was briefly paralysed by the big left. Briefly that is. Something was keeping him up. The bell rung with the two men exhausted but still trading. Frazier also had the last say in the war of words, offering some departing quip from his gory mouth. Unanimous scores were prepared.

Muhammad was firmly knocked into second place, though how bitterly he had resisted defeat. "I never thought I would live to hear Ali described as a "fighter that can take it"[244] conceived a reporter. As it was, Ali's second career was *built* on a reputation to be able to take it. He would take a lot in the years to come but nothing like the beating Joe put on him. In two successive meetings Ali had his way, admittedly not without a struggle, but Frazier was never the same fighter; the tenacity, the speed, the fitness levels, all the vital components dithered. He entered hospital and didn't come out for two weeks. Retirement still troubled his mind. He would not retire, but Smokin' Joe already had.

Four years later the two diminished fighters collided for fourteen gruelling rounds in boxing's most beloved rubber match, the Thrilla in Manila. Frazier did everything his degraded body would permit. Ali was nowhere near prime condition either but age was not as incriminating. It was a fight undoubtedly worthy of the championship though there would be no last round heroics as Eddie Futch explained to Joe he was going to pull him out. Frazier remonstrated in vain, spitting out blood, shaking his head. Once aware of the surrender Ali crashed to the floor to escape a swarming audience. Back in the calm of the dressing room he tried his modest best to pay Joe a tribute; "He is the greatest fighter of all time, next to me." Until his dying day, Joe grunted at the remark, but while he may have lost the case, some hard evidence continues to smoke; a date. That night when the greatest wasn't good enough.

---

[244] Eugene Register-Guard, 1971, Mar 9th, p.3-B

AARON PRYOR
VS.
ALEXIS ARGUELLO

November 12th, 1982
WBA Light-Welterweight Title
Miami, Florida

On a warm Miami evening, encased before 23,800 spectators, Aaron Pryor offered his fractured attention to the following spiel.

"Give me the other bottle…the one I mixed." Al 'Panama' Lewis' call for a plastic bottle is one of those endlessly entertaining chapters. Hand-feeding Pryor the mysterious tipple, Lewis assumed his dastardly role. In seven months' time he would remove the padding from Luis Resto's gloves, in turn destroying the career of Billy Collins (just in case you weren't sold on his crookedness). There must have been something in the bottle, something illegal, some kind of unapproved substance. Maybe we've seen too many movies. Whatever it was it can't have made a difference, not at that point, not after the way they had been fighting. And while we may find it silly to entertain the idea that Pryor ingested turbo it would be a shame to dispel such a bizarre story. Besides, it fits snuggly inside Pryor's helter-skelter life. His opponent's life was no picnic either.

Though the classy Nicaraguan had a peaceful air to him, even when fighting, much of his spare time was dedicated to the problems of his country, and they weren't few. Alexis Arguello developed his compassionate ethos as a teenager, learning his trade in the tropical, earthquake prone capital, Managua. As his country's foremost sportsman he would witness some of the worst events in its one hundred and twenty year history. In the ring it was patience which separated Arguello from the herd. He was neither quick nor slow, but steady with a serrated edge. One of boxing's paradoxical commandments, to be relaxed in a hectic situation was a speciality of Alexis'; ice cool under fire was 'El Flaco Explosivo'. His strict economy gave him a subdued appearance as if he was supervising rather than fighting, but this deliberate tempo could disarm your radar, clearing the runway for his straight right. Arguello's honey punch was a rare treasure. Unlike Joe Frazier who had his left stuck on repeat Alexis' right was sent in every now and then. Contrary to those who believe in working three minutes a round, this sporadic malice axed seventy of its eighty-nine victims.

Alexis learnt to take his time from the get go. School was strangely enjoyable but his father was unable to fund him and so he had to leave at fifteen. A trip to the local boxing gym proceeded and, right then and there, it became his new home. 58-2 with 48 knockouts wrapped up a solid amateur record and then came the professionals where Omar Amaya showed Alexis that a treadmill awaited, stopping him in four rounds. He recovered well as he began to forge that essential, championship stamina. Arguello endured his second loss in 1972 during a bout where he injured his hand. He was back after a few months but, as he fell asleep on the evening of the 22nd December, something far more disastrous was in store for him.

Half an hour into the 23rd an earthquake hit Managua. Aftershocks were gravely felt days after killing around 20,000 and making hundreds of thousands homeless. Opportunists were killed for looting and the government had many more buildings dynamited for fear of them collapsing. Young Alexis recalled, after having decided to sleep on the coach for no particular reason that he awoke to see "one of the walls lying on my bed."[245] Less than a week of tremors created a problem which would take

[245] The Glasgow Herald, 1981, Jan 9th, p.24

decades to repair, and while diggers got to work on clearing the rubble, Arguello tried to clear his own path with his fists.

Ernesto Marcel's world title gave the twenty-one-year-old his big chance in 1974. It was a little too early for the mustachioed string bean to take on such responsibility and he was outpointed in the Panamanian's backyard. Marcel retired straight after, vacating the belt for Ruben Olivares to snatch it in an alteration Arguello was soon part of. The Mexican was not the butcher of bantamweights he used to be at 126lbs but had oodles of experience. The odds preferred youth and Arguello was made the slight favourite. For a man touching 5'10" Alexis looked every bit a 124lbs man with ribs protruding. It was his first fight out of Nicaragua, no less against a modern legend, but he handled the pressure very well, wearing the impassive look of a man in a friendly spar. Olivares fought a gutsy fight but strength was with the challenger. A second knockdown in the thirteenth rid Olivares of everything and Arguello was world champion, one with aspirations. Gaining the featherweight championship allowed Arguello to flex his passport. He went as far as Japan for one of his four defences, all of which ended before the distance. Nobody could stand his power but possible victims were spared when he moved up to super-feather. The 130lbs class gave his body just enough leeway; it would neither sap his strength nor dull his natural advantages. Those ribs healthily regressed back into his chest cavity but his ability to finish a fight didn't disappear.

Alexis got his first taste of the Garden in 1977 where three opponents amounted to less than seven rounds. No longer hindered by weight or experience issues, his talent for boxing shifted into top gear, and with Alfredo Escalera up ahead, Arguello would need to be firing on all his spindly cylinders. The Puerto Rican champion was young, powerful and had ten defences to back up his boastful talk. Brimming with confidence, Escalera put his whole body into his punches from the onset. He quickly learnt that trying to phase, let alone hurt Arguello was tough going. Knocked down in the second, bleeding from the mouth and cut around both eyes before the fifth, the harder he pressed Alexis the more he incurred injuries like a man wrestling with barbwire. "Some feel you can outbox Arguello only for so long" remarked Howard Cossell. Escalera began to meet the gaze of his corner with a helpless expression. With a greased brow and heavy lungs he made a defiant stand in the ninth, cutting Arguello and showing he was no paper champ. A sneaky right made Alexis give ground in the twelfth and Escalera punched in synchrony with the non-stop, ceremonial drumming. Referee Arthur Mercante did not condone the champion's facial damage and waved it off in the thirteenth. It was a cruel way to lose but Escalera got a chance to reclaim his title next year. For Arguello it was the chance to leave no question as to who was the best at 130lbs. He came through loud and clear. Escalera made it all the way to the thirteenth again. The determined challenger wore the same bloody mess on his face and had been down twice. Another cuts stoppage was possible; instead Arguello threw a short hook off the jab and Escalera, though he had a stab at rising, was incapable of controlling his body.

Alexis, though conscious of his country's problems had moved into the sunny, cheerful ambience of Miami. Back in Nicaragua it was just sunny. President Anastasio Somoza Debayle, the third in the bloodline was guilty of utilising national aid for the earthquake to enrich the regime. The growing revolt was pushed over the edge with the assassination of Pedro Joaquín Chamorro, the editor of Managua's foremost, anti-Somoza newspaper, and the country was thrown into civil war. One of Arguello's six brothers was killed during the turmoil. The super-featherweight champion did not wish to take sides. Highlighting the difference between violence inside and outside of the ring, "the bombs" said Arguello, "don't respect anybody."[246] And with respect came focus. Alexis had no problem testing his might against the best. Rafael 'Bazooka' Limon and Bobby Chacon were to rule the 130lbs landscape after he had left, but until then they were cut up and expelled. The proposition of a fight with Roberto Duran sizzled for a few years but when Arguello climbed into the 135lbs class the fiery man from Panama was preoccupied terrorizing welterweights.

Scotland's Jim Watt had defended the World Boxing Council version of the title four times and was the first to put a dent in the undefeated record of the Olympic gold medallist, Howard Davis Jr; against Arguello, the difference in calibre was evident. The Nicaraguan was too much for the tough Scotsman and the title duly changed hands after fifteen. The win made Alexis only the sixth man to have won titles at three weights but he wasn't done. At 135lbs Arguello revived the tradition of defeating future champions when Ray 'Boom Boom' Mancini smashed into the tanned reed of a fighter. Big cheers went up as he rotated the champion's head with quick punches but the later rounds was when it got hot with Arguello. Come round ten Mancini began the respiratory battle. That unsettling poise eyed him in the twelfth when a straight right caused his knee to scrape the floor in a drunken cloud. There was nothing left and in the fourteenth Arguello delivered a wonderful finale. Three more defences took Arguello into his third decade of life. A fourth title was, seeing as it had never been done, ambitious, but that is precisely what Arguello sought as he walked out into that warm Miami evening.

And so to his bellicose rival, the one called 'The Hawk'. On the streets of Cincinnati, Pryor's "you hit me, I'll hit you" attitude unearthed boxing at a tender age for a thirteen year amateur career. He became a National AAU champion in 1972 and four years later outpointed a young Thomas Hearns to win a National Golden Gloves championship. The stylish Howard Davies Jr prevented him going to the Montreal Games, handing him one of his sixteen defeats. In the remaining two hundred and four Aaron was the victor. Pryor seethed at his conqueror's pretty contract. $250,000 was there for Davies in his pro debut, dwarfing Pryor's measly $400. Insult followed injury as Pryor became one of Davis' sparring partners for $250 per week though that arrangement was speedily undone when he floored the rising star. In twenty-four fights just two men managed the distance. Pryor was not an atomic puncher, but he threw them in amazing quantity, pursuing every moment. He made it part of his

[246] Harlan Daily Enterprise, 1979, Jul 9th, p.2

character to rush at you from the opening bell, and usually only a few rounds were necessary to finish what he started.

Aaron could do nothing but laugh when Davis flopped against Jim Watt in June of 1980. With his own world title challenge looming against Antonio Cervantes his mind needed to be clear. 'Kid Pambelé' as Cervantes was known had taken the World Boxing Association light-welterweight title way back in 1972, and save for a close loss to Wilfredo Benitez in '76 it had been his since. Aaron realised the importance of a quick start as Cervantes was a solemn customer to deal with once he found his stroke. At the opening bell Pryor was the embodiment of aggression, running close to his target, setting the legs wide apart to pump his arms in that crazed, highly-enjoyable fashion. This strategy made him a little easy to hit and got him floored before the rounds close, but his bountiful attack was eye candy. The short right that caused a touchdown riled the madman in him. He was not one to neglect the belly and constructed outrageous combinations. At no point was Cervantes comfortable. The short challenger had it all his way and in the fourth he cornered his worried opponent to start a new reign with a ten count. The Cincinnati supporters were nearly as happy as the new champion.

From the winter of 1980 to the summer of 1982, Pryor stopped another five men who went for his title. It was never dull. Charisma, excitement and a big finish shaped every one of those defences, but the name opponent was missing, and there sure as hell wasn't a shortage of name fighters in the early '80s. Sugar Ray Leonard was already the prince of the box office. He was the glorious realisation of the false prophet that was Howard Davis Jr. If you wanted the big pay day, you fought Leonard, alas Roberto Duran and Thomas Hearns were much higher than Pryor in Ray's list of enriching adversaries. 1981's ticket-shifting showdown between Leonard and Hearns marked the second irony in Pryor's boxing life. Now it was the man he had *defeated* in the amateurs who was part of the richest fight in history. A seven digit purse is many fighters' primary goal but Leonard went into exile in 1982, killing whatever slim chance there was of a Pryor fight. The light-welterweight division was definitely not the place to be. The stars of welterweight were about to climb higher while Wilfredo Gomez, Salvador Sanchez and Lupe Pintor happily mingled below. Jamaica's Saoul Mamby held the World Boxing Council version of the title but since the championship was split attempts to unify had become rare. By the time Pryor had chosen the man to define his legacy, Mamby was an ex-champion.

Alexis Arguello knew how it felt to be the favourite, and he was due a refresh. Nobody had ever captured a fourth world title but the odds favoured "the most chivalrous man in the fight game"[247] to conquer uncharted land. The date was set for November 12th. There wasn't quite the $8-10 million pay packet that Leonard could produce, but $1.6 million wasn't half bad. $1.5 million went to Arguello. Two men, so very different, physically and as well as culturally, were linked by something besides boxing. Usually this is the cue to emphasise how much they despised each

[247] The Miami News, 1982, Nov 4th, p.18

other, but the ostensible thug from Cincinnati had only pleasant things to say of his opponent. There was class to go with that animal in the ring. Alexis was his respectful, complimentary self. Noting his pristine etiquette it was joked that "he out-Louises Joe."[245]

Due to the anarchy, Nicaragua had banned professional boxing. The profession which Arguello swore by for discipline, for success, was no longer an option for young men. Furthermore his old property, estimated to be worth around $2 million, had been expropriated. Times were pressing to keep focus, but boxing had this hypnotic effect on Arguello, reducing the outside world and all its problems to a simple case of mano-a-mano. Trainer Eddie Futch remarked how Arguello would never break his gaze from the opponent, "even between rounds, while I'm talking to him, he is looking across the ring right at the other guy."[248] Pryor had his own method for sharpening his mind. Taking a pew for the medical examination, the calmed champion wore a pair of gloves. When asked what was the purpose of them were he explained, "They keep my mind occupied on what is first."[249] It's a classic pitfall to think one fight ahead, but for a life short on opportunity, Pryor refused to charm himself with notions of stardom.

When he made the long walk out to meet his destiny, recognizable as a short bundle of energy inside a black satin robe, his expressive face was frozen with determination. To say the same of Arguello would be an oxymoron. The pencil-shaped Nicaraguan was no different before the tens of thousands than he was when jumping rope. Pryor pointed at Arguello, signalling his demise. You could bet your bottom dollar that he was going to try to finish his man in that first round. "We'll see what happens." said Alexis, "If I have to start fast, I will."[250] He wasn't to have a choice in the matter as Pryor jumped on him in record speed. Excited volleys were launched upwards at the taller challenger, pounding him into his defence. After the initial wave Arguello clipped Pryor's unguarded head with a right. It staggered his feet and the Nicaraguan support made themselves heard. Aaron reacted in earnest with a smile.

The champion, though a few pounds heavier, was every inch the smaller man. Arguello could have gone up another weight and still looked short of a good meal. He extended his left warily against the crazed one. Getting the range of Pryor was near impossible when in this fearless state. Thoughtful combinations slammed into Arguello's head and they exchanged fiercely in the last moments to conclude a brilliant opener. Greater quantity was landed by Pryor but the defensive vulnerabilities were on show again in the second when that cross zipped in. Every time this happened his head bounced precariously on his neck, ripe for another blow. Apparently he was too hostile to be dazed. Arguello looped punches to the gut and fought effectively off the ropes. The third was Pryor's but Arguello spied him trying to take in air near the bell and landed crisp single punches. Between Aaron's lunges and Arguello's hurried countering there was little structure to the fight. It was difficult for either to find their tempo but in the fourth Pryor reminded the crowd of his weighty amateur pedigree.

[248] Gettysburg Times, 1982, Nov 10th, p.17

[249] Williamson Daily News, 1982, Nov 10th, p.21

[250] Record-Journal, 1982, Nov 11th, p.13

The ring was put to good use and smooth jabs kept Arguello off balance. When he shot with the right, Pryor niftily slipped to the outside and came between his opponent's guard with an uppercut. "It's really impressive to see Aaron Pryor as a boxer" mused Ray Leonard, commentating for HBO. "You Da Man!" blurted from Pryor's corner. Faced with this light-footed pretender it was hard to tell whether Arguello was genuinely bemused or purposely standing off. With that internal clock ticking he responded at the close of the round, and when he did the audience loved it.

Pryor had created a nice point's cushion. From the fourth to the ninth he was tactically superior. A sharp right sliced Arguello's left eye in the sixth and his infrequent contributions became rarities. The ninth gave him that lease of life when a right knocked Pryor's whole body sideways. The champion's swish feet resumed control, but the warning signs were getting brighter. Those attacks weren't as overwhelming as before. You got the sense that Aaron was the one more prone to fade than the thirty year old assassin. For the expert in championship disaster, fatigue was preparing ideal sniper conditions.

With the eleventh a minute old, referee Stanley Christodoulou scorched Al Lewis for flapping his lips and then Alexis blasted the pupil with his best yet. The whiplash caused a circular mist to spray from the champion's head. Strangely, Pryor barely reacted to the punch but Alexis was beginning to find his wicked range. The fight was back on and Pryor adapted wonderfully, slipping straight shots through Arguello's high defence. His winged punches sometimes had a pushy appearance but there was no denying their quality; the fluidity of his head-to-body and body-to-head rallies were good enough to please sixty-nine-year-old Henry Armstrong, one of the many getting their money's worth. Arguello took his licks and persevered with that subtle body attack, each blow guided by an experience most believed would make the difference. The thirteenth round came, and with it a milestone, for nobody had lasted this long with Pryor in thirty contests. Halfway through things slowed down. Pryor was content with jabbing when Alexis let go with a straight right. It couldn't have landed more squarely had it been guided by a set of coordinates. It was, as HBO's Larry Merchant jested, "batting practice." The gasping audience waited for the delayed reaction but there was nothing. Pryor stared back like a man impervious. They went back to their corners; Arguello to the calm tuition of Eddie Futch, Pryor to Al Lewis who was looking for his bottle.

Pryor came out fresh with the knowledge that six minutes remained. He got back to jabbing and went in with his lead right-straight left combination. Both connected and Arguello grimaced. He soon capitalised with another flurry and the durable stalker became helpless. That famous composure perspired from his body as he staggered into the ropes. Aaron suddenly had the energy of ten men and sent in his right hand, again and again. Arguello's head bounced back and forth. Christodoulou had the good sense to end what Ring magazine would go on to dub the fight of the decade. Aaron had his big win, and nothing, not allegations of cocaine abuse or a Howard Davis Jr could take it away from him. Alexis slumped to the floor where he was given oxygen during an uneasy interlude. He had sustained a bad concussion, cuts around both eyes and a broken nose, but compared to the pain of losing it was trivial.

The big rematch went ahead next year and Arguello was done in ten. Entertaining, it had nothing on the original. Arguello sat hugging his knees when dropped, glancing at Richard Steele reluctantly. It wasn't a look of defeat. Alexis knew his time as a fighter was up. Technically he had four more fights, but it's best to forget pointless additions to great careers. Arguello urged Pryor to continue on his war path, but The Hawk had reached his summit. The unbeaten fighter became one of many champions to fall foul of drugs. By 1985 he was an ex-champion. Boxing gave him a reason to detox but in 1987 he suffered his lone defeat when Bobby Joe Young put him on the floor. Unlike days of old, Pryor did not spring up but rose to sample the grim effects he had caused thirty-one opponents. Three more fights and he faced a difficult future, though through religious speaking and training young fighters he avoided the abyss. Arguello's personal troubles were not an entirely private matter but he carried on and looked to have made it to the autumn of his life in one piece.

Despite the continuing struggle with his homeland his people did not think anything less of him than a hero. In 2008 he held the flag for the introduction of Nicaragua into the Beijing Olympics and shortly after became mayor of Managua. His relationship with Pryor went beyond the respective small talk that occurs when rivals reunite. Alexis could be happy of Pryor's rehabilitation. The warmest, most sincere good wishes were waiting for Aaron whenever they met up. He couldn't however cleanse a tormented soul. On July 1st, 2009, Nicaragua lost its most famous personality when a bullet went through his heart. It is widely believed that Arguello is the one who pulled the trigger. Thousands upon thousands of motorists preceded and trailed the hearse which took his body to Jardines del Recuerdo cemetery. A single pair of blue Reyes gloves rested on the beautiful casket.

As for that bottle, Lewis explained that it was only tap water mixed with Perrier (carbonated mineral water) to help with a recent spell of diarrhoea. Bill Miller, Arguello's agent, saw things differently. Without his fighter's consent, Miller tried to have the fight declared a no contest though he didn't make the most believable case when he said that whatever Pryor had consumed made him able to withstand "shots that would have stopped King Kong."[251] According to Eddie Futch, "Pryor took at least 10 shots that would have knocked anybody else out"[252] and to pique the interest of the seventy-one-year-old was no easy thing. Eddie believed that Alexis could have won had he not been trying to look for single shots, but his student felt differently about the encounter.

"Every time I hit this guy they don't affect him, I don't hurt him...and I'm pissing him off."

---

[251] Bangor Daily News, 1982, Nov 15th, p.25

[252] The Milwaukee Sentinel, 1982, Nov 13th, p.1 Part 2

MIKE TYSON
VS.
JAMES 'BUSTER' DOUGLAS

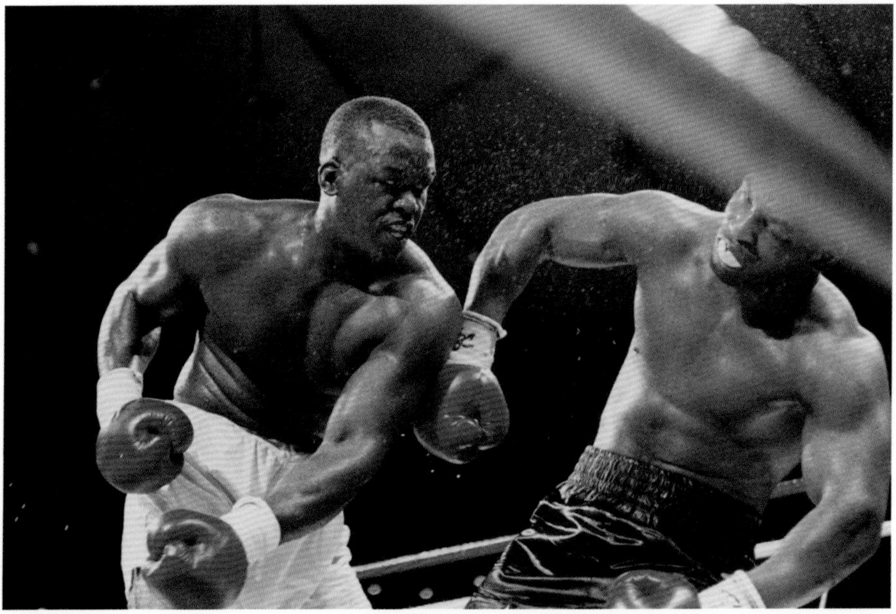

February 11th, 1990
Undisputed Heavyweight Title
Tokyo, Japan

"Cut him and he bleeds, insult his wife or take his money and he hurts. But when he steps into the ring he becomes inhuman in his brutal efficiency. He is a machine that might have been fashioned by the gods of war."[253] This was the kind of effect Mike Tyson had on mere mortals.

On June 27th, 1988 the one man who might have a shot at overcoming the baddest man on the planet was annihilated. 'Once and For All' they called Tyson's acid test and it lasted a whole ninety-one seconds. Undefeated Michael Spinks was expected to, if not win, indemnify his credentials, but the lineal champion was no harder to demolish than Hector Mercedes. Once in the ring Spinks was a picture of disbelief. A few notable sages had chosen him to pip Mike at the finish line, like he did Larry Holmes. 'Whisper it, but Spinks might win' ran a headline. It wasn't a time for wishful thinking. Every motion Tyson made at the former light-heavyweight got him flustered, and you know what they say about sharks smelling blood. The undisputed champion marched his coy opponent into the ropes where a gut blaster forced him to take a knee. Fighting back was quickly ruled a bad idea as another right (this time to the head) went one better and got him horizontal. The starry-eyed victim was given ten and the doubters quickly made themselves scarce.

The slugger with the oak tree neck was hot property ever since he was starching kids as an amateur, but in the months after the Spinks fight many wondered whether there had *ever* been a heavyweight as good as the ferocious twenty-two-year-old. It was a tender subject, but a large percentage were happy to concede that not Joe Louis, not Muhammad Ali, nobody would have survived Tyson's machine-gun bursts. It wasn't just a case of you knew what you were going to get with Tyson but that he looked deeply involved in his line of work. Cranking his neck, restlessly traipsing his end of the ring, the pre-fight ritual was no act. When there was a gap between the officials he'd balefully eye his target. In post-fight interviews he'd often ramble. His personality was odd. The real Mike Tyson seemed to be the fighter and the audience revelled in this apparent rapport with inflicting damage on another person.

A resemblance to Jack Dempsey was no coincidence. As a reformed thirteen year old Mike had watched old films of Dempsey storming after his opponents and it did more than catch his attention. For a time he cropped his hair in that severe '20s style and it became his trademark to wear the old, sockless shoes. A single towel draped over his shoulders to put the finishing touches on a no frills presentation. Fellow New Yorker Kevin Rooney had the privilege of training him and he got Tyson's see-saw clobbering down to a numerical science. It was a winning recipe but their roots were to be found in the spiritual teachings of Constantine D'Amato. Famous for taking Floyd Patterson to the title, he would pass shortly before Tyson became the youngest heavyweight champion ever at twenty.

Cus made Mike. He didn't purge him of his street tendencies, but he supplied the youngster with crucial moral and emotional support. Life had not been easy. Mike's dad died when he was just two, at thirteen his juvenile mishaps landed him in Tryon's Boys' school, and at sixteen his mother passed away. His soprano voice was riddled

[253] Daily Express, 1988, Jun 29th, p.35

with a lisp, making him an obvious target for bullies. One time an older kid went too far, breaking the neck of a pigeon. Many an evening Mike would sit on the rooftops of Brownsville to keep his feathered friends company. He grew to love the city bird and gave the bully a good thrashing. It was the first time Tyson had snapped, therein becoming conscious of his strength. On first contact with boxing there was a spark.

Amongst the many tombstones at St. Patrick's Cemetery lies Cus'. Engraved on his slab are his own words; a beautiful soliloquy on the essence of his teachings:

> "*A boy comes to me with a spark of interest,*
> *I feed the spark and it becomes a flame,*
> *I feed the flame and it becomes a fire,*
> *I feed the fire and it becomes a roaring blaze.*"

Patterson was his chief pupil, but Tyson too perfectly fit this idea of cultivating a human bonfire.

Mike's love affair with boxing ran deeper. He was as much a scholar in his profession as he was a brute. For hours upon hours he would slave over old film reels. The aged mentor happily bunked with numerous fighters, but none were more enthusiastic, more *interested* in boxing than Mike. We're not talking about some dime-a-dozen black kid in the 1930s whose hero was Joe Louis; Tyson could list fighters from any era. He could give you the lowdown on Johnson's 'dive' against Willard or write an essay on why it's unfortunate that Owen Moran is not more fondly remembered.

By the 1980s Cus was working his way into his seventies, far removed from the tricky negotiations and pond-hopping which came with managing Patterson. He had spent a lifetime helping troubled minds and had time for Mike. He would listen to what he had to say and offer advice which was respected with stone silence. Tyson later credited him as the closest thing he ever had to a father figure. Whatever was asked of him he would do, and this made him a very dangerous person. As a physical specimen Tyson was incredibly gifted. He suffered from small-man syndrome in his early teens and made it a point to spar with larger men, but he soon filled out, and when he did he was sight to see; huge thighs, bumbling arms, and that neck which was just a shade off twenty inches. He looked very much like a human rendition of a bulldozer, but he didn't move like one. Tyson was Patterson with added firepower. He could deliver four, five punches in under a second, and not messy flurries, but good, solid punches; phenomenal for a 215lbs man. Friedrich Nietzsche once defined life as a "discharge of strength". When Tyson trained it looked like he was trying to discharge the strength of an elephant. On the speed bag, the heavy bag, and while skipping he came alive with great intensity. Cus equipped him with the same 'peek-a-book' defence but taught him to stay close, roll under hooks, jump to the side for a surprise attack. Jaded reporters would only see the power, but this was a clever fighter.

"Your head's coming up a little bit" Mike was once told while being watched bludgeon the heavy bag. "Is it?" he responded apologetically. "Just a little, we need to make it perfect." This scrutiny rubbed off on Rooney. He saw how Cus spoke to

Mike and blended in. Teddy Atlas had trained Tyson for his win in the 1984 National Golden Gloves tournament, even lending him a shoulder to cry on during a pre-fight breakdown. An incident involving his daughter brought a gun into the middle of their relationship, and they unpleasantly parted.

After wiping his eyes dry, Tyson registered an amazingly quick knockout over Jonathan Littles and he was dubbed the eight second kid. There was a preference for achieving maximum damage in the shortest space of time, and it was the same approach as a professional. Not to put too light a word on it, Tyson's preference for a quick night ended fifteen of his first twenty-seven fights in the first round. His competition wasn't much cause for worry but it was the manner in which he got rid of his opponents that scored brownie points. Tyson could make a knockout look spectacular. He had the compact, shotgun delivery of Joe Louis, but different to the Brown Bomber's economy, with Tyson it was overkill. Once he got the opponent going, before the rules could put a curfew on the carnage, he tried his best to wreck them. "You would never intentionally hit a man while he was down would you?" once asked Harry Carpenter. "Absolutely not" replied Tyson, though later admitting that in the ring "it's different." That he once expressed a desire to drive Jesse Fergusson's nose bone into his brain tells of that difference. Two men had the misfortune of stretching Mike the distance. Mitch 'Blood' Green and James 'Quick' Tillis had enough experience to escape the big knockout, but they were unable to cause much trouble in their quests to survive.

Cus passed away in November of 1985, but there was a prophecy to fulfil; Tyson would become heavyweight champion of the world. Trevor Berbick captured the World Boxing Council version of the title after upsetting Pinklon Thomas. The thirty-two-year-old Jamaican had worked hard to get to the top and made it known he wasn't spooked by the young destroyer. The challenger, still too young to purchase alcohol, was favoured to rewrite history. Berbick's antics looked to be born of insecurity. Tyson was overeager in the first, missing wildly a few times, but once in range with his hooks he started belting the champion across the ring. Faces were made as he walked back to his corner but Trevor wasn't fooling anybody. Ten seconds into round two he was dropped hard and before the round was over he had lost complete control of his legs, falling over three times. Referee Mills Lane had to call it off.

Rooney was first to congratulate Mike, manager Jim Jacobs was given a kiss, and Don King slipped into his best friend routine. There was a new heavyweight champion, the youngest ever, but different to Patterson, Tyson intended to have an honest reign. A nice level of activity was kept as champion with Mike making four appearances in 1987. Larry Holmes had been a regular champion but he never unified the titles. In March, Tyson outpointed James 'Bonecrusher' Smith for the WBA, in May he knocked out Pinklon Thomas, in August he outpointed Tony Tucker for the IBF and in October he knocked out Tyrell Biggs. It was strange to see Smith last the distance but he stuck to Mike like glue whenever he got the chance. Tucker didn't do too bad either, relatively speaking that is. Both managed to tangle Tyson up in the clinches which was always a problem, even when fighting well a good clinch could paralyze his attack.

Awkwardly decked out in royal garb during his coronation as the undisputed heavyweight champion, it was easy to forget the sacrifice that went into boxing's most exciting fighter. He could already hear the rattling of speed balls during the post-fight interview, and when back in training his body would clock fifty-five hours, from Monday through to Saturday, climbing towards two hundred rounds of sparring. Tyson expressed that if people had to go through what he did "they would cry." Tyson was no less explosive in the gym as he was fighting and it was Rooney's lasting contention that only 50% of Tyson's potential was realized in the ring. However the strain, at least socially, began to take its toll, and the twenty-one-year-old's need for an outlet got him in the print for reasons outside of boxing.

Larry Holmes had made his contempt of Tyson public and King was only too happy to put the former champion in the path of his concussive piggy bank. Though he hadn't fought since losing to Spinks, thirty-eight-year-old Holmes was adamant that the two year break had done him the world of good. For three rounds he managed to avoid the big punches and at the start of the fourth he nearly made Tyson look silly. A perfectly short right cracked his temple moments later, ending the birth of wild thoughts, and he was sent to the canvas twice more; the last time like a brick. March was another instance of success inside the ring but loss outside. Tony Tubbs' head absorbed a big left hook to score Mike's sixth defence. At first stung, the effect coursed its way through his body. At last he fell to the floor, slimly avoiding a savage follow up. You couldn't fault the fighter but Tyson was given a low blow when manager Jacobs died of leukaemia. A month prior Mike's life was made that bit more complicated when he married actress Robin Givens. Blasting Spinks put a lid on the critics, but Robin's financial intentions were exposed when she attempted to sue Tyson for $125 million following a predictable divorce. In the end she had to make do with a $10 million settlement, but as a result of the emotional rollercoaster Kevin Rooney was fired. And with Mike's final tie to that winning formula severed, Don King moved in for checkmate.

Against England's Frank Bruno, the cracks in the paint began to show. The heavyweight with the body-builder physique momentarily shook Mike in the first with a left hook. That vicious right-to-the-body, uppercut-to-the-head combination dismantled Bruno in the fifth, but it had been a scrappy fight. The press were quick on the uptake, a few predicting his demise, but you're as good as your last fight, and when Tyson starched Carl Williams five months later all those puns about Iron Mike rusting were readily pardoned. James 'Buster' Douglas was the next designated piñata, and the chances of him saying otherwise were so far-fetched that some bookies flat-out refused to give him any odds. An underdog of 42-1 in Las Vegas, never before had victory been such an impossibility. Realistically these odds were more indicative of Tyson's mystique than Douglas' actual chances. 8-1 was more like it, but that still made him a bigger underdog than Cassius Clay when he challenged Sonny Liston.

Douglas had bags of talent, but discipline and focus were sore points. The son of William 'Dynamite' Douglas, you'd have thought focus would come naturally, but he was constantly at war with his weight. The chance to become IBF heavyweight champion evaporated at the end of Tony Tucker's fists. It was agreed that Douglas was the one in control but in the tenth he abruptly sagged on the ropes and was stopped. Had Tyson not delved his division into famine it is unlikely that Douglas would have received his shot, but victories over Berbick and Oliver McCall were nice ones at a time when contenders were thin. McCall, a sparring partner of Tyson, was firmly outpointed in a performance where Douglas' loose-armed style was working in top gear. He had a very long reach and threw a jab which could put you on your heels. For a 230lbs man he shifted his weight well. Four, five punch combinations came easily. Few bothered to notice, but Douglas was an accomplished fighter. Though he may as well have been talking to a bust of Beethoven, the challenger swore to make good of his opportunity. What he didn't account for was the tragedy that befell him before his big moment in Japan.

Twenty-three days before the lonely walk into the Tokyo Dome, Douglas' mother died of a stroke. His wife had left him and his father was one of the millions who forecast his destruction. That the mere sight of Tyson may dissolve the last shreds of remaining spirit was a fair bet, but the bad news was more motivating than distracting. "A lot of people think we're crazy, but we think we're going to win"[254] sounded manager John Johnson. Even Tyson was an advocate of the ruling that anything is possible, but most were willing to make an exception.

It was the second time Tyson had graced Japan and the fascination with the undisputed champion was suffocating. Admittedly, it was a little scary to discover that he was a bigger star in a place six thousand miles removed from his home country. Ready for the press, King had himself and Mike dressed in especially distasteful white fur coats. Cameras nervously flashed at them regardless of what they were doing. In a training session it was written that Tyson "exuded an almost bored sense of confidence."[255] One may remember the champion's berating comments towards gym work, and at a pinch over 220lbs, it was possible that commitment was becoming an issue. Problem was Douglas' weight was not too pretty either. At 231 and a half he was a good 10 pounds heavier than he had predicted. Tyson now had a fat lamb to slaughter.

Douglas entered the arena first jogging. Warmly wrapped in a bright white rope, he looked positive. Tyson was next, making his grumpy way to the ring. A white towel ornamented those big shoulders, increasing that no-holds-barred shtick. It took a bit longer than normal for Jimmy Lennon Jr. to complete the introductions while both men focused on staying warm; Douglas bouncing about, Tyson prowling. The Japanese crowd applauded champion and challenger respectfully. With jeering at a minimum, the atmosphere was more like one you'd find at a concerto. The religiously attuned Douglas had explained that the only man he feared was Jesus Christ. Mike Tyson was as intimidating as the next man. With his gloves anxiously squeezed against his chin the champion readied himself for demolition but James used the ring well enough to stop Mike flattening him. All eyes were on Mike but the huge underdog

[254] Spokane Chronicle, 1990, Feb 11th, p.C3

[255] News Straits Times, 1990, Feb 10th, p.19

was there to earn his $1 million purse. A few lefts proved the best work in the opener. It wasn't the first time Tyson had dropped his favourite round. Tony Tucker had had his best moment during the first three minutes and Tony Tubbs looked like he may provide a decent challenge when he started quickly. The ominous champion closed in at the beginning of round two but Douglas had obviously been watching the tapes and tangled his arms. Drifting apart, James made some space and suddenly battered the top of Mike's head with a four punch combination. He calmly moved away, unsurprised by his success. Tyson was slow to react, the inner tiger still dormant it would seem, and he caught more punches, a few flush. You could always rely on HBO's Larry Merchant for an amusing remark as he lethargically quipped, "I dunno if he's gonna shock the world, but he's shocked me so far."

Tyson was livelier in the third and got his body punching into action, but the punches came in ones and twos. Those quick, ninety degree sidesteps were nowhere, but then Douglas was making things very difficult. At the end of the third (a round in which Tyson deserved a share of if you were being generous) Douglas opposed Mike and watched him drag his feet back to his corner. "You're too flat-footed in there" explained unfamiliar second Aaron Snowell. The champion needed to be sharper, but there was little worry on his face. If anything, he looked slightly fed up, as if his latest contract was for $2700, not $27 million. The fourth was another good one for Douglas. He began to double up on his jab and socked Mike with a clean right. Tyson was shown to be amazingly ineffective. The timid crowd, sounding more like a conference room than a packed arena, still waited for the big bang.

"You gotta use that seven to get in." Tyson partially listened to instruction. There was a decided glum about him. Douglas' stamina issues were thrown into conversation but the pace wasn't demanding. In the fifth the pattern repeated itself and a right-left combination thudded into Mike's head, punishing his indecision. A hook was telegraphed in anger which dissolved into the rest of his messy offerings. The heavyweight destroyer was particularly unorganized, and so was his corner. The tissue underneath Mike's left eye began to flare up, but his corner was an enswell light. Just as some betting houses had not bothered to offer any odds, team Tyson had not bothered to bring standard equipment. Snowell was reduced to filling a plastic glove with cold water and crudely applied the makeshift item to the injured eye.

Douglas' contributions dropped off in the sixth, but Tyson's were dire. The man who had sculpted a reputation for burning after his opponents moved like a man weary from anaesthetic. James had yet to budge from the driver's seat and remained in control during a quiet seventh. Mike christened the eighth with a quick combination. Had he been working the bag those explosive arcs would have won the adulation of any spectator, but against the tall, slippery frame of Douglas every one missed. Those huge thighs struggled to shift Mike's body. Douglas flowed with his punches and backed Tyson into the ropes. It appeared as if he was about to turn a boxing lesson into a beating. Suddenly a big right uppercut came to save the day. Mike had dug low for this one and it cranked Douglas' neck, sure to make a nice addition to the greatest hits reel. All that good work was headed for the trash. Referee Octavio Meyran gave him the count. A little distracted at six, it was a tad slower than customary. Douglas arose at nine. Then the bell came. The moment had gone.

Tyson was nearly enthusiastic in the ninth but Douglas gave better than he got, thumping the champion in retaliation. Another minute in and Tyson was wobbled. Iron Mike was indeed malleable. "Come on, Mike…come on" whispered Snowell. Even the trainer was having trouble convincing himself. That inflated glove was still being applied. Tyson made full use of the minute rest, getting off his stool at the bell. A big right came Douglas' way but, apart from that uppercut, nothing had worked. After each effort he seemed to lose a step, and in the tenth the knockout machine was dead on his feet.

The champion clumsily stumbled into Douglas where a right uppercut near took off his head. The follow up was wonderfully fluid and a wicked left smashed Mike to the canvas. The impact caused his mouthguard to eject. Improving himself on to all fours, Tyson was hopelessly groggy. He scanned for his mouthpiece which was unsuccessfully crammed sideways into his gob as he tried in earnest to pull himself together. At nine and a half he was vertical again and straight into the arms of Meyran who stopped the drunken stumbles. The cryptic believers huddled around the new champion who raised his arms into the air. It was easy to hear their cries of elation over the Japanese crowd which quietly hummed in reflection, suggesting nothing of the result's magnitude. One-eyed Mike brooded around the ring until Snowell found him with a hug. The ex-champion was not the only one in need of a cuddle as Don King hid his true feelings behind that moronic grin. The result had undone his million dollar plans with Mike and he was willing to rewrite history to get them back on track. He soon had the WBC and WBA under pressure to reverse the decision on the basis of Douglas' eighth round long count. It was arguable that James had been down for around twelve seconds, but then the same could be said of Tyson. Justice had the last say. The better man stayed champion.

Now that Douglas was the one with the belts, Evander Holyfield was headed his way. Evander entered the ring ripped n' ready, but James had been busy coveting his $20 million purse and looked every inch his 246lbs. One man was ready for the full twelve but only three were required to end Douglas' reign. The short right that cracked off his nose was more a stinging than fight-ending shot, but rather than punch the canvas and rise as he had against Mike, Douglas stayed put.

Some attributed Tyson's defeat to poor preparation, but when it was seen how quickly Douglas fell the theory of a fluke was replete with subscriptions. The Tyson-Holyfield mega fight was rescheduled for 1991 and the prospect was just as exciting as it had been. Record purses were on the cards but a rib injury postponed the bout and a year later Tyson was behind bars on the charge of rape. When released in 1995, King was all too obliged to charm his golden goose. The fascination with Tyson refused to subside, and on his return that fearsome aura remarried his movements. Unofficially, Mike Tyson was invincible again. Save for a spooked Frank Bruno he had not fought anyone of note. He could still produce the big finish, and that's all that mattered. Thirty-four-year-old Holyfield was considered meat in 1996, but he ate up the odds along with Tyson's punches and, for a second time, the boxing world was rumbled to its core. Six years and one suspension later, many were picking a thirty-five-year-old party worn Mike Tyson to dethrone Lennox Lewis. Biting Holyfield's ear showed how far removed he was to his attentive, respectful youth, but that impulse to believe in boxing's bad boy would not die. When Danny Williams beat him in 2004 the unfavoured Brit became, along with Douglas and Holyfield, the man who beat Mike Tyson.

"I haven't loved this sport since 1990." Despite a catalogue of quizzical remarks, you could believe Tyson after losing to Kevin McBride. The stocky teenager who got a kick out of making men unconscious had officially run out of bad intentions. "Everything he said that would happen came true" Mike once said of Cus. Had the old sage lived on, you wonder if he could have gone one better than predicting the rise and prevented the meltdown.

MARCO ANTONIO BARRERA
VS.
ERIK MORALES

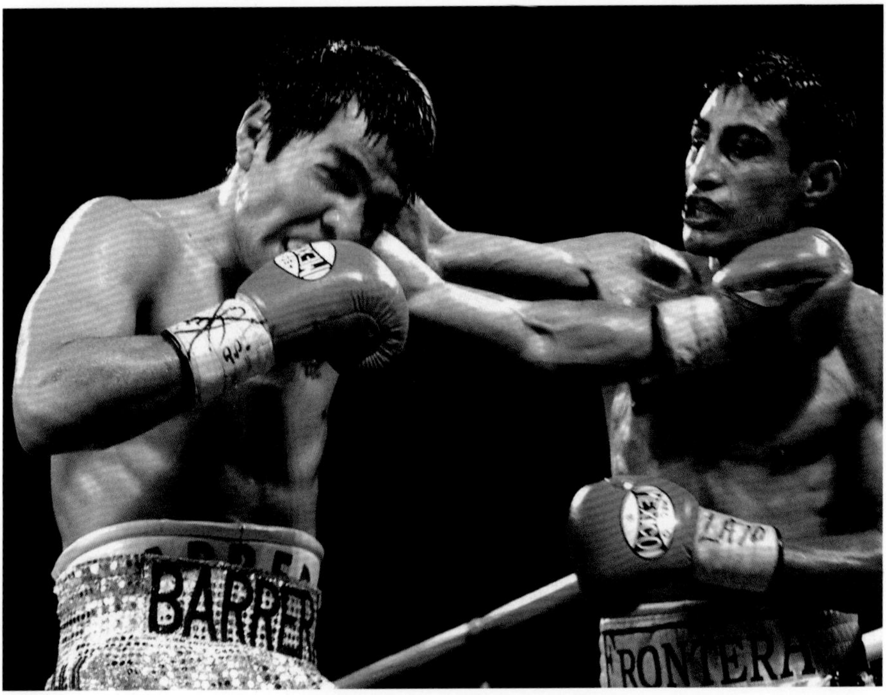

February 19th, 2000
WBC & WBO Super-Bantamweight Titles
Las Vegas, Nevada

Mexican fighters are different. The distinction runs deeper than the presentation; the olive, leathery skin, the solid black hair and the trunks with family names sewn into them. It's probably easier to tell a Mexican fighter from any other, but they're more than a defiant breed. Mexico fashions adorable contradictions; men who are ill-treated by their country but come into the ring smouldering with patriotism, like an estranged unit of a battalion, certain he'll be stronger on his own. Within the debauched streets that connect the city centres there is a daily obstacle course of guns, drugs and every other evil truancy spawns. More accurately, many can't afford schooling, and so the would-be mentors are already playing the devil's hand. With a bit of luck he might set himself straight, start a business or receive an education. Maybe he'll have something as a fighter. For special cases an assortment of local titles will colonise their windowsill, but only the select few will march before tens of thousands, punching the air, converting mariachi notes into energy.

Julio Cesar Chavez remains the benchmark for the Mexican fighter. The image of the man who didn't lose until his ninety-first fight, wearing his flag as a headband was one which inspired a new legion of single-minded militia. In 1996 Oscar De La Hoya delivered the upsetting message that Chavez was on his way out. It was insuperable to eclipse such a legacy but Marco Antonio Barrera got to work on shortening the mourning process.

Barrera comprehensively debunked the idea that you need a sorry childhood to make a competent fighter; for a time he was fighting *and* studying to become a lawyer at the University of Mexico. Intentions to rediscover his more vocal, less physical lifestyle ultimately died and he made a fantastic fighter. You had to take two at first glance. The build, the position of the hands, the haircut, the committed body attack; he looked like the lost younger brother of Chavez. The WBO 122lbs champion was cool, efficient and had been magnificent in defeating the American, Kennedy McKinney. Junior 'Poison' Jones was another American, a heavy puncher with a reputation for splattering Mexicans. Barrera's class was supposed to burst that reputation but a big right led to his first loss in five rounds. The scorecards had Barrera winning at the time of the stoppage, producing a rematch which delivered a second loss, surprisingly on points.

From the prostitution tolerant Zona Norte, Tijuana came Erik Morales; three years Barrera's junior and without a single grade to his name. He was born on the first floor of a building that housed a boxing gym and had the gloves on before he could connect his letters. Father Jose encouraged his son to set the trail rather than follow the path but it was like cutting meat out of a piranha's diet. A long amateur career developed a savvy boxer, one who carried bounce in his step and could destroy nine stone men with his right hand. He was very different to Barrera; quite tall, slender (skinny almost) and had a chiselled face with dark, piercing eyes. Experience is what they had in common, and that is what he used to wear down Daniel Zaragoza to win the WBC title. The long-serving Mexican was applauded by Erik for his valiant efforts to defend his belt. When finally put down by a body shot he saluted the better man.

"This really isn't the sad death of a king, so much as the passing of the torch to a new generation" surmised Larry Merchant.

In his first three defences Morales made a mess of his opposition. For whatever may have been said against their credentials he did his part getting rid of them, changing the delivery of his punches, creating angles out of nowhere. An attractively even record of 30-0 brought a smile to promoter Bob Arum. Next up was Junior Jones. McKinney had gotten the better of Jones in his last fight, but seen as he was American it didn't impede on his image as a Mexican terror. In total he was 35-0 against Mexican's and Morales was to fight him in front of his home city.

Erik was more mobile than Barrera. You needed to move against a puncher like Jones and he jumped in, and then out of range effectively. A chopping right sent the American over in the fourth and accurate punches made sure he did not hear the bell. Morales' win over Barrera's master turned the fans' attention to the potential of an all-Mexican showdown. Barrera had restored some lost respect since losing, recapturing his WBO super-bantamweight championship and showing no loss of confidence, though it was Morales who was now established as Mexico's número uno. Weight complaints hinted at Erik's featherweight future, but there was work to be done at 122lbs. After drumming super-tough Wayne McCullough it was time for Barrera, or as the posters put it, 'Campeon vs. Campeon'.

Boxing entered the 21st century scanning for new peaks. Lennox Lewis had control of the heavyweight division having outboxed Evander Holyfield, Oscar De La Hoya and Felix Trinidad were sent in different directions after their collision and Roy Jones was still shy of a good challenge. The return of Mike Tyson always created a buzz though pasting Julius Francis meant nothing. A surprise was overdue. When the fight was set Barrera was made the firm 7/2 underdog. A lively one was expected, but a clear winner. The event was partly viewed as a prelude to a big money featherweight bout with the overtly flamboyant 'Prince' Naseem Hamed. The fact they were competing at super-bantamweight (a division just outside the commercial loop) stopped it receiving the royal treatment. And the bottom line, it was a crossroads fight. Twenty-six-year-old Barrera was a fighter *probably* on the slide, so said the critics. It is a more or less true theory that the game chickens of the ring work best at an age when heavyweights are considered babies. There is no maturing stage; when they lose a step they are quickly found out. Barrera was sharp in outpointing Pastor Maurin but the wild Argentinean was no gauge to see how many miles were left on the clock. Fifty-two fights was no picnic and they were ominously referenced.

Mexico's 'Baby-Faced Assassin' ended his judicial studies after five whole semesters. He hadn't flunked the opportunity most families would have killed for to lay down. Columns of doubt became fuel for inspiration and he explained that he had not been up for a fight like this since his thrilling triumph over McKinney. Something else was apparent as the fight drew nearer. Barrera had explained that it mattered not who he was fighting but for Morales he seemed to make an exception. Marco was not one to badmouth opponents. In interviews he was respectful, realistic, never overly polite or sentimental. This unmoved attitude towards his line of work was disturbed by his Tijuana rival. The only explanation was that he was Mexican.

It was Puerto Rico that shared a bitter rivalry with Mexico; your classic case of two countries with next door neighbour syndrome. Carlos Ortiz vs. Sugar Ramos, Wilfredo Gomez vs. Carlos Zarate, Wilfred Benitez vs. Carlos Palomino, Chavez vs. Edwin Rosario; there had been some classic battles through the years. The two fighters may have been Mexican but they came from different worlds and were insistent on underlining those differences, reinforcing their dislike for one another. One of them was a native imposter. "The fighters in Tijuana are chicken" taunted Barrera, "they don't like to be hit." This insult, while amusingly blunt had a whiff of strategy behind it. Clearly it was in the interest of the close-quartered Barrera to goad his opponent into a ruckus. For the public, the fight was to decide who the best 122lbs boxer in the world was. For the fighters it was to decide who the best fighter in Mexico was. Suddenly those WBC and WBO world titles felt little more valuable than the plastic toys inside Christmas crackers. On their appointed date Morales spoke with calm austerity, "I have to win this fight because it is for honour and very personal."[256]

Around 7,000 people filled about half of the Mandalay Bay arena; not quite the glitzy ensemble for the De La Hoya-Trinidad fight five months ago. There had been a good squabble over the gloves during the last week. Barrera's camp had threatened to walk out on the fight when a coin toss was to decide the brand to be worn. He wasn't there to see he had won the game of chance but it was later ruled that they were both required to wear the same brand. A second coin toss was to decide who would have the pleasure of entering the ring last. Barrera couldn't argue with that but he had another reason to dislike Morales when the coin landed with the letter 'M' facing up. As the evening drew in, fighter and spectator continued with their opposing lives; one relaxing following a strict programme while the other got suited n' tipsy. From the outside in, boxing may be the hardest sport to comprehend, but without fans there is no spectacle. As customers made tracks towards the Mandalay Bay, tearing down each other's predictions, lifted by the primary colours of Vegas, all the pieces were coming together for a memorable night.

The underdog emerged from his dressing room in an attractive silver and blue robe covered with sparkles. He had ditched his curtains and buzz-cut for a nondescript haircut and his round face wore one expression which didn't alter as he closed on the ring. When the robe was removed the word 'TAPIA' (his mother's maiden name) decorated his waist band. There was lots of space available but the crowd made enough noise to convince the TV audience that the aisles were overflowing. Not a moment was lost and Morales was ready to enter in a less spectacular white robe with black stripes. He had given his military-esque, short back n' sides a trim. A quartet of trumpeters beckoned him into the ring where Barrera was pacing.

"Uuuuuuh, Let's get Ready to Ruuuummmbuuuuhhll!" After Michael Buffer's infamous catchphrase the Mexican introductions gave him ample opportunity to show his talent for rolling his R's. It was a dead heat in terms of reception. Referee

[256] Los Angeles Times, 2000, Feb 19th, Part D

Mitch Halpern was amazingly quick with the instructions; was it possible he was as excited as everybody else?

Three seconds into the fight Barrera tried some scare tactics and got off with a three punch combination. Back into stance his arms made for excellent barriers with the hands protecting either side of his head and elbows hiding all the soft spots. He moved with his steady plod. Morales darted about, swiftly and inquisitively, stopping his bounce to scout openings. He was tentative, for about the first ten seconds. Barrera gave him little choice but to fight and so he fired back. A one-two-uppercut combination was a favourite for Barrera and he ripped it in with contempt. Near the bell Morales jumped in and out of range to confuse Barrera but it was the latter's round. The crowd exploded in applause.

Erik was considered the puncher but he had yet to land with something clean. In the second Barrera shifted back to make space; Morales overreached with his fists and caught body punches that sounded like Barrera's gloves were connected to an amplifier. Halfway through the second a right knocked Morales back and in came the WBO champion to hack away at his rib cage. This kind of fight was not, as happy as Morales was to oblige, playing to his strengths. The ten second reminder excited the fighters in a chance to steal the round but nothing significant landed. Beginning the third, Morales seemed to have had a rethink and kept his range. This did not ruffle Barrera but it did stop him landing. This lasted for all but a minute when Erik threw a flurry to address his Tijuana faction. He did better this time and had Barrera disorganized in a couple of the exchanges. Despite the good work, Marco was still told off. "He's hitting you, you be first...don't wait!" They wanted the absolute best out of their fighter.

Every one in four of Morales' punches started to get through. It was getting more competitive and the crowd were getting more rowdy. Erik's angular face caught punches easier than Barrera's. His loose guard didn't help and reddened cheeks told of the punches he had shipped. Progressively he warmed to the fight and began to give some angles. Bending left and right, jumping back and forth had Barrera reacting as he had hoped and in went a right. It was Erik's best punch yet but he lost momentum after slipping. Chants of "BAH-RER-RA! BAH-RER-RA!" went off. The variety of punches from Morales gave the artful spectator plenty to appreciate. Barrera's contributions were fewer but slammed home. The undefeated and younger fighter was making things harder for himself though his creative spearing started to shape the rounds. The ten second reminder went off again and Barrera punched Morales into the ropes for a possible steal. "You're the master, the teacher." There was a different tone in each corner. Praise may have cooled Barrera's fight. For Morales it was fuel. Into the fifth they went.

A neat hook came off a straight and Erik bounced to keep his man guessing. Barrera got close again and punished Erik with a wicked double shot to the body and head. Another blow had Morales intentionally saunter to the ropes where there was a vicious, defence-be-damned exchange. They couldn't wait to get at each other but it was Morales' turn to do damage. Uppercuts and crosses were linked with confusing pauses.

A right pinged Marco's chin and everyone could see its effect. The unpredictable attack continued as he feinted lefts and threw rights. Barrera got flustered near the ropes and went into a shell. Erik now looked irresistible as he pressed his advantage which is why it was so shocking to see Barrera suddenly blast him in a spontaneous rage.

Morales' exposed head was thumped back as the adrenalin temporarily rid Barrera's arms of any fatigue. He pressed on with this violent change of current, creating such drama that the word exciting seemed insolubly mundane. The crowd stood to attention, no longer customers but witnesses. Many of those near ringside stood up in amazement, temporarily leaving their amazingly cheap $300 seats. Sky Sports' Ian Darke estimated their current value at "three times as much." Partner Glenn McCrory figured "five times" was just as fair. For the remaining minute they punched slowly while maintaining disregard for their health. They came to for a mutual rest but Halpern separated them instantly as if one of the fans had the official hooked up to a remote control. The bell went and the crowd sounded with delight. "TEH-REE-BLEH!" "TEH-REE-BLEH!" bounced off every wall. There was no fan-favourite inside those ropes.

Tiredness helped Morales concentrate on his boxing in a mellow round six; mellow of course by comparison. Barrera's contributions were light and his attempt to steal the round in the last moments was attractively negated by Morales' feet. That defensive sheen of the WBO champion was dulled and liable to error. Morales' tin-opening combinations stopped cuffing and started to thump Barrera's head. Sometimes they were arm punches but Morales could turn lazy efforts into effective blows. Barrera's right hand was an unsuspecting shot and landed nearly every time. After pursuing Erik to the ropes they went all out again in an exchange of incredible intensity. The seventh and eighth rounds were very even and the ten-second call sent them into a mutual frenzy. The thick skin of Barrera had resisted injury long enough and his left cheek came out with a purple swelling. Another round's worth of aggravation had it dripping blood.

The ninth was a good one for the man from Mexico City. He got that left back into action, alternating between the hook and uppercut which greeted Erik's mouth with a crash. There was no particular injury on his face, just red blotches lending him a distressed look. Barrera had the last say after Morales fell short, nailing him with a one-two-hook, everyone on the button. The tenth was brilliant as, once again, clever boxing erupted into something furious. Morales looked more vulnerable than he was. A hook knocked him off balance but he came back half a second later. One thing was for sure, the odds were completely inaccurate. Morales was probably entitled to the eleventh, probably. Trying to score a fight so close was anybody's game, no less a fight in Vegas.

"The twelfth aaaannd FINAL round!" Buffer's theatrical bulletin got the fans to their feet, half in appreciation for the last eleven rounds, the other half in anticipation for the next one. They didn't need Halpern to force a touch of gloves. The best of enemies saluted one another. Barrera nodded at Erik and then seconds later he was trying to sever his torso from the hip with a savage body attack. The scrapping quickly moved into the opposite corner and Morales had an adverse reaction to a Barrera left. He tried to make some space but he was the weaker man. A short left went to his head as he ducked, putting him down. The replay would show no punch to have landed but Halpern called it a knockdown. A 10-8 round was like gold dust at this stage of the fight. Morales shook his head and ran back into the melee, arms flailing. The final pictures saw the two swinging for keeps. Win, lose or draw a fight like this didn't need a decision.

It's an automatic reaction to dig into the filing cabinet after watching a great fight. It was a tall order to reference a better one. Short-lived shootouts like Hagler and Hearns, up-and-down slugfests like Zale and Graziano, come-from-behind knockouts like Chavez and Taylor; everyone has their favourite, but in terms of sustained ferocity there was nothing like it. "A round of applause please, for two fighters at 122lbs that fought their hearts out here at the Mandalay Bay." Buffer read out of the scorecards. The one thing the fight was missing (controversy) was corrected when Morales was made the winner via split decision. Two rounds to Barrera was a fair card. Close but clear. One was made the winner, but how could you call either a loser? Boxing's nifty CompuBox had Morales landing 319 to Barrera's 199, though just about all of Marco's were of the nerve-killing variety. More impressive was how few he threw, 618, an amazing economy for such a furious battle.

Boos went up around the arena while Morales was given a shoulder ride. "I really don't know what you have to do in Las Vegas to win a fight" sighed Barrera. It wasn't as ludicrous as the draw rendered after Lennox Lewis had given Evander Holyfield a boxing lesson, but that didn't stop the WBO refusing the decision. Considering the 'knockdown' Dalby Shirley's card of 115-112 was a little suspicious, and we all know politics and boxing go together like spaghetti and meatballs.

Morales went up to featherweight as planned, stopping old dog Kevin Kelley and outpointing Gutsy Espadas Jr. to swap his WBC super-bantamweight title for the featherweight version. Barrera stayed at 122lbs for three more fights, seemingly alienated from the big paydays. Everything changed when he got the chance to face Naseem Hamed. Being the underdog only made Barrera grin. Hamed's record was rather fearsome with only four opponents lasting the distance in thirty-five contests. The elastic southpaw had C4 in his left but Barrera had steel in his jaw. He also had talent which the over-confident Hamed was not prepared for and he put on a blinding display over twelve rounds. Fourteen months ago he was the bitter loser, now he was the featherweight king and part of the pound-for-pound elite. Morales trudged on, struggled with Espadas and was then given a tough fight with In-Jin Chi. This reversal of themes set the stage for the highly anticipated rematch with his nemesis.

Fight two was virtually the opposite of what the first had been. They were cautious and deliberate. Fans prayed for the fight to catch fire but they had to settle for lukewarm. To see them both opt for a more tactical approach was surprising as Barrera had punched Morales at a press-conference. Naturally Erik retaliated with both fists before getting restrained. This was a far cry from the sugar-coated insults and pretend shoving that goes on. Just in case anyone hadn't got the hint, these men didn't like each other. The fight itself was decent; engaging, one to separate the casuals from the die-hards. This time the fight remained on the outside, favouring Morales who deserved the nod. When the cards were read out they were unanimous for Barrera, clearly atoning for the much discussed wrongdoing of the original. The Hamed win purchased Barrera global fame, and the win over Morales, however legitimate, sealed him as the best 126lbs fighter. Defeating Johnny Tapia and Kevin Kelley helped Barrera acquire that unbeatable chevron. It's hard to imagine that praise going to his head but Barrera was not all there for the Philippines' Manny Pacquiao. 'Pacman' as he was known looked a lot like Barrera had in his first fight Morales, motivated and razor sharp. Through eleven rounds the Baby-faced Assassin was beaten into a puffy-faced casualty. Huge as the surprise was, it remained 1-1 between the two best fighters in Mexico. That Barrera had lost did not distract fans from the most compelling aspect of his career. When one faltered the other thrived. Morales decided to add five more pounds to join the super-featherweights, and while Barrera suffered his fourth loss Morales won the WBC and IBF titles off Jesus Chavez and Carlos Hernandez in fine performances.

The decider gave the fans more of what they wanted in a splice of the previous two bouts. They swapped rounds, beginning with jabs and counters, but things heated up to revisit the toe-to-toe action of the original. It was probably the closest of the three. Paul Smith's draw was overruled by Jerry Roth's card of 115-113, and Larry O' Connell's 115-114 gave Barrera the majority decision by a single point. Morales was not in the mood for a hand shake and refused pleasantries. A second loss to Barrera was ghastly and he went away with emotions running high. The stomach for battle was not lost; far from it. Morales welcomed the Philippine terror.

It was high-tempo from round one. Pacquiao came alive with his bursts of power and speed. When a clean one got through he may as well have spat in his opponent's face. Erik raised his arms in defiance and chased him halfway across the ring. For the full twelve the Mexican veteran had it out with the Asian powerhouse. Brains superseded brawn and Erik climbed to the top again. Assured that he was ahead, in the last round Morales dared Pacquiao to knock him out, switching southpaw and pressing forward. Fight-ending blows rocked him but Erik continued to box from the unfamiliar stance until the final bell. Escorted over to Larry Merchant, the battle-worn hombre from Tijuana was asked why he'd pulled that dangerous stunt. "Did you like it?" A warm smile concluded the interview and Erik left the building. For those who had doubted him, this victory made Morales' all-time status undisputable. Admittedly, there was a more personal reason for that broad grin.

Jim Lampley had observed that Erik is "always fighting Marco Antonio Barrera, in some sense or another". It caused a chuckle amongst coworkers, but it wouldn't have been funny had there not been some truth there. The man who hated to concede anything knew he had cleared a hurdle Barrera had tripped on; the next best thing after jawing that wannabe lawyer. Before mention of 'him' got the blood boiling again, cheers helped drown any hecklers. Remind him at your own peril. Erik still trails 2-1.

ACKNOWLEDGEMENTS

I would like to thank the following people for their contributions to the book, however big or small they were: Graham A. Pritchard, Nick D. Pritchard, Tony Triem, Daniel Riley, Neil Sutcliffe, Springs Toledo and Clay Moyle.

I would also like to give a shout out to Monte Cox, Mike Casey, Robert Ecksel and the late Joe Rein for their influence and encouragement.

And to the following websites that continue to feed my interest in this sport.

www.boxing.com

www.eastsideboxing.com

www.cyberboxingzone.com

www.checkhookboxing.com

www.boxingscene.com

www.boxrec.com

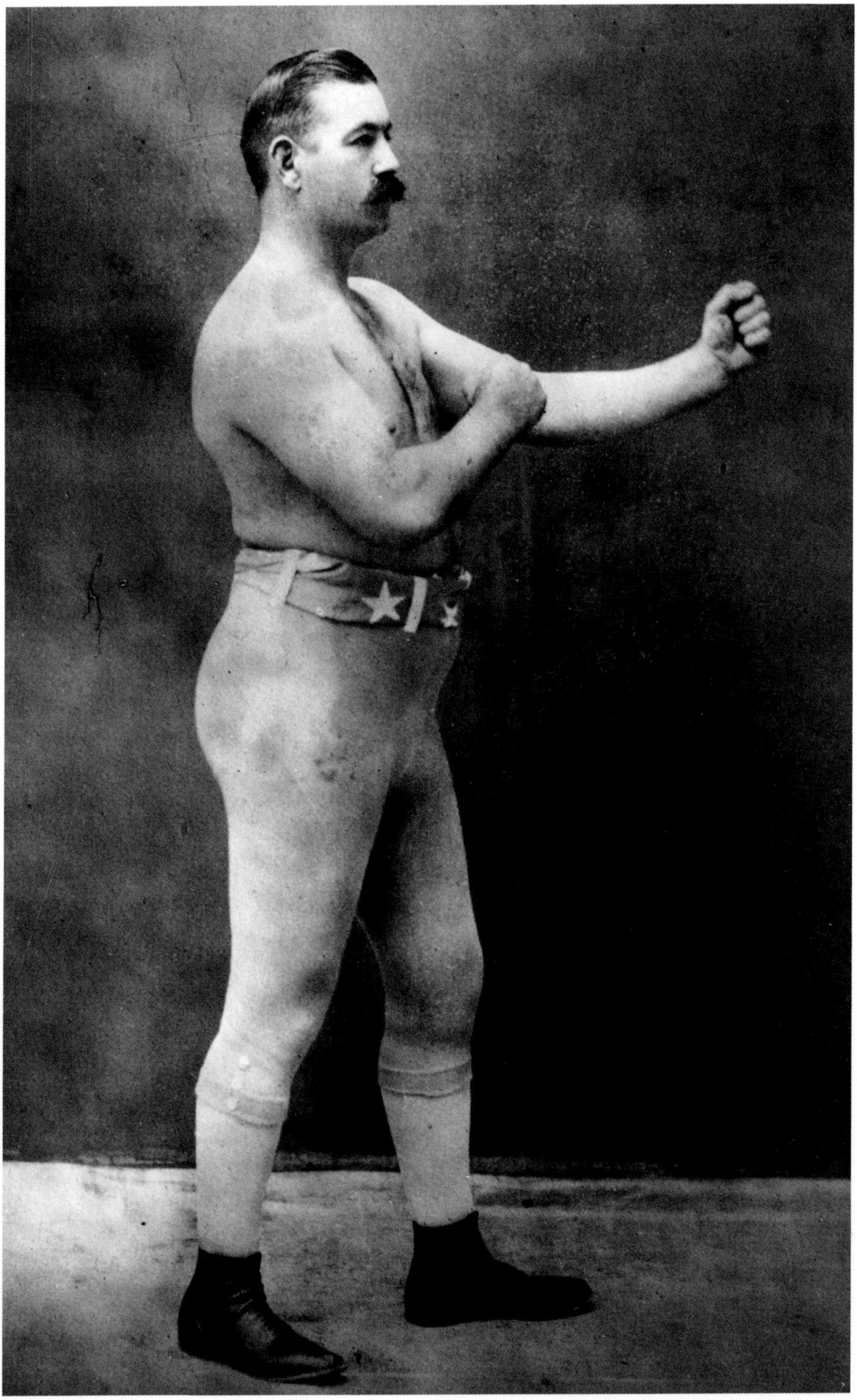

FRAGER

VEN
REYES

PACQUIAO
head & shoulders
WBO
CAFÉ PURO
WBC
MOTOLITE
MGM GRAND